REMAKING THE
AMERICAN MAINSTREAM

REMAKING THE AMERICAN MAINSTREAM

Assimilation and
Contemporary
Immigration

RICHARD ALBA

VICTOR NEE

HARVARD UNIVERSITY PRESS
Cambridge, Massachusetts, and London, England 2003

Library of Congress Cataloging-in-Publication Data

Alba, Richard.
    Remaking the American mainstream : assimilation and contemporary immigration /
Richard Alba and Victor Nee.
        p. cm.
    Includes bibliographical references and index.
    ISBN 0-674-01040-X (cloth : alk. paper)
    1. United States—Emigration and immigration—Social aspects.
2. Americanization.   3. Immigrants—United States—Social conditions.
I. Nee, Victor, 1945–   II. Title.

JV6475.A433 2003
303.48′273—dc21   2002191300

For the next generation
    William Nee, Michael Alba
    Sarah Alba, David Nee

CONTENTS

PREFACE

The mainstream of American life has demonstrated since the colonial period a remarkable capacity to draw into its swift currents the descendants of successive waves of immigrants. Individuals and families descended from the mass immigrations of the late nineteenth and early twentieth centuries have joined the mainstream despite the fierce nativist hostility directed toward immigrants from southern and eastern Europe and East Asia. The descendants may choose to celebrate their ethnic identity and cultural roots, but their ethnicity has greatly diminished as an ascriptive trait that decisively shapes life chances. The processes that brought about this outcome are the motor of American assimilation, and the goal of this book is to demonstrate their continued relevance.

A new era of mass immigration beginning in the late 1960s has dramatically increased the diversity of ethnic groups in American society. In contrast to the immigration of the past, the new immigrants hail predominantly from the developing societies of Latin America, Asia, and the Caribbean Basin. The 2000 U.S. Census documents the tremendous surge in the number of immigrants and their children, who now constitute 20 percent of the total American population. The new immigrant and second generations are a significant presence in neighborhoods, schools, and workplaces in virtually all metropolitan areas of the United States. Their widespread influence on American society prompts the question: Do differences in national origin and cultural background negate in a fundamental manner the assimilation pattern experienced by earlier European and East Asian groups? Many social scientists and other observers appear to believe that they do and have pointed to a number of factors, from the presumed racial distinctiveness of the new groups to the restructuring of the American economy, to argue that today's immigrant populations face an essentially novel predicament: either they maintain their cultural and communal distinctiveness, thus selectively acculturating while keeping some distance from the mainstream, or they will be forced into the position of racial minorities, imposing great disadvantages on themselves and their children.

We have written this book to respond to what we see as the prevailing pessimism about the prospects for the assimilation of the new immigrants and their second generation. This pessimism is partly rooted in outmoded views of assimilation and simplistic accounts of how the descendants of past immigrants entered the mainstream. Indeed, there has been no systematic comparative study of assimilation for over two decades, since Stanley Lieberson's then authoritative *A Piece of a Pie*. Much has changed in the United States since Lieberson's book appeared in 1980. What has been lacking, in our view, is a sophisticated, up-to-date account of assimilation: a definition of the concept that avoids the problems of many past definitions, especially their implicit ethnocentrism; a theory of assimilation that specifies the causal mechanisms that make assimilation relevant for new groups; and an outline of the evidence that demonstrates assimilation as a continuing pattern in the incorporation of immigrants and their children. In broad terms, our book seeks to compare the experience of two major waves of immigrants to the United States and their descendants: the late-nineteenth- and twentieth-century immigration from Europe and East Asia and the contemporary immigration from Latin America, Asia, and the Caribbean Basin.

In reworking ideas about assimilation, we have sought to avoid any normative implications suggesting that immigrant groups *should* assimilate. Our reformulation is intended to illuminate and make comprehensible existing aspects of the contemporary American experience—to have social-scientific validity, in other words. We recognize that assimilation is but one of the patterns of immigrant-group incorporation in American society and that, at this moment in history, there can be no guarantee that it will be the dominant one. In the very complex landscape of present-day immigration, however, only with a clear conceptual lens can one detect the powerful elements of continuity that connect the assimilation of past immigrations with what some are experiencing in the present. This continuity does not mean, of course, that the present simply replicates what happened in the past. History does not repeat itself in mechanical fashion. Nevertheless, the attempts to assert the uniqueness of the present era have gone too far, we believe. Grasping the continuity between past and present also carries implications for the future: as we will indicate in the final chapter, contemporary assimilation suggests scenarios for the future that differ from current visions.

This continuity indicates the utility of assessing contemporary events against the background of past processes of inclusion, which were often anything but straightforward and seemed quite problematic to observers at the time. As we were completing this book, the devastating attacks on the World Trade Center took place in New York City. In their aftermath, Muslim immigrants and the second generation have come under intense scrutiny because of anxieties about the presence of terrorist cells in their midst. Combined with a worsening economy, the fear of terrorist attacks could ignite a new period of nativist reaction and intolerance directed against immigrants. Would these developments not blunt the dynamics of assimilation we describe here? A glance backward, however, demonstrates indisputably that many groups now regarded as part of the mainstream went through periods when their suitability as Americans was in doubt. Germans, and central Europeans more generally, were under suspicion during World War I, when laws were even passed in many states to limit the use of the German language. After the war there was a spasm of hysteria over Bolsheviks among immigrants, which led to the Palmer Raids of 1919–20, when thousands were arrested. During the 1920s, the Sacco and Vanzetti case aroused passions about Italian immigrants, and the presidential candidacy of Al Smith ran afoul of deep unease about the loyalty of Catholics to Rome. This produced one of the most humorous moments in American nativism: throughout the South, a picture was distributed showing Smith, then governor of New York, cutting a ribbon for the opening of a subway tunnel, but which, according to the caption, was a secret passageway to the Vatican. World War II produced the most infamous moment: the internment of all Japanese Americans on the West Coast. During the McCarthy period in the early 1950s, the beam of suspicion was focused on Jews and increased in intensity as a result of the trial and execution of Julius and Ethel Rosenberg for espionage. And so on. Although we do not wish to engage in exact predictions about the course of the current concerns over terrorism and Muslim fundamentalism, we think it safe to say that they are not an ultimate bar to assimilation processes.

In more personal terms, this book is the fruit of conversations that we began as assistant professors at Cornell University in the late 1970s. They have led to a writing partnership of two equal and complementary voices. Yet we only began working on the book because of an invitation extended by Josh DeWind of the Social Science Research Council to produce a paper on assimilation theory for a conference in Sanibel, Florida, held in January 1996. The reactions of participants there, and especially of the discussant Philip Kasinitz, signaled to us that we were onto something and that there was a need for a new formulation of assimilation. We are grateful for the opportunity provided us by the SSRC, which resulted in our collaboration. A few sections of the book first appeared in our paper from that conference, "Rethinking Assimilation Theory for a New Era of Immigration," *International Migration Review* 31 (Winter 1997): 826–874. We thank the *International Migration Review* and Russell Sage Foundation, which subsequently published *The Handbook of International Migration,* where the essay was reprinted, for their permission to use it here. We likewise express our gratitude to *The Public Interest* for permission to use sections of Richard Alba's essay, "Assimilation's Quiet Tide" (Spring 1995): 1–18.

Books almost inevitably demand more in the end of their authors than seems likely at the outset. That has been true here, and we owe much to our colleagues who have supported us along the way. A number of them read the entire manuscript and gave us detailed comments. These include Douglas Massey and Roger Waldinger, who read the manuscript for Harvard University Press. Other readers were Frank Bean, Nancy Denton, Reynolds Farley, Nancy Foner, Herbert Gans, Nathan Glazer, Charles Hirschman, Suzanne Model, Orlando Patterson, Joel Perlmann, Richard Polenberg, Rubén Rumbaut, and Mary Waters. We also wish to thank our editor, Michael Aronson, who expressed enthusiasm and support for our book from the time we started it. Thanks to Rachel Davis for excellent editing of the entire manuscript.

Richard Alba could not have completed his portion of the book without support that made it possible for him to take time out from other academic responsibilities. During the spring of 1999, a residential fellowship at Russell Sage Foundation was one such source of support. A Guggenheim Fellowship and sabbatical leave from the University at Albany, SUNY, for the academic year 2000–2001 were also critical. The book has been improved by his collaborations with Nancy Denton, Reynolds Farley, and John Logan, which provided important empirical findings. Additional data were produced by Albany students; for their efforts, Dalia Abdel-Hady, Kyle Crowder, Tariqul Islam, Olga Krolmalnaya, Xiaojie Liu, Amy Lutz, Karen Marotz, Brian Stults, and Charles Zhang can only find their reward here. The technical support provided by the Center for Social and Demographic Analysis at SUNY-Albany was indispensable. At the Russell Sage Foundation, John Smelcer proved an invaluable assistant. In addition, Alba's thinking has been stimulated by discussions with many colleagues; among those not yet acknowledged in this preface are Hartmut Esser, Donna Gabaccia, Gary Gerstle, Jennifer Hochschild, Peggy Levitt, Alejandro Portes, David Reimers, Gregory Rodriguez, Peter Salins, Walter Zenner, Min Zhou, and Aristide Zolberg.

Victor Nee gratefully acknowledges the generous support of the College of Arts and Sciences at Cornell University, which provided him with financial support for leaves from his teaching obligations during 1996–97 and 2000–2001. During his residential year (1994–95) at the Russell Sage Foundation, he benefited from discussions about the new institutionalism with Robert K. Merton, and from conversations on immigration with Nancy Foner, Alex Stepick, Louise Tilly, Eric Wanner, and Min Zhou. The Russell Sage Foundation generously provided Nee with funding for a conference on the new institutionalism in sociology that same year. A year as a Fellow of the Center for Advanced Study in the Behavioral Sciences in Palo Alto (1996–97) and a grant from the National Science Foundation (SBR-#9022192) allowed further opportunity for sustained work. Many stimulating conversations with the late Roger Gould as well as with David Card, Roberto Fernandez, Russell Hardin, Sigi Lindenberg, and Saskia Sassen contributed to clarifying ideas. During his sabbatical leave in 2000–2001, the Department of Sociology at Harvard University lent Nee a quiet office to hang his hat. Thanks to Daniel Bell, Lawrence Bobo, John Lie, Stanley Lieberson, Jeffrey Reitz, Barbara Reskin, and Mary Waters for discussing revision work in progress while in Cambridge. Other colleagues and former students will find their influence in the making of this book through collaborative work and engaging discussion: David Grusky, Douglas Heckathorn, Paul Ingram, Michael Macy, Rebecca Matthews, Jimy Sanders, Scott Sernau, and David Stark.

Both of us have experienced personally some of the processes we write about. This is true above all in our happy family lives, which, despite Tolstoy, are each distinctive. For Richard Alba, the love and support of Gwen, Michael, and Sarah have made it possible to focus his intensity in ways he never imagined. For Victor Nee, there is, above all, profuse gratitude and appreciation for Brett de Bary, whose kindness and keen readings as a humanist scholar contributed much to more nuanced and careful formulation; and William and David, who embody the remaking of the mainstream project, provided inspiration.

REMAKING THE
AMERICAN MAINSTREAM

CHAPTER ONE

Rethinking Assimilation

Assimilation is a contested idea today. Since the 1960s it has been seen in a mostly negative light, as an ethnocentric and patronizing imposition on minority peoples struggling to retain their cultural and ethnic integrity. The very word seems to conjure up a bygone era, when the multicultural nature of American society was not comprehended, let alone respected, and there appeared, at least to white Americans, to be a unitary and unquestioned American way of life. The sociologist Nathan Glazer, in an essay tellingly titled "Is Assimilation Dead?" describes the present attitude thus: "'Assimilation' is not today a popular term. Recently I asked a group of Harvard students taking a class on race and ethnicity what their attitude to the term 'assimilation' was. The large majority had a negative reaction to it. Had I asked what they thought of the term 'Americanization,' the reaction, I am sure, would have been even more hostile."[1] The rejection of the old assimilation canon is not limited to students and the young. Assimilation was once unquestionably the foundational concept for the study of ethnic relations, but in recent decades it has come to be seen by sociologists and others as an ideologically laden residue of worn-out notions. For many, it smacks of the era when functionalism reigned supreme and when ethnic and racial groups could be rated according to a cultural profile presumed to be required for success in an advanced industrial society. The assimilation concept of the earlier era is now condemned for the expectation that minority groups would inevitably want to shed their own cultures, as if these were old skins no longer possessing any vital force, and wrap themselves in the mantle of Anglo-American culture. The one-sidedness of this conception overlooked the value and sustainability of minority cultures and, in addition, masked barely hidden ethnocentric assumptions about the superiority of Anglo-American culture. Indeed, it has been viewed as a form of "Eurocentric hegemony," a weapon of the majority for putting minorities at a disadvantage by forcing them to live by cultural standards that are not their own.[2]

This old conception of assimilation has become passé. It was done in by many forces and events, but perhaps above all by the sociological equivalent of Arthur Conan Doyle's telltale "dog that didn't bark": namely, the virtually universal failure of social scientists to predict the broad impact of the civil rights movement and the identity politics it spawned. Ever since, the argument has been that their view was blinkered by the uncritical acceptance of an assimilation model of American life, which led them to assume that black Americans sought no more than quiet integration with white America.[3]

Without question, many of the intellectual sins now attributed to assimilation can also be documented in the mid-twentieth-century literature that describes the adjustments made by ethnic and immigrant groups to enter the mainstream of American society. They can be found, for instance, in W. Lloyd Warner and Leo Srole's *Social Systems of American Ethnic Groups* (1945), a classic study of ethnic assimilation in "Yankee City." Warner and Srole conclude that American ethnic groups are destined to be no more than temporary phenomena, doomed by the egalitarian values of the United States and by widespread social mobility: "The future of American ethnic groups seems to be limited; it is likely that they will be quickly absorbed. When this happens one of the great epochs of American history will have ended. . . . Paradoxically, the force of American equalitarianism, which attempts to make all men American and alike, and the force of our class order, which creates differences among ethnic peoples, have combined to dissolve our ethnic groups."[4] As part of this assimilation process, ethnic groups must, according to the authors, "unlearn" their cultural traits, which are "evaluated by the host society as inferior," in order to "successfully learn the new way of life necessary for full acceptance."[5] Even more disturbing to the present-day viewpoint, Warner and Srole correlated the potential for speedy assimilation with a hierarchy of racial and cultural acceptability, ranging from English-speaking Protestants at the top to "Negroes and all Negroid mixtures" at the bottom. Whereas the assimilation of fair-skinned Protestants, whether English-speaking or not, was expected to be unproblematic and therefore of short duration, that of groups deviating from this ethnic prototype in any significant respect would be considerably more prolonged, if not doubtful. Thus, the assimilation of "dark-skinned" Mediterranean Catholics, such as the Italians, was expected by Warner and Srole to demand a "moderate" period, which the authors equate with six generations or more! The assimilation of non-European groups was even more problematic and was expected to continue into the indefinite future or even, in the case of African Americans, to be delayed until "the present American social order changes gradually or by revolution."[6]

Exhibited here are some of the features of the old assimilation conception that scholars now vigorously reject in relation to new immigrants and their American-born children. One is the seeming inevitability of assimilation, which is presented as the natural end point of the process of incorporation into American society. Even black Americans, blocked by the racism of U.S. society from full pursuit of the assimilation goal, are presumed by Warner and Srole to be assimilating, albeit at a glacial pace. Further, by equating assimilation with full or successful incorporation, these and other earlier writers viewed African Americans and other racial minorities as, in effect, incompletely assimilated, rather than as incorporated into the society on some other basis. In relation to black Americans in particular, this older assimilation conception was consistent with liberal incrementalist strategies for pursuing racial justice, which, on the one hand, sought to remove legal and institutional barriers to equality and to combat white prejudice and discrimination and, on the other, urged blacks to seek integration and to become more like middle-class whites.[7] In his classic work, *An American Dilemma*, Gunnar Myrdal stated this premise baldly: "We assume that it is to the advantage of American Negroes as individuals and as a group to become assimilated into American culture, to acquire the traits held in esteem by dominant white Americans."[8] By this standard, black Americans and other racial minorities should want to assimilate rather than seek support and protection in the company of their racial/ethnic peers.

Another feature that has been found objectionable in the old formulation of assimilation is its apparent ethnocentrism, which elevates a particular cultural model, that of middle-class Protestant whites of British ancestry, to the normative standard by which other groups are to be assessed and toward which they should aspire. This is bluntly apparent in the ranking of groups by Warner and Srole, which places groups higher in the scale, and thus more rapidly assimilating, the closer they are at the outset to the Anglo-Saxon cultural (and physical) model. Assimilation, then, meant becoming more like middle-class Protestant whites. That this was in fact the cultural prototype for assimilation was quite explicit in the most authoritative discussion of the concept in the post–World War II era, Milton Gordon's *Assimilation in American Life* (1964). Gordon wrote, for instance, that "if there is anything in American life which can be described as an overall American culture which serves as a reference point for immigrants and their children, it can best be described, it seems to us, as the middle-class cultural patterns of, largely, white Protestant, Anglo-Saxon origins."[9] He did not argue that this cultural standard enjoyed its preeminence because of inherent superiority, just that it was the first one established by the European colonists and was associated with the ethnic core of U.S. society. He recognized, moreover, that the mere acquisition of this cultural prototype did not guarantee acceptance by the core group and thus social assimilation to it; discrimination could still be practiced against minority individuals, even if they perfectly mimicked the behavioral repertoire of the WASP upper-middle class.[10] But what Gordon and other writers on assimilation failed to recognize was the possibility of successful incorporation into the society on a cultural basis other than that of the WASP mainstream. Insofar as individuals and groups retained ethnic cultural distinctiveness, they were presumed to be hampered in achieving socioeconomic and other forms of integration and, of course, to be incompletely assimilated, with the implication that over time their similarity to the middle-class Anglo-Saxon standard would grow.

The one-sided nature of the assimilation process, as traditionally conceived, and the cultural and ethnic homogeneity it allegedly produces have also provided the basis for disputing it. As Warner and Srole's reference to an "unlearning" process suggests, the old assimilation concept assumed that the minority group would change almost completely in order to assimilate (except for areas where it already resembled the majority group), while the majority culture would remain unaffected. Gordon was quite explicit about this. In a well-known passage, he asked whether acculturation was "entirely a one-way process? Was the core culture entirely unaffected by the presence of the immigrants and the colored minorities?"[11] Although he took pains to stress the contributions to American life of many minority individuals, his answer was for the most part affirmative: other than in the area of institutional religion, and aside from what he characterized as "minor modifications" made by minority cultures, the culture of the Anglo-Saxon core was accepted intact by assimilating ethnic groups and thus took the place of their own. From the contemporary standpoint, this view of the predominance of the culture of Anglo-American groups that settled in North America in the colonial era downplays the multiple cultural streams that have fed into American culture, affecting even the English language as spoken by Americans.[12] And it presumes that assimilation will impose a cultural homogeneity where diversity previously reigned. Not only does this view seem in contradiction to the riotous cultural bloom of the United States, but also, in the contemporary, rapidly globalizing world, it seems quite undesirable to extinguish the distinctive cultural and linguistic knowledge that immigrants could pass on to their children.

The final fatal flaw in the old assimilation canon, according to a common view, is that it allows no room for a positive role for the ethnic or racial group. The ethnic community could provide temporary shelter for immigrants and their children seeking to withstand the intense stresses associated with the early stages of immigration to a new society; according to frequently used images, the ethnic community was a "way station" or a "decompression chamber." But, past a certain point, attachment to the ethnic group would hinder minority individuals from taking full advantage of the opportunities offered by American society, which require individualistic mobility, not ethnic loyalty. What assimilationist scholars appeared to overlook was that, in some cases, the ethnic group could, by dominating some economic niches, be the source of better socioeconomic opportunities for ethnic entrepreneurs. In New York's garment industry throughout the first half of the twentieth century, it was an advantage for businessmen to be Jewish or Italian, and it would have been difficult for members of other groups to establish themselves in the industry's network of particularistic transactions. There are also important non-economic ways in which the ethnic group can contribute to the well-being of its members, such as through the solidarity and support provided by co-ethnics with whom one shares a diffuse sense of a common heritage.[13]

Clearly there are marked deficiencies in the old assimilation canon. Events and intellectual trends since the 1960s have brought about social changes that make these deficiencies very apparent. The 1960s were a watershed period shaped by social movements that raised probing and far-reaching questions about the constitution of American society, especially with respect to the status of minorities and women. In light of the institutional changes that followed in the wake of these social movements, future historians may view this period as just as transformative for American society as was the Protestant Reformation for European civilization. Intellectual trends responding to the unfolding events emphasized the rights of groups whose history of exclusion and discrimination was viewed as justifying remedial action. Criticism of the old canonical formulation of assimilation reflects a new consensus involving a mandate for the inclusion of all groups in civil society and for remedial action to secure *equality of rights,* interpreted broadly as meaning parity in life chances. This logic has permeated thinking about the incorporation of immigrant minorities, imparting a strong momentum to the rejection of the old assimilation canon.

Alternative models have developed describing how immigrants adapt in a new historical context of globalization and non-European immigration. One such alternative envisions enhanced prospects for a vigorous ethnic pluralism in the contemporary world, generated partly by the advantages to be derived from welfare-maximizing features of ethnic connections and partly by globalization driven by enormous advances in information technology, market integration, and mass air transportation—all of which make it feasible for immigrants and perhaps the second and later generations to maintain significant relationships with their homeland and with the relatives and towns that hold a special place in their hearts and memories. So remarkable has the prospect for such relationships seemed that a substantial body of scholarship has mushroomed around it under the somewhat faddish name of *transnationalism* (though the phenomenon is not entirely new, as we will observe in a later chapter).[14] The pluralist alternative envisions that, in the contemporary world, the choice to live in an ethnic social and cultural matrix need not be associated with the loss of the advantages once afforded almost exclusively by the mainstream.

The prospect that pluralism will flourish to a degree not seen before in the United States begins with the observation that some level of pluralism has in fact survived all along, though often at the societal margins. Growing interest in multiculturalism has led to a recognition that minority cultures have retained a vitality that was not acknowledged during the period when the melting pot was the paramount metaphor for American society. Native American languages such as Navaho (178,000 speakers in 2000) continue to thrive, for instance, as do African American religious traditions and numerous customs brought by immigrant groups. Recent scholarship adds the innovative claim that ethnic individuals can derive advantages from a group's culture and institutions. The claim comes in varied forms: the argument that bilingual individuals possess cognitive advantages over those who speak only one tongue; the suggestion that ethnic sub-economies, epitomized by the extensive Cuban sub-economy in Miami, can provide opportunities for income and mobility equal to those in the mainstream economy; and the observation that involvement with an ethnic culture and institutions offers protection to second-generation adolescents from some of the hazards of growing up in the inner city.[15] In each case, it is implied that ethnics have a motivation to reject assimilation, at least in its crassest forms.

Transnationalism may strengthen that motivation. The idea of transnationalism emphasizes the prospects for achieving an almost seamless connection between workaday lives in America and the origin society through a web of border-spanning cultural, social, and economic ties. An example of a style of transnationalism rooted in globalization is seen in the large Japanese business community in America, where corporate executives and technical personnel maintain close linkages with their home offices and business associates in Tokyo through information technology and frequent air travel to Japan. Another example of transnationalism is the new form of sojourning by low-wage laborers and entrepreneurs from the Caribbean Basin and Central America.[16] Border-spanning social networks enable sojourners to send remittances, operate cross-national small businesses, invest their savings in the hometown economy, and sustain ongoing communal life in two countries.

While the pluralist alternative to assimilation envisions opportunities that are at least the equivalent of those found in the mainstream, another alternative model foresees a form of incorporation associated with constricted opportunities. It focuses on the possibility that many in the second and third generations from the new immigrant groups, hindered by their very humble initial locations in American society and barred from entry into the mainstream by their race and their class location, will be incorporated into American society as disadvantaged minorities. This approach is associated with the terms "segmented" and "downward" assimilation.[17] In application to low-income nonwhite immigrants, the term refers to a route of assimilation guided by the cultural models of poor, native-born African Americans and Latinos, a route which has probably been traveled in previous immigration eras—for example, by the Afro-Caribbean immigrants of the early twentieth century and their children, many of whom gradually became part of the black American population.[18] The segmented assimilation concept thus alerts us to an emergent social problem: individuals in the second generation who perceive that they are likely to remain in their parents' status at the bottom of the occupational hierarchy and are then tempted to drop out of school and join the inner-city underclass.

Yet the segmented assimilation concept risks essentializing central-city black culture in the image of the underclass, which the American mainstream views as the undeserving poor.[19] This image overlooks the variety of cultural models found among urban African Americans and inflates the magnitude of the underclass population.[20] To be sure, the black underclass may exercise a greater influence in shaping the cultural practices of the inner city than its relative size warrants.[21] But the great majority of adult urban African Americans and Latinos hold down jobs, have families, and aspire to a better future for their children.[22] For this group, middle-class aspirations and norms are an important feature of ordinary lives in the central city.[23] Thus, segmented assimilation, which has value in calling attention to an emergent social problem facing Afro-Caribbeans and arguably Mexicans and other Latinos,[24] may predict an excessively pessimistic future for central-city minority youths.

The demographic realities of the United States have given additional momentum to the rethinking in progress on the assimilation of immigrants and their descendants. The emerging demographic contours of an American society that has received more than 20 million legal immigrants since the passage of the Immigration Act of 1965 can be found sharply etched in the data from the 2000 U.S. Census. The foreign-born and their children now constitute about 20 percent of the American population. They are concentrated in a number of large states such as California, Florida, New York, Texas, and Illinois, magnifying the regional impacts of immigration. Their presence has been dramatically visible in California, the nation's most populous state, where one in eight Americans resides. The state's robust population growth during the 1990s, almost 10 percent, was largely driven by the rapid increase in the Hispanic and Asian populations, which grew by 33 and 43 percent respectively. Within the span of two decades, the population of non-Hispanic whites declined from two-thirds to slightly less than half of the state's population.[25] Hispanics and Asians have become the two largest minority groups, with African Americans' share of the population declining. The pace of demographic change is even more intense in an immigrant metropolis such as Los Angeles, where Hispanics were 45 percent of the county's population in 2000, followed by non-Hispanic whites (31 percent), Asians (12 percent), and African Americans (9 percent). Although it should be noted that nearly half of Hispanics identify themselves racially as white,[26] a mainstream that constitutes a majority of California's population will need to be racially diverse, especially in the largest metropolitan areas. The profundity and rapidity of California's demographic change are unlikely to be replicated on a large scale elsewhere in the United States in the near future; but in some other large states and metropolitan areas, nonwhites and Latinos have achieved a critical mass sufficient to exercise a strong, if not increasingly dominant, influence on regional developments.

What can assimilation look like in such a diverse and ethnically dynamic society? The aim of this book is to address this question by providing new ways of theorizing assimilation as a social process stemming from immigration. We argue that, while both of the alternative models of incorporation—pluralist and segmented—possess their own spheres of validity, neither rules out the possibility that assimilation in the form of entry into the mainstream has a major role to play in the future. Despite the accuracy of some of the criticisms of the canonical formulation of assimilation, we believe that there is still a vital core to the concept, which has not lost its utility for illuminating many of the experiences of contemporary immigrants and the new second generation.

The contemporary debate over assimilation and the changing realities of the United States point to the need to rethink some of the classical writings on assimilation, including those of the early years of the Chicago School of sociology. The founders of the Chicago School were responding to the transformative changes and social problems associated with the mass immigration of their time, which have some similarities with those of today. In reflecting on the issues raised by the ethnic and racial diversity of immigrant groups, they posited a conception of the mainstream as rooted in what now must be viewed as a *composite culture* evolving out of the interpenetration of diverse cultural practices and beliefs. By "composite culture," we refer to the mixed, hybrid character of the ensemble of cultural practices and beliefs that has evolved in the United States since the colonial period. By contrast, the idea of multiculturalism, though it may appear to be similar, implies more or less autonomous cultural centers organized around discrete ethnic groups, with much less interpenetration of cultural life.

The Chicago School's definition of assimilation envisioned a diverse mainstream society in which people of different ethnic/racial origins and cultural heritages evolve a common culture that enables them to sustain a common national existence.[27] This more flexible and open-ended specification of assimilation largely receded into the background in the later writings of Warner and Srole and Gordon, which we identify with the old assimilation approach. The view of American culture and society that emerged in the subsequent assimilation canon was heavily influenced by the functionalism of Talcott Parsons and other sociologists who built structural functionalism into the reigning paradigm.[28] This paradigm conceived of society as a largely homogeneous social system integrated around core values and norms, in which stable equilibrium between the structures and functions of component subsystems sustained social order. Such a conception of society is built into the old assimilation formulation of the core Anglo-American middle-class culture and society—the putative mainstream—which was the end point of assimilation. In rethinking assimilation, we have sought a reformulation of the concept that adheres in spirit to the classic Chicago School definition; but we extend this foundation with the aim of adapting assimilation to the demographic realities of American society stemming from contemporary immigration.[29]

How then should assimilation be defined, given the prospects for a more racially diverse mainstream society arising from large-scale immigration of non-Europeans? A viable conceptualization must recognize that (1) ethnicity is essentially a social boundary, a distinction that individuals make in their everyday lives and that shapes their actions and mental orientations toward others;[30] (2) this distinction is typically embedded in a variety of social and cultural differences between groups that give an ethnic boundary concrete significance (so that members of one group think, "They are not like us because . . ."); and (3) assimilation, as a form of ethnic change, may occur through changes taking place in groups on both sides of the boundary. Consequently, we define assimilation as the decline of an ethnic distinction and its corollary cultural and social differences. "Decline" means in this context that a distinction attenuates in salience, that the occurrences for which it is relevant diminish in number and contract to fewer and fewer domains of social life. Individuals' ethnic origins become less and less relevant in relation to the members of another ethnic group (typically, but not necessarily, the ethnic majority group), and individuals on both sides of the boundary see themselves more and more as alike, assuming they are similar in terms of some other critical factors such as social class; in other words, they mutually perceive themselves with less and less frequency in terms of ethnic categories and increasingly only under specific circumstances. To speak in terms of extremes, at one time an ethnic distinction may be relevant for virtually all of the life chances of members of two different groups—where they live, what kinds of jobs they get, and so forth—while at a later time it may have receded to the point where it is observed only in occasional family rituals. Yet assimilation, as we define it, does not require the disappearance of ethnicity; and the individuals undergoing it may still bear a number of ethnic markers. Assimilation can occur on a large scale to members of a group even as the group itself remains a highly visible point of reference on the social landscape, embodied in an ethnic culture, neighborhoods, and institutional infrastructures.

Our definition of assimilation intentionally allows for the possibility that the nature of the mainstream into which minority individuals and groups are assimilating is changed in the process; assimilation is eased insofar as members of minority groups do not sense a rupture between participation in mainstream institutions and familiar social and cultural practices. Given demographic trends, the mainstream is likely to evolve in the direction of including members of ethnic and racial groups that were formerly excluded. Given the plasticity of the mainstream, an obvious question is, How does one bound or define it? The American mainstream encompasses a core set of interrelated institutional structures and organizations regulated by rules and practices that weaken, even undermine, the influence of ethnic origins per se. For example, university admissions committees operate within the framework of formal and informal rules that specify guidelines for selecting incoming students. Once they are admitted, the university's rules governing the treatment of students do not distinguish among them by their ethnic origin. A useful way of defining the mainstream is as that part of the society *within* which ethnic and racial origins have at most minor impacts on life chances or opportunities.[31] This conception, we want to underscore, allows for ethnic and racial origins to be powerful determinants of opportunities in the society as a whole, particularly when those outside the mainstream are compared to those in it. Moreover, it does not imply that full equality of opportunities obtains within the mainstream, because life chances are still strongly differentiated by social class and other non-ethnic factors. Thus, we do not limit the mainstream to the middle class: it contains a working class and even some who are poor, not just affluent suburbanites. One objection to our definition could be that the boundary between the mainstream and the rest of the society is not as clear as the definition makes it seem. We concede that there is undoubtedly some fuzziness at the boundary, but we see the definition as a valuable heuristic conception.

Historically, the American mainstream, which originated with the colonial northern European settlers, has evolved through incremental inclusion of ethnic and racial groups that formerly were excluded and accretion of parts of their cultures to the composite culture. Although cultural elements from the earliest groups have been preserved—in this sense there is great cultural continuity—elements contributed from subsequent immigrant groups have been incorporated continually into the mainstream. Such elements are most easily seen in cuisine and in highbrow and middlebrow forms of entertainment and artistic expression; and in many cases they have diffused well beyond the regions where the groups that brought them have concentrated. For example, the recreational practices of Germans played an important role in relaxing puritanical strictures against Sunday pleasures and left a deep mark on what is now viewed as the quintessentially American culture of leisure: "American culture in the century after 1880 moved in fits and starts toward the values cherished by German Americans. A love of music and drama and liberal attitudes about card playing, drinking, and Sunday relaxation ceased to be regarded as foreign imports."[32] This influence was in addition to the most obvious cultural borrowing—German Christmas customs, including the decorated Christmas tree. The mainstream can even encompass alternative institutional forms. For instance, when Jewish and Catholic immigrants were pouring into the United States at the beginning of the twentieth century, the mainstream was still defined as Christian, even Protestant; but during and shortly after World War II, the boundary shifted to include Judaism and Catholicism as mainstream American religions, as they are viewed today (see Chapter 3).

Thus, the mainstream culture, which is highly variegated in any event—by social class and region, among other factors—changes as elements of the cultures of the newer groups are incorporated into it. The composite culture that we identify with the mainstream is made up of multiple interpenetrating layers and allows individuals and subpopulations to forge identities out of its materials to distinguish themselves from others in the mainstream—as do, for instance, Baptists in Alabama and Jews in New York—in ways that are still recognizably American.

This process of incorporation is certain to continue and to encompass portions of the new immigrant groups and their cultures. We can see this in the ready acceptance of intermarriage between whites and Asian Americans and the ongoing incorporation into the American mainstream of cultural practices and cuisine from East Asia. This will likely lead to a break with the conventional equation of the mainstream with white America. We view it as unlikely, in other words, that the assimilation of the near future will be accomplished by redefining non-European groups as "white," even though this did happen in the past to the racially "in-between" European groups, such as the Italians and eastern European Jews.[33] Rather, in the next quarter century, we expect some blurring of the main ethnic and racial boundaries of American life. For portions of nonwhite and Hispanic groups, the social and cultural distance from the mainstream will shrink: these individuals will live and work in ethnically and racially mixed milieus, much of the time without a sense that their social interactions are greatly affected by their origins; some will be the products of intermarriage, or they or their children will intermarry. Indeed, this process is already visibly under way, but it will expand in the future. This will not, we want to underscore, mean an end to the profound racial and ethnic inequalities of the United States. But it will alter the racial compartmentalization of American society to an important extent. These considerations leave a fundamental question: What will contemporary assimilation mean for the most intractable boundary, the black-white one? In our concluding chapter, as we spell out the implications for the future, we address this difficult question.

Any effort such as this requires a theoretical base to give coherence to its argument. The theoretical approach we take is influenced by the new institutionalism, a cross-disciplinary paradigm oriented to explaining the stability and change of institutional structures.[34] An underlying claim of the new institutionalist approach is that institutionalized incentives matter in channeling the action of individuals and groups.[35] Our rethinking has led us to formulate a "new assimilation theory" that specifies the mechanisms of assimilation. This is outlined in the second half of Chapter 2. We argue that one key to understanding trajectories of incorporation lies in the interplay between the purposive action of immigrants and their descendants and the contexts—that is, institutional structures, cultural beliefs, and social networks—that shape it. The mainstream encompasses structures of opportunity offering powerful incentives that make assimilation rewarding for many immigrants and their descendants.[36]

Another crucial factor lies in the ability and willingness of established groups in the white majority to resist and exclude the newcomers, which are presently greatly reduced from what was the case during the first half of the twentieth century. The children of immigrants from southern and eastern Europe experienced intense nativist hostility and some discrimination. Nevertheless, their constitutional rights based on European origins (and their legally unchallenged whiteness) differentiated them from nonwhite migrant groups of the time, such the Chinese and the Mexicans, who were denied these rights. As we will show in Chapter 3, civil rights—and the political incorporation that followed from them—were critically important to the gradual assimilation of these European groups, who continued to face prejudice and discrimination. Because of the subsequent extension of civil rights to nonwhites, the monitoring and enforcement of formal rules that once worked to effect exclusion from the mainstream now contribute to lowering the barriers to entry for immigrant minorities and the new second generation. The institutional boundaries of the mainstream are more open now to the entry of nonwhites than they have been in any other period of American history. In Chapter 2 we argue that by attacking racial discrimination, the institutional changes of the civil rights period introduced a tidal shift, even if they have not been successful in eradicating racism. In addition, the legitimacy of overtly racist belief and practice has never been lower in the eyes of most Americans. These changes have subtly but noticeably shifted societal incentives in the direction of promoting improved, predictable chances for minorities. Even as we make this argument, we recognize that these improvements are still small for some minority groups, especially non-immigrant ones, such as African Americans.

As with social mobility in industrial societies for all ethnic groups, majority or minority, assimilation into the mainstream mainly occurs as an individual, family-based process.[37] The extent of intergenerational upward mobility is more limited in industrial societies than is commonly assumed, and there is a divergence in outcomes for all ethnic groups, whereby many experience upward social mobility while most move laterally, and some even move downward in the stratification order. Hence, assimilation linked to actual social mobility proceeds unevenly and varies across ethnic groups and within the same group. It depends in part on the forms of capital that immigrants bring, as we elaborate in Chapter 2. In a high-technology society, immigrant families who bring large volumes of human and cultural capital obviously have an advantage over low-wage laborers with little formal schooling.

The conception of assimilation that we put forward is neither normative nor prescriptive. We recognize that the separation between positive and normative science has been, and still is, difficult to achieve in the study of human affairs, and that much of the conceptual literature in the field of ethnicity and race mixes the two together. A normative slant on assimilation is exemplified by the earlier quotations from Warner and Srole and could be amply illustrated by quotations with a similar character from elsewhere in the classical literature. It was commonly assumed that assimilation is not only a "normal" outcome for an ethnic minority in American society but also a beneficial one, bringing an end to prejudice and discrimination and a liberation from the constricting bonds of parochial group loyalties. As numerous critics have pointed out, the classical assimilation literature thus appears to presume, or at least seems consistent with, a now outdated view that ethnicity is a primordial bond destined to weaken as a consequence of the spreading rational individualism and enlightenment of modern society. Part of our task is to free the concept of assimilation from this unnecessary baggage.

Much of the skepticism today about the relevance of assimilation for the immigration of the current era is mirrored by perceptions about immigrants in past eras. Needless to say, the mere existence of such parallels does not prove that contemporary immigrants and their descendants will undergo a process of assimilation comparable to that of the past; it only alerts us to the possibility that there may be more continuity than our sense of the uniqueness of the present moment may readily grant. Therefore, after laying out the basis for a new theory of assimilation in Chapter 2, we take up the historical record and its relevance. In Chapter 3, we examine in some depth the evidence about assimilation among the European-ancestry groups and East Asian groups from the earlier era of mass immigration. This evidence is instructive, for it demonstrates the complexity of the historical assimilation process, which differs in some important respects from the stereotyped view. It leads us to a consideration of frequently advanced claims about the differences between past and contemporary immigration eras, which is the subject of Chapter 4. There we assess the various arguments that express skepticism over the relevance of assimilation for contemporary immigration. Suffice it to say here that we find these putative differences less decisive than they seem at first sight. In Chapters 5 and 6 we turn our attention fully to the new immigrant groups. Chapter 5 depicts the historical background of the new immigration and provides illustrative capsule summaries of some of the new groups. In Chapter 6 we sift recent data for clues concerning the potential relevance of assimilation, considering the domains of language, socioeconomic standing, residential situation, and intermarriage. Chapter 7 summarizes our argument and also attempts to address implications for the American future and for the place of ethnic and racial cleavages in it.

CHAPTER TWO

Assimilation Theory, Old and New

Whatever the precise words, conceptions of assimilation have been central to understanding the American experience at least since colonial times. Even then, assimilation was a contested idea, reflecting different visions of a society that was coming into being. Nation building through immigration has been a source of contention throughout America's history as a settler society. The alarm expressed by Benjamin Franklin about the swelling number of Germans in Pennsylvania has a very contemporary ring: "Why should the Palatine boors be suffered to swarm into our settlements and by herding together establish their language and manners to the exclusion of ours? Why should *Pennsylvania,* founded by the *English,* become a colony of aliens, who will shortly be so numerous as to germanize us instead of our anglifying them?"[1] Implicit here is an early version of what has since become known as Anglo-conformity, the expectation that immigrant groups should swallow intact the existing Anglo-American culture while simultaneously disgorging their own.[2] A different spirit runs through the now well-known words of the French-born J. Hector St. John Crèvecoeur, who in his *Letters from an American Farmer* (1782) gives an early articulation of the melting pot conception of assimilation:

> What is the American, this new man? He is either an European, or the descendant of an European, hence that strange mixture of blood, which

you will find in no other country. I could point out to you a family whose grandfather was an Englishman, whose wife was Dutch, whose son married a French woman, and whose present four sons now have four wives of different nations. *He* is an American, who leaving behind him all his ancient prejudices and manners, receives new ones from the new mode of life he has embraced, the new government he obeys, and the new rank he holds. . . . Here individuals of all nations are melted into a new race of men, whose labours and posterity will one day cause great changes in the world.[3]

In 1845, Ralph Waldo Emerson extended the melting pot idea beyond Europeans when he referred to the energy not only "of Irish, Germans, Swedes, Poles, and Cossacks, and all the European tribes," but also "of the Africans, and of the Polynesians," who would contribute to "a new race, a new religion, a new state, a new literature, which will be as vigorous as the new Europe which came out of the smelting-pot of the Dark Ages."[4]

These quotations reflect different visions of assimilation that existed even during the early experience of nation building through the incorporation of immigrants and their descendants. They also illustrate how ideas regarding assimilation are rooted in historical experiences of immigration, from the colonial era of immigration from northwestern Europe to the nineteenth-century transition to mass immigration from southern and eastern Europe and Asia. Each new wave of immigration expanded the range of groups that contributed to the ethnic diversity of American society, which in turn stimulated new thinking about the assimilation of newcomers. More recently, conceptions of assimilation have undergone further rethinking in response to the contemporary nonwhite immigration from Asia, the Caribbean, and Latin America. Assimilation is not a static or unchanging concept; its definition and specifications have evolved steadily as American society has changed in its more than several-century experience of immigration. Conceptions of the American mainstream likewise have changed as immigration has contributed to the growing diversity of ethnic and racial groups that inhabit the United States.

Assimilation and the Chicago School

Assimilation as a paradigm for the social-scientific understanding of immigration is traceable to the Chicago School sociologists of the early twentieth century and especially to the work of Robert E. Park, W. I. Thomas, and their collaborators and students.[5] That a scientifically oriented conception of assimilation should have arisen there is understandable, for the members of the Chicago School achieved distinction partly through the close observation of the urban environment around them, and Chicago was then a city growing by leaps and bounds as a result of massive migrations and industrial growth.[6] As late as 1833, when Chicago was incorporated as a town, its site was almost bare, and its population numbered some 350 souls. Scarcely three-quarters of a century later, its population had swelled to more than 2 million. The migrations responsible for this growth brought people from rural areas of the United States but even more from other countries. In 1910, 70 percent of the city's population consisted of immigrants and their children, who came from numerous, primarily European countries and frequently from peasant backgrounds.[7] The next decade witnessed the initial large-scale migration to the city of blacks from the rural South and the resulting intense racial conflicts. All around the city in this era, one could observe the difficult adjustments that ethnic minorities and rural migrants were making to urban American life.

At the newly founded University of Chicago (1890), sociologists took up the challenge to understand the experiences of migrants to the city. Robert Park and E. W. Burgess provided a widely known early definition of assimilation—"a process of interpenetration and fusion in which persons and groups acquire the memories, sentiments, and attitudes of other persons and groups and, by sharing their experience and history, are incorporated with them in a common cultural life."[8] When read closely, this definition clearly does not require what many critics of assimilation theory assume, namely, the erasure of all signs of ethnic origins. Instead, it equates assimilation with changes that bring ethnic minorities into the mainstream of American life. It is in its way a critical response to the total Americanization of immigrants that at the time was being aggressively promoted by many Americans. The limited nature of the assimilation Park envisioned was made even clearer by another definition that he later created for the *Encyclopedia of the Social Sciences,* whereby "social" assimilation was "the name given to the process or processes by which peoples of diverse racial origins and different cultural heritages, occupying a common territory, achieve a cultural solidarity sufficient at least to sustain a national existence."[9] This definition expresses an understanding of assimilation with contemporary appeal, leaving ample room for the persistence of ethnic elements set within a common national frame.[10]

Nonetheless, Park's legacy is closely identified with the notion of assimilation as the end stage of a "race-relations cycle" of "contact, competition, accommodation, and eventual assimilation," a sequence that, in his best-known formulation, was viewed as "apparently progressive and irreversible."[11] In depicting the race relations cycle, Park was rather deliberately painting with broad brush strokes on a large canvas, for the cycle refers obliquely to the processes in the modern world economy, including long-distance labor migrations, that bring once-separated peoples into closer contact. Competition is the initial, unstable consequence of contact, as the groups struggle to gain advantages over one another, eventuating in the more stable stage of accommodation, where a social structure of typically unequal relations among groups and a settled understanding of group positions have emerged.[12] But no matter how stable this social structure, ethnic differences would eventually diminish, according to Park, who wrote that "in our estimates of race relations we have not reckoned with the effects of personal intercourse and the friendships that inevitably grow up out of them."[13]

The Chicago School of sociology contributed to the elaboration of the concept of assimilation through important empirical studies directed at informing social policy. One of the early ones, *Old World Traits Transplanted* (1921), which was originally published under the names of Robert Park and Herbert Miller but is now known to have been written largely by W. I. Thomas, was self-consciously formulated against the campaign for rapid and complete Americanization waged during and immediately after World War I.[14] In a profound insight that remains current today, Thomas, Park, and Miller recognized that assimilation would proceed more unproblematically if immigrant groups were left to adjust at their own pace to American life, rather than being compelled to drop their familiar ways: "A wise policy of assimilation, like a wise educational policy, does not seek to destroy the attitudes and memories that are there, but to build on them. There is a current opinion in America, of the 'ordering and forbidding' type, demanding from the immigrant a quick and complete Americanization through the suppression and repudiation of all the signs that distinguish him from us."[15]

Members of the Chicago School were pioneers in the study of city life, and the most enduring empirical studies of assimilation they produced examine it as a social process embedded in the urban landscape. These studies take as their point of departure Park's axiom that "social relations are . . . inevitably correlated with spatial relations; physical distances . . . are, or seem to be, indexes of social distances."[16] From this it follows that upwardly mobile immigrants and their descendants will leave ethnic enclaves, since "changes of economic and social status . . . tend to be registered in changes of location."[17] When combined with E. W. Burgess's zonal model of the city, in which immigrants settle initially in dilapidated areas in a city's industrial and commercial center, Park's dictum implies a correspondence among assimilation, socioeconomic mobility, and spatial mobility outward from the city center toward the suburban ring. In Burgess's formulation, immigrant groups initially enter slums "crowded to overflowing with immigrant colonies," move in the next generation to ethnic working-class neighborhoods, and may eventually disperse into the "Promised Land" at the city's edge.[18]

In *The Ghetto* (1928), Park's student Louis Wirth analyzed this process for Jewish neighborhoods in Chicago. Where "a steady influx of new immigrants has replenished the . . . community, there a ghetto, with all the characteristic local color, has grown up and maintains itself." But the ghetto is weakened as many residents increasingly desire to break free from the narrowness of ghetto existence. Immigrants, or more typically their children, consequently leave it for "the more modern and less Jewish area of second settlement," a neighborhood with "a new complexion, unmistakably Jewish, though not quite as genuine as that of the ghetto itself." Since aspects of the ghetto follow the "partially assimilated Jews" into the new area, some move on again to a third neighborhood, changing their character and institutions at each of these stages.[19]

The seminal ideas of the Chicago School on assimilation were formulated during the final decades of mass immigration from southern and eastern Europe. These ideas guided the empirical studies of immigrant adaptation that established the University of Chicago as the preeminent center for research on the social problems of American urban society. But the empirical study that had the greatest subsequent impact, extending the Chicago School's ideas to the study of the descendants of turn-of-the-century immigrants, was W. Lloyd Warner and Leo Srole's *Social Systems of American Ethnic Groups* (1945). Concentrating on an older industrial city in New England, Warner and Srole observed a series of corresponding changes that occurred over the course of successive generations of various European ethnic groups following the end of mass immigration in the 1920s and the Great Depression of the 1930s. Their study was conducted during World War II, which contributed to lifting the New England economy out of the long slump stemming from the depression. They documented the decline of white ethnic enclaves in the context of the wartime economic boom as the native-born generations shifted out of the working class to higher occupational and class positions and better residential neighborhoods. In addition, they identified behavioral changes in the private spheres of ethnic groups, in the relations between husbands and wives and between parents and their children, as well as in the friendships formed by the children. In interpreting their findings, Warner and Srole posited that assimilation was the direction in which all groups were moving, but that there was great variation among them in the time required for it to occur. For virtually all groups of European origin, including the groups they characterized as "dark Caucasoids," such as Armenians and Sicilians, the time required was no more than "short" to "moderate," though, as we noted in the previous chapter, the scale of time involved could be longer than these terms might appear to imply, since the authors defined a "short" duration as a period anywhere in the range of one to six generations. For non-European groups, all of whom were in their view racially distinct, assimilation would be "slow" or "very slow," with the adjectives actually conveying the uncertainty of the process: "slow" refers to "a very long time in the future which is not yet discernible," while "very slow" indicates that "the group will not be totally assimilated until the present American social order changes gradually or by revolution."[20] "Dark-skinned" Jews were the one European group to whom this uncertain prognosis also applied. Despite the uncertainty about the prospects for assimilation of nonwhites and some Jews, the assumption that assimilation was the point on the horizon toward which all groups were moving, albeit in some cases with glacial slowness, was unquestioned. The stage had been set for the post–World War II synthesis.

The Canonical Synthesis

By the middle of the twentieth century, the apogee of the "melting pot" as metaphor, assimilation was integral to the American self-understanding as the pivot around which social science investigations of ethnicity and even of race turned. Yet, oddly, the concept itself was loosely specified and quite murky. There existed a broad consensus about the scope of assimilation, stemming from the early Chicago School formulation; but relatively little had been accomplished in the way of developing clear and consistent operational concepts that could be employed, in an analytically useful fashion, to measure the extent of assimilation of individuals and groups. Over the decades, a proliferation of definitions, created by anthropologists, sociologists, and others to fit the needs of particular research agendas, had accumulated, with attendant confusion generated by definitions that partly overlapped and partly did not.[21] The problem of disentangling the strands associated with assimilation to reveal its distinct elements and thereby fashion a set of operational concepts with analytic value in a broad range of research settings was not solved until Milton Gordon's *Assimilation in American Life* (1964). It is with his book that a canonical account takes on a sharply etched conceptual profile.[22]

Gordon's singular contribution was to set down a synthesis that elaborated a multidimensional concept of assimilation. Acculturation, he argued, was the dimension that typically came first and was, to a large degree, inevitable. He defined acculturation very broadly as the minority group's adoption of the "cultural patterns" of the host society—patterns extending beyond the acquisition of the English language and such other obvious externals as dress to include aspects normally regarded as part of the inner or private self, such as characteristic emotional expression or core values and life goals. The specific cultural standard that represented the direction and eventual outcome of the acculturation process was the "middle-class cultural patterns of, largely, white Protestant, Anglo-Saxon origins," which Gordon also described as the "core culture."[23] In his view, acculturation was a largely one-way process: except in the area of institutional religion, the minority group adopted the core culture, which remained basically unchanged by acculturation. Gordon also distinguished *intrinsic* cultural traits, those that are "vital ingredients of the group's cultural heritage," exemplified by religion and musical traditions, from *extrinsic* traits, which "tend to be products of the historical vicissitudes of the group's adjustment to the local environment" and thus are deemed less central to group identity.[24] The distinction seems to imply that extrinsic traits are readily surrendered by the group in making more or less necessary accommodations to the host society, but its implications are less clear about intrinsic ones. Certainly, Gordon had no expectation that the fundamental religious identities (e.g., Catholic, Jewish) of different immigrant groups would be given up as a result of acculturation.[25]

Acculturation could occur in the absence of other types of assimilation, and the stage of "acculturation only" could last indefinitely, according to Gordon. His major hypothesis was that structural assimilation—that is, integration into primary groups—is associated with, or stimulates, all other types of assimilation (*"Once structural assimilation has occurred, . . . all of the other types of assimilation will naturally follow"*). In particular, this meant that prejudice and discrimination would decline, if not disappear, that intermarriage would be common, and that the minority's separate identity would wane.[26] The hypothesis suggests a relationship of cause and effect, but it should not be given the causal inflection Gordon's language implies. Gordon did not develop a theory of assimilation specifying which causal mechanisms impede or promote the assimilation of individuals and ethnic groups. It could be just as true that a decline in prejudice allows structural assimilation to take place as the reverse. Gordon's contribution was the codification of a conceptual framework through lucid specification of some of the key dimensions of assimilation. His synthesis identifies various indicators of assimilation, which are not causally distinct but describe different dimensions of the same underlying process. These seven dimensions—cultural, structural, marital, identity, prejudice, discrimination, civic—provided a composite multidimensional index of assimilation that was useful as a guide in determining the extent of a group's assimilation according to both individual- and group-level criteria. Such specification of empirical indicators of assimilation was readily adapted to the variable research of quantitative sociology, which in the 1960s was in rapid ascendance.[27]

As noted, Gordon assumed that acculturation involved change on the part of an ethnic group in the direction of middle-class Anglo-American culture, which remained itself largely unaffected, except for what he described as "minor modifications" in areas such as food and place names.[28] An obvious difficulty, one that Gordon recognized elsewhere in his work (in his concept of the "ethclass," for instance), is that American culture varies greatly by locale and social class; acculturation hardly takes place in the shadow of a single middle-class cultural standard. But what was lacking more profoundly was a more differentiated and syncretic concept, a recognition that American culture was and is mixed, an amalgam of diverse influences, and that it continues to evolve "from the unsystematic fusion of various regional and racial customs and traditions," as Michael Lind points out in his discussion of what he calls the "vernacular" culture.[29]

It does not require a radical shift in perspective to recognize that assimilation and acculturation processes can occur not just through changes in one group that make it more like another, but also through changes in two (or more) groups that shrink the differences between them. In short, acculturation can result from processes of group convergence. Moreover, acculturation need not be limited to the substitution of one cultural element for its equivalent, whether the replacement comes from the majority or minority cultures, though such substitution certainly takes place; this narrow conception of acculturation is at the root of the frequently encountered notion that one group "adopts" the cultural traits of another. In a process of convergence, the impact of minority ethnic cultures on the mainstream can occur also by an expansion of the range of what is considered normative behavior within the mainstream; thus, elements of minority cultures are absorbed alongside their equivalents of Anglo-American or other origins or are fused with mainstream elements to create a composite culture. The cultural fusion that results, especially evident in urban life, remakes the repertoire of styles, cuisine, popular culture, and myths, and incrementally becomes incorporated into the American mainstream.

Gordon's legacy also includes codification of alternative conceptions of assimilation in the United States. Gordon described these as the "theories" of Anglo-conformity and of the melting pot, but they are more appropriately viewed as alternative popular beliefs or ideologies about the composition and nature of civil society. The model of Anglo-conformity, which corresponds in spirit with the campaign for rapid, "pressure-cooker" Americanization during and immediately after World War I, equated assimilation with acculturation in the Anglo-American mold. It ignored other aspects, and was therefore indifferent with regard to structural assimilation. The model of the melting pot has enjoyed several periods of popularity in American discussions of ethnicity, most recently in the aftermath of World War II. It offers an idealistic vision of American society and identity as arising from the biological and cultural fusion of different peoples; and while its exponents have usually emphasized the contributions of Europeans to the mixture, it allows for recognition of those of non-European groups as well. In terms of Gordon's scheme, the model emphasized cultural and structural assimilation. It forecast widespread intermarriage; a well-known variant, the triple melting pot, foresaw intermarriage as taking place within population pools defined by religious boundaries.[30] The cultural assimilation portion of the melting pot idea was rather ambiguous, however. Many early exponents spoke in ways that suggested a truly syncretic American culture blending elements from many different groups, but later commentators were more consistent with Gordon's own conception that acculturation is a mostly one-directional acceptance of Anglo-American patterns.[31]

Gordon discussed a third model, cultural pluralism, which, though not strictly speaking a part of the assimilation canon, nevertheless tended to bolster the assimilation concept by providing an unconvincing alternative. Here Gordon hewed rather strictly to an early-twentieth-century conception of pluralism articulated by the philosopher Horace Kallen. The basic idea was quite simple: that a society benefited when the different ethnic elements in it retained their cultural distinctiveness, analogous to the way that the sound of an orchestra gains in richness from the distinctive voices of the assembled instruments. Cultural pluralism is thus the intellectual ancestor of contemporary multiculturalism.[32] The difficulty, as Gordon recognized, is that Kallen's conception more or less required preservation of the cultural integrity of different groups and thus largely overlooked the cultural change and mixing arising from their interactions.

Interestingly, Gordon himself espoused none of these models. This may come as a surprise to many who know his views only in the context of the present-day, disparaging discussion of assimilation, for he has often been identified with a school that portrays assimilation as an almost inevitable outcome for groups that have entered the United States through immigration. But this is not, in fact, a fair characterization. Although Gordon left little doubt that, in his view, acculturation was inevitable to a large degree, he did not see structural assimilation as similarly foreordained. His analysis of American society led to the conclusion that *structural pluralism* rather than cultural pluralism was the more accurate description. He envisioned the United States as constituted from ethnic subsocieties, in whose institutions and social networks most individuals spend the major portion of their social lives.[33]

Another prominent element of the canonical synthesis is the notion of "straight-line assimilation," popularized by Herbert Gans and Neil Sandberg. (Gans later changed the straight line to a "bumpy" one.)[34] The straight-line idea envisions a process unfolding in a sequence of generational steps: each new generation represents on average a new stage of adjustment to the host society, that is, a further step away from ethnic "ground zero," the community and ethnoculture established by the immigrants, and a step closer in a variety of ways to more complete assimilation.[35] The idea of an inherent generational dynamic is well illustrated by the hypothesis of third-generation return, which has an ambiguous relationship to the assimilation thesis.[36] The logic behind the hypothesis is that the second generation, the children of the immigrant generation, feels impelled to assimilate by the need to demonstrate that it is truly part of the society and no longer foreign, while the third generation, in no doubt about being American, can afford to exhibit signs of ethnicity. "What the son wishes to forget, the grandson wishes to remember" was Will Herberg's pithy formulation that helped to popularize the idea.[37]

Extending the Canon

Gordon described his multidimensional schema as "assimilation variables"; and although he illustrated its applicability with a chart that employed only qualitative measures such as "yes," "no," "mostly," and "partly," his synthesis nonetheless opened the way for the development of quantitative indicators of assimilation. The specification of precise measures of assimilation gained ground in the 1960s, inspired by the breakthrough in quantitative research, especially in the field of stratification. Following the publication of seminal studies such as Peter Blau and Otis Dudley Duncan's *American Occupational Structure* (1967),[38] researchers shifted their focus in the 1970s from structural assimilation—integration into primary groups, intermarriage—to what became identified as "socioeconomic assimilation."

Status-attainment research reinforced the view that assimilation and social mobility are inextricably linked (and, conversely, that there is no assimilation if social mobility has not also occurred). Although this view had been adumbrated earlier, the explicit link between socioeconomic attainment and assimilation represented a conceptual reformulation, one that was in accord with the postwar interest in comparative research on social mobility. According to the most common conception, socioeconomic assimilation was equated with the attainment of average or above-average socioeconomic standing, as measured by indicators such as education, occupation, and income. It was deemed to have occurred to the degree that the socioeconomic distribution of the minority group resembles that of the majority.[39] Since many immigrant groups, especially those coming from agricultural backgrounds, such as the Irish, Italians, and Mexicans, entered the American social structure on its lowest rungs, this meaning of socioeconomic assimilation was often conflated with social mobility.

A more sophisticated conception of socioeconomic assimilation is needed to recognize that immigrant groups no longer start inevitably at the bottom of the labor market, that contemporary immigration includes numerous groups that bring substantial educational credentials, professional training, and other forms of human capital. One way to avoid the historical specificity in the conventional formulation is to define socioeconomic assimilation as minority participation in mainstream socioeconomic institutions (e.g., labor market, education) on the basis of parity with ethnic-majority individuals of similar socioeconomic origins. If the emphasis in the first conception falls on equality of attainments or position, the emphasis in the second is on equality of treatment: members of the immigrant minority and others similarly positioned have the same life chances in the pursuit of contested goods, such as desirable occupations. In this sense, the ethnic distinction has lost its relevance for processes of socioeconomic attainment.[40] In this sense, too, one can assimilate into the working class, and many do.

Also added to the quantitative repertoire of assimilation studies was a focus on residential mobility, which was not included in Gordon's synthesis either. This was a curious omission in that the settlement of immigrants in segregated ethnic communities, from which a gradual dispersal took place in tandem with other forms of assimilation, frequently after a generation or two, was one of the best-known observations of the Chicago School of sociology. The inclusion of residential mobility would appear to be consistent with Gordon's thinking on structural assimilation because it can be viewed as a "determinant" of spatial opportunity, that is, it expands the ethnic mix of everyday social contacts, especially for the generation growing up. Douglas Massey's "spatial assimilation" model formalized the significance of residence for the assimilation paradigm.[41] The model, a continuation of the Chicago School's ecological tradition, treats the spatial distribution of racial and ethnic groups as a reflection of their human capital and the state of their assimilation, broadly construed. Its basic tenets are that residential mobility follows from the acculturation and social mobility of ethnic families, and that residential mobility is an intermediate step on the way to structural assimilation. As members of minority groups acculturate and establish themselves in American labor markets, they attempt to leave behind less successful members of their groups and to convert socioeconomic and assimilation progress into residential gain by "purchasing" residence in places with greater advantages and amenities. But because good schools, clean streets, and other amenities are more common in the communities where the majority is concentrated, and these communities have been largely suburban since the 1950s, the search by ethnic minority families for better surroundings leads them toward suburbanization and greater contact with the majority.

Status-attainment and segregation research provided assimilation studies with quantitative measures, by means of powerful statistical methods, of the extent to which the life chances of immigrants and their descendants were similar or dissimilar to the mainstream experience. The study of ethnic and racial groups was linked to the general interest in understanding social and spatial mobility in a manner that shifted analytic interest from the examination of the cultural and interpersonal dimensions of assimilation to questions of comparative ethnic stratification. Accordingly, ethnic and racial minorities were regarded as moving in the direction of assimilation insofar as their educational, occupational, income, and residential characteristics approached, equaled, or exceeded those of Anglo-Americans or native-born non-Hispanic whites. Findings of persistent inequality in life chances, measured quantitatively with large public-use data sets, could be interpreted as evidence of discrimination and restrictions on the opportunity for assimilation.

A Return to the Chicago School's Roots

Gordon's analysis, the touchstone for all subsequent studies of assimilation, focused attention on the last stage of Park's race relations cycle. This has had the effect of influencing subsequent researchers to conceive of assimilation as an outcome expected to be rapidly achieved. Often they are quick to conclude that if signs of incipient assimilation are not abundant in the first and second generations, as in the naïve view that assimilation is contingent on attainment of middle-class status, the theory should be rejected. Yet the race relations cycle pioneered by Park took the long view of ethnic and race relations as a protracted historical process. (Warner and Srole, as we have noted, viewed six generations—the period they thought would be required by groups such as the Armenians and the Italians—as a "moderate" time to assimilation. Moreover, they did not conflate assimilation with entry into the middle class but identified it with the reduction of differences with Anglo-Americans, including presumably those in the laboring classes.) What later got eclipsed was the ethnic stratification in the period of accommodation for the first and second generations after immigration. In other words, the modal experience of these generations is within an ethnic stratification order, not rapid assimilation.

At virtually the same time as Gordon's seminal volume, another book appeared that represented a plausible attempt to formulate a complex and sophisticated theoretical analysis of ethnic stratification and assimilation. What distinguishes Tomatsu Shibutani and Kian Kwan from Gordon is their interest in reviving and updating the Chicago School approach to studies of assimilation. Although their study has had only a limited influence in shaping the subsequent literature on assimilation, it was an important early effort to specify causal mechanisms within the assimilation paradigm. Shibutani and Kwan employed a worldwide canvas for their study of assimilation—the case studies they used to ground their theoretical analysis included such diverse instances as Manchu rule over Han Chinese and ethnic stratification in the Roman Empire—and their underlying aim was to gain a deeper understanding of the American experience of race relations through comparative analysis of systems of ethnic domination in diverse historical and societal settings.

Shibutani and Kwan drew upon core conceptual themes of the Chicago School—George Herbert Mead's symbolic interactionism, Robert Park's race relations cycle, and Charles Darwin's evolutionary theory as extended by human ecologists—which they then applied to the study of assimilation and stratification of ethnic and racial minorities. The starting point of their analysis was the assertion that genetic differences between groups, if they even exist, cannot explain the social distances between them. Instead, differences giving rise to social distances are created and sustained symbolically through the human practice of classifying people into ranked categories. Following Mead, Shibutani and Kwan argued that how a person is treated in society depends "not on what he is" but on the "manner in which he is defined." Placing people into categories, each associated with expected behavior and treatment, allows humans to deal in a routine and predictable manner with strangers and acquaintances outside their primary groups. "Except in a small village one cannot possibly treat each individual he encounters as a unique human being, for he has neither the time nor the opportunity to acquire all the pertinent details. In such contexts as these, ethnic categories assume importance."[42] The claim that the classification of human beings into ethnic and racial groups stems from a *cognitive* mechanism embedded in social interactions, not biological difference, has a very contemporary ring, so much so that a name has been fashioned for it: *social construction*.[43]

Social distance is the linchpin concept in the explanation of the color line that segregates minorities and impedes assimilation. By social distance, Shibutani and Kwan refer to the subjective state of "nearness felt to certain individuals," not physical distance between groups.[44] In their account, change in subjective states—reduction of social distance—precedes and stimulates structural assimilation (in contradiction to Gordon's reasoning about structural assimilation, we may note). When social distance is small, there is a feeling of common identity, closeness, and shared experiences. But when social distance is great, people perceive and treat the other as belonging to a different category; and even after long acquaintance, there are still feelings of apprehension and reserve.

Shibutani and Kwan's use of the Chicago School's evolutionary approach contributed a vital macroscopic dimension which was missing from Gordon's synthesis. The large processes behind Park's race relations cycle, they argued, stem from competition and natural selection arising out of human migration and intergroup contact, as individuals, through groups, compete for resources and symbolic domination in a territorial space. Following the lead of the Norwegian anthropologist Frederik Barth, Shibutani and Kwan emphasized the social processes governing the boundary between ethnic groups rather than the attributes of specific groups.[45] Majority and minorities, they argued, must be studied in terms of their relationship to each other rather than separately. There are usually multiple groups sharing a territorial space, rather than only two, and they are bound by mutual interdependencies in such a way that the unit of analysis is the community as a whole, not distinct, enclosed ethnic groups.

Shibutani and Kwan linked the processes governing the symbolic construction of ethnic differences to the economic and status interests of corporate actors at the community level. Not only did this insight allow them to bring power—a concept absent from Gordon's scheme—into their analysis of assimilation, but also it pointed to the linkages between large-scale institutional processes and change at the individual level. For Shibutani and Kwan, a stable system of ethnic stratification is embedded not just in informal arrangements—social norms, customs, and conventions operating at the micro-sociological level—but also in an institutional order in which the dominant group upholds its position and privileges through control of formal institutions, the state, and coercive forces. Thus, the subordination of ethnic minorities is maintained not merely by moral consensus but ultimately by institutionalized power and outright coercion.

Their comparative analysis uncovered many exceptions to Park's optimistic conception of assimilation: interethnic contacts that resulted in the segregation, expulsion, or even the extermination of minority groups. It thus provides a soberly realistic assessment of the prospects for assimilation of non-European minorities. Domination is gained through competitive advantages accruing to the group whose culture is best adapted to exploit the resources of the ecology. Competition and natural selection push minorities into the least desirable residential locations and economic niches. Ethnic stratification orders tend to be long-lasting once established and institutionalized. They are based on a moral order in which the dominant group is convinced that its advantages derive from natural differences, and minorities come to believe in their inferiority and accept their lot at the bottom of the stratification order. Individual minority group members may achieve social mobility within the stratification order and gain economic parity, but as exceptions to the rule. Such upwardly mobile individuals, often of mixed race, acquire a marginal status that gives them a modicum of privilege and respect, but they are fully accepted neither by the dominant group nor by their own ethnic community. In a stable ethnic stratification order, individual assimilation occurs even while the system maintaining dominance remains intact.

In most of the cases Shibutani and Kwan analyzed, the assimilation of racial minorities occurs only incrementally as social distance is gradually reduced and the color line begins to break down. The mechanisms that bring about the reduction of social distance stem from structural changes that occur at the macro level. In the absence of such changes, ethnic stratification orders tend toward stable equilibrium. In other words, the segregation of racial minorities into ethnic enclaves would persist indefinitely in the absence of exogenous change. In explaining the changes that alter stable ethnic stratification orders, Shibutani and Kwan emphasize the importance of technological innovation, which in turn induces alterations in the mode of production. Changes in the economic system associated with technological shifts often introduce opportunities for minority groups to acquire new competitive advantages that make them indispensable to employers. These in turn lead employers to seek institutional changes favorable to the interests of minority groups, changes that, in a capitalist system, are relatively easy to institute when elites find this in their economic interest. As a contemporary example, one could point to the role of employers in supporting the immigration of workers, both skilled and unskilled, legal and undocumented, despite the public clamor for greater limits on legal immigration and a curtailing of illegal immigration. At one end of the economic spectrum, there is the growing labor market demand for highly skilled workers (e.g., Silicon Valley's use of foreign-born computer programmers), given the post-industrial transformation of the American economy; at the other end, there is a continuing need for elastic sources of low-wage labor in the agricultural sector, in "degraded" manufacturing sectors such as the garment industry, and in personal services such as child care.[46]

The most immediate source of a decline in social distance, Shibutani and Kwan assert, occurs when institutional change stimulates the introduction of new ideas that challenge values and cultural beliefs previously taken for granted, as in the discrediting of white supremacist ideologies in the postcolonial world, and a "transformation of values" ensues. "Systems of ethnic stratification begin to break down when minority peoples develop new self-conceptions and refuse to accept subordinate roles. As they become more aware of their worth in comparison to members of the dominant group, what they had once accepted as natural becomes unbearable."[47] Social movements, often involving protests and rebellions, are the motor that sparks interest among the political elite in instituting changes and reforms to alter the relationship between majority and minority in a manner that promotes assimilation.

In sum, their analysis of assimilation focuses attention on the extent to which change at the macroscopic level opens the way for concomitant change in subjective states at the individual and primary group levels. Their study adds several features that are missing in the canonical account. One is a complex causal analysis that allows for the introduction of contingency (i.e., variable group trajectories), in contrast to the uniformity produced by the reliance on generationally induced change. Another is the preservation of the distinctions among levels of aggregation so that the interaction among individuals, groups, and the larger social environment is incorporated into the analytic accounting. Their analysis acknowledges exogenous influences, such as technological innovations, along with shifts in conditions at the societal and group levels as affecting individual decisions and actions that do or do not advance assimilation. Finally, their analysis quite explicitly recognizes the centrality of stratification in the ethnic experience; it does not, as the canonical formulation does, slight the persistence of social inequalities while presenting assimilation as the seemingly universal experience of immigrant minorities.

These advances notwithstanding, Shibutani and Kwan's theoretical analysis proved to be less influential than Gordon's, in part because it was not amenable to the multivariate design of quantitative sociology. Nevertheless, recognition of a theoretical impoverishment of quantitative sociology, which tacitly came to conceive of theory as the "sum of variables," has given rise to an interest in explanation that specifies the causal mechanisms which produce the outcome to be explained.[48] In light of this development, Shibutani and Kwan's synthesis of the Chicago School provides useful clues for the construction of a new institutionalist theory of assimilation, one that specifies causal mechanisms which explain the coexistence of both segregating and blending processes in society.

New Assimilation Theory

The aim of theory is to help us understand the causes of a phenomenon. In constructing a theory of assimilation, we follow the "new realists" in the philosophy of science in moving away from the "covering law" approach to explanation associated with classical positivism.[49] Causation, instead, is identified as *a central cluster of diverse and specific processes conceived as mechanisms that produce or generate the phenomenon to be explained.*[50] In other words, a theory is the approximately true description of the underlying causes of what one seeks to explain.

In any era, theorizing about a particular domain is shaped by a more general theoretical language, the modalities of conceptualizing social processes that are current at that time. As we noted, Shibutani and Kwan's theoretical analysis was deeply imbued with the principal elements of the Chicago School approach, including Darwinian evolutionary theory. The language these presuppositions gave rise to accounts for some of the limitations of their framework. For instance, Shibutani and Kwan wanted to address theoretically events at an institutional level, but institutions, properly defined as the formal and informal rules of the game, are poorly conceived as features of a physical ecology within which competition and natural selection operate. For one thing, the selection processes stemming from institutions are constrained by cultural beliefs and social networks, which set institutional processes apart from natural selection in the biotic world where Darwinian evolutionary theory has demonstrated its explanatory mettle.

The Conceptual Framework

We draw for our theoretical language on recent advances in institutional analysis in the social sciences. Institutional theories evolved out of two distinct traditions, the methodological individualism of Max

Weber's comparative institutional analysis, and methodological holism, stemming from the influence of the French sociologist Emile Durkheim, which asserts that institutional structures cannot be reduced to the action of individuals.[51] These rival traditions have gradually moved in the direction of convergence, through efforts to integrate purposive action with large-scale institutional processes.[52] In the new institutionalist approaches, explanations for institutional change generally refer to causal mechanisms embedded in the purposive action of individual and corporate actors, which in turn are shaped by cultural beliefs, relational structures, path dependence, and changing relative costs.

Institutions structure incentives and specify the rules of legitimate social action within which individuals and organizations compete for control over resources. Institutions, defined as a web of interrelated norms, formal and informal, govern social relationships.[53] As Durkheim argued, they serve as constraints shaping social and economic exchange at all levels of society. Institutions are not merely constraints, however, but are also resources that make possible the achievement of goals not otherwise attainable; hence, individuals and organizations compete for influence and control over institutional structures. Those who control the direction of institutional change can remake the rules of the game to favor their interests. Thus, firms lobby to change the legal environment in a manner that accrues to their competitive advantage, and political parties compete for control. Changes in formal rules are enacted by formal organizations such as the state. Change in the informal rules such as customs, conventions, and social norms involve a more bottom-up evolutionary process of cultural and social change. Consequently, informal constraints often are resilient to efforts at change imposed by the state. For instance, changes in the formal rules legislated by Congress in the wake of the civil rights movement in the 1960s brought about institutional changes dismantling de jure segregation in the South and increasing the cost of discrimination in the workplace nationwide. The subsequent backlash, first expressed through informal resistance and then through formal challenges to federal programs, suggests the resilience of the informal constraints—the customs, conventions, etiquette, and social norms—regulating the color line between blacks and whites.

History matters in understanding the deep patterns of stability and change in institutional structures.[54] Opposition to changes in the formal rules of the game often arises out of social groups whose interests are adversely affected by the new rules. Whereas self-reinforcing mechanisms in institutions tend to frustrate efforts to bring about change, other aspects of the institutional environment may facilitate changes in certain directions.[55] As individuals and organizations attempt to innovate institutional change to open the way for new opportunities, they undermine or remake the existing institutional framework, often with effects not anticipated by those initiating the change. This is seen in the landmark Immigration Act of 1965, whose supporters in Congress never envisioned that their legislation, aimed at eliminating national origins quotas restricting southern and eastern European immigration, would result in altering profoundly the racial and ethnic composition of major cities and even regions of the United States. In order to ensure continuity in the ethnic mix of immigration, they drafted a family reunification clause to the new immigration law. But they did not anticipate that family members of European Americans would prefer to remain in Europe and that relatively small existing ethnic populations would generate a high volume of chain migration from Asia through the family reunification option.

Our theory of assimilation builds on the behavioral assumptions of the new institutionalism in sociology. Agents act according to mental models shaped by cultural beliefs—customs, social norms, law, ideology, and religion—that mold perceptions of self-interest. They follow rule-of-thumb heuristics in solving problems that arise, and make decisions in the face of uncertainty stemming from incomplete information and the risk of opportunism in the institutional environment. For this reason, new institutionalists view rationality as *context-bound* and contingent in contrast to the rationality assumption of neoclassical economics that individuals maximize their utility with complete information and unbounded cognitive capacity. Context-bound rationality focuses analytic attention on integrating accounts of choices made by individuals with an analysis of the institutional context.[56] It involves a "thick" as opposed to a "thin" view of rationality. The latter depends on an abstract account of goals as motivated by a self-interest rooted in utility or preferences and posits utility maximization as the mode of reasoning for actors who calculate costs and benefits of alternative courses of action in selecting the most efficient means to an end. By contrast, a context-bound rationality views agency as stemming from choices made by actors according to perceptions of costs and benefits embedded in the institutional environment. It assumes limited cognitive ability on the part of actors and interprets rationality partly as a product of institutional processes. Adaptations based on unintended consequences of action that result in success or rewards also fall within the purview of context-bound rationality.[57] If an unintended consequence results in success, actors are likely to repeat the action. Similarly, if the informal norms of a close-knit group contribute to producing unintended beneficial outcome, the group will reinforce these norms.

Mechanisms of Assimilation

Our aim in this section is to specify a repertoire of mechanisms operating at the individual, primary-group, and institutional levels that shape the trajectories of adaptation by immigrants and their descendants. The causal mechanisms we propose fall broadly into two groups that are general to social behavior: the *proximate* causes which operate at the individual and social network (primary-group and community) levels and are shaped by the forms of capital that individuals and groups possess, and the *distal,* often deeper causes, which are embedded in large structures such as the institutional arrangements of the state, firm, and labor market.

We do not assume that assimilation is a universal outcome, occurring in a straight-line trajectory from the time of arrival to entry into the middle class. The assumption of inevitability assumes away what requires explanation. Assimilation, defined as the attenuation of distinctions based on ethnic origin, is not an inevitable outcome of adaptation by ethnic and racial minorities, as even a cursory reflection on the extent and scope of ethnic conflict around the world would suggest.

To the extent that assimilation occurs, it proceeds incrementally, usually as an intergenerational process, stemming both from individuals' purposive action and from the unintended consequences of their workaday decisions. In the case of immigrants and their descendants who may not intentionally seek to assimilate, the cumulative effect of pragmatic decisions aimed at successful adaptation can give rise to changes in behavior that nevertheless lead to eventual assimilation. Assimilation occurs at different rates within different ethnic and racial groups, so that within the same ethnic group there is very considerable variation in the extent of assimilation—as is clear, for example, in the sharp contrast between intermarried Jews and the residents of socially encapsulated Hasidic communities.

Finally, we assume that no single causal mechanism explains immigrants' adaptation to their host society; instead a variety of mechanisms operating at different levels are involved. Similarly, the set of mechanisms varies across ethnic and racial groups, sometimes involving more collectivist modes of accommodation (e.g., among Jews, Japanese, Cubans, and Koreans) and sometimes more individualist modes of adaptation (e.g., among Germans, Scandinavians, Italians, and Filipinos). Moreover, for most ethnic groups a mix of collectivist and individualist mechanisms contributes to shaping the trajectory of adaptation, so that even while the modal experience is defined by the purposive activity of individuals, this does not rule out the importance of collectivist efforts at the group level which help to secure opportunities for gain at the individual level.

Purposive action. Although individual and corporate actors typically meliorize, rather than maximize—that is, their choices are "intendedly rational, but only limitedly so"[58]—their actions are purposive in the sense that interest and incentives obviously matter. A satisfactory theory of assimilation must, at the individual level, conceptually incorporate agency stemming from purposive action and self-interest and provide an account of the incentives and motivation for assimilation.

Like all of us, immigrants and their descendants act in accordance with mental models shaped by cultural beliefs that mold perceptions of self-interest. They follow rule-of-thumb heuristics in solving problems, and make decisions in the face of uncertainty stemming from incomplete information. Their choices are inevitably context-bound, shaped not only by cultural beliefs but also by institutional constraints.

This is illustrated in the story of a Mexican laborer named Flores who was interviewed by a *New York Times* correspondent along the Mexico-Arizona border. That border is known to be the most dangerous point of entry for illegal migrants because it adjoins the vast Altar Desert. Flores is described as a stout man with the coarse and stubby fingers of someone who works the land. He had "heard of dozens of stories about immigrants who had died from exposure to the heat and cold" crossing the desert and readily "acknowledged that the journey ahead might seem foolhardy." Yet even without full information of the harsh conditions he would expose himself to, Flores planned to risk his life to cross the desert on foot. The *Times* correspondent writes that after stating his intention, "he talked about the needs of his wife, and of their dreams for their three children, especially his newest son, born just two weeks earlier. He said he was determined to try. 'Of course I am scared. . . . But it's better to be scared and try to make a better life for my family than to stay and watch them go hungry.'"[59] Shaped relationally, motivated by concern for his family as opposed to his immediate self-interest, Flores's choice is influenced also by the more effective enforcement of immigration laws along the California and Texas borders where immigrants have crossed in the past. He weighs not only the risks of attempting to cross the desert but also the probability of being caught by the border patrol should he try crossing at another point where the terrain is less threatening but more intensely monitored. But his information is incomplete, since those who died in the crossing did not return to tell their stories, while those who made it through and found jobs in Arizona report through the grapevine that the desert is traversible and not so well monitored.

The sheer regularity of such context-bound choices is what renders purposive action by individuals a potent causal mechanism. Although they may not face the same life-and-death circumstances in their calculation of risks as Flores, it is the aggregation of similar choices by many thousands of Mexican peasants that gives rise to sustained large-scale undocumented migration to the United States. These choices are not well accounted for by the "thin" rationality assumption of neoclassical economics, as they are embedded in the cultural belief that a man *ought* to be willing to sacrifice for the well-being of his family. The normative content of such cultural beliefs imparts direction and purpose to the rational action of individuals.[60] Like Flores, the young Mexican people who cross the border at night and experience the uncertain circumstances of underground lives as illegal aliens in migrant labor camps have more than their own immediate self-interest in mind, as reflected in the high volume of remittances sent by undocumented migrants back to their families.[61]

In their adaptation to life in the United States, many descendants of immigrants face choices in which the degrees of risk and of benefit are similarly hard to gauge; it is also usually the case that these choices involve long-term consequences that are unforeseeable. In contemplating the strategies best suited to improve their lives and those of their children, immigrants and the second generation weigh the risks and potential benefits of "ethnic" strategies, dependent on opportunities available through ethnic networks versus "mainstream" ones, which involve the American educational system and the open labor market. Often enough there may be little choice in these matters; when immigrants have little human and financial capital and/or they are undocumented, they will usually be limited to jobs located through ethnic networks and constrained to reside in ethnic areas. But others, where possible, may try mixed strategies, built from ethnic and mainstream elements, as when second-generation young adults obtain jobs through family and ethnic networks while continuing their education, thus leaving multiple options open.

Individuals striving for success in American society often do not see themselves as assimilating. Yet the unintended consequences of practical strategies and actions undertaken in pursuit of familiar goals—a good education, a good job, a nice place to live, interesting friends and acquaintances, economic security—often result in specific forms of assimilation. For example, it is not uncommon for first- and second-generation parents to raise their children speaking only English, or at least to avoid placing their children in bilingual educational settings, in the belief that their chances for success in school will be improved by their more complete mastery of the host language. This is often true of families that instill aspirations for professional careers in their children. As we will document in a later chapter, surprising numbers of second-generation Asian children speak only English at home, which suggests that their families have adopted this strategy. For another example, also explored more fully later on, the search for a more desirable place to live—with good schools, safe streets, and opportunities for children to grow up away from the seductions of deviant models of behavior—leads immigrant professionals and entrepreneurs to move to the suburbs (if and when socioeconomic success permits this), since residential amenities tend to be concentrated there. One consequence, whether intended or not, is increased interaction with families of other backgrounds; such contacts tend to encourage acculturation, especially for the children. Human-capital immigrants (i.e., professionals, managers, skilled workers and technicians) optimize their investments in human capital through individualist strategies that increase their children's chances of entering into mainstream society.

Associated with acculturation are culturally codified notions of appropriate behavior which, when learned, serve as cues to others as to an individual's level of cultural and social competence.[62] Such competence contributes to reducing social distance by signaling behavioral attributes that appear familiar and trustworthy. Physical differences may persist, but their effect on perceived social distance attenuates as cultural competence modulates social behavior in ways that highlight shared understanding and cultural attributes. For employers, such cues are a "market signal" providing a ready rule-of-thumb measure of the individual's cultural capital, especially with respect to the linguistic and social competence needed to perform effectively in the workplace.[63] It is not surprising, given the emphasis on successful adaptation common to immigrant families, that the second generation strives to acculturate. Institutionalized incentives are such that regardless of ethnicity, pragmatic individuals signal that they have the cultural and social competence to compete and perform in schools, the workplace, and other institutional contexts, especially when they believe that they have a predictable chance of success in mainstream institutions. The exploitation of opportunities often carries some ramifications for further assimilation, even if unforeseen ones.

Network mechanisms. Network mechanisms are the *social processes that monitor and enforce norms within close-knit groups.* Strictly speaking, social networks and norms do not constitute causal mechanisms insofar as they are concepts referring to elements of social structure—the relationship connecting two or more actors and the informal rules governing the relationship—rather than to the social processes that give rise to and sustain cooperation.[64] A more analytically tractable approach to understanding the causal properties of networks and norms is to focus on the *social exchange mechanisms that enable actors to engage in joint action as a means to achieve collective goals.*[65] In close-knit groups, the mechanisms are the social rewards and punishments.[66] Observations showing how network mechanisms work to shape the performance of individuals in a close-knit group can be found in William Foote Whyte's *Street Corner Society* (1943), a study of unemployed Italian American youths in Boston during the Great Depression.[67] Monitoring and enforcement of norms occur spontaneously in the course of social interaction among members of the group through the exchange of social approval for behavior conforming to the group's norms, and disapproval and ostracism for violating them.[68] Robert Axelrod's *Evolution of Cooperation* develops a formal model showing in game-theoretic terms how the mechanisms of reward and punishment operate to promote cooperation in repeated exchanges.[69] The model demonstrates that the network mechanism conforms to the assumption of rational action, albeit within ongoing social exchange in which actors' appraisal of future interactions influences how they behave in the present. In other words, actors are more likely to cooperate in ongoing relationships than in one-shot transactions between strangers.

Norms are the informal rules that provide guidelines according to which joint action in close-knit groups or social networks is sustained. They arise from the problem-solving activity of individuals striving to improve their chances for success through cooperation. Members of a close-knit group or social network will informally encourage one another to engage in cooperative behavior by jointly enforcing its norms. Individuals cooperate because not only are their interests linked to the success of the group but their identity is as well.[70] No claim is made that the norms of close-knit groups operate to benefit society as a whole. Indeed, the norms that benefit members may impoverish those outside a group—for example, the norm of solidarity among a band of thieves and the norms of racial segregation in the Jim Crow era in the South.

Network mechanisms in close-knit groups sustain norms that maximize the welfare of members of the group.[71] Ethnic minorities often exhibit many of the same qualities as close-knit groups in their capacity to monitor and enforce norms of cooperation, especially evident during periods of extreme societal hostility and social isolation.[72] Welfare maximization is seen in the central role of migrant networks in initiating, sustaining, and expanding streams of labor migration linking small communities in Mexico to destination points in California.[73] It is seen in the norms of close-knit groups in the immigrant community. Newly arrived immigrants turn to relatives, acquaintances, and friends for direct assistance in meeting practical needs from the first weeks following their arrival to establishing the sequence of jobs and residences that form the basis of their long-term accommodation.[74] The welfare-maximizing feature of norms in close-knit groups is assumed in studies of ethnic economies showing extensive cooperation to secure competitive advantages in markets.[75] Studies of immigration show that social networks lower the risks of international migration and increase the chances of success in making the transition to settled lives in America. They support the view that network ties are a fungible form of social capital, providing an array of tangible kinds of assistance, especially timely and accurate information about the availability of start-up jobs and places to live.

A study of Chinese in the Mississippi Delta illustrates the role of network mechanisms in maximizing a group's welfare and thereby its assimilation.[76] Chinese migrated to the delta in the 1870s in response to white plantation owners' effort to recruit an alternative supply of cheap labor, thus weakening the bargaining power of black share-croppers. Soon after their arrival, the Chinese left farming to establish grocery stores serving the black community, a niche shunned by whites. In the institutional context of racial segregation under Jim Crow, where the only racial categories were black or white, the Chinese laborers were classified as black. As male sojourners, they lived in the black community, in back of their grocery stores, and eventually a number of them married black wives or brought Chinese wives to the delta region. In the early 1920s, by now affluent merchant families sought admission for their children in white schools, which were vastly superior to public schools for blacks, but these efforts were rebuffed by the white community, anxious about establishing a precedent that could weaken the norms and etiquette of racial segregation by opening a way for others to cross the color line. In response to a legal challenge, a decision by the state Supreme Court (subsequently upheld by the U.S. Supreme Court) sustained the 1890 Mississippi constitution, which stipulated that "separate schools shall be maintained for children of the white and colored races."

After their legal setback, the close-knit Chinese American community mobilized to demonstrate through their adoption of white social norms and etiquette that they should not be treated as if they were black—that is, to change the de facto racial definition of "Chinese." Social pressure was brought to bear on merchants with black wives to leave them, and those who refused were ostracized from ethnic associations and social events. The children of mixed Chinese–African American marriages were also socially excluded from the Chinese community to demonstrate that the Chinese accepted the white norm against racial mixing. Eventually, the strategy succeeded. Despite de jure segregation, Chinese American families moved into white residential neighborhoods and their children gained admission into white schools. When James Loewen did his field study in 1967, the Chinese community of about 1,200 scattered across the small towns of the Mississippi Delta region continued to enforce the norms of their collectivist strategy of adaptation to the racial segregation of the Jim Crow era. As one man remarked, "I tell my boy not to get in trouble or foul up, or they won't say 'that boy,' they say 'that *Chinese* boy!'" Or as another emphasized, "If some Chinese starts getting out of line, the others of us would talk to him, straighten him out."[77]

We see in this field study the workings of purposive action directed at changing the definition of the situation (cognitive mechanisms) and of network mechanisms in a close-knit group enforcing welfare-maximizing norms. In general, *when discriminatory barriers block an individualistic pattern of social mobility, assimilation, when it occurs, depends on collectivist strategies.*

Other ethnic groups have relied on collectivist strategies of assimilation to a greater or lesser extent, even though the dominant pattern of assimilation conforms to the individualistic mold. The experience of the Mississippi Chinese is an exceptional case of collectivist assimilation involving a close-knit community in the extreme circumstances imposed by racial segregation in the South. More commonly, assimilation occurs through a path-dependent process involving interaction between collectivist and individualist modes of adaptation. For instance, Irish Americans, in their effort to shed the stereotype of "shanty Irish," also socially distanced themselves from African Americans as a group strategy to gain acceptance from Anglo-Americans, ostracizing those who intermarried with blacks. Likewise, assimilated German Jews encouraged the acculturation of eastern European Jews through their charitable activities in the immigrant neighborhoods of New York City, lest the impoverished eastern European Jews blemish the favorable image of the American Jewish community. More recently, South Asians who settled in an agricultural town in northern California evolved social norms encouraging selective acculturation while discouraging social contact with local white youths who teased and taunted the Punjabi youths.[78] The Punjabi immigrants' strategy, according to the anthropologist Margaret Gibson, emphasized academic achievement in the public schools as a means to improve their children's chances for success, which they defined not locally but in terms of the opportunity structures of the American mainstream.

The welfare-maximizing feature of a close-knit group renders network ties a form of capital, a fungible asset, which, like human or financial capital, can be converted into material gain. Such social capital is generally accumulated as a by-product of ongoing social relationships, manifested in the buildup of good will and trust among members of a group and among acquaintances who have cooperated in the past.[79] For immigrants, it consists of the webs of network ties that they have accumulated over the course of the migration experience, starting with the strong ties of family, kinship, and friendship and extending to the weak ties of acquaintanceship.

Forms of capital. The forms of capital brought by today's immigrants differ significantly both within the same immigrant stream and among ethnic groups. Exemplifying the former, immigration from Mexico, though made up overwhelmingly of manual laborers from rural towns and villages, also includes a large number of urban professionals and technical workers. Moreover, Mexican immigration includes those from largely European ethnic origin, as well as migrants from Indian and mestizo stock. And to further complicate matters, a large proportion of Mexican migration includes undocumented workers. At the same time, ethnic groups can be seen as broadly differentiated from one another on the basis of the forms of capital they typically tend to bring. At one end of the continuum are the East Indian, Korean, and Filipino immigrant groups, which include high proportions of professionals and technical workers holding college or postgraduate degrees. At the other end are the low-wage laborers from Mexico who come generally with a primary school education. Today's immigrants also arrive with varying amounts of financial capital, which can be important in easing the transition to workaday lives, as in the case of middle-class Korean immigrants who sell their homes and assets before they emigrate. The financial capital they are thus able to bring helps to explain the high rate of Korean small-business ownership.[80] By contrast to middle- and upper-middle-class immigrants, labor migrants commonly have no financial capital to speak of. Those who have to borrow money to cover the cost of undocumented immigration often unwittingly become trapped in a modern form of indentured servitude, working for ethnic entrepreneurs who exploit them as cheap labor. This diversity in forms of capital, as well as in the racial and legal status of the contemporary immigration, stands in contrast to the earlier era of mass immigration, which was primarily a labor migration of peasants with similar levels of education arriving from Europe.[81]

Assimilation into the mainstream society is affected not just by the social, financial, and human capital of immigrant families but also by the ways individuals use these resources within and apart from the existing structure of ethnic networks and institutions. A forms-of-capital model, developed by Victor Nee and Jimy Sanders in a study of Asian immigrants in Los Angeles, emphasizes the mix of family capital that immigrants bring with them as strongly influencing the decisions they make in adapting to daily circumstances in the United States and thus helps us to understand why patterns of adaptation vary among groups. For example, three Asian immigrant groups have in common a high percentage of professionals with educational credentials from their countries of origin. Members of the two English-speaking groups—Filipinos and Indians—have found jobs in the mainstream labor market, reside in mixed residential neighborhoods, and have shown no special proclivity for self-employment or interest in building an ethnic enclave economy. By contrast, Korean immigrants, who do not come from a culture where English is widely spoken, optimize their human and financial capital by investing in small businesses and developing an ethnic economy in which their native cultural competence is advantageous. All three Asian groups appear to be on pathways of assimilation insofar as their children acculturate, frequently go beyond secondary school to attend four-year colleges followed by professional and graduate schools, and often marry outside the ethnic group. Although the proportion of professionals in the other large immigrant streams may not be as high, the forms-of-capital model predicts that immigrant professionals and their children, whether Chinese or Mexican, are likely to have a similar pattern of entry into the American mainstream.

Human capital is gained through education and work experience. The concept is widely used in the social sciences, in part because it is readily measured by years of schooling and work and is demonstrably correlated to ultimate socioeconomic attainment. Notwithstanding, cultural dimensions are often critical in shaping social mobility, as Pierre Bourdieu has shown in his study of the French elite.[82] Although the concept of human capital can be expanded to include linguistic competence, its definition does not encompass cultural tastes and references, as it is a concept that originated in economics to distinguish skills embodied in workers from physical capital. This is why Bourdieu criticized the concept of human capital for being too narrowly economic in its specification. While it might be useful in the study of the French elite, however, his conception of cultural capital, which emphasizes knowledge of high culture, has limited utility for the study of immigrants. The concept of *human-cultural* capital can serve to integrate the two ideas in such a way that insights from both can be extended to the study of immigrant adaptation.

One implication of the forms-of-capital model is that it enables us to offer an account of mechanisms of assimilation in which skin color is not reified as an unyielding barrier to assimilation. To be sure, racial differences have important effects; but skin color is not the only trait by which immigrants and their children are evaluated. If it were, then we would not have an explanation for the experience of East Indians, whose skin color is often dark but who do not live in racially segregated ghettos nor concentrate in enclave economies; instead they find jobs mainly in the mainstream labor market and tend to reside in mixed residential neighborhoods.[83] Moreover, the second generation appears to be on the pathway to assimilation insofar as U.S.-born East Indians combine a native's knowledge of the American mainstream culture with the same human-cultural capital and even professional-managerial-technical occupational profile of the immigrant generation.

A characteristic feature of professional immigration is its tendency to be family-based. This is in part due to the original intent to immigrate, rather than to migrate as sojourners and transnationals (the latter is a variant of sojourning for businessmen and -women). Professional immigrants hope to reestablish their middle-class lifestyle by building careers in the United States, whether as entrepreneurs or as technical workers if they are unable to secure professional jobs in their areas of training. The transfer of human-cultural capital from the immigrant to the second generation is often the focal point of parental attention in the families of professional immigrants; for many, this entails moving to suburban communities to secure a high-quality education for their children and learning how to mix socially with neighbors who are not of the same ethnic group.

By contrast, labor migrants, whether they come from Mexico, Central America, or the Caribbean Basin, lack the same stock of human-cultural and financial capital as immigrant professionals. Labor migrants from Mexican villages and rural towns are often barely literate and arrive first as sojourning males. Over time, and after several return visits to marry and establish a family in Mexico, most eventually settle in America as immigrants. The most valuable capital that labor migrants possess is their stock of social capital, the network ties that span the distance from their home villages and towns to their destination point in the United States. The migration network significantly reduces the risks of international migration for labor migrants who rely on word of mouth for timely information about labor market conditions, help in crossing the border, finding a first job, and other practical aspects of workaday lives.[84] Reliance on social capital, however, gives rise to dependence on the ethnic community. In the case of ethnic entrepreneurs, this is helpful to their small businesses but does not necessarily limit their social world to the immigrant enclave, as is evident from the Korean entrepreneurs who move to the suburbs though their stores are located in the central city. For Asian immigrant laborers in Los Angeles, reliance on ethnic ties leads to pathways of incorporation that are associated with low-wage, low-skill labor, either in the ethnic economy or in the open economy.[85] This in turn constrains opportunities for the second generation compared to the children of immigrant professionals.

In analyzing the prospects for the children of low-wage labor migrations, the forms-of-capital model does not emphasize the community's ability (or mobility) to shield their youth from exposure to the influence of inner-city minority youth, as does the segmented assimilation approach.[86] Instead the focus is on the mechanisms within the immigrant family that transfer human-cultural capital from one generation to another, and the consequence of low-wage labor on the family's ability to do so. Given the low level of formal education of Mexican and Central American labor migrants, it is not surprising that a smaller percentage of the Hispanic second generation compared to other immigrant populations goes on beyond a high school diploma. A high school education is already substantially more education than that of the immigrant generation. A recent study shows that Hispanic females drop out of high school at a higher rate than any other ethnic group.[87] It is not convincing to attribute the higher dropout rate to the influence of domestic minority youth culture. Instead, the forms-of-capital approach asks whether immigrant parents with a primary school education from rural villages and towns and who work at low-wage labor have the same human-cultural resources as parents who graduated at least from high school. Path-dependent transfer of human-cultural capital from the parents' generation to the second generation may offer a more credible interpretation of the relatively low educational attainment of the children of labor migrants from Central America.

In sum, the forms-of-capital model provides an empirically based approach to understanding the different patterns of purposive adaptation. If we assume that an institutional environment ensuring predictable chances for assimilation into the mainstream is maintained, it predicts that the descendants of immigrant minorities will assimilate at varying rates depending on the mix of family capital that the immigrant generation brings. As with the general pattern of social mobility in industrial societies, intergenerational mobility is likely to be most constrained in the move from the bottom to the middle, and from the middle to the top, of the stratification order.[88] It is reasonable to assume that a similar pattern of *divergent outcomes* will obtain for the descendants of contemporary immigration as for native groups in industrial societies. Hence, many in the second generation are likely to experience upward social mobility into the American socioeconomic mainstream, while the children of immigrant professionals and entrepreneurs may start there and, in fact, enjoy better life chances than white Americans from less advantaged social origins. But other members of the second generation may experience instead lateral or, at best, short-distance mobility, thus remaining close in their socioeconomic position to their immigrant parents. Children of low-wage labor migration are likelier to experience downward mobility into the urban minority underclass than children of human-capital migration from the same ethnic group.[89] This forecast of very unequal attainments for the contemporary second generation suggests one reason why many observers believe that assimilation is problematic for new immigrant groups. But it should not be forgotten that divergent outcomes were apparent also among the children of European immigrants, many of whom entered the urban working class.[90]

Institutional mechanisms. Although we began by specifying the proximate mechanisms, our theory of assimilation turns on the structure of incentives embedded in the institutional environment. This is because the same proximate mechanisms can also account for segregating behavior given *different* institutionalized incentives. For instance, it is well known that some structures of opportunity readily accessible to poor immigrants and minorities are illicit, from the organized criminality of a mafia to the street corner opportunities of minority youth gangs. Oppositional norms, a feature of a reactive subculture formed in defiance of perceived rejection by mainstream authorities (such as teachers), contribute to maintaining the level of solidarity critical to group success. Viewed from the perspective of the mainstream, oppositional norms have a negative effect, insofar as they are associated with social behavior that opposes mainstream values and hence reinforces negative stereotypes. But from the viewpoint of members of the close-knit group of youths, conformity with opposition norms is boundedly rational because it contributes to the survival and success of the group and its members. Examples of ethnic groups in which purposive action and network mechanisms give rise to segregating rather than blending behavior are numerous in studies of immigrant adaptation.

The pre–World War II Japanese American ethnic economy provides a useful case study.[91] Japanese immigration to the West Coast followed in the wake of the anti-Chinese movement that culminated in the legal exclusion of Chinese laborers in 1882. As the Chinese returned to China or moved away from the western states to the East and South, white farmers in California turned to Japanese immigrants for a source of agricultural labor. Soon after their arrival, the Japanese shifted rapidly out of agricultural labor into self-employment. The Japanese laborers, despite their better education, confronted a society deeply hostile to Asian immigrants. Like the Chinese in the Mississippi Delta, the close-knit Japanese immigrant community evolved pragmatic welfare-maximizing norms that promoted a high level of internal solidarity and cooperation in the ethnic economy they built around truck farming and commerce. Ethnic solidarity was manifested in a variety of institutional arrangements, from the *tanomoshi,* or rotating-credit associations providing start-up capital for small businesses, to patron-client relations between employer and employee wherein workers perceived their interests to be bound up with that of the enterprise. This helped Japanese immigrant farmers and merchants to build a vertically integrated ethnic economy, enabling them to compete effectively for market share and control against larger white-owned farms. This economy supported a sizable yet socially cohesive community featuring a diversified occupational structure that was ethnically bounded: ethnic networks controlled opportunity and mobility within the Japanese enclave economy. The ethnic economy provided jobs for the nisei, or second generation, who even with a college education could not find employment in the open economy because of racial discrimination. Dependence on the ethnic economy contributed to a high level of cooperation in the Japanese community, evidenced by the use of *network mechanisms* "to distribute resources efficiently and to control internal competition."[92] The result was a highly specialized Japanese American economy which was culturally distinct and socially isolated, but which produced goods for the society as a whole. The Japanese enclave economy soon established a dominant niche in the produce market by virtue of its competitive advantage.[93]

But white farmers quickly came to view the Japanese ethnic economy as a serious competitive threat to their livelihood. They responded accordingly, mobilizing public opinion against Japanese immigrants in order to eliminate competition by means of legal restrictions on property ownership and on further Japanese immigration. An institutionally embedded causal dynamic developed in which the Japanese collectivist pattern of adaptation incited fierce white hostility, which in turn reinforced norms strengthening ethnic solidarity among Japanese Americans and heightened their dependence on the ethnic economy. On the eve of the Pacific war, Japanese Americans were among the most socially isolated ethnic groups in America. The structure of opportunity and incentives for the second generation was nearly entirely bounded within the ethnic economy by virtue of their exclusion from the mainstream. It was only after the demise of the ethnic economy, undermined by the internment of Japanese Americans during World War II, that the causal dynamic reinforcing racial segregation was finally broken. During the postwar era, Japanese Americans assimilated rapidly according to the individualistic pattern, following the ensuing decline of societal hostility, shifts in the occupational structure stemming from sustained economic growth, and the institutional changes arising from the civil rights movement.

Institutional mechanisms constitute the deeper causes insofar as they determine whether the proximate mechanisms—purposive action and network mechanisms—advance blending or segregating processes. Earlier we implicitly discussed institutional mechanisms by pointing to the importance of institutionalized incentives in shaping purposive action. Whether this is viewed as a micro-macro link or as an agency-structure relationship,[94] purposive action by individuals and within close-knit groups cannot be understood apart from the institutional framework within which incentives are structured. This is the essence of the idea of context-bound rationality. The hallmark of the new institutionalist approach is a cheek-by-jowl relationship between the purposive action of individuals and the informal (i.e., networks and norms) and formal (i.e., rules and laws) constraints.[95]

The striking feature of the institutional environment of advanced industrial societies such as the United States is not so much the variability of localities and regions, but the extent to which there is homogeneity in the enforcement of laws and regulations of the federal government. For instance, the rules governing personal and corporate income tax are invariant despite state and regional differences in economic conditions. Federal laws and regulations extend the power of the central state uniformly despite variability in local and regional customary practices. Variations in local institutional contexts may limit the effectiveness of monitoring and enforcement, but they do not occasion different federal rules. The vastly expanded reach of centralized authority in modern societies highlights the importance of the institutional mechanisms at the command of the state. The state is the sovereign actor in specifying the framework that sets the underlying rules for competition and cooperation in a society. It is the ultimate source of coercion in its geographic area. It has the powers of taxation to mobilize resources in order to achieve its objectives, to redistribute wealth and income by enacting laws and regulations, and to create wealth by devising and enforcing property rights. It has the capacity to enact and enforce laws and carry out institutional changes in order to secure public goods (e.g., defense, environmental protection, civil rights) and to respond to changing relative prices (e.g., through interest rates, minimum wage, money supply). Thus the institutional mechanisms of *monitoring and enforcement of formal rules of the state organizations constitute a potent causal force.* "The costs to the individual of opposing the coercive forces of the state have traditionally resulted in apathy and acceptance of the state's rules," argues the economic historian Douglass North, "no matter how oppressive."[96]

Viewed from the vantage point of institutional mechanisms, the different experiences of the descendants of European and nonwhite immigrants to the United States are readily explained. Despite a history of nativism and discrimination directed against southern and eastern European immigrants and their descendants, their constitutional rights provided basic legal safeguards that kept channels of mobility open. By contrast, for nonwhite minorities prior to World War II, the formal rules of the game and their enforcement, from immigration laws to legal rights, forcefully bolstered the informal constraints—the norms and etiquette of the color line—excluding them from civil society. For example, Asian immigrants were ineligible for citizenship (until the McCarran-Walter Act of 1952), and faced many discriminatory local and regional laws that restricted their property rights and civil liberties, while informal racism blocked the chances of mobility into the economic and social mainstream for the second generation. It required institutional change directed at extending formal rights and their enforcement to racial minorities before assimilation was a possibility, despite the preference of native-born Asian Americans to join the mainstream as evidenced by their high level of acculturation already apparent in the pre–World War II era.

It is beyond the scope of this chapter to review the history of post–World War II institutional change culminating in the extension of fundamental constitutional rights to racial minorities. Suffice it to say, *in the post–civil rights era, the institutional mechanisms for monitoring and enforcing federal rules have increased the cost of discrimination in nontrivial ways.* Title VII of the Civil Rights Act of 1964 allows the Equal Employment Opportunity Commission (EEOC) the right to intervene in private bias lawsuits when it deems that the case is of "general public importance." A follow-up law, the Civil Rights Act of 1991, allows victims of bias to collect up to $300,000 in compensatory and punitive damages. Although enforcement of Title VII has been inconsistent under different administrations, corporations and nonprofit firms have become more attentive in observing its guidelines, with increasing numbers of firms offering diversity and multicultural training workshops for managers and employees and instituting company rules against racial and gender discrimination. This stems from technical improvements in the monitoring of firm behavior by agencies of the federal government. EEOC's district offices now routinely collect data on the pay and promotion practices of large organizations and analyze them to discern patterns of discrimination. The government has sought to demonstrate a credible commitment to enforcement of Title VII. In 1997 the landmark federal discrimination case against Texaco resulted in well-publicized threats of boycott, damage to the firm's reputation, and a costly $175 million settlement to minority employees. It also compelled Texaco to implement extensive organizational changes aimed at eliminating racial discrimination in hiring, promotion, and the workaday organizational environment. Similarly, the 1999 federal discrimination case filed by black employees at Coca-Cola was resolved at a cost of $192 million dollars to the firm. In a gesture of commitment to change the corporate culture, Coca-Cola's management agreed to an external oversight structure to monitor progress in eliminating bias in all areas of the firm's operation. These landmark settlements of federal discrimination lawsuits have rendered the cost of discrimination more transparent for corporations and nonprofit organizations.[97] They also provide the federal government with useful case histories and lessons in dealing with discrimination lawsuits. Recent federal cases, such as the one filed by black employees against the large defense contractor Lockheed Martin, contribute to increased attentiveness to Title VII guidelines in corporate America.

In light of the credible commitment to enforcement of Title VII, firms may be more reluctant to hire minority workers since it is more difficult to prove discrimination at the point of hiring than after minorities are in the firm. This may reinforce a preference to employ immigrant workers whom employers believe are more acquiescent and less likely to cause trouble.[98] It also contributes to fierce partisanship in national elections as political parties vie for control over the monitoring and enforcement of federal rules. Nonetheless, firms do enforce rules against discrimination, not only owing to more effective external monitoring, but also because an increasingly diverse labor force creates positive incentives for management to evolve norms in the workplace that promote a climate of racial tolerance and avoid costly ethnic conflict and tensions. Microsoft, among the largest American corporations, maintains a "zero tolerance" rule against discrimination. With 22 percent of the company's employees nonwhite, corporate performance is dependent on a high level of cooperation among employees regardless of race.

It might be argued that we overstate the importance of institutional changes for assimilation and that what is more important is economic development since the end of World War II, which has resulted in the concomitant transformation of the American occupational structure and expansion of higher education to train the cadre of professionals and technical workers needed by advanced capitalism. Economic development is certainly important, but one should note that an earlier period of sustained economic growth sparked by the industrial revolution of the nineteenth century led to a radically different outcome. This earlier era paralleled the imposition through violence and legislation of the racial segregation in the South under Jim Crow laws, segregation of blacks in central cities in the North, virulent anti-Asian movements directed at exclusion and segregation in the West, and nativist mobilization against immigrants and their descendants from southern and eastern Europe. Hence, modern economic development in itself is not a sufficient cause of assimilation.

Notwithstanding, economic growth can be viewed as a necessary condition for assimilation on a wide scale. In combination with the institutional changes we have described, growth can make an important difference in motivating shifts out of ethnic enclaves into mainstream America, as we detail in Chapter 3. Moreover, there is another aspect of growth that can be considered propitious for entry into the mainstream by some previously excluded groups: it has been associated throughout the nineteenth and twentieth centuries with the development of new economic sectors and new occupations. At the dawn of the twenty-first century, the obvious—but hardly the sole—example is the so-called new economy associated with electronics and the computer industry. The significance of such new economic domains is that they create "space" for economic and social mobility that is outside the complete control of established elites. Granted, these elites are hardly irrelevant for the way new domains develop: Bill Gates, after all, is the son of a Seattle banker, and his family's connections originally helped him to sell Microsoft's operating system to IBM and thus contributed directly to his firm's dominance. Nevertheless, institutional changes and their enforcement have extended equal rights in asset ownership to racial minorities, which were denied before World War II. Consequently, of the entrepreneurs in Silicon Valley, a large proportion come from new immigrant groups (25 percent are Chinese and Indian immigrants), testifying both to the openings the new economy affords for the creation of new elites and to the effectiveness of institutional mechanisms in the post–civil rights era in enforcing the property rights of immigrant entrepreneurs.

But the more important institutional changes are those that have not only increased the cost of discrimination but also led to changes in values. One of these is the remarkable decline in the viability of racist ideologies since the end of World War II. This is evident in the shift from the nineteenth- and early-twentieth-century emphasis on the value of racial homogeneity, as in the white supremacist vision of America, to an institutionalized consensus on the value of diversity. An impressive body of survey evidence shows that many Americans have embraced the principle of racial equality, even if they are also ambivalent about positive policies, such as affirmative action, intended to bring about equality as a matter of fact. An examination of more than half a century of survey data demonstrates unequivocally that the belief in racial separation endorsed by a majority of white Americans as late as the 1940s has been steadily eroded. In the early 1940s, only a third of whites believed that "white students and black students should go to the same schools." By 1965 the percentage had risen to 70 percent, and by the early 1980s it had attained 90 percent.[99] Other changes were not so dramatic, but they were large in scale and occurred in the same direction. But we must note also that whites have been much more reluctant to accept many state interventions to enforce racial equality, especially where these might interfere with what they see as their own rights. Thus, the fraction of whites willing to support a communitywide "open housing" law that would prevent racial discrimination by individuals selling their own homes changed little during the 1970s and 1980s and remained at less than a majority.[100]

While the ideological shift has not ended racial prejudice and racist practice, it has changed their character. They are more covert and subterranean; and racism as belief has lost its public legitimacy and can no longer be advocated in public without sanction. Today, many white Americans are anxious to demonstrate that they are not racists.

Implications for the New Immigration

We have argued that institutional mechanisms extending civil rights to minorities and women have increased the cost of discrimination in nontrivial ways in American society. Despite this, a wealth of research in the social sciences has documented the persistent effect of racism in limiting the life chances of minorities, especially African Americans. Clearly, implementing formal rules is not tantamount to effectively re-

alizing the rules' intent. Whether in government-led efforts to safe-
guard the civil rights of minorities by outlawing discrimination, or in
the attempts in post-communist societies to construct market economies by means of drastically altering property rights, changing the
formal rules of the game at best incrementally results in path-dependent change. This is because the legacy of past practices, vested interests, and custom imposes a powerful constraint limiting efforts to
implement institutional change. In some cases the rules become too
costly to enforce effectively owing to the strength of persistent racism,
or prove so unpopular that informal opposition gives rise to political
efforts to overturn them.[101]

Despite persistent racism and unevenness in enforcement under different administrations, in the post–civil rights era a watershed change
has taken place in the institutional environment. Immigrant minorities other than African Americans have derived considerably more
benefit from institutional change, in part because their relationship to
the mainstream is much less burdened by the legacies of the historic
norms and etiquette governing race relations. The examples of the
Asian American groups offer the most compelling testimony in this
respect. Stigmatized by racism throughout the first half of the twentieth century, barred by law from immigration and from naturalization,
confined residentially to ghettos and prevented by some state laws
from intermarrying, they are now widely admired as "model minorities" who enjoy higher average incomes than white Americans and
not infrequently attain extraordinary academic success, reflected in
their visible presence on elite campuses from the Ivy League to Stanford. The Asian American story is not a uniformly positive one about
the openness of American society, for there is still racism directed
against Asian Americans, who suffer from glass ceilings in many
American companies and are subjected occasionally to racist violence.
But acknowledging that racism still exists should not blind us to the
profound nature of the changes that have occurred.

The stories of other immigrant minorities are less compelling at first
glance, though this does not mean that they are not also affected
by institutional change. As a rule, the groups immigrating from the
Americas (other than Canada) bring lower levels of human-cultural
capital than do Asian immigrants, and they are therefore less able to
make conspicuous use of openings in the mainstream. In addition,
their opportunities are affected by complications of race. Hispanics

are a racially diverse population: about half self-classify on the U.S. Census as "white," while some describe themselves as "black." Many of the remaining, who fit in the "other" racial category, presumably have an appearance reflecting an indigenous heritage. In general, black immigrants, whether from Latin America, the Caribbean, or Africa, and their children face racial barriers similar to those confronting African Americans.[102] And social scientists have not yet assembled the evidence to address this issue systematically for Hispanics who are neither white nor black.

The ultimate point is that race in American society, while it has not really lost its bedrock importance, has become much more complex and differentiated as a result of institutional changes. It has become more permeable, especially to immigrants and their children who are outside the troubled arena of black-white relations. Consequently, for at least part of the contemporary immigration, the proximate mechanisms that we identified earlier in the chapter as promoting assimilatory steps apply.

Assimilation and Boundaries

A key to assimilation, as we have defined it, is boundary spanning and altering. A social boundary is, in effect, a categorical distinction that members of a society recognize in their quotidian activities and that affects their mental orientations and actions toward one another. Such fundamental aspects of interaction as whether one individual extends even a modicum of trust toward another person casually encountered are determined by social boundaries.[103] These boundaries are almost always associated with numerous concrete social and cultural differences between groups, such as the occupational and residential differences between whites and blacks that contribute to each group's ignorance about the actual life conditions of the other.

Our theory of assimilation specifies a repertoire of proximate and distal mechanisms. The theory explains why assimilation is likely to remain a central social process in the adaptation of immigrants and their descendants and why it will encompass divergent outcomes in American society. It indicates that institutional mechanisms enforcing equal rights, in combination with the forms of capital immigrants bring with them, open the way for assimilation of ethnic minorities by providing predictability in the chances of success for those who try.

But it does not specifically address *how* ethnic boundaries change. In fact, relatively little is understood in the social sciences about the dynamics of social boundaries. Population ecology argues that competition gives rise to segregating processes, which reinforce ethnic boundaries; but it does not analyze what promotes blending processes that weaken boundaries.[104] When competition between ethnic groups involves split labor markets, in which a minority group offers to sell its products or labor for less than the going price, the sociologist Edna Bonacich argues that the majority group responds by seeking to exclude the source of competition, whether through legislation or through violence.[105] An example is the Chinese Exclusion Acts and the segregation of Chinese in racial ghettos in the late nineteenth century. Competition between ethnic groups, especially when ethnic markers confer differential treatment, generates ethnic conflict and hardens boundaries. Against this, the well-known integrative features of markets can operate to sustain blending processes, a view of markets emphasized by Max Weber.[106] It is common, however, for both blending and segregating processes to occur simultaneously in large urban markets where immigrants concentrate, because contemporary urban centers have both bounded ethnic markets and open markets. A study of labor markets in Los Angeles highlights the growth of a "mixed economy," with immigrant workers appearing to move with relative ease across social boundaries of the ethnic and mainstream labor markets in the course of job changes.[107] Overall, we may conclude that blending tends to occur to the extent that competition for scarce resources based on principles of ethnic identity attenuates, and competition instead is perceived as involving individuals rather than ethnic groups.

It is useful to distinguish among three boundary-related processes: boundary crossing, boundary blurring, and boundary shifting.[108] These are ideal types, we want to underscore, and are hard to operationalize in a precise way. Boundary crossing corresponds to the classic version of individual-level assimilation: someone moves from one group to another without any real change to the boundary itself (although if such boundary crossings happen on a large scale and in a consistent direction, the social structure is altered). Boundary blurring implies that the social profile of a boundary has become less distinct, and the clarity of the social distinction involved has become clouded.

This sort of change is invoked by many recent discussions of racial mixture, a consequence of the increasing occurrence of interracial marriage; many commentators seem to envision the mixed-race population as constituting an interstitial social grouping, one that creates a new racial/ethnic zone and begins to break down the rigidities of racial division.[109] The final process, boundary shifting, involves the relocation of a boundary so that populations once situated on one side are now included on the other: former outsiders are thereby transformed into insiders.

The assimilation of immigrant groups of prior eras has involved all of these processes, as we will discuss in the next chapter. At this moment in history, the first two are the ones that are relevant to new immigrant groups. Boundary crossings, undoubtedly in both directions, have occurred continuously throughout American history and are consistent with the conception of assimilation as Anglo-conformity. They are exemplified by the members of racial and immigrant minorities who pass as members of the majority by changing their names and taking on its habits of speech, dress, and behavior. The ability to pass also presumes a physical appearance that is not identified with minority status; cosmetic surgery has been used sometimes to achieve this.[110] Boundary crossing can occur as an intergenerational process when intermarriage in one generation produces individuals in the next whose social appearance is indistinguishable from majority group members of the same social class and region.

Boundary crossing need not alter a stable order of ethnic stratification, but boundary blurring, which changes the character of a boundary, usually does. The concept, described by Aristide Zolberg and Long Litt Woon, is illustrated well by the family cultures in the increasing number of American extended families that include couples married across the major religious boundaries. All the evidence shows that many of these families recognize both of the religions involved. Thus, Protestants may attend midnight Mass on Christmas Eve with their Catholic relatives, and in Christian-Jewish families it is common to celebrate both Christmas and Passover.[111] While the boundaries have not disappeared, and the individuals involved usually identify with a single religious affiliation (as we know from abundant survey data), they also participate in some of the rituals of another religion, know much more about it, and grant it greater validity than adherents of their religion would have done in the past. In some cases they may even view themselves, or be viewed by others, as members of both religions. This is the ultimate form of boundary blurring.

How does boundary blurring come about? Contact between groups is not enough. Stable, ongoing, and even vital social relationships are routinely maintained across boundaries without diminishing ethnic distinctions. Especially when ethnic markers assign differences in treatment, whether preferential or discriminatory, distinctions based on ethnic identity can persist despite cross-ethnic social relationships and interdependence.[112] Social psychologists and population ecologists have observed that increasing contact (e.g., competition) can even produce a heightened sense of difference between groups.

The key, we believe, lies in the sustained equal-status contact between the members of different groups that is produced on a substantial scale by the socioeconomic and residential opportunities available to many members of the new groups—*supported by institutional mechanisms enforcing equal rights*. These bring the new groups into contexts where members of the majority population are numerous or predominant. For example, an unheralded development associated with the new immigration is the widespread decline of the exclusively Anglo residential neighborhood, even in the suburban pastures that were once the preserve of middle-class whites. Although the effectiveness of monitoring and enforcement of rules—institutional mechanisms—outlawing racial discrimination in the real estate business has been debated, the evidence of increased heterogeneity in suburban neighborhoods nonetheless suggests that discrimination in the housing market has declined. By 1990, in the fifty largest U.S. metropolitan regions, nine of ten suburban tracts included a noticeable proportion (defined as at least 2 percent of residents) of nonwhites and Hispanics in their population.[113] Two-thirds had a minority population of at least 5 percent. Both fractions were sharply higher than two decades earlier, largely as a consequence of immigration. By 2000, the average suburban white in the United States lived in a census tract where one of every six neighbors was Hispanic or nonwhite.[114] These data indicate that most whites now encounter a new racial and ethnic diversity in their proximity, when they shop or attend PTA meetings, or even when they walk down their street. And the fact that minorities have percolated so thoroughly throughout the residential mix means that whites have difficulty moving entirely away from diversity (though, admittedly, they can lessen their exposure to it).

As such interactions proceed on a substantial scale, boundaries can indeed become blurred. Individuals on either side of a boundary can see that the differences between them are less than they previously thought.[115] Over significant periods of time, the social categories that distinguish the sides can become less and less relevant, as Shibutani and Kwan have emphasized. A critical point for contemporary immigration is that this can happen for some members of a group but not others, just as some members of immigrant groups reside in ethnically integrated settings while others are found in enclaves.

If the processes of intergroup contact take the pathway that leads to boundary blurring, one cannot rule out in the long run that even perceptions of physical difference—that is, of a racial distinction—will change. As we discuss in more detail later, some of the major European immigrant groups—the Irish, Italians, and Jews are the best-documented cases—were viewed as racially different from native-born whites at some point; their eventual achievement of white racial status was not just a matter of relabeling the same populations, though this is hardly a simple shift. But, in fact, the perceptions of, and social values attached to, different physical features changed over time; standards of beauty stretched. In the past, cosmetic surgery was used as a device of assimilation, to make minority individuals look more like the ethnic majority to which they desired to gain entry, as when Jews had their noses altered to make them smaller and more like those of WASPs. But the heyday of the "nose job" is past. In the interim, the "ethnic look" has become an acceptable form of beauty.[116]

Our approach to rethinking assimilation extends and revises the conceptual foundation laid down during the twentieth century, in order to meet the challenges of understanding a new era of immigration in which movement across borders appears to have become a permanent condition of modern life. Since the early days of the Chicago School, assimilation has evolved as a primary concept for understanding and interpreting the adaptation of immigrants and their descendants. Robert E. Park's "race relations cycle" of "contact, competition, accommodation and eventual assimilation" represented an early effort to analyze the large-scale human migrations of the nineteenth and early twentieth centuries. Researchers at the University of Chicago applied this race relations cycle to empirical studies of new ethnic and racial communities that grew out of the mass migrations to the city. The intellectual stamp of the Chicago School proved to have a long-standing influence on subsequent sociological research on ethnicity. Warner and Srole's study of ethnic groups in Yankee City seemed to confirm Park's optimistic prognosis of eventual assimilation. In the postwar study of ethnic and racial groups, the canonical synthesis was provided by Gordon's formulation of a multidimensional set of indicators. These opened the way conceptually for the application of quantitative methods to the study of assimilation, even as a lack of specification of causal mechanisms strengthened the impression that assimilation would be a universal outcome. Shibutani and Kwan's attempt to revive the Chicago School tradition identified anomalous findings showing that assimilation was not an inevitable outcome of intergroup contact. Competition between ethnic groups could also result in genocide, and ethnic stratification orders subordinating racial minorities can remain indefinitely in stable equilibrium. Their synthesis emphasizes that ethnic stratification orders are embedded in informal constraints—stereotypes, customs, norms—that are resilient to change because they arise from cognitive mechanisms which are fundamental to how humans conduct social life outside their immediate primary group. They argued that because of the stability of such local stratification orders, change must be exogenous, stemming from institutional processes at the macroscopic or ecological level.

Our rethinking is intended to remedy the now visible deficiencies in earlier conceptions. One was the ethnocentrism that was sometimes explicit and sometimes implicit in the notion that assimilatory change was almost exclusively one-directional, that the minority changed to make itself more like the majority, whose role was limited to accepting or rejecting the minority "petitioning" to be allowed into the mainstream. This blinkered vision of the assimilation process overlooked the historical reality that the majority changes too, and that the American mainstream has been continually reshaped by the incorporation of new groups. This historical reality is mirrored today in the view that American society increasingly reflects a composite culture made up of diverse ethnic elements. We find this debatable as a statement about the contemporary era compared to the past (for example, the level of everyday use of languages other than English may have been higher in the past than it is today). Insofar as it expresses something valid, it is that Americans today are more self-conscious about their cultural borrowings and more comfortable with cultural syncretism. This is not inconsistent with assimilation as we understand that concept.

Another problem in earlier conceptions was that they lent themselves too easily to the view that assimilation was inevitable. Critics of assimilation theory have correctly pointed out that there are other patterns of incorporation into American society—that some groups are incorporated as racialized minorities, as happened to the Chinese and Japanese during the nineteenth and early twentieth centuries and happens now to black Caribbean immigrants; while other groups or parts of them are able to sustain a pluralistic pattern, maintaining distinct communities and cultures that organize the lives of those who remain in the ethnic matrix, as exemplified by the Amish or white ethnic communities. These patterns are hardly absent from the American past, but many argue that they will have even greater relevance to contemporary immigrant groups because most immigrants now come from outside of Europe and because transnationalism and racialized enclaves provide reinvigorated incentives to maintain ethnic affiliations.

Ironically, perhaps, these arguments were even more applicable to American society prior to World War II, when the formal rules buttressing racial separatism reinforced the color line between whites and nonwhites. Following World War II, far-reaching institutional changes opened the way for predictable chances of social mobility for ethnic and racial minorities into the American mainstream which were not possible before changes in the formal rules and ideology. It is our contention that, consequently, the assimilation pattern will prove to be an important pathway for many descendants of the post-1965 immigration. The theory outlined in this chapter addresses the need to explain why immigrants and their descendants seek to assimilate, or so frequently end up assimilating as an unintended consequence of their pursuit of other goals. Unlike the earlier literature on assimilation, the theory does not assume that assimilation is inevitable, nor for that matter do we assume it is even irreversible. Instead we view assimilation as a contingent outcome stemming from the cumulative effect of individual choices and collective action in close-knit groups, occurring at different rates both within and across ethnic groups. Assimilation is brought about by a repertoire of causal mechanisms, the precise mix of proximate ones varying considerably across groups. For some groups, especially human-capital immigrants, assimilation is shaped mainly by individualistic adaptation conforming to a "straight-line" or perhaps "bumpy-line" intergenerational pattern. Others—traditional labor migrants with a low stock of human and financial capital in particular—follow a collectivist pattern in which network mechanisms shape the trajectory of adaptation. Such groups also include middlemen minorities who adapt through reliance on ethnic solidarity to achieve economic security and success, and then employ their resources through collective action to fight barriers to entry and gain acceptance in mainstream institutions. Various combinations of individualistic and collectivist adaptation emerge through the mix of purposive action of individuals and reliance on network mechanisms of close-knit groups. Our theory of assimilation turns on distal causes stemming from the institutional mechanisms of monitoring and enforcement that structure incentives in the institutional environment. These are the deeper causes insofar as they determine whether the purposive action of individuals and network mechanisms result in blending or segregating behavior on the part of both majority and minority groups.

The test of a theory lies in the power of its application to empirical reality, in the reach of its ability to organize and give interpretive coherence to otherwise disparate facts. We turn now to this sort of test, beginning with the story of the assimilation of the descendants of European and East Asian immigrants, the foundation for the canonical account.

CHAPTER THREE

Assimilation in Practice:
The Europeans and East Asians

Assimilation is viewed today as having dubious relevance for contemporary immigrant groups. Yet there is abundant evidence that it has been a process of major import, the master trend, in fact, among the descendants of immigrants from Europe and of earlier immigrants from East Asia. There is an element of paradox here, for what was the usual or normal pattern among earlier immigrant groups, who suffered grievously at times from nativism, is said not to be characteristic (or desirable) for the new immigration, in a period when nativism has been mild by historical standards. But this view should not be too readily accepted. Before one can assess the prospects of assimilation for new immigrant groups, one needs to examine in depth the emergence of assimilation as a widespread pattern among previous ones. Only then can the elements of continuity and disjuncture between the experiences of past immigrant groups and those of the present day be fairly evaluated.

Behind the skepticism about the relevance of assimilation for new immigrant groups, there is frequently a mythic conception of its course among earlier groups: that assimilation was unproblematic for European immigrants in particular because they were white and desired to be accepted by the mainstream society, and because opportunities for mobility, the siren call to assimilation, were abundant. Yet even a glance at the history of various earlier immigrant groups should convince us that this picture is too simplistic. At equivalent points in their history, assimilation was far from taken for granted as a prevalent outcome; indeed, it appeared not just problematic but, to the pessimistic, even outside the realm of possibility.

For one thing, the willingness of immigrants and their progeny to assimilate could not be presumed. While undoubtedly that willingness varied considerably from individual to individual and group to group, there is ample evidence to show that many earlier immigrants frequently did not want or expect their children and grandchildren to assimilate and, in their eyes, thus disappear into American society. During their early decades in the United States, some groups, such as the southern Italians, kept a distance between their families and agencies of Americanization, such as the schools, in part because their goals were still focused on returning to their home villages; a small percentage of early-twentieth-century Italian immigrants went so far as to keep their children out of American schools altogether, while many others withdrew them from school as soon as the law allowed and sent them to work.[1] For another, it is clear that native-born Americans frequently rejected even European immigrants and their children as inferior, even racially so, and ultimately unassimilable. Irish Catholics, eastern European Jews, southern Italians, and other immigrants from southern and eastern Europe at the turn of the twentieth century were particular targets of nativist hostility. The vehemence of this hostility has been largely forgotten because of the recent successes of these groups in joining the American mainstream, but it boils up out of the historical record.

Consider just a single exemplary quotation, from an 1896 *Atlantic Monthly* article by Francis A. Walker, president of the Massachusetts Institute of Technology, superintendent of the U.S. Census, and one of the leading intellectual lights in the nativism of his day. With the Darwinian framework of natural selection in mind, he issued a warning about the dangers posed by the new immigrants, characterizing them as "beaten men from beaten races; representing the worst failures in the struggle for existence. . . . They have none of the ideas and aptitudes which . . . belong to those who are descended from the tribes that met under the oak trees of old Germany to make laws and choose chieftains."[2] While others may have lacked his gift for creating phrases (which, in this case, are tinged with irony in the light of twentieth-century history), the denigration of immigrants from southern and eastern Europe was reiterated many times over. And hostility was not limited to words; there was also violence. Immigrants were occasionally lynched or gunned down by the forces of putative "law and order," especially when they became economic competitors of native-born white men or joined in labor unrest. A famous incident is the lynching of eleven Italians in New Orleans in 1891, but it is far from the only one.[3]

Immigrants from East Asia were subject to even more widespread and systematic racism because of the color of their skin. Despite the nativism directed against immigrants from southern and eastern Europe, owing to their European cultural heritage there were categorical differences between the hostility and discrimination they experienced and that suffered by immigrants from China and Japan. The response of white Americans to Asian immigration quickly escalated into racial conflict and legalized exclusion as the whites, guided by the ideals of manifest destiny and white supremacy, forcefully organized and passed racist legislation. The threat that whites felt from unfettered immigration from Asia is illustrated in these remarks of James D. Phelan, a California politician active in the anti-Japanese movement in the early twentieth century: "Wherever I went in the beautiful and productive regions about Los Angeles, I could not but feel a shudder at witnessing the disappearance of the white man's family. . . . I am sure that rural Los Angeles county, where for every three births one is a Japanese, will realize before it is too late that there is a duty just before us which we will have to perform. We must stop this yellow tide and regain the soil for our own people."[4] Chinese immigration was effectively curtailed by the passage of the Chinese Exclusion Act of 1882, and later Japanese immigration was ended with the so-called Gentlemen's Agreement of 1907–8 and the Immigration Act of 1924. The restrictions on Asian immigration continued, with minor changes, until the passage of the Immigration Act of 1965.

Further, although immigrants from southern and eastern Europe faced societal hostility, they and their descendants were never legally excluded from civil society and confined to a subordinate racial caste, as were Asian immigrants. Chinese and Japanese immigrants were ineligible for citizenship through naturalization and hence lacked the political and legal rights of their European counterparts. For Asian immigrants and the native-born generation in the first half of the twentieth century, the reality of workaday and community life was shaped by an apartheid stratification order in which the issue of assimilation was all but moot. As George P. Clements, a prominent civic leader in Los Angeles in the 1920s—the site of the largest Japanese community in North America—testified about the Japanese: "The question can he be assimilated is beside the mark. We do not want to assimilate him."[5] Even in the early 1940s, not a single schoolteacher in Los Angeles was of Japanese ancestry, despite the fact that a large proportion of the acculturated second-generation nisei were college-educated.

Despite this virulent racism, the color line that barred the descendants of the early immigration from East Asia from entry into the American mainstream gradually attenuated in the post–World War II era. Without fanfare, the native-born generations quietly assimilated as they secured jobs in the mainstream economy and moved out of the racial ghettos of Chinatown and Little Tokyo.[6] Still, some might argue that the legacy of racism experienced by these nonwhite immigrant groups—and the Asian phenotype—rules out the full scope of assimilation that has resulted in the "twilight of ethnicity" for European Americans. Thus, even though the descendants of the early Chinese and Japanese immigration may be third-, fourth-, and even fifth-generation Americans, they continue to be seen and treated as other, as perpetual foreigners.[7] Such skepticism is understandable and needs to be addressed in rethinking assimilation for nonwhite groups.

Assimilation has its variants and degrees, of course. Among Americans descended from the European and Asian immigrants of the nineteenth and early twentieth centuries, assimilation is more accurately viewed as a direction rather than an end state that has already been attained.[8] It does not imply the obliteration of all traces of ethnic origins nor require that every member of a group be assimilated to the same extent. Thus, it is not necessarily evidence against the thesis of assimilation that ethnic communities continue to exist in many cities, nor that many individuals continue to identify with their ethnic origins and to put their identities on display at symbolic moments, whether these are family occasions or festivities like Saint Patrick's Day.[9] Assimilation refers to the results of long-term processes that have gradually whittled away the social foundations for ethnic distinctions: diminishing cultural differences that serve to signal ethnic membership to others and to sustain ethnic solidarity; bringing about a rough parity of life chances to attain socioeconomic goods such as educational credentials and remunerative jobs while loosening the attachment of ethnicity to specific economic niches; shifting residence away from central-city ethnic neighborhoods to ethnically mixed suburbs and urban neighborhoods; and, finally, fostering relatively easy social intercourse across ethnic lines, resulting ultimately in high rates of ethnic intermarriage and mixed ancestry.

Ultimately, the distinctions themselves have been eroded. As we shall see, not only the descendants of southern and eastern Europeans have experienced all of these processes associated with assimilation but the descendants of the early Asian immigration as well. It is therefore not surprising that despite her skepticism about their acceptability to white Americans, the sociologist Mia Tuan acknowledges that Asian Americans may be experiencing today the rites of passage most groups have traversed; and that from the vantage point of a longer time horizon, "we might indeed find that Asian ethnics are entering that 'twilight' period of their ethnicity."[10]

The assimilation associated with these processes should not be viewed as imposed on resistant individuals seeking to protect their cultural identities—a common image in negative discussions of assimilation—nor as self-consciously embraced by individuals seeking to disappear into the mainstream (though, in both instances, there may be some who fit the description). Rather, as we argued in Chapter 2, it is in general the cumulative by-product of choices made by individuals seeking to take advantage of opportunities to improve their life chances and well-being through purposive action. For many ethnic minorities of immigrant origins, these opportunities opened especially in the period following World War II, through interlocked institutional changes and economic growth, including more favorable attitudes toward groups such as Jews, Japanese, Chinese, and Italians; the expansion of higher education and middle-class and upper-middle-class employment; and the mushrooming growth of suburban communities. The impact of one generation's decision to take advantage of enhanced opportunities has sometimes been greater on the following generations, as when socially mobile families forsake the old ethnic neighborhood, where the stamp of ethnic ways on everyday life could be taken for granted, for a suburb where children grow up in multiethnic, if not non-ethnic, surroundings.

Evidence of Acculturation

European-ancestry groups and those deriving from early Asian immigration have changed over the course of the twentieth century in profound ways that are consistent with assimilation. Declines in overt cultural differences are a prominent part of this picture. Some cultural shifts represent more or less necessary accommodations to the surrounding society. But by diminishing the differences among groups, such changes lower some of the barriers to their social mingling and thereby advance assimilation on other fronts. For example, although second-generation Japanese Americans grew up within racially segregated communities, after the Second World War the acculturated nisei were able to take advantage of the new opportunities for employment available in the corporate economy and in government.[11] As a result, within a remarkably short period of time, the occupational profile of native-born Japanese Americans shifted from a nearly complete concentration in the ethnic economy to a high representation in professional occupations and in the corporate economy.[12] This shift would have been impossible without considerable prior acculturation.

The pace of acculturation has varied for different aspects of social life.[13] Perhaps most telling for acculturation in general and the prospects for resistance to it is linguistic assimilation. Language is crucial here in at least two respects. Many aspects of ethnic culture are embedded in the mother tongue and thus are diminished, if not lost, as fluency wanes. In addition, communication in a mother tongue marks a largely impenetrable social boundary which includes all who share the same ethnic origin and can speak its language and excludes everyone else.

All the evidence about the European and early Asian groups reveals a powerful linguistic gravitational pull that has produced conversion to English monolingualism on a wide scale within three generations; only a small minority of any group has escaped its grip.[14] This process has generated a massive implosion of European ethnic language communities (other than Spanish) within a short historical span, as fluency in these mother tongues and even exposure to them at home have dropped off; Asian language communities have been spared such an implosion only because recent immigration has replaced the losses to assimilation. Anglicization occurred quite precipitously among those of European or East Asian ancestry who are descended from late-nineteenth and early-twentieth-century immigrants. Many older members of these ethnic groups spoke, or at a bare minimum heard, their mother languages in the immigrant homes and communities where they grew up. For example, data collected by the Census Bureau's Current Population Survey in the late 1970s show that three-quarters of southern and eastern European ethnics born in the United States before 1930 grew up in homes where a language other than English was spoken.[15]

The situation at the end of the twentieth century among U.S.-born white and Asian Americans, as depicted in the 1990 Census, is presented in Figure 3.1. The key language data in the census come from a question on languages spoken at home. The American-born, with rare exceptions, speak English fluently, but some also speak a language other than English, probably more at home than anywhere else.[16] In order to uncover change, we need some means to dissect groups: the picture obtained by looking at entire ethnic or ancestry categories will be muddled because they mix individuals who are at different points on a broad spectrum of assimilation. For instance, a category containing U.S.-born individuals of Italian ancestry would include older members of the still large second generation (the children of immigrants), who typically grew up in ethnic Italian families and communities, often speaking Italian dialects at home and on the streets (plus a smaller number of younger second-generation individuals, the children of a modest wave of Italian immigrants who came during the decades following World War II); and younger members of the third and fourth generations (the grandchildren and great-grandchildren of immigrants), many of whom are the offspring of intermarriages and grew up in ethnically diverse communities. A similar account of complex intergenerational linguistic transition can be told for individuals of Chinese ancestry descended from the mid-nineteenth-century immigration.[17] The changes associated with assimilation are most fully reflected in the experiences of recent birth cohorts and of the third and fourth generations, who have been raised under a different regimen of opportunities and contacts than their parents were. While it is possible from 1990 census data to make only very limited generational distinctions among the U.S.-born, the characteristics of different cohorts can be measured.[18] Those of younger cohorts are indicative of the future for Americans of European and East Asian ancestry.

Figure 3.1 focuses on the Japanese and on the southern and eastern European ancestry categories that represent the last and largest wave of mass immigration from Europe.[19] (The Chinese are not presented here because their U.S.-born children include many from the post-1965 immigration.) These groups can be regarded as the acid test of historical assimilation because of the relative recency of their arrival and the continued prominence of their ethnicity in some American cities and regions. Also included are two ancestry groups, French and German, that are associated with earlier migration waves but whose languages have left an enduring legacy in the United States. To establish a baseline, language data are presented for the population that demographers describe as "non-Hispanic whites," a population overwhelmingly of European ancestry at this point in American history; they approximate the ethnic majority population.

For the European groups, 95 percent or more of the younger cohort, who were children aged five to fourteen at the time of the census, speak only English at home.[20] There are scarcely any differences to be noted among the ethnic categories, except perhaps for the slightly higher percentage of German children who speak only English. Speaking a mother tongue at home (along, no doubt, with English) is more common among the older members of these groups. Even

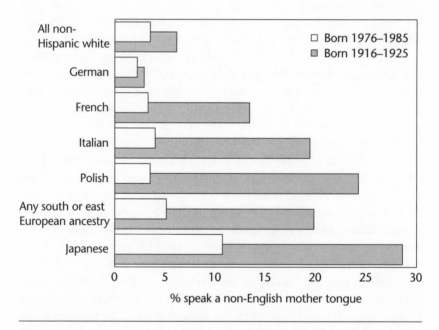

Figure 3.1. Current home language by ethnic ancestry and cohort of the U.S.-born, 1990. *Source:* Tabulations from the 5% Public Use Microdata Sample of the Census.

in the older cohort, the Germans are exceptionally monolingual in English, testifying to the crushing impact of wartime hostility on the survival of German in the United States.[21] For the Italians, Poles, and other southern and eastern Europeans, however, about 20 percent of their older members continue to speak a mother tongue, possibly on a daily basis. The figure is nearly as high for the French. Of course, much higher percentages spoke mother tongues during childhood, as already noted. A major transition in language has been accomplished in less than seventy-five years, as the proportion of children from the southern and eastern European groups who are raised in a mother-tongue home has plummeted from the great majority to 5 percent or less.

Linguistic decline is also evident for Japanese Americans, a turn-of-the-twentieth-century immigration, for which the first wave of the second generation was born in the decade 1916–1925. As of 1990, more than a quarter of that cohort speak a language other than English at home. Among those born in the later period, the fraction has slipped to one-tenth. While this is not as low as in the European ethnic categories, it does indicate a very similar trajectory. Moreover, the group of U.S.-born Japanese children undoubtedly includes some who are the children of Japanese managers posted temporarily to the United States, a group that bulks large among foreign-born Japanese residing here today. Since their families will ultimately return to Japan, these children are obviously likely to be raised speaking Japanese at home; they are not indicative of the language predispositions of later-generation Japanese Americans.

Although the comparable census data for the Chinese are not as meaningful for this examination because they include many children of contemporary immigrants, we can still bring the Chinese into this picture by looking at the children in homes where the parents were born in the United States. By definition, such children belong to the third or a later generation, and, given the onset of the contemporary Chinese immigration in the late 1960s, virtually all the third-generation Chinese children in the 1990 census are descended from the immigrants of an earlier era.[22] Of this group, we find that 8.6 percent speak a Chinese language (Mandarin, Cantonese, etc.) at home, a figure like that for the Japanese, which is higher than the rates observable among European groups but quite low in an absolute sense.

Still, it would not be reasonable to forecast the disappearance of the

European languages or Japanese, even though they are not sustainable by immigration inflows. (Quite obviously, the situation of the Chinese languages, spoken by many recent immigrants, is different.) The languages of earlier immigrations may still be sustained within geographically delimited "language islands," to borrow Joshua Fishman's term. Indeed, while the numbers of speakers of most European languages declined between the censuses of 1980 and 1990, the figures are certainly not trivial; for instance, 1.3 million speak Italian at home and 720,000 Polish.[23] To a limited extent, then, linguistic pluralism survives even among the descendants of earlier waves of European and East Asian immigrants.

Despite such sharply etched patterns of linguistic decline, some scholars nevertheless believe they see limits to the extent of acculturation among Americans of European and Asian ancestry. Generally, they point to values and behaviors in the family realm as the domain where distinctive ethnic cultural patterns are most likely to persist. The acculturation required to take advantage of opportunities for social mobility in American society leaves ample room for maintaining distinctive cultural practices in private spheres, they argue, and this compartmentalization is part of the American understanding of ethnicity.[24] Fictional literature about ethnicity, which emphasizes its subtle influences in family settings, adds its own resonance, as exemplified in works such as Maxine Hong Kingston's *Woman Warrior,* William Kennedy's *Ironweed,* and Mary Gordon's *The Other Side;* many examples for other groups could be identified. A corollary argument, whose origins can be seen in Nathan Glazer and Daniel Patrick Moynihan's seminal account *Beyond the Melting Pot,* holds that cultural distinctions among ethnic groups can survive the inevitable erosion of the immigrant cultures themselves by a process of regeneration: "As the old culture fell away—and it did rapidly enough—a new one, shaped by the distinctive experiences of life in America, was formed and a new identity was created. Italian-Americans might share precious little with Italians in Italy, but in America they were a distinctive group that maintained itself, was identifiable, and gave something to those who identified with it, just as it also gave burdens that those in the group had to bear."[25] More recently this argument has taken on a new vitality, as some scholars have come to view ethnicity as an "invention" subject to periodic reappraisals and re-creations. The implication is that unpredictable ethnic "reinventions" can blunt the seeming inevitability of cultural assimilation and even reverse it. Accordingly, ethnic cultural distinctions are seen as capable of arising like the phoenix from the embers left behind by assimilation.[26]

We accept that some cultural differences may persist over generations, and that others may emerge among the U.S.-born descendants of immigrants. But we do not believe that contemporary cultural differences, absent those emanating from differences in religion, have the depth and prominence necessary to shore up ethnic distinctions per se. This comment from a third-generation Chinese American indicates how ethnic culture gets intermingled with popular culture in contemporary American society: "My dad . . . does have a background in Chinese culture because he hung out with all these Chinese people in the Bay Area in that generation in Berkeley. There are a lot of Chinese people around, so he had the culture, he knows some of the stuff. He didn't practice it but he knew it. He hung around Chinese people a lot. He's definitely Chinese but a lot of the things they did as kids were like *Happy Days,* American stuff. Cars, girls, and baseball. That's kinda cool."[27] Arguments that emphasize the persistence of ethnic cultures in private spheres typically fail to address some difficult questions about their significance—for example, how the contemporary expression of such differences compares to that in the past, and whether they set ethnic groups apart or, rather, are within a range of "normal" variation to be observed in the mainstream of a multiethnic society. Arguments that highlight ethnic reinventions have so far failed to present convincing evidence of their differentiating nature.

Increasing Parity in Life Chances

Historically, part of the bedrock of ethnic differentiation has been socioeconomic inequality. Ethnicity has, to an important degree, been anchored in the concentrations of different ethnic groups in specific socioeconomic strata. Consequently, the members of any ethnic group are brought together by life circumstances apart from ethnicity and share specific material and other interests arising from their common situations. As Glazer and Moynihan observed several decades ago in *Beyond the Melting Pot,* for New York City ethnic groups of the 1950s and 1960s, "to name an occupational group or a class is very much the same thing as naming an ethnic group."[28] Class concentrations of such groups were reflected in and supported by the different uses they made of educational opportunities.

In the interim, however, there has been a growing and impressive convergence in the *average* socioeconomic life chances of U.S.-born members of the various groups from the earlier immigration. In particular, the disadvantages that were once quite evident for some groups of largely peasant origins in Europe and Asia have mostly faded, and their socioeconomic attainments increasingly resemble, and even surpass, those of the average white American. This convergence has not necessarily diminished the exceptional achievements of some relatively small groups, such as eastern European Jews, Chinese, and Japanese. But differences that once lay heavily *between* ethnic categories now lie mainly *within* them.

This convergence is quite demonstrable for education (a convenient indicator because its level is, for the great majority, fixed by the mid-twenties), but it is hardly limited to this sphere. Figure 3.2 presents the educational attainments of younger and older cohorts for the major southern and eastern European and East Asian ancestry categories. (We can include Chinese here because individuals born in the United States between 1956 and 1965 descend from the earlier immigration.) Two comparison groups are presented to evaluate changes: one comprises all non-Hispanic whites, and the other individuals whose ancestry is solely from the British Isles (exclusive of Ireland). The latter represents one conception of the higher-status ethnic core in the United States (Because of the large amount of information in Figure 3.2, we have streamlined the presentation of group data, excluding some important white ethnic categories, such as the Irish.)[29]

Given their initial disadvantages and uneven educational records during the first decades after their arrival, the groups from southern and eastern Europe and from Japan best reveal the trajectory of convergence. (Though the Chinese came from rural areas, as did most of the southern and eastern Europeans, their educational successes were revealed very early, as the data in Figure 3.2 show.) For southern and eastern European and Japanese males who were born between 1916 and 1925, moderate disadvantages are evident in comparison to the average non-Hispanic white; the disadvantage appears more substantial when the comparison is to men of exclusively British ancestry. For instance, only a quarter to a third of Italian and Polish men attended college, compared to almost half of the British men; and about one in

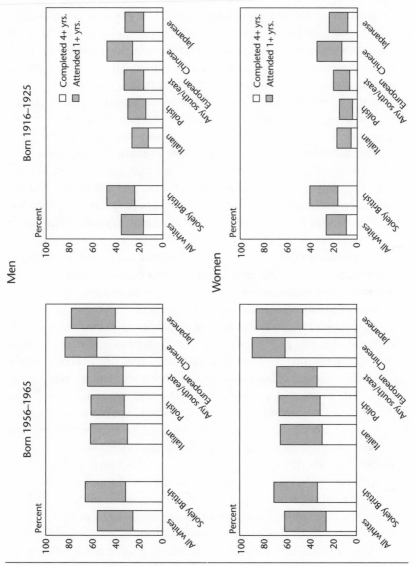

Figure 3.2. College education among U.S.-born cohort for selected ethnic groups, 1990. *Source:* Tabulation from the 5% Public Use Microdata Sample of the Census.

eight Italians and Poles completed bachelor's degrees, compared to nearly one in four British men. In the cohort born between 1956 and 1965 (whose education was largely complete by the time of the 1990 census), the southern and eastern Europeans have just about pulled even with the British men and are ahead of the average white: in particular, the figures for baccalaureate completion (about a third in each case) and postgraduate education (not shown here, but completed or ongoing for 10–15 percent of each group) are very similar. The Japanese have forged even further ahead: their educational attainment exceeds that of all categories of whites. The figures for southern and eastern Europeans in general and for Poles may be affected by the extraordinary accomplishments of Jewish men (who are nevertheless minorities within these categories), but the same argument cannot be made in the case of the Italians.

The process of convergence is even more striking among women. For groups such as the Italians, Japanese, and Poles, with heavy representations of immigrants from rural areas, the education of daughters once took a distinctly secondary place compared to the education of sons. In the older cohort, Italian and Polish women had rates of college attendance and graduation that were less than half those of their British contemporaries. This disparity, too, has been largely eradicated in the younger cohort: Italian and Polish women are slightly behind British women in college attendance and graduation, but tied with, if not slightly ahead of, the average non-Hispanic white woman. The younger women in the general southern and eastern European category have above-average educational attainments similar to those of British women; this parity represents a marked improvement over their situation in the older cohort. Chinese and Japanese women in the younger cohort exhibit exceptional educational attainment, which was not apparent among those born in the 1916–1925 period.

To be sure, these data and conclusions represent broadly drawn trends about quantitative levels of education. They cannot tell us—no census data can—about the possibility of remaining differences in qualitative aspects of education, such as access to elite schools.[30] The very high relative percentage of Asian Americans enrolled in elite universities, however—private and public—highlights the potential for this kind of social mobility for Asian Americans in the post–civil rights era. Of course, differences in educational opportunities still exist within ethnic categories, most obviously along lines of social class origin. It is also the case that the above-average attainments of younger whites of southern and eastern European ancestry are not equaled by those of some more established European groups such as the Germans and the French, but the differences are not large. Geographical placement may play a part here: the southern and eastern Europeans tended to settle in economically dynamic metropolitan regions, where educational and occupational opportunities expanded rapidly in the post–World War II period.

The convergence seems remarkable, nevertheless. In the thirty years that separate the two cohorts, differences that once bordered on, or even exceeded, a 2-to-1 margin have shrunk dramatically. For groups of largely peasant origins in Europe and Asia whose disadvantages were once quite evident, educational attainments now resemble, or surpass, those of the average white American. Moreover, not only is socioeconomic convergence revealed in the increasing parity of educational life chances, but also it has been demonstrated by other research for occupational position and income, which shows, for example, a decline in differences among white ethnic groups in average occupational standing by the third generation; a gradual erosion of ethnic economic niches, such as the former concentration of Germans among bakers; and income parity, if not superiority, for the descendants of Catholic immigrants from the European peasantry.[31]

Yet convergence does not mean an end to all socioeconomic differences associated with ethnicity. As noted, it does not erase the higher-than-average educational and occupational attainments of some groups such as eastern European Jews, Chinese, and Japanese. Nor does it imply the complete disappearance of ethnic economic niches, the disproportionate representation of some groups in particular occupations or trades, to the point at times of ethnic domination. These niches can still be found in and around New York, as is probably the case for other regions where immigrants settled in large numbers in the early twentieth century: thus, Jews still dominate the diamond trade, centered on Forty-seventh Street in Manhattan, and Italians the refuse business. Yet over time, many other niches, such as the concentration of Jews and Italians in the garment industry, have weakened or disappeared, in some cases because the niches have undergone a process of ethnic succession and been taken over by new immigrant groups.[32]

Nor does convergence in life chances imply the complete absence of discrimination. The descendants of the early immigration from Asia made impressive socioeconomic progress in the latter half of the twentieth century. U.S.-born Chinese and Japanese have, on average, higher incomes than whites, particularly at the household level. But studies of income parity that control for education and occupation show that there still exists a wage gap, albeit very modest, between native-born whites and Asian ethnics.[33] In other words, the higher income of Asian ethnics stems from their higher educational attainment; but Asians with the same educational and occupational attainments as whites earn somewhat less than their white counterparts. Likewise, concerns persist about the existence of a glass ceiling limiting the mobility of Chinese and Japanese onto the highest rungs of management in the corporate economy, despite the high relative percentages of professionals and managers within these groups. But, in contrast to the complete exclusion of Asians from jobs in both the corporate economy and government prior to World War II, the trend in life chances has been robustly in the direction of convergence with those of whites. This trend is likely to continue, given the high educational attainment of Asian ethnics, their high proportional enrollment in elite institutions that prepare their students for entry into management suites, and high rates of intermarriage with whites.

Finally, convergence should not be understood to imply that the routes taken by different ethnic groups into the economic mainstream were uniform and that there was thus a single process of assimilation for all groups. To the contrary, groups with peasant backgrounds that settled in urban settings in the United States, such as the Irish and Italians, entered the labor force at much lower levels than did groups that brought urban experience and industrial skills with them, eastern European Jews being perhaps the preeminent example. Even between the Irish and Italians, there were major differences in the processes of upward mobility, as the Irish came to dominate the politics of many cities and took advantage of opportunities in government employment to move up, while the Italians were far more inclined toward small-business ownership in diverse areas, such as barbershops, construction, grocery stores, and garment factories.[34] As for East Asian immigrants, the destruction of the Japanese ethnic economy following forced internment during World War II removed an alternative ethnic base of employment for young native-born Japanese, resulting in a more rapid shift after the war into the corporate economy than might have been the case had the ethnic economy remained intact.[35] The economic assimilation of native-born Chinese proceeded parallel with that of Japanese Americans, but at a more gradual pace because Chinatown continued to provide a viable economic base for self-employed Chinese American professionals. While the mobility ladders for large immigrant groups that settled in cities have been studied in some depth, less is known about groups that settled heavily in rural areas, such as the Germans, Dutch, and Swedes. Were their stories to be added, we would undoubtedly see even more the ethnic diversity in economic pathways to the mainstream.

Growing Residential Assimilation

Without exception, European and Asian immigrant groups had distinctive geographic patterns of initial settlement, generally linked to their periods of arrival and their economic intentions and opportunities, and the resulting regional concentrations of different ancestries are still very visible on a population map of the United States. Thus, nineteenth-century German immigrants went in large numbers to the Midwest, at a time when farmland was readily available. Italians, coming later and frequently lacking the money to travel far into the American interior in search of work, settled mainly in or near the eastern seaboard ports. Chinese and Japanese immigrants settled in the western coastal states and Hawaii. Dispersal from areas of initial concentration has been slow, as subsequent generations have grown up with attachments to family and place that tend to keep them from moving very far away. German ancestry (now frequently cited as one element in ancestry mixtures) is still the most common in many midwestern states, while even in 1990, about half of all Americans of Italian ancestry were located in just six northeastern states. The West Coast remains the center of Asian settlement despite some dispersion to the U.S. interior. One analysis of patterns of interregional mobility concluded that even long-distance moves are not changing such regional concentrations very much, because some moves are to new areas of group concentration, such as the clusters of Frostbelt ethnic groups that have emerged in the Sunbelt, while others bring group members back into the original areas.[36] The ethnic implications of these geographic concentrations have not been thoroughly explored, but some are clear. Most obviously, a group's contributions to the public culture are most salient in regions where it is concentrated: a

German Oktoberfest has a significance in Milwaukee that it does not have in many other parts of the country, and the same point can be made about Chinese New Year in New York and San Francisco, Saint Patrick's Day in Boston, Chicago, and New York City, and Mardi Gras in New Orleans.[37] That such ethnic festivities often are no longer the exclusive property of one group—that Saint Patrick's Day celebrations involve some participants who are minimally or not at all Irish—illustrates a point we made earlier: the mainstream culture is not a homogeneous monolith but an evolving, syncretic agglomeration, a composite culture that incorporates what were once exclusively ethnic elements.

Within the regional concentrations of ethnic groups, however, substantial residential changes have taken place, spurred by socioeconomic mobility and language acculturation, combined with the rapid postwar development of the suburbs and, starting in the 1960s, the potent catalyst of competition with racial and new immigrant minorities over urban turf. The result has been a decline in the scale of ethnic neighborhoods and, more generally, in residential separation of European and Asian ethnic groups descended from the earlier immigration. Ethnic neighborhoods have been weakened especially by the migration of many ethnics—or perhaps, more accurately, former ethnics—out of inner-city areas (or, in some cases, such as the Japanese, out of farming communities) and into suburban settings, where ethnic residential concentrations tend to be diluted, when they exist at all. Because of the continued visibility of surviving ethnic neighborhoods, some of which have become meccas for those seeking "authentic" ethnic experience, the magnitude and implications of residential shifts are sometimes less appreciated than they should be.

The term "segregation" is often applied to the distinctive distributions of white ethnic groups across areas, but this is not in general segregation as the term is understood outside of the technical literature of social science. Even in the mass immigration era, European immigrant groups did not experience the extreme degree of concentration in homogeneous neighborhoods that characterized urban African Americans throughout the twentieth century and the Chinese and Japanese prior to World War II. European immigrant neighborhoods for the most part were not homogeneous but juxtaposed cheek-by-jowl individuals and families from several groups.[38] In the white ethnic context, then, "segregation" refers to the pattern showing each group overrepresented in a particular set of neighborhoods, so that its distribution across areas within a city is dissimilar to a greater or lesser extent to the equivalent distribution for any other group.

The residential segregation of European ancestry groups weakened during the transition from the first to the second generation, though this weakening appears to have been only modest by mid-century.[39] In the postwar era, the paramount factor behind residential assimilation has undoubtedly been suburbanization, which has siphoned off many socially mobile white families from central-city enclaves. About 70 percent of non-Hispanic whites who live in metropolitan areas now live outside the large (i.e., central) cities and thus in suburban communities, as these are defined in census data. Suburbanization has spread uniformly throughout the major ethnic ancestry categories in the white population, as Table 3.1 demonstrates. The proportions of these groups residing in metropolitan areas (as opposed to nonmetropolitan rural areas and small towns) varies in accordance with the settlement patterns of their immigrant ancestors—Italians and Poles being noticeably more likely to live there. Within metropolitan areas, however, all the white groups are distributed in a remarkably similar way between city and suburbs: in each case, the suburban percentage is within a few points of the figure for all white. Overall, this urban-

Table 3.1. Suburbanization of white and Japanese ethnic groups, 2000

	Pop. size (millions)	% in metro. areas	% of metro. pop. in suburbs
Non-Hisp. whites	194.6	76.6	70.6
Germans	42.9	77.6	71.7
Irish	30.6	82.2	71.4
English	24.5	78.2	70.8
Italians	15.7	91.2	73.5
French/French Canadian	10.8	79.3	70.7
Scots/Scots-Irish	9.2	79.4	68.5
Polish	9.0	88.3	73.5
Japanese	0.8	91.0	55.0
All other Americans	86.1	88.5	45.9

Source: U.S. Bureau of the Census, "Census 2000: Demographic Profiles" (*www.census.gov*).

suburban ratio is quite different among America's non-European racial and ethnic groups, about 55 percent of whose metropolitan inhabitants reside in the city itself. This is due in large part to the urban concentration of African Americans, roughly 60 percent of whom live in large cities. Some new immigrant groups are becoming predominantly suburban, but in the aggregate the populations growing rapidly from immigration are close to evenly divided between urban and suburban space.

As the descendants of the earlier East Asian immigration entered the American mainstream, they too joined the migration to the suburbs. Chinatowns in cities and rural towns scattered throughout the western states were gradually dying out in the late 1950s, as native-born Chinese Americans assimilated and the older sojourning male bachelors declined in number.[40] In the 1950s, second-generation Chinese moved out of the Chinatown ghetto to homes in the fashionable "Avenues" near the Pacific Coast area of San Francisco.[41] Japanese Americans quietly moved into suburban communities and to the Midwest and eastern states; today more of them live in suburbs than in cities, unlike the rest of the nonwhite population.[42] Although the larger Chinatowns have been revived by recent immigration—for, like earlier European immigrants, contemporary Chinese immigrants tend to settle on arrival in predominantly immigrant neighborhoods, in both older Chinatowns and new ethnic enclaves such as Monterey Park in Los Angeles and Flushing in Queens—the descendants of the earlier Chinese immigration now frequent Chinatowns on weekends mainly to shop for groceries and to dine out. Likewise, Little Tokyos in San Francisco and Los Angeles continue as centers of commerce but are no longer residential communities.

Focusing on a specific metropolitan region, where the neighborhood context is not lost entirely in aggregate indices of residential patterns, reveals all the more clearly the growing residential integration of earlier groups. The greater New York metropolitan region, a broad swath of cities and suburbs stretching from the Hudson Valley and Long Island in New York to the New Jersey shore, was home to 17 million people in 1990.[43] Because of the New York region's historic role as a gateway for immigrants, European ethnic communities continue to play a visible role in its ethnic geography, despite the ending of mass immigration from Europe in the 1920s. If such communities are important anywhere, they are sure to be so here. We trace residential patterns for three large groups: Germans, Irish, and Italians. Each group numbers 2 to 3 million members in the region, according to census data from 1980 to 2000. Each has figured in significant ways in the region's ethnic neighborhoods in the past, but based on their histories, the Germans could be expected to be the least residentially distinctive (i.e., represented by the fewest ethnic areas), while the Italians should be the most.

In fact, all three of these groups are now found mainly in the suburbs, where ethnic residential concentrations are demonstrably milder (though not nonexistent). By 1980, roughly three-quarters of both the Germans and the Irish were already living outside central cities, compared to two-thirds of all non-Hispanic whites (but just one-quarter of Latinos and nonwhites). Moreover, in suburbia, these groups are residentially dispersed, their distributions barely distinguishable from those of other non-Hispanic whites. Students of residential segregation use a statistic known as the Index of Dissimilarity, calculated across census tracts, which are small and relatively homogeneous areas, to measure the distinctiveness of one group's residential distribution compared to that of a reference group (all other non-Hispanic whites in this case); the numeric value of the index can be interpreted as the proportion of the group that would have to be moved to match the residential pattern of the target population. As shown in Table 3.2, for the Germans and Irish in the suburbs, these values are approximately .15, quite small in absolute terms and much less than the benchmark value of .3, conventionally taken as the threshold for meaningful segregation.

The Italians present a different but more dynamic picture. In 1980, they were slightly less likely to be found in suburbs than the average white (64 versus 66 percent), but by 1990, 70 percent resided in suburbs; while they were still not as suburbanized as the Germans and Irish, they were more so than the average non-Hispanic white. For the Italians, too, suburban residence increases the probability of living in an ethnically diverse community. As of 1990, their segregation index value in suburbs was a modest .20, a bit higher than the low values exhibited by the Germans and Irish but considerably below the Italian value in cities, .42.

For all three white ethnic categories, the regional values of the index have been affected by the large proportions of these groups now resident in suburbs. The contrast in overall segregation between these

Table 3.2. Urban-suburban distribution and residential segregation of the Germans, Irish, and Italians in the New York region, 1980 and 1990

	Metropolitan region		Central cities		Suburbs	
	1980	1990	1980	1990	1980	1990
Urban-suburban distribution:						
Germans	100.0%	100.0%	22.8	20.6	77.2	79.4
Irish	100.0%	100.0%	27.4	24.1	72.6	75.9
Italians	100.0%	100.0%	36.5	30.0	63.5	70.0
All non-Hispanic whites	100.0%	100.0%	34.5	31.6	65.5	68.4
All others	100.0%	100.0%	76.1	72.1	23.9	27.9
Index of Dissimilarity:						
Germans	.223	.215	.260	.263	.148	.151
Irish	.222	.223	.307	.301	.160	.164
Italians	.292	.267	.422	.422	.220	.196

Source: Summary Tape File 3 of the 1980 and 1990 U.S. Censuses; Richard Alba, John Logan, and Kyle Crowder, "White Ethnic Neighborhoods and Spatial Assimilation: The Greater New York Region, 1980–1990," *Social Forces* 75 (March 1997): 883–912.
Note: The Index of Dissimilarity values, which measure residential segregation, are based on comparisons of all members of each ancestry category to all other non-Hispanic whites.

groups and non-European groups, both immigrant and non-immigrant, is strong. African Americans represent the most extreme form of segregation, and the 1990 index value in their case over the whole metropolitan region, .81, is three times the highest metropolitan-wide value among the white groups (the Italians at .27).

How does this modest level of residential concentration translate to the level of ethnic neighborhoods? To answer this question, the researchers identified the region's ethnic neighborhoods in 1980 and 1990 census data, based on clusters of census tracts where any of the three ancestry groups has a concentration of more than a third of the population, a threshold value that, according to a preliminary investigation, tends to be associated with comparatively high levels of ethnic traits, such as speaking a mother tongue. For the Germans and Irish, these neighborhoods are, generally speaking, few and small; only tiny fractions of each group could be considered to reside in them (just 4 percent of the Irish in 1990, for instance). For the Italians, however, there are a number of these neighborhoods, some of which are quite large and most of which take on familiar outlines, identifiable with well-known Italian areas, such as Brooklyn's Bensonhurst, which has become widely known through its appearance as an archetypal Italian neighborhood in a number of films, including popular Mafia movies. (Other neighborhoods—Belmont, Canarsie, and Greenpoint—have also been studied by ethnographers.)[44] Nevertheless, it is still the case that just a minority of the group—a quarter in both 1980 and 1990— resides in Italian neighborhoods.

The most ethnically Italian neighborhoods have been shrinking. Many of these neighborhoods have not held onto their young people for several decades. Now, their older Italian residents are dying off or moving to retirement regions, while their children are joining the outflow to the suburbs. Bensonhurst is an exemplar: In 1980, it was the largest contiguous Italian area in the region, home to nearly 150,000 persons of Italian ancestry. The neighborhood was then more than 60 percent Italian and contained census tracts that reached as high as 90 percent Italian; moreover, 90 percent of its Italian residents were of exclusively Italian parentage, an indicator of limited intermarriage, and nearly 40 percent spoke Italian at home. By 1990, the Italian areas had shrunk in spatial extent and in Italian population to less than 100,000. The contraction is continuing, as Bensonhurst is becoming home to new immigrant groups.[45] Some of these neighborhoods are even facing imminent "death" as Italian residential areas. Ironically, this has already happened to Manhattan's famed Little Italy, which, though it retains its street-level facade of Italian restaurants and stores, now houses primarily Chinese immigrants.

The suburban areas with growing numbers of Italians are very different in character from inner-city Italian neighborhoods, and the great majority of suburban Italians reside outside anything resembling an ethnic neighborhood. Population growth has bypassed inner-suburban ethnic neighborhoods, such as the Italian areas of Yonkers, New York, or Belleville, New Jersey, which often have developed as the suburban mirror to urban ethnic neighborhoods that lie just across a city border (in the Bronx in the case of Yonkers, and in Newark in that of Belleville). During the 1980s, much of the growth of the Italian suburban population took place in non-ethnic communities, and insofar as growth was funneled into areas of ethnic concentration, these were not very ethnic.

In sum, even in the New York region, the ethnic mosaic par excellence, trends favor the further residential assimilation of white ethnic groups. The Irish, long a prominent ethnic group in the region, are already residentially intermixed, except for a very small minority. The Italians, some of whose ethnic communities are still conspicuous, reside mostly in non-ethnic areas, and their continuing suburbanization is eroding the most ethnically Italian neighborhoods. Nevertheless, it would be a mistake to conclude that the Italian neighborhoods are fated to disappear in the foreseeable future, just as it would be to infer that they represent the everyday living situations of most Italian Americans. Thus, the analysis of New York shows that, for white ethnics, residential assimilation is an incomplete and ongoing process, without a predictable end point, and that a minority of ethnics continue to reside in ethnic milieus. Assimilation and pluralism are thus compatible with each other to some extent. We suspect that the patterns of residential change, combined with the persistence of some ethnic neighborhoods, are rather similar in other metropolitan regions where European immigrants settled in large numbers.

The Growth of Intermarriage and Mixed Ancestry

The most compelling evidence of assimilation among descendants of the mid-nineteenth- and early-twentieth-century immigration from southern and eastern Europe and Asia comes from data on intermarriage. Intermarriage, a strong form of what Milton Gordon called "structural assimilation," can be viewed as the visible tip of a denser mass of interethnic contacts, occurring throughout the social body, but below the surface in the sense that they are not usually measured directly by research instruments. But intermarriage also has an obvious importance in and of itself. It is generally regarded, with justification, as the litmus test of assimilation. A high rate of intermarriage signals that the social distance between the groups involved is small and that individuals of putatively different ethnic backgrounds no longer perceive social and cultural differences significant enough to create a barrier to long-term union. (In this sense, intermarriage could be said to provide a test of the existence and salience of a social boundary between ethnic categories.) Further, intermarriage carries obvious and profound implications for the familial and, more broadly, the social contexts in which the next generation will be raised. Its significance in these respects is not much diminished by a high rate of divorce. For the vast majority of individuals, marriage is still a fateful act and not undertaken lightly.

Intermarriage is occurring at a robust level in the white population and, at this point in history, primarily involves mixtures of European ancestries (and Native American ancestry, which is claimed by a non-negligible fraction of whites). A substantial majority of marriages among non-Hispanic whites involve some degree of ethnic intermixing. The 1990 census data show that more than half (56 percent) of U.S.-born whites have spouses whose ethnic background has no element in common with their own (included in this count are spouses whose ethnic ancestries are described as just "American" or in some other non-ethnic way).[46] Only a fifth have spouses with an identical ethnic background. The remainder, not quite a quarter, have spouses whose ancestry overlaps their own in some respect but differs in some other, one or both partners in these marriages having mixed ancestry (as when, for instance, a German-Irish groom takes an Irish-Italian bride). Intermarriage is so commonplace among whites that its occurrence is no longer remarkable. In this sense, one could even say that it has ceased to be intermarriage to its participants because they no longer recognize that a social boundary is being crossed.[47] Social scientists still do, however.

Among those aged twenty-five to thirty-four in 1990, a majority of each of the seven largest ancestry categories of whites had married unambiguously outside of it, choosing a spouse with no ancestry from it (see Figure 3.3). Such a marriage is more common among the smaller groups, having an especially deep impact on the groups from southern and eastern Europe. Close to three-quarters of the younger Italians have spouses without Italian ancestry; for Poles, the equivalent figure is higher still. A comparison to the older cohort shown in the figure reveals that intermarriage has increased substantially over time, although even older members of these groups had surprisingly high rates of intermarriage. The smaller size of these groups (in comparison, say, with the German ancestry group) makes them more susceptible to out-marriage; the higher intermarriage rates of smaller groups are well documented by intermarriage studies.[48] These groups are also more concentrated in regions of the nation where ethnic diversity is greater among whites (the Northeast and Midwest compared to the South), increasing the likelihood that they will have close relationships with individuals of diverse backgrounds. For the large, long-established categories, the English, Germans, and Irish, their size alone implies a statistical pattern of endogamy; that is, even under a hypothetical assumption of mating without regard to ethnic origin, a substantial fraction of each group would marry someone who shares that ancestry.

The acid test of intermarriage among Americans of European ancestry is the case of Jews. Not only does a substantial religious divide, accompanied by a historical legacy of anti-Semitism, come between Jews and Gentiles, but also Jews have made strenuous efforts to promote endogamy among their young people. For much of the twentieth century, these efforts seemed to bear fruit: Jewish-Gentile intermarriage remained at low levels. But in more recent decades, it has surged. According to data from the 1990 National Jewish Population Survey, about half of Jews wed since 1985 married partners raised in other religions; just two decades earlier, only 11 percent did so.[49] The consequences of Jewish-Gentile intermarriage are still debatable,

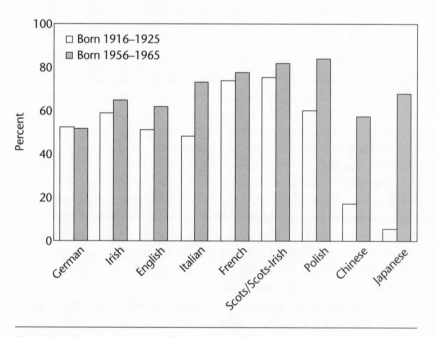

Figure 3.3. Percent intermarried by group and cohort, 1990. *Source:* Tabulation from the 5% Public Use Microdata Sample of the Census.

at least in principle, because of the possibility that the non-Jewish spouse will convert or the children will be raised as Jews, though the data suggest that neither occurs in a majority of intermarried couples. In any case, it is clear that religious origins play a lesser role in the choice of a spouse than they once did.[50]

Still, marriages involving spouses who have some ancestry in common are more frequent among whites than they would be if marriage were "random" with respect to ancestry. There is, moreover, some sign that the increase in intermarriage may be leveling off among the southern and eastern European groups, where it has risen most sharply since the end of World War II. The frequency of intermarriage in the younger cohort in the 1990 data is not much different from what it was in the 1980 census. A reasonable forecast is that intermarriage will continue at high levels, but that a significant minority of each white ethnic group will continue to look within it for marriage partners. In this bottom-line sense, then, intermarriage could be said to resemble residential assimilation, where the wide breadth of a pattern of assimilation does not negate some ethnic persistence among a minority of whites.

For the descendants of the earlier East Asian immigrants, intermarriage rates have also risen sharply in recent decades, from levels that were, at the middle of the twentieth century, drastically lower than those among white ethnic groups and suggestive of racial exclusion.[51] Nearly 70 percent of young U.S.-born Japanese Americans were intermarried in 1990, compared to just 5 percent among Japanese born in the United States four decades earlier (see Figure 3.3). The out-marriage rate of the group is such that without sizable new immigration from Japan, which is unlikely, this ethnic group appears to be on the road to amalgamation with whites and, to a lesser but growing extent because of pan-Asian marriages, other Asian groups. Indeed, there is growing concern among Japanese Americans that continued marital assimilation might result in a loss of community and identity as ethnic boundaries continue to erode.[52] For the offspring of Japanese and white intermarriages, the choice of identity is often dependent on physical appearance or the specific context of extended family relations; in any case, their mixed ancestry and social connections lead to a more contingent involvement with Japanese ethnicity.[53] The intermarriage rate is not quite as high for young native-born Chinese, of whom 50–60 percent intermarry. Post-1960s immigration from

China, Taiwan, and Hong Kong has made the Chinese among the fastest-growing ethnic groups, which may lower the out-marriage rate for the native-born as the base of marriageable Chinese increases in number. Notwithstanding, by 1997, one in five Asian Americans, including foreign-born, had a non-Asian spouse; these interracial marriages have produced about 750,000 mixed-race children under eighteen years of age.[54]

An obvious consequence of intermarriage is ethnically mixed ancestry, which holds potentially profound implications for ethnic groups. Although the mere fact of mixed ancestry is certainly no bar to ethnic feelings and loyalties, it is likely to reduce their intensity, especially because most individuals of mixed ancestry are raised with limited exposure to ethnic cultures and social circles in their most robust form. Among the non-Hispanic white children born during the 1980s, more than half (56 percent) were described by their parents as having mixed ancestry (because of simplifications in the reporting of ancestry to the census, this understates the actual extent of ethnic mixture); another 13 percent were described as "American" or in some other non-ethnic way. Just 31 percent were reported as having a single ethnic background only. In accordance with the frequency of intermarriage, mixed white ancestry is even more common among those of southern and eastern European descent. About 80 percent of children with Italian ancestry born during the 1980s were reported to have some other ancestry as well; for children with Polish ancestry, close to 85 percent. The number is somewhat lower among Japanese born in the 1980s but stunning nevertheless: 63 percent have mixed ethnic ancestry, suggesting the erosion of a racial boundary.[55]

Shifting Modes of Identity

Although increases in these more or less objective forms of assimilation are clearly evident, observers have seen the persistence of some of the more subjective dimensions of ethnicity, or ethnic identity, among objectively assimilated individuals, such as intermarried suburban whites, as a direct challenge to assimilation theory. Others have elaborated a concept of ethnic identity, generally labeled "symbolic ethnicity," that is more consonant with assimilation.[56] The latter is a form of limited-liability ethnicity that allows individuals to "feel ethnic" occasionally in family and leisure-time activities but carries few commitments in everyday social life. For whites, it has been described as a set of "ethnic options" that they can exercise but are not compelled to.[57] Herbert Gans argues that symbolic ethnicity is consistent with the straight-line theory of assimilation, but is agnostic about whether it can persist indefinitely among whites. Richard Alba suggests that it can, because symbolic ethnicity is the social-psychological expression of a European American group in the process of formation. Like all ethnic groups, the European American group expresses a common identity in terms of a perceived common historical experience, which in this case is based partly on immigration and its aftermath. Family memories of European ancestry and immigration (whether factually accurate or not) serve to link individuals to this validating experience.

Such symbolic ethnicity increasingly characterizes Asian ethnics as well. Like white ethnics, third- and later-generation Asians speak English as their mother tongue, often knowing only scattered phrases of Chinese or Japanese. They enjoy ethnic cuisine when they like, and observe ethnic rituals and holidays with an often superficial understanding of their cultural content. They may or may not choose to learn more about their cultural heritage. They may feel an awkwardness in not speaking the native language of their grandparents and a sense of loss in not being part of a cohesive ethnic community; and there may also be "hidden injuries" associated with racial slurs. But Asian ethnics are closer to the experience of symbolic ethnicity of white ethnics than is commonly acknowledged.[58]

In discussing ethnic identity, one must distinguish it from ancestry. Ancestry can be defined as the beliefs about the racial or ethnic identities of forebears. Ethnic identity, by contrast, is fundamentally a matter of the ethnic labels accepted as suitable for oneself (including "American") and of the emotional intensity attached to them. Survey research and census data demonstrate that the great majority of Americans do not say just "American" when asked their ancestry; they name some extra-American origin. Ethnic ancestry data were collected by the U.S. Census for the first time in 1980. Between the 1980 and 2000 censuses, there was surprising flux in these ancestry reports for white Americans, suggesting that, for many, ethnic ancestry is not a solid anchor of their self-identity. The question on the census is open-ended, and to suggest the nature of the answer desired, examples are listed just under the line provided for a response.[59] The examples were different on each census, and their influence on the resulting responses implies that many whites are quite suggestible when it comes to the way they describe their ancestry. For instance, in 1980 "English" was among the first examples given, and 49.6 million Americans claimed English ancestry; in 1990 it was omitted from the list of examples, and the number who identified themselves as of English ancestry fell to 32.7 million, a decline of one-third. Similarly, in 1990 "German" was the first example, and the number claiming German ancestry rose by nearly 9 million persons, to make it the most populous ancestry category in the 1990 census; in 2000, when the "German" category was no longer among the examples, it lost 15 million claimants. There is no conceivable demographic explanation for such mercurial flux.

A similar pattern of inconsistent reporting of ancestry can be expected for the rapidly growing mixed-race groups whose ancestry does not fall readily into preexisting ethnic and racial categories, as in the offspring of white and Asian intermarriages. The trend toward increasing pan-Asian intermarriage could likewise contribute to flux in the self-reported ancestry of Asian ethnics in a manner paralleling the inconsistent reporting of ancestry found among white ethnics.[60]

Still, it is clear from in-depth surveys that many think of themselves at times in terms of ethnic labels and show some preference for one origin over others when their ancestry is mixed; they attribute some importance to their ethnic origin; and they have specific conceptions about the characteristics associated with these origins, although these conceptions frequently exhibit surprising commonalities across different ancestries. But certain hallmarks of contemporary ethnic identity for whites seem symptomatic of widespread assimilation.

One hallmark is malleability.[61] For the same individual, the salience, the intensity, and even the definition of ethnic identity may vary from situation to situation. Increasingly, then, ethnic identities are situationally specific. This malleability is partly due to the complexity of ancestry for many whites and to the weak social constraints on how white Americans identify themselves (since their ethnic backgrounds are frequently not self-evident). Only a small minority of whites hold intensely to ethnic identities that are likely to be manifest in a wide range of situations; at the other extreme, only a minority believe that ethnic origin has little or no personal importance. In between these extremes is a much larger group, possibly a majority, at least in areas of European immigrant settlement in the Northeast and Midwest,[62] for whom ethnic background and identity are of middling significance. For these individuals, ethnic identity is typically an occasional feeling, experienced perhaps with certain family members, at weddings and other family celebrations, on holidays like Saint Patrick's Day, or in moments of solidarity with friends and acquaintances.

Another hallmark is the weak reflection of ethnic identity in everyday experience. Most who identify at all with their ethnic backgrounds can point to some experiences they regard as "ethnic." But few have many such experiences or very regular ones, aside from eating ethnic food. And eating ethnic foods, the prime example, is an experience mostly in the private, rather than public, realm; it is innocuous, unlikely to give offense or attract negative comment; and it need not be ethnically exclusive (ethnic foods can be shared with people of other backgrounds). Though some whites may have encountered ethnic stereotypes, very few believe themselves to have suffered discrimination because of being Irish, Italian, or whatever.

"Privatization" is itself a hallmark of contemporary white ethnicity, reducing its expression to largely personal and family terms. For many whites, there is only a loose connection between ethnic identity and ethnic social structures larger than the family. A larger ethnic community is only hazily discerned at best. Of course, most whites live and work in highly intermixed social settings (at least as far as European ancestries are concerned). But even when it comes to voluntary memberships that make only modest claims on people's lives, such as memberships in ethnic organizations, few whites join.[63]

The kind of ethnic identity whites hope to instill in their children, insofar as they imagine one at all, frequently seems little more than a sense of family background—as when intermarried parents, or those of mixed ancestry themselves, tick off the ethnic variety of their children's ancestries with fairly equal weighting. Few white Americans care strongly about their children's ethnic identities; most accept what Gans has labeled "middle-American individualism" and consider the nature and extent of ethnic commitment ultimately a matter for the children themselves to decide. As a consequence, the intergenerational transmission of ethnicity is more and more tenuous.

The evidence that we have about the identities of later-generation Chinese and Japanese Americans is less complete, but it does suggest that these conditions extend also to them, though perhaps to a lesser extent.[64] Ethnic identity among these groups is complicated by the arrival of new immigrants from Asia, whose presence reinforces the view among whites that Asians are recent arrivals on the American scene. This has led to a vigorous assertion of American identity by native-born Asian Americans descended from the earlier immigration. Asian American writers like Frank Chin, author of *Chickencoop Chinaman and Year of the Dragon,* and the playwright David Henry Hwang, whose plays include *The Dance and the Railroad* and *My American Son,* explore the American roots of Asian ethnic identity arising from being neither immigrant nor white. The assertion of an American identity among Asian Americans is in part defensive, an attempt to emphasize the distinctiveness of the American experience at a time when newly arrived immigrants from Asia outnumber the native-born Asian American population. As with white ethnic identity, ethnic identity among later-generation Asian ethnics is malleable. With the high rates of intermarriage among descendants of the earlier Asian immigration, white spouses, in-laws, and friends are often present in Asian American family life. The experiences of relationships with friends and acquaintances from other ethnic groups and of mixed-race children increasingly define Asian American ethnic identity. Where the differences mainly lie between whites and Asian ethnics in the experience of ethnicity is with respect to how race matters when prevailing stereotypes about Asians intrude, often during unguarded moments in everyday social life. For native-born Asian Americans this typically may be experienced as annoyance at being praised for fluency in English or being asked, "Where are you really from?" But the new reassertion of nativist sentiment in some regions of the United States has caused concern over hate crimes directed at Asians, such as the bludgeoning to death of Vincent Chin, a third-generation Chinese American who was mistakenly identified by white youths in Detroit as a Japanese businessman. Awareness of a degree of vulnerability may make Asian Americans more attentive than white Americans to the continuing salience of ethnic identity.[65]

The Limits to Assimilation

Not all critics agree with the depiction of assimilation as the master trend among whites of European ancestry and East Asians descended from earlier waves of immigration. Some, as already noted, have pointed to evidence of the incompleteness of acculturation to suggest that a sufficient basis for ethnic distinctiveness and solidarity remains.

Others have pointed to surviving ethnic social structures that mesh with ethnic economic and political interests. They argue that ethnic solidarity, the self-conscious recognition of ethnic origin as a social bond, crystallizes under certain conditions, namely, where ethnic group membership overlaps substantially with occupation and with neighborhood. Under these conditions, the interests held in common by individuals who share more than ethnicity alone come into play in its support.[66] Decades ago, these conditions could be readily observed, as Glazer and Moynihan's previously cited remark about the correspondence of occupations with ethnic groups in the New York City of the 1950s and 1960s indicates. But this description is less valid today. This is not to deny that some economic niches remain, nor that ethnic neighborhoods can still be found in the cities where immigrants settled in large numbers at the beginning of the twentieth century.

Even those who argue that the powerful tide of assimilation is undeniable must recognize the importance of variations in its extent. For instance, while rates of intermarriage are high in an absolute sense and appear to have increased over time, they are still not at the levels that would obtain if marriage choice were indifferent to ethnic origin. Rates of endogamy, in other words, are considerably higher than would occur by chance, thus suggesting the presence in all groups of pools of individuals who either seek out mates of the same background or, because of the social contexts in which they are embedded, have relatively little opportunity to choose mates from other backgrounds.[67]

This points up the significant role of the remaining ethnic neighborhoods, which by sheer force of propinquity are one factor behind endogamy. Individuals who grow up and continue to reside in ethnic neighborhoods are more likely to exhibit characteristic ethnic behavior and to participate in ethnically based social networks. The analysis of the white ethnic neighborhoods in the greater New York City region is illustrative, demonstrating that those who reside in census tracts where their ethnic group is concentrated are more likely to have ethnically undivided rather than mixed ancestry and to speak a mother tongue at home. For the Italians, whose ethnic areas are the most extensive, it is also possible to examine intermarriage patterns directly, and the predictable pattern obtains: intermarried couples are much less common in ethnic neighborhoods than outside of them (some of this association is probably produced by migration after a marriage partner is chosen). The disparity between central-city ethnic neighborhoods and suburban non-ethnic ones is substantial. For instance, the residents of the former are two and a half to four times more likely than residents of the latter to speak the mother tongue. There is thus tremendous variation in the probability of hearing a language other than English on the streets, in the stores, and elsewhere.[68]

On a larger scale, regional concentrations of ethnic groups play a major role. In the regions where a group is densely represented in the population—Germans in and around Milwaukee, say—its cultural and institutional infrastructures are likely to be robust and ethnic economic niches, or even sub-economies, present.[69] In such regions the supply side of ethnicity, in the form of cultural symbols, organizations, and economic opportunities, is typically richer and therefore likely to provide incentives to identify in non-symbolic ways with the group and to participate in its networks and institutions; these incentives may well be attractive even for those members of an ancestry group who seem relatively assimilated. Group size is also important. Its impact on the rate of intermarriage, for instance, is well established.[70] Since an individual's "taste" for a mate of the same or a similar ethnic background is just one of the competing preferences that influence his or her final choice, the size and composition of that pool affect the likelihood that these inclinations can be satisfied within the group. More generally, group size determines whether a critical mass exists to create and sustain ethnic infrastructures such as enclave economies.[71]

Such social-structural factors help to explain the rare cases of groups that appear resistant to the assimilatory trends we have described. One is the Cajuns of Louisiana, who have an unusually high rate of endogamy. In addition to being a sizable, regionally concentrated group, the Cajuns exhibit a distinctive occupational profile: once a rural proletariat, they are now concentrated in the petroleum and textile industries in southwestern Louisiana. Their unusual history also figures in their persistent ethnicity. Though European in origin, Cajuns are less an immigrant group than a "colonized" one, to employ a familiar distinction. The ancestors of present-day Cajuns originally settled in Canada but were forcibly uprooted by the British in 1755. After resettling in Louisiana, they were not incorporated into an English-speaking society until the United States purchased the territory; and even then Louisiana promulgated its laws in French as well as English until the middle of the nineteenth century. Their experience of involuntary incorporation as an already settled group with its own communities and institutions is quite distinct from that of the typical immigrant who enters a larger society. The Cajuns' persistent ethnicity resembles that of the French-speaking Canadians, the European group most resistant to assimilation in North America.[72]

Ethnicity involves both social structure and the more elusive factors of subjective meaning. The changes in social structure are more easily measured and described than the subjective ones, which are analytically separate from and to some extent independent of them. Some people can and do persist in seeing the world in ethnic ways and in making ethnicity central to their lives, even though ethnic structures have weakened and their own personal characteristics, such as generational position, might seem to predispose them otherwise. In different ways, some Italians and Jews exemplify this behavior. Some Italians express an unusually intense sense of ethnic identity and a preference for preserving as much as possible the warm embrace of the family-centered lives they grew up with. Because of the dual character of the Jewish population as an ethnic and a religious group, Jews have an especially broad spectrum of options for ethnic commitment. At an extreme, such a commitment can involve an ultra-Orthodox way of life that sets its participants apart in cohesive enclaves such as the Hasidic communities of Brooklyn.[73]

Assimilation is nonetheless the master trend, and for the majority of whites and Asians descended from the earlier era of mass immigration, ethnicity does mean considerably less than it did a generation or two ago. A study of mostly white working-class men in New Jersey observed:

> Workers rarely use ethnic categories to understand and explain their own position in contemporary America. They see a large part of economic and political life happening to them as working men or as the middle class or as Americans. But very little happens because they are Italians or Poles or Irish or Germans. . . .
>
> Ethnic beliefs concern the area of interpersonal relations as well as the sociopolitical world. Thus in some forms they contain the idea that those of similar ethnic origin should spend their social life together and should intermarry. Here too such beliefs are of secondary or tertiary importance. There was a time, among the first generation, when exogamy, if not taboo, was viewed with disapproval. People were expected to

marry within their ethnic groups. But among the second and third generations such norms are widely disregarded. . . . As a third-generation worker of Irish origin explained: "You know, years ago in the 1930s if you wanted to marry an Italian or Pole your family would give you all kinds of trouble. . . . Now things have changed. It doesn't matter anymore."

Beliefs that those of similar ethnic origin should spend their social life together are even weaker. No one [in the study], younger or older, first or third generation, ever expressed such a view.[74]

How Did Assimilation Happen?

In Chapter 2 we laid out the repertoire of causal mechanisms to explain *why* so many descendants of immigrants assimilate. Here we now turn to the question: *How* did assimilation happen for the descendants of the late-nineteenth- and early-twentieth-century mass immigration? The short answer is that scholars don't know for sure. A large part of the reason lies in what might be called the problem of the "missing decades," which can be illustrated with a group that, at the time of its immigration, most seemed to challenge optimism about assimilation—the Italians, who came mainly from southern Italy, a largely agricultural and industrially undeveloped area. Historians have thoroughly documented their story up to the end of the immigration era, around 1930.[75] At that point the Italians as a group seemed generally isolated from mainstream society, concentrated in the ranks of low-wage labor, beset by social problems such as school failure, and subject to widespread prejudice and discrimination. Then, as if to seal their fate as an underclass, came the Great Depression and the gathering clouds of fascism and war in Europe, which cast a further shadow over them. Sociological studies from the 1930s portray a group in distress, unsure of its acceptability in American society, with many young people dropping out of school, into unemployment, and onto street corners.[76] Yet by the time the Italians come into focus again, this time in the 1970s as social scientists once more took up the study of ethnicity in contemporary society, the group had more or less entered the American mainstream, notwithstanding the existence of pockets of more resilient ethnicity. Because the picture of the intervening decades provided by research is sketchy at best,[77] we can only speculate about how the bulk of the group got from there to here.

Adding to the complexity is the variety of pathways that different ethnic groups appear to have taken into mainstream society and the difficult-to-evaluate role of historical contingency in the balance and sequence of proximate mechanisms that shape the *modal* path of adaptation. The modal path for the Irish, who took unusual advantage of politics and government employment, is different from that of, say, eastern European Jews, who distinguished themselves in small-business ownership and educational attainment; and both look different from the paths of the Italians and the Germans, whose trajectories in turn do not resemble each other, as well as from those of the Chinese and Japanese. Moreover, the course of assimilation for the European and Asian groups was affected by unpredictable and unique historical sequences, such as the abrupt end of immigration at the close of the 1920s and the two world wars, whose different effects we discuss later on. These add to the difficulty of evaluating the relative contribution of systemic forces and of applying lessons from the descendants of the earlier immigration of Europeans and Asians directly to the prospects for the new immigrant groups.

Narrowing our focus to a critical period enables us more clearly to distinguish and evaluate contributing historical events, demographic trends, and institutional conditions. The most critical for our purposes falls in the middle of the twentieth century, for this was when the children of the last, largest, and, to many Americans, most unacceptable wave of immigrants, mainly from southern and eastern Europe and from East Asia, came of age. Of the nearly 38 million immigrants who entered the United States from 1830 to 1930, half arrived during the last thirty years of that time span. In the early part of the twentieth century, immigrants and their children made up astonishingly large percentages (even by today's standards) of the population in many American cities: in 1920, 72 percent of Chicago's population, 69 percent of Cleveland's, and 76 percent of New York's.[78] The incorporation of the second and third generations of the last wave of immigration a century ago was a challenge of huge import for American society, probably no less consequential than the incorporation of the descendants of the newest immigrants will prove to be.

For all the complexity of the story of this incorporation, it is largely put together out of several prominent but deceptively simple themes. One is social mobility: without opportunities on a very wide scale to move upward within the American social structure, assimilation might not have occurred on the scale that it did. Second, there was a cultural shift toward greater acceptance of groups that had previously been excluded from the mainstream. So-called native-born Americans, the descendants of immigrants from the British Isles and to some extent other countries of western and northern Europe, had resisted with prejudice and discrimination the entry of the children and grandchildren of new immigrants into their social and economic spheres. To some degree, they even defined southern and eastern Europeans as racially different; and they certainly did so with Asians. Their attitudes toward the new groups—European and Asian ethnics—underwent broad shifts in more positive directions, especially during and immediately after World War II; and the growing acceptability of these groups facilitated the social processes that led to their fuller assimilation. Finally, some of the newer groups, such as Jews and the Japanese, made strenuous collective efforts to overcome the prejudice and discrimination of the ethnic majority and to break out of their disadvantaged position. Their successes helped not only themselves but also other groups that were behind them in the queue of educational and occupational mobility. Their efforts led to institutional openings that were subsequently widened by the civil rights movement and the politics of inclusion of the 1960s and to a weakening of the ideological support for all forms of ethnic and racial discrimination.

Social Mobility

The availability of social mobility during the nineteenth and early twentieth centuries in the United States, the period of mass immigration from Europe and of the approaching zenith of the industrial economy, is a matter of some debate among historians. One synthesis of the historical literature has arrived at a rather bleak view of mobility prospects for immigrants and the second generation. Not only was upward mobility "an unrealistic expectation in their [immigrants'] lifetimes," but also "the status of a father usually foretold the social positioning of a son."[79] Nevertheless, other scholars draw a considerably more optimistic picture, concluding that "social mobility in America had indeed been considerable," though "it was not as salient as stated in the most naive versions of the rags-to-riches stories of the Horatio Alger type."[80]

There can be much less doubt about the availability of social mobility in the middle of the twentieth century. Much of this mobility was generated by a far-reaching transformation of the American workforce, which narrowed or closed out some occupational slots while opening up others, and thus reshaped economic opportunity over time. A comparison of 1930 and 1970, marking a period that covers the century's economic extremes from the Great Depression to post–World War II prosperity and also spans generations—the working lives of, say, southern and eastern European immigrants and those of their children and/or grandchildren—suggests some ramifications of this process. In this forty-year period, the percentage of the national workforce engaged in agricultural pursuits declined precipitously, from 21 to 3 percent, thus forcing many grandchildren and great-grandchildren of earlier immigrants to rural areas into more urban lines of work. Further, even though the overall proportion in blue-collar and service occupations hardly changed, remaining at slightly less than 50 percent, significant realignments were taking place within these categories: in particular, unskilled laborers, a category that included many of the immigrants in the early part of the century, declined sharply from 11 to 4 percent of the labor force. Finally, white-collar occupations expanded robustly, from 29 to 45 percent. Nearly half of this increase was concentrated in the generally high-ranking occupations of the professional and technical category, whose share of the labor force doubled from 7 to 14 percent.

A consequence of such massive shifts is structural mobility, as a substantial proportion of each new generation entering the workforce is more or less constrained by a drastically altered regime of opportunities to take jobs different from those held by their parents.[81] For the children and grandchildren of many immigrant groups, the most significant aspect of the occupational transformation was that it entailed a sharp contraction at the lower end of the occupational spectrum and a corresponding expansion in its middle and upper reaches. Jobs in the sectors where the immigrants and perhaps the second generation had established themselves—Italians on the docks, for instance—were growing scarcer. The choice for ethnic youth was clear: get enough education to advance to the white-collar jobs that were proliferating; find a place, frequently through kin connections, in one of the skilled trades; or face diminished economic prospects.

Structural mobility of this sort holds a special significance for the advancement of disadvantaged ethnic groups because it does not have a "zero-sum" character. The advancement of some does not require the downward drift of others, since a large-scale transformation of the occupational structure creates additional space in some sectors that cannot be filled by those already there and their children. Hence, advancement can occur without the already advantaged perceiving a great threat to their interests, and therefore without a fortification of group boundaries to keep the disadvantaged in their place. Structural mobility, in other words, suggests the possibility of a gradual erosion of ethnic boundaries, as steady, large-scale mobility allows for an increasing amount of equal-status contact between members of more and less advantaged ethnic groups.

An unresolved issue concerns the extent to which the arrival in urban America of groups below the white and Asian ethnics in the queue of employer preference facilitated this upward mobility. This in-migration reached its zenith in the decades after World War II, the period when the strides taken by the children and grandchildren of the immigrants were at their greatest. Certainly, the availability of African Americans, Puerto Ricans, and Mexicans to take the jobs at the bottom must have made it easier for some second-generation Italians and Chinese to escape the socioeconomic fate of their parents. Moreover, many working-class white ethnics made strenuous efforts to keep blacks in particular from gaining parity with them in the labor market. For example, many unions, by virtue of their constitutions or practices, prevented blacks from joining and so remained all-white preserves. This exclusion, along with a great deal of informal discrimination, locked blacks into the bottom strata of jobs, which were redefined as not suitable for the groups now being accepted as "whites." Yet, much upward mobility would have happened in any event. One suggestive clue is that patterns of white ethnic advance seem to have been very similar in many cities, some of which received large numbers of black and Hispanic migrants after World War II and some of which did not. Another is that signs of second-generation socioeconomic advance were already apparent in the 1940s, at a point when the massive migration to northern cities by blacks and Puerto Ricans was just getting started.[82]

To highlight social mobility, which looks frictionless when discussed in the abstract, is not to deny the pain felt by white working-class families who experienced the decline, and even the disappearance, of the economic worlds that had supported ethnic ways of life. Some of the actual turmoil has been portrayed in an analysis of the fortunes of the French Canadian textile workers of Woonsocket,

Rhode Island. French Canadians had migrated into the area beginning in the middle of the nineteenth century and found a somewhat
precarious economic foothold in the textile mills. Although wages
were low and full-time employment was not always available, new
generations were able to find jobs in the mills with the assistance of
their older relatives. Many French Canadians apparently found this
situation tolerable because their lives were focused on *la survivance,*
the persistence of a traditional way of life focused on family and
church rather than on economic mobility. As late as the 1920s and
1930s, community leaders viewed their city as "la ville la plus fran-
çaise aux États-Unis."[83] Most French Canadian children attended
Catholic schools where French was the primary language of instruction, even for those subjects that state law mandated be taught in English; French was also the dominant language at home into the third
generation. But the signs of erosion gnawing at the economic base of
this way of life were already evident. During the 1920s, employment
in cotton manufacturing and related industries began to decline in
New England because of competition with southern mills, and this
process was accelerated by the depression. This left woolen manufacture as the economic bulwark of *la survivance;* but following a brief
period of prosperity at the end of World War II, it too succumbed to
competition with low-wage manufacturers elsewhere. The big mills of
Woonsocket shut down, and by 1952 almost a third of the city's
workers were unemployed. Obviously, young French Canadians
could no longer follow in their parents' footsteps. By then, English
was also achieving hegemony over French, and parochial schools
switched to English as the main language of instruction.[84] An ethnic
world went into eclipse.

For those ethnics elsewhere who had their sights set from the start
on social mobility, the process was also not without friction, as the
then largely Protestant middle and upper classes attempted to block
routes of access in order to preserve their privileges.[85] The experiences
of Jews are a good barometer of these attempts at social closure because they were so frequently the target. The efforts of WASPs to exclude Jews from spheres of privilege became salient during the 1920s
when eastern European Jews acquired the educational credentials to
gain entrance to Ivy League schools in large numbers; Harvard responded by imposing a quota on the number of Jewish students who
could be admitted, and in one form or another, many other elite col-

leges followed its lead.[86] The efforts to exclude Jews or restrict their numbers did not end there. From the 1920s onward, many Jews were denied admission to professional schools; they were not hired by elite law firms and could not gain faculty positions at universities; and they were systematically excluded from elite social clubs.[87] Anti-Semitism in the general population intensified during the 1930s and early 1940s as a result of the stresses brought on by the depression and World War II. But when the war came to an end, the grip of anti-Semitism relaxed in a way that was palpable to many observers, both Jewish and Gentile. A number of factors contributed: some were cultural, such as the perception of many Americans that Hitler and the war had rendered anti-Semitism, and to some extent ethnic and racial intolerance more generally, unacceptable; and some were institutional, such as the ultimately successful attempts by Jews to bring legal and political weapons to bear on the exclusionary policies of universities and professional schools.[88] But, we suggest, privileged WASPs would not have been willing to accept these changes if they were in strong conflict with their own socioeconomic interests. The expansion of opportunities in the middle and upper reaches of the social structure was an essential ingredient in the sea change of attitudes and practices with respect to Jews.

Structural mobility in the labor market was accentuated by parallel changes in the educational system. At mid-century there was a rapid expansion of higher education from a selective to a mass system. In 1940, only 15 percent of the college-age group actually attended college, but by 1954 it was 30 percent, and by 1960 almost 38 percent.[89] (Currently, about 45 percent of twenty- and twenty-one-year-olds are enrolled, and an even higher percentage will have attended some form of post-secondary education for at least a year by the time they reach their mid-twenties.) The expansion of higher education went hand in hand, of course, with the expansion in the upper reaches of the occupational system—the great increase in the number of jobs requiring technical and professional training. And it provided a route for white and Asian ethnics to take advantage of the occupational openings.

Although this mobility is often popularly depicted as a consequence of individual initiative within a market system and thus as not dependent on government largess, the not-so-invisible hand of government can be glimpsed. The initial impetus came in part from the GI Bill, passed in 1944 in anticipation of the flood of servicemen returning at the end of the war. The intent behind the legislation was to deflect some of this huge inflow away from the labor market, where it might have generated a surge in unemployment. As a consequence of the institutional change in access to higher education induced by the GI Bill, the enrollment in college of males eighteen to twenty-one years olds soared during the late 1940s, doubling the prewar level and raising total enrollment throughout the nation by 75 percent.[90] (At its peak, in 1947, veterans accounted for two-thirds of all male students and one-half of *all* students enrolled in college.) The GI Bill permanently changed the public's attitude toward higher education: no longer would it be seen as a privilege restricted to the very talented or the offspring of the affluent; instead, it became the normal expectation for average students from average families. "Middle-class groups increasingly came to depend upon higher education as a means of ensuring that their children would do as well or better than themselves, instead of relying on inherited wealth or on family, union, or personal contacts."[91] Nonetheless, the increased access to a college education largely benefited whites and Asians at first; the extension of access to blacks had to wait until the civil rights era.

The institutional transformation of higher education into a mass system was also very much a product of growth and consolidation within the public, rather than private, sectors. In response to the demand for higher education after the war and to forecasts of changes in the labor market, public colleges and universities came into being or expanded robustly; most private colleges and universities did not have the elasticity to respond quickly to surging demand. Just after the war—when the first enrollment data are available separately for the public and private sectors—approximately equal numbers of students were enrolled in both types of institutions. But the number enrolled in public colleges and universities soared more rapidly during the 1950s and 1960s, exceeding by 1965 the number in private higher education by a margin of nearly 2-to-1. Some of this growth was in two-year colleges, which have been seen as diverting the first generation of ethnic-minority families to attend college away from the more rewarding baccalaureate and post-baccalaureate degrees, but it is still the case that growth in four-year college and university enrollments occurred disproportionately in the public sectors.[92]

The growth of the public college and university system in New York State suggests the order of magnitude of these changes. New

York already had a highly developed system of private higher educational institutions, including elite universities such as Columbia and Cornell, numerous Catholic colleges such as Fordham, and many nondenominational two- and four-year schools. Students in New York City were also served by several well-regarded public colleges, one of which, City College, dated back to the middle of the nineteenth century. Yet in 1948 the governor and the legislature authorized the formation of a state university system, which initially encompassed about thirty previously independent publicly supported colleges, with a total enrollment at the time of fewer than 30,000 students. This system expanded very rapidly during the 1960s, in anticipation of the enrollment surge associated with the baby boom cohorts. New campuses, such as Stony Brook, were founded, while others were rebuilt. By the early 1970s, the system consisted of seventy-two campuses and enrolled a total of more than 350,000 students. At that point, these students were overwhelmingly European American: the first ethnic census, in 1976, shows the student body to have been more than 90 percent non-Hispanic white. The formation and expansion of New York's state university system especially benefited students from upstate communities and from the suburbs of New York City. When the City University of New York inaugurated its open enrollment policy in 1970, the initial beneficiaries also were disproportionately European American.[93] The California public system of higher education also expanded tremendously after World War II, as evidenced in the rapid growth of both the University of California and the state university system. Many Asian Americans took advantage of this development.

The children and grandchildren of European and Asian immigrants were the ones waiting at the head of the queue, so to speak, the ones who were positioned by virtue of their parents' socioeconomic achievements—whether in wage employment or small businesses—and their families' location in the more economically dynamic urban areas of the nation to take advantage of any openings in the opportunity structure. African Americans and Native Americans, the latter still largely confined to reservations, continued to suffer racist handicaps. The ethnic effects of these structural changes in the labor market and in education have been traced through cohorts of the second generation of the southern and eastern European groups by Stanley Lieberson in *A Piece of the Pie*. His analyses reveal a substantial upgrading among all these groups for the cohort born between 1925 and 1935, which came to maturity during and after the war. In the case of second-generation Italians, the educational gap separating them from third- and later-generation white Americans, who would have been overwhelmingly of northern and western European ancestry in this era, was fairly constant for the cohorts born before 1915; it declined somewhat for that born between 1915 and 1925, and narrowed more substantially for the next cohort. The proportion of second-generation Italian men employed as professionals rose less gradually, with the big leap occurring between the cohort of 1915–1925 and that of 1925–1935, most of whom entered the labor market after the end of the war.[94]

A third transformation, in residential setting, also contributed to assimilation. In contrast to the preference for the city center with its cultural amenities that marks urban life in Europe, suburbanization has long represented the American ideal of individual property ownership in a leafy ambience, distant from congestion, pollution, and the intrusions of the workplace. But for much of the nineteenth and early twentieth centuries, it was an ideal attainable mainly for the economic elite, while the inner city was largely given over to the working classes, in which immigrants and their children were heavily represented.[95] This was to change radically in the middle decades of the twentieth century, and in this case, too, the state played a central role by offering the prospect of home ownership to the majority of whites and enabling them to flee the city for the suburbs. The key event was the creation of the Federal Housing Administrations (FHA) home mortgage insurance program in 1934. The impact of this institutional change was widened by the establishment in 1944 of a similar Veterans Administration (VA) program aimed at returning GIs. By insuring mortgages that met certain criteria, these programs enabled banks to relax the miserly terms under which they had previously granted mortgages, which then became affordable to a much wider range of families. Consequently, in just three decades, between 1940 and 1970, the proportion of American households owning their homes soared from 44 to 63 percent. Because of the emphasis in the programs on new single-family home construction in socioeconomically and racially stable neighborhoods, their overwhelming impact was felt in the suburbs, where they promoted rapid development after the end of the war. In any given year during the 1950s, for instance, FHA- and

VA-insured loans were responsible for between a quarter and 40 percent of all new housing starts in the United States.[96] The consequence was a tidal wave of suburbanization: in a single decade from 1950 to 1960, the population in the suburbs shot up by nearly 50 percent, from 41 million to 60 million.

In its postwar heyday, the exodus to suburbia was predominantly a movement of whites. This was, in significant part, also a consequence of federal policy, one of the more fateful, if little-known, effects of federal action in the twentieth century, for it imposed a continuing racial division on the city-suburb boundary in many parts of the country. The FHA approval process was, at the outset, explicitly biased against neighborhoods that contained African Americans or were deemed likely to undergo any mixing of races; even after the FHA was forced away from overt consideration of race, it did little or nothing to challenge the institutionalized discrimination in the real estate industry. Nor was it in the interest of developers to do so; as William Levitt, a member of the family that perhaps did as much to transform the postwar suburban landscape as all others combined, observed, "We can solve a housing problem or we can try to solve a racial problem. But we cannot combine the two."[97] Until the 1960s, the developers of the Levittowns refused to sell homes to blacks. (The effects of the exclusion of black home buyers have been long-lasting; fifty years after the founding of the first Levittown, on Long Island, the suburb is still overwhelmingly white, and less than 1 percent of its population is African American.)[98]

But suburbanization drew little distinction among whites on ethnic, as opposed to class, grounds. Moreover, the rapid construction of large developments of tract houses, which tended to attract families at the same stage of the life cycle, undoubtedly worked against the reconstitution of urban ethnic neighborhoods in the suburbs and thus favored the residential integration of whites of different ethnic backgrounds. Herbert Gans, in a 1967 study of a Levittown in New Jersey, observed that the suburb's residents came from a variety of European ethnic backgrounds: "Thirty-seven percent reported being of Northern European origin (English, German, or Scandinavian); 17 percent were eastern European (mostly Russian Jewish with a scattering of Poles); 10 percent, Irish; 9 percent, Southern European (mainly Italian), and the remainder a heady mixture of all of these backgrounds."[99]

Although their smaller numbers made them less noticed in this mix, upwardly mobile Asian ethnics also joined in the migration to suburban neighborhoods in the postwar era. The presence of Asian ethnics did not significantly alter the ethnic balance of suburban neighborhoods, which remained almost entirely white. Many of the third-generation Chinese and Japanese interviewed by Mia Tuan recall growing up in white suburbs where their families were the only, or among the few, nonwhites in the community.[100]

Some ethnic concentrations did arise in suburbia, often in inner suburbs to which working-class ethnics moved from nearby urban neighborhoods. In some other cases, suburban ethnic neighborhoods dated back to the era of immigration, when they arose because they were near places of immigrant employment; this was the story behind some Italian areas on Long Island, for instance. Finally, there were to some extent religious divisions in suburbia, and these especially affected Jews.[101] But all in all, suburban ethnic concentrations tended to be much more diluted than those in cities. For the most part, the suburban exodus promoted migration to areas without the kind of overt ethnic character that was stamped onto a large number of urban neighborhoods.

Together these post–World War II institutional changes, in education, occupation, and residence, tended to diminish once-salient social distinctions among the European and Asian ethnic groups, while scoring deeply the lines separating them from blacks, Puerto Ricans, and Mexicans. Among the Europeans and Asians, the changes prompted individual mobility, which in many cases drew those who took advantage of it away from their ethnic communities of origin: vertical mobility up the social ladder was also frequently horizontal mobility out of intense involvement in the ethnic group. Broadly speaking, the net effect of the opportunities for mobility was to weaken ethnic communities, especially as those who left generally were not replaced by newly arriving immigrants, for immigration came to a grinding halt for southern and eastern Europeans and Japanese in the middle of the 1920s as a consequence of restrictive legislation followed by the depression.[102] This hiatus in the immigration stream from Europe and Asia, which, aside from brief episodes involving the resettlement of refugees, was to last until 1965, is a historical contingency whose effects on the course of assimilation are hard to calculate. Had it not occurred, and had the ethnic communities established by southern and eastern European immigrants and by East Asians remained more vibrant and therefore more attractive to the upwardly mobile, perhaps assimilation would not have become the master trend.

Almost certainly, though, it still would have been a prevalent pattern. In thinking about the impact of this hiatus on assimilation, one needs to bear in mind that it came after at least a century of continual mass immigration. Immigration record keeping began only in 1821 and was incomplete until the early twentieth century (for instance, immigrants from Canada and Mexico were not fully counted until then); thus, the nineteenth-century immigration is underestimated by the data. Even so, these show that from the 1820s to the 1920s, the volume of immigration relative to the entire American population was as large as, and mostly larger than, the equivalent measure during the several decades of contemporary immigration.[103] It seems to us highly implausible that assimilation of the descendants of the European immigrants was not occurring during this period, that it held off until the gates more or less shut in the 1920s. It seems equally implausible that the entire assimilation process for such a huge addition to the American population could have been limited to the few decades following this caesura. This is not to deny that the immigration hiatus had an impact on assimilation, but merely to urge caution in assessing its magnitude.

Cultural Shifts

Institutional changes enacted by Congress and implemented by the federal government aimed at opening mass access to higher education and home ownership were not the only forces behind the assimilation of ethnics. Cultural shifts, twists in the meanings and themes associated with ethnicity, were also at work. The cultural shifts partly depended on social-structural changes—it is hard to imagine that they could have occurred to the degree that they did without the increases in opportunities for mobility—but they were also responsive to other events and, to this extent, independent of the structural forces. Changes in attitudes toward ethnic whites, in particular, resulted especially from the two world wars, for during both the themes of national loyalty and foreign origin became entangled and took on great significance. During World War I, which began just after the high-water mark of immigration, the presence of many recent immigrants from central Europe engendered a national anxiety attack over their potential to form "fifth columns," acting at the behest of enemy powers, and to subvert American institutions from within. Wartime xenophobia dealt the first and deeper of two lethal blows to the long-standing effort to maintain a German-language culture in the United States, a culture that was still widespread in the first decade of the twentieth century and was inculcated in numerous bilingual public education systems; many states with large German populations took legal steps to prohibit teaching, publishing, and even speaking German. Xenophobia had carried over into the postwar period, giving renewed energy to the movement for immigration restriction and spurring a campaign for the immediate "100 percent Americanization" of the immigrants.[104]

Although World War II also engendered anxieties about subversion from within, which were manifested at their most repugnant in the internment of Japanese Americans on the West Coast, the response to ethnics of European origin was quite different from before. By the 1940s, the flood tide of immigration had receded, and the European groups once perceived as having the potential for loyalty to enemy nations were increasingly composed of the second and later generations. Instead of mass xenophobia and cultural suppression, white ethnic groups were bathed in the cultivated warmth of a campaign for national unity, which symbolically promoted the unification of Americans of different national backgrounds with festivals to celebrate the contributions of immigrant groups to America, an early form of multicultural ritual. In addition, wartime reporting and films about the war made for domestic consumption self-consciously portrayed the American military as a national cross-section and fighting units as a melting pot in miniature. *Time* magazine, reporting on a raid in France, claimed that its participants "sounded like the roster of an all-American eleven. . . . There were Edward Czeklauski of Brooklyn, George Pucilowski of Detroit, Theodore Hakenstod of Providence, Zane Gemmill of St. Clair, Pa., Frank Christensen of Racine, Wisconsin, Abraham Dreiscus of Kansas City. There were the older, but not better, American names like Ray and Thacker, Walsh and Eaton and Tyler. The war . . . was getting Americanized."[105] Ethnics responded to the appeal for unity with a wave of acculturation. For example, the number of radio stations broadcasting in immigrant languages dropped by 40 percent between 1942 and 1948.[106]

The self-conscious wartime unity was a precursor of a different vision of America, which for the first time included white ethnic Americans in the charmed circle of full-fledged Americans. Nonwhite Americans, however, remained outside; their men fought in segregated military units, their accomplishments little noted by mainstream media, the exception being the Japanese American 442nd Brigade, which the Truman administration publicly recognized as the most decorated unit of the U.S. Army in conferring on its regimental colors the Presidential Unit banner.[107] Nevertheless, the wartime period and that immediately following could be said to represent the zenith of the melting pot ideal, at least for Americans of European origin. It permeates the popular novels about the war, published during that time and afterward, such as Norman Mailer's *The Naked and the Dead,* James Jones's *From Here to Eternity,* Harry Brown's *A Walk in the Sun,* and John Hersey's *A Bell for Adano,* all of which were also made into successful films and served to interpret the war experience for a large segment of the American population. The novels portrayed military groups that represented the white ethnic diversity of American society in miniature. At the same time, they openly acknowledged the prejudice present in American society. Indeed, that was one of their major themes, as they showed ethnic Americans in the lower ranks subordinated to prejudiced or incompetent WASP officers.[108] But where their vision was triumphant was in their portrayal of ethnic Americans, who were lifted out from behind a curtain of stereotypes and presented as the moral equals of other Americans and as men who were contributing to American victory with everyday heroism and sacrifice.

The hero of a *A Bell for Adano* (1944), written by the war correspondent John Hersey, is the decent Major Victor Joppolo, an Italian American from the Bronx serving in wartime Sicily. His moral foil is General Marvin, who is depicted as prejudiced against the Italian people. Marvin says of the hero: "Joppolo . . . Remember that name. That goddam Major's a wop, too. . . . He's a goddam wop himself." But this book belongs to the decent ethnic American, who, according to Hersey, "happened to be a good man" and therefore "his works represented the best of the possibilities." Hersey captured what seemed to many white Americans at the time to be an essential truth about their country when he explained in the foreword to *A Bell for Adano* that "America is the international country. Major Joppolo was an Italian-American going to work in Italy. Our Army has Yugoslavs and Frenchmen and Austrians and Czechs and Norwegians in it, and everywhere our Army goes in Europe, a man can turn to the private beside him and say: 'Hey, Mac, what's this furriner saying?' . . . And Mac will be able to translate."[109]

The vision reflected in the novels and films represented a sea change in attitudes toward many of the white ethnic groups. No doubt these artistic works gave voice to the Zeitgeist as much as they themselves helped to produce it. This shift in the cultural landscape reverberated in widely felt ideals for American society, in the attitudes they entailed toward the ethnics in its midst, and in the encouragement to integrate felt by the ethnics themselves. Surveys measuring anti-Semitism—attitudes toward Jews, we note again, are a sensitive index of intolerant attitudes toward white ethnics more generally—captured the shift as it occurred. One survey question that was repeated periodically—"Have you heard any criticism or talk against the Jews in the last six months?"—measured the extent to which anti-Semitic sentiments were openly discussed, and probably allowed respondents who harbored such sentiments themselves to report them without having to acknowledge personal responsibility. During and immediately after the war, a majority of Americans—the high-water mark was 64 percent in 1946—answered the question affirmatively, and no doubt many of them also contributed to the prejudiced speech they reported. But in the late 1940s and the early 1950s, the number giving this response plummeted: by 1951, it was down to 16 percent; and in 1956, it was only 11 percent.[110] Even if some of this decline came from respondents telling interviewers what they thought the interviewers wanted to hear, it still represented a dramatically rapid change in norms.

Thus, it appears that cultural change is a part of any plausible and complete explanation of white ethnic assimilation. That this cultural change coincided with a period of "opening up," of increasing educational, economic, and residential opportunities, gave it an efficacy it would have lacked in more stagnant times, but does not negate its independent contribution.

Collective Actions and Institutional Changes

The postwar confluence of historical, demographic, and institutional changes that facilitated assimilation was not an entirely bloodless affair, in which, as in an upbeat Hollywood ending, privileged groups experienced a change of heart and welcomed previously scorned new-

comers into their midst. As the attempts to exclude Jews from elite social spheres imply, considerable struggle was involved, and to some
extent less privileged groups had to fight their way, overcoming sometimes determined resistance.[111] For example, the lowering of discriminatory barriers to admission to elite universities and to professional
schools was not purely a matter of enlightened self-interest on the
part of their leaders. Jewish organizations campaigned against the use
of religious and racial criteria in admissions; they pressed the case for
antidiscrimination legislation, especially in New York State, where a
good number of prestigious, exclusionary institutions, such as Columbia and Cornell, were located. An initial success was achieved in
1946, when the New York City Council adopted legislation threatening the tax-exempt status of nonsectarian colleges and universities
that discriminated based on race or religion. Columbia was thereby
forced to revise its admissions procedures, and some other schools,
seeing the handwriting on the wall, did the same. New York State followed with an antidiscrimination statute in 1948. That these laws
were in fact successful is demonstrated by, for example, the increase in
the percentage of Jews among New York's medical students from 15
percent in 1948 to about 50 percent by the mid-1950s.

To be sure, the powerful hand of social and cultural changes in the
majority population can be glimpsed in the outcome of some of these
battles. It is apparent in the suddenness with which the barriers fell in
many cases, indicating that a good number in the WASP group were
ready to accept, if not to assist in, ethnic change. The ending of the
anti-Semitic quotas in higher education has been attributed to the
"new legal and social environment" stemming from institutional
changes of the immediate postwar period.[112] Leonard Dinnerstein,
who asserts that colleges and universities "were being influenced by
the changing tone in society," notes that "in 1948 Jewish undergrad-
uates at Yale protested being automatically assigned other Jews as
roommates. As soon as they raised the issue, the practice ceased."[113]

As the American economy expanded robustly in the immediate
postwar period and opportunities to establish footholds in privileged
sectors grew, the competition between talented and ambitious newcomers and the entrenched group often forced the hand of the latter.
Within the legal profession, elite firms with major corporations as cli-
ents had refused before mid-century to accept Jews as partners, and
WASP dominance of the profession had managed to confine Jews to

the lowest-status legal work, "such as bill collecting, criminal law, petty negligence suits, bankruptcy cases, small real estate closings, and the like." But in the postwar period, the nature of the legal profession began to change because of changing power relations and increasing complexity in the society. New specialties, such as labor and tax law, came to the fore, and Jewish lawyers emerged as leaders in these fields. At the same time, the ties of tradition that bound large corporations to exclusively WASP law firms weakened. The path was now open for new, more ethnically diverse firms to establish themselves; and as they competed successfully with older firms, it was no longer sensible, or profitable, for the latter to maintain their ethnic exclusivity. Around 1960, the barriers to partnership began to fall. While there may be some overstatement in the claim that "today the law may well be the most religiously and ethnically, if not yet racially integrated profession,"[114] the law has plainly been transformed from the bastion of WASP exclusivity that it was even at mid-century.

The struggles of white ethnics were not only with the groups above them, who were seeking to keep the newer arrivals in a subordinate position, but also with non-European groups, African Americans above all, that at one point had the potential for parity with some white groups, in particular those of peasant origins in Europe, who flooded the lowest tiers of the urban labor market on arrival in the United States. These struggles predate the period on which we have focused this discussion, though they continued into it. At the time of their mass arrival in the mid-nineteenth century, the Irish, for example, were not clearly distinguished in social terms from African Americans; and both groups did some of the same jobs. In attaining ascendancy over these competitors, the Irish and other disparaged European-ancestry groups aggressively laid claim to the status of "white" and used a variety of means to mark their separation from "nonwhites."[115] Segregation in the labor market was a key prong in this strategy: "To be acknowledged as white, it was not enough for the Irish to have a competitive advantage over Afro-Americans in the labor market; in order for them to avoid the taint of blackness it was necessary that no Negro be allowed to work in occupations where Irish were to be found."[116] White ethnic workers often refused to work alongside African Americans; and as we noted earlier, a large number of unions, such as those in the construction trades, prevented blacks from joining. Segregation in residence and thus in schooling was another key factor, and many scholars have noted its growing rigidity in the second decade of the twentieth century, as European ethnics and then in-migrating African Americans bumped against each other in many industrial cities.[117] The race riots of 1917–1919, in which whites in more than twenty cities attacked blacks and drove them out of what would become white areas, marked a critical moment, after which blacks were largely confined to racially homogeneous ghettos. The stage was set in urban America for the incorporation on unfavorable terms of post–World War II migrants—blacks from the South, as well as Puerto Ricans and Mexicans.

This mid-century portrait, though complex, has not been exhaustive. Other factors also played a role—for example, meso-level institutions such as unions, churches and synagogues, and political clubs, where ethnics of different origins came together and worked out ways of cooperating with one another, thus bridging former ethnic cleavages.[118] But we are convinced that, in broad outline, the themes we have traced capture the aspects of the assimilation of descendants of earlier immigrants that matter most for evaluating contemporary immigrants' prospects for assimilation: social mobility, which provided many white and Asian ethnics with a motive to assimilate and brought them out of ethnic communities; cultural change in the majority group, which contributed to a lowering of the barriers keeping ethnics in a subordinate place; and institutional changes stemming partly from collective action by the ethnics themselves, challenging exclusion by the majority group. It is tempting to add a fourth: social closure directed against African Americans as a way of marking racial out-groups and enhancing the racial bond presumably shared by whites. Whether the existence of racial out-groups is essential to the process of assimilation is the most vexed question in the entire American literature on ethnicity and race. We have already noted one element of a negative answer: the socioeconomic advance of the southern and eastern European second generation seems to have depended to no more than a modest degree on the arrival of blacks and Hispanics in northern cities. But this is not sufficient to close such a complex question, which emerges also for the assimilation of contemporary immigrant groups. We will meet this question again in our concluding chapter.[119]

The experiences of the descendants of the earlier era of high-volume immigration demonstrate the usefulness of assimilation concepts and theory. The dimensions of assimilation defined by Gordon and others appear to describe in meaningful ways a set of tremendous changes that have taken place, largely since the middle of the twentieth century, in the white and Asian populations. The American mainstream has been transformed: in the early 1900s, the lives of a majority of whites and Asians were firmly embedded within an ethnic matrix—including native-born Protestants, who then drew a sharp ethnic distinction between themselves and the children and grandchildren of new immigrants—but by century's end this was true of at most a minority, and one moreover that has been declining in size. In the earlier period, the jobs that whites and East Asians obtained, the places where they lived, the people with whom they associated, and the values and symbols they cherished were all determined in substantial measure by the country from which their ancestors, or they themselves, had immigrated; moreover, these influences were usually not subtle and hidden from view but were salient and acknowledged. Samuel Freedman's book *The Inheritance* evocatively describes this thickly ethnic reality for one suburban New York family during the 1920s and 1930s:

> A trolley line linked the West End [of New Rochelle] to the downtown district, but most of the Italians rode it only for Christmas shopping and other exceptional occasions. In their own half-mile-square enclave stood a public school named for Christopher Columbus, a Catholic Church dedicated to St. Joseph, and mutual-aid societies serving immigrants from several separate regions. Every manner of shop operated within walking distance from home—Marciano's bakery, DiNapoli's stationery, Uzzi's tavern, . . . even Zito the druggist with his patent medicines and leeches.[120]

Realities such as this have been steadily eroded by acculturation and the various other forms of assimilation, structural (or social), socioeconomic, and spatial. Granted, assimilation has not entirely erased ethnicity as a significant form of social difference in the majority population; but it has reduced it to a matter of largely symbolic weight for most and narrowed its meaning to a small set of social contexts.

It seems difficult to decide, based on a narrative of the assimilation of descendants of the earlier mass immigration, whether assimilation was more the product of systemic forces in American society or of his-

torical contingency—unique sequences of events, unlikely to be repeated. Even though social mobility might be counted among the former, there is no certainty that the level of upward mobility in mid-
twentieth-century America will be repeated; it could therefore also be
placed on the other side of the ledger, where events such as the closing
down of mass immigration and the ethnic impact of World War II
must be placed. But, inevitably, large-scale social processes express
themselves through, and are entangled with, unique historical sequences. It is the task of social science to attempt to lift the veil of
history and to extract abstract models of the social dynamics that lie
behind its visible surface. We recognize that such models should generally be proposed in a tentative manner, for they may be subject to
contingencies that the analyst cannot discern from the available empirical data.

In mid-century America, changes in the "life chances" of ethnics
were generated by a fairly drastic shift in the changes in the occupational structure and hence in the kinds of opportunities available for
those entering the labor market, accompanied by a rapid expansion of
the opportunity for education beyond high school. This dynamic, the
motive power for assimilation, could be expressed in an even more
general manner: whenever the opportunities for ethnics are greater in
the mainstream than in the ethnic economy, there is a motive for assimilation, as the theory outlined in Chapter 2 emphasizes. The case
of eastern European Jews, the European group with probably the
most prosperous ethnic economic enclaves, demonstrates this. Two
other conditions are of course assumed: that ethnics are interested in
taking advantage of these opportunities, which in turn presupposes
that they have already acculturated to the status standards of the
United States; and that they are in a position to reach for them, which
in turn requires a large measure of linguistic assimilation and access
to education.

Other cultural changes, especially in the dominant group's ideology
of superiority over minority ethnic groups, are also key to the processes bringing about assimilation. The central events in this respect
may have been associated with World War II, ultimately convincing
many Americans, both WASP and ethnic, that they should place their
faith in the vision of America as a melting pot. The struggles of some
minority ethnic groups, especially Jews (and, earlier, Irish Catholics),
also challenged, albeit in different ways, the exclusionary dominance

of WASPs, contributing to the perception of WASP dominance as unfair and opening up particular sectors of opportunity for colonization by mobile ethnics. The main criterion here is that the dominant group not be in a position to achieve social closure, barring all but token members of the ethnic minorities from achieving parity.

These changes, in turn, increased the degree of social contact among members of European-origin ethnic groups, as Shibutani and Kwan could have predicted. In one phase, this led to a great deal of residential intermixing among groups, especially in the suburbs. In another, it has produced the high ethnic (and religious) intermarriage rates that prevail today among whites and extend to Asian ethnics. As a consequence, there has been an effective melding of ethnic groups, producing a dramatic reduction in the social distances among different ethnicities that prevailed in an earlier era.

The European American and Asian American experiences of assimilation, though entangled with many historical contingencies and thus impossible to replicate precisely at the beginning of the twenty-first century, nevertheless offer useful clues as to what to look for again in contemporary immigration.

CHAPTER FOUR

Was Assimilation Contingent on Specific Historical Conditions?

There is impressive evidence of a powerful tide of assimilation among European and Asian ancestry groups with very different characteristics at the time of their immigration and quite varied histories in the United States: Germans, whose ancestors populated sections of the Midwest during the nineteenth century, often in rural areas, where they could continue to use German as a language of daily life; Irish Catholics, a rural proletariat that crowded into American cities during and after the potato famine and provided a corps of raw labor power that built railroads and canals until political success enabled them to gain control over municipal employment in major American cities; Italians, also a rural proletariat but one that arrived late in urban America and for a good part of the twentieth century seemed consigned to a permanent place in the working class; East Asians, excluded by racist legislation and practices from civil society until institutional change in the post–World War II era dismantled legal barriers to their mobility; and eastern European Jews, who, while they came at the tail end of mass immigration from Europe, possessed entrepreneurial drive and a variety of industrial skills and consequently soon distinguished themselves by rapid upward mobility but also by a strong group consciousness. All these groups exhibit telltale signs of advanced stages of assimilation. This does not mean, of course, that all are assimilated in precisely the same ways or to the same extent, nor does it imply that all members of these groups are assimilated to the same degree. Nevertheless, the rough uniformity of outcome is hard to overlook, and it suggests the possibility that forces promoting assimilation are well entrenched in the American social order, despite all the historical contingencies that must be aligned in order to explain how assimilation has come about. Above all, these forces appear to be concentrated in the structure of opportunities, a factor that has compelled the descendants of immigrants to choose between the optimum range of mobility chances, on the one hand, and strong attachment to an ethnic community and culture, on the other. Those confronted with this choice have not always been aware of its ultimate implications.

Despite this picture, many scholars of contemporary immigration reject assimilation as a likely outcome on a mass scale for post-1965 immigrant groups. They argue that assimilation is specific to a set of historical circumstances that characterized mass immigration from Europe but does not, and will not, apply to contemporary immigrant groups:

> Underneath its apparent uniformity, contemporary immigration features a bewildering variety of origins, return patterns, and modes of adaptation to American society. Never before has the United States received immigrants from so many countries, from such different social and economic backgrounds, and for so many reasons. Although pre–World War I European immigration was by no means homogeneous, the differences between successive waves of Irish, Italians, Jews, Greeks, and Poles often pale by comparison with the current diversity. For the same reason, theories coined in the wake of the Europeans' arrival at the turn of the century have been made obsolete by events during the last decades.[1]

Such declarations that the new immigration is sui generis and not comparable to past immigrations are widespread in the recent literature.

In this chapter we address this viewpoint in some detail and also consider several countervailing perspectives. We argue that the distinctions between contemporary and past immigrations have been overplayed and that they are based to a significant extent on simplistic readings of the historical experiences of European groups (much less so in the case of Asians) which overlook features that might have worked against assimilation and certainly made it seem far more problematic to past observers than it appears in hindsight.[2] Of course, even if distinctions have been exaggerated, they do still exist; further, even if the similarities between past and current immigrations outweigh the differences, this fact would not by itself demonstrate that the outcomes of both will be the same. But our key point is that the significance of differences for the integration of the second and later generations of the new groups is much less clear-cut than it is frequently made out to be.

If many contemporary observers are skeptical about the prospects for assimilation, what do they foresee as the fate of the descendants of contemporary immigrants? In the final part of this chapter, we consider the two main alternative conceptions of the incorporation of ethnic groups into American society: segmented assimilation and reinvigorated pluralism (introduced in Chapter 1). If the assimilation perspective is problematic because of contingencies and limitations, one has to ask whether the same is true for the alternatives. And indeed we find them no less problematic. There are no grounds for viewing the assimilation model as intrinsically inferior.

The Distinctiveness of the New Immigration

Observers have pointed to a number of actual or possible differences between the circumstances of past and contemporary immigrations as a basis for arguing that the fate of new immigrant groups will likely differ from that of past groups. Let us consider these differences in more detail.

Absence of a Foreseeable Hiatus in Immigration

The decisive halt in the stream of mass immigration from Europe in the late 1920s, induced by legislated restrictions followed by the Great Depression, is widely thought to have been fateful for those ethnic groups.[3] Scarcely had immigration begun to recover from its depressed level during World War I when it plummeted once again as a consequence of the immigration acts of 1921 and 1924, which excluded immigration from Asia and erected quota barriers against southern and eastern Europe, then the principal source of American immigrants. In a series of abrupt steps, the change in immigration rules led to a precipitous decline in total European immigration, which fell from 650,000 in 1921 to a tenth of that figure just ten years later. (The number had exceeded 1 million at its height in 1907.) Immigration from Europe did recover somewhat after World War II, fed in part by the resettlement of refugees; and the Immigration Act of 1965, the centerpiece of current immigration policy, was enacted partly in the expectation of increasing immigration from those European countries that had been the objects of discriminatory quotas in the 1920s. But any such effect was modest and short-lived for most groups. Although immigration from Italy, for instance, rose quickly to about 25,000 a year in the late 1960s, the potential was quickly exhausted, and after 1970 the number of Italian immigrants dropped, to 11,600 in 1975 and 5,500 in 1980. By 1985, down to 3,200, it had all but collapsed.

The hiatus starting in the 1920s virtually guaranteed that ethnic communities and cultures would be steadily weakened over time. The social mobility of individuals and families would drain population from these communities and undermine the cultures they sheltered, since there were few newcomers to replace those who were departing. Generational shifts would have a similar impact because there was little replenishment of the immigrant generation. Over time, then, the modal generation shifted from the immigrant to the second and then from the second to the third. Since ethnic communities and the culture and infrastructure they support play a pivotal role in providing incentives for individuals to maintain loyalty to the group, the hiatus undoubtedly contributed to the extent of assimilation among Americans of European and Asian ancestry.

Many observers believe that a similar halt in the contemporary immigration stream is unlikely. One reason is the apparent disinclination of the federal government to ratchet down the level of immigration, though this could change if the political temperature generated by immigration issues rises sharply.[4] Legislation since 1965 such as the Immigration Act of 1990 generally has raised the level of legal immigration; and given the strong constituencies supporting the various provisions of modern immigration law, it seems unlikely that legislation could reverse this course in the near future. Moreover, recent attempts to control the immigration flow have generally had unanticipated and even counterproductive consequences, perhaps, many suggest, because the immigration-generating forces in the United States and in sending societies are so powerful that they thwart or bypass the feeble attempts of the U.S. government to harness them. A common view is that restrictions on legal immigration will simply generate equivalent surges in the illegal flow.[5]

The counterproductive effects of restrictive legislation are nowhere better illustrated than by the Immigration Reform and Control Act of 1986 (IRCA), conceived at the time of its passage as a major step toward the control of undocumented immigration. IRCA appears to have exerted no more than a temporary check on the undocumented flow, as its employer-sanctions provisions, intended to undermine the labor market footholds of the undocumented, have turned out to be largely ineffective and, if anything, have spawned an underground industry producing fraudulent identity documents.[6] In addition, many argue that the amnesty the law provided to long-resident illegals, allowing them to legalize their status, has created an incentive for further illegal immigration that will have lasting effects. Indisputably, it will contribute also to legal immigration, because of the ability under U.S. law of the legalized immigrants to bring in their relatives.

Movement across national borders appears to be an endemic feature of the contemporary world, and this adds to the difficulty of substantially limiting contemporary immigration. UN projections of the world population suggest very large population increases in the near future (by 2025), which will occur mostly outside the highly developed nations and thus add to the huge reservoir of people available to move.[7] Of course, emigration from less developed countries is a product not just of population pressure but also of the curve of economic development, such that broad segments of their populations have desires that cannot be satisfied by their native economies, and of the historical linkages that exist between less and more developed nations in the international system.[8] The ubiquity of American cultural products in the form of movies, television series, and popular music advertises the individualism and material standards of American society (albeit with considerable distortion) and enhances the magnetic power of the United States for potential immigrants. Finally, it is more difficult for national governments to control emigration than was the case a century ago, given the frequency of international travel. All these forces seem likely to engender huge, difficult-to-control population movements far into the future, as exemplified by the large legal and illegal flows from Mexico to the United States.

If immigration to the United States continues indefinitely at its current level, then population projections show that many of the ethnic groups involved will be dominated by the first and second generations for the next half century or more.[9] This will create a fundamentally different ethnic context from that faced by the descendants of European immigrants, for the new ethnic communities are highly likely to remain large, culturally vibrant, and institutionally rich under such a scenario, and ethnic sub-economies, though they may not remain affixed to particular niches, are likely to continue to offer channels of mobility. In sum, there are likely to be strong incentives to keep ethnic affiliations alive even for the third generation, as long as the distance between the generations does not grow so great as to alienate them from one another.

But however plausible the scenario just sketched seems from to-day's perspective, there is no guarantee that it will occur. If there is any proven rule regarding population projections, it is that the patterns of the present cannot be projected indefinitely into the future, for they will change in unforeseeable ways. The level of immigration could go up, to be sure, but it could also go down—as a result of restrictive legislation backed up by tougher enforcement, a decline in the attractiveness of the United States to one or more of the main source populations, a weakening of the forces generating emigration from these countries, or some combination of these changes. Despite the current pessimism about efforts to control immigration flows to the United States, more effective control is not impossible, as the example of Germany shows. Like the United States, Germany has land borders with countries containing large numbers of potential immigrants, Poland in particular.[10] But it has strict limits on immigration and only a small resident population of illegals. A greater use of identity documents, which are required even of citizens, and a more unforgiving attitude toward illegals are a large part of the explanation for Germany's ability to control illegal immigration. To be sure, there are serious impediments in American political culture to the use of identity cards. But if the control of immigration, and especially of its extralegal component, continues to grow as a social problem, then the pressures for having some rigorous form of internal verification of legal residence will grow in tandem. (We do not intend this statement as an endorsement of identity cards.)

Moreover, the attractiveness of the United States to potential immigrants could decline for any of a number of reasons—such as changes in the labor market that eliminate some of the niches exploited by immigrants, a decrease in the relative quality of life in the metropolitan regions that are the main receiving areas for immigration, or a rise in the relative attractiveness and accessibility of other countries as immigrant destinations. Recent immigration history gives empirical force to this point. When the Immigration Act of 1965 was under consideration by Congress, the common argument was that it would lead to greatly increased immigration from the countries of southern and eastern Europe, whose applicants would qualify under the family reunification provisions. Italy alone was said to have a backlog of a quarter million visa applications.[11] Yet, although there was a temporary, modest rise in immigration from Italy, the anticipated surge did not occur. In the interim, the United States had become less attractive to prospective Italian immigrants because of the emergence of the European Common Market, as it was then known. Why should Italians come to the United States when they could go instead to Germany and be able to return home at frequent intervals?

Raising the prospect of a future decline in the general level of immigration is admittedly speculative. We are on firmer ground, we believe, in predicting that the immigration of *some* groups will decline and will not live up to the assumption of continued inflow far into the future. One reason for suspecting such declines is that the level of economic development of some sending nations may approach or even catch up with that of the United States, eliminating the principal motive for immigration. This has happened in the case of Japan, which sent many immigrants around the turn of the twentieth century but currently is the source of few immigrants other than managers of Japanese companies and their families doing tours of duty at U.S. branches. As of the beginning of the twenty-first century, it may also be happening in Ireland, Korea, and Taiwan. Indeed, during the 1990s there were marked declines in Irish and Korean immigration: between 1990 and 1994, the number of immigrant visas allocated to Koreans fell by half, while the number returning home surged. South Korea's sustained economic growth, interrupted only briefly by the Asian financial crisis, has altered the incentives such that those who might have considered emigration in the past now remain at home. In the case of Ireland, one of the world's major sources of immigrants for a century and a half, rapid economic growth in the 1990s appears to have brought at least a temporary halt to emigration and even to have induced a significant return migration.[12] For groups whose immigration abates, the prediction of ethnic communities continually revitalized by new immigration will prove inaccurate.

Even immigration from Mexico, at present the largest flow into the

United States and generally regarded as the most difficult to control, may not be immune from decline. Although economic trends in Mexico during the last decades of the twentieth century generally had emigration-enhancing impacts—unemployment rose, as did employment in informal sectors of the economy, while real wages fell—demographic trends have been pointing for some time in the opposite direction. Falling rates of fertility have slowed population growth, a trend that is expected to continue. The biggest impacts of these demographic shifts will be on the youthful and working-age portions of the population, from which future new migrants are most likely to come. The high level of emigration of the 1980s and 1990s was associated with rapid growth of the working-age population (persons fifteen to sixty-four years of age), placing great strain on the Mexican economy. The stabilization of this age group, the most critical one for migration, has been delayed because of a backlog of large birth cohorts. But its rate of growth will fall off rapidly after 2010 and is expected to come to a stop five years later. Should economic trends turn in a more favorable direction, then it is likely that there would be some decline in immigration.[13]

Racial Distinctiveness of New Immigrant Groups

It is commonly argued that the descendants of earlier European immigrations, even those composed of peasants from economically backward parts of Europe, could eventually assimilate because their European origins made them culturally and racially similar to American ethnic core groups. The option of assimilation will be less available to the second and later generations of new immigrant groups because their non-European origins make them more distinctive, with their distinctiveness of skin color especially fateful.

While we wish to avoid at all costs a Panglossian optimism about American racism, we find this argument less than compelling. For it ignores the experience of the descendants of the earlier immigration from Asia, who, despite "looking different" and despite a history of discrimination against Asians, are showing strong tendencies toward assimilation, including high rates of intermarriage with whites, as discussed in Chapter 3. Further, it treats perceptions of racial difference as more rigid than they have proved to be historically.

Even in the European case, the view that the pathway to assimilation was smoothed by a white racial identification is an anachronism, inappropriately imposing contemporary racial perceptions on the past. There is ample evidence that native-born whites perceived some of the major European immigrant groups, such as the Irish, Jews, and Italians, as racially distinct from themselves and that such perceptions flowered into full-blown racist theorizing during the high-water period of mass immigration in the early decades of the twentieth century.[14] This is not just a matter of language usage in which "race" was treated as a synonym for "nation" or "ethnic group." Many Americans believed that they could identify the members of some groups by their characteristic appearance (e.g., "Jewish" facial features), and nineteenth-century caricatures of the Irish frequently gave them a distinctly simian cast. At first, these Europeans, beginning with the Irish, were not clearly distinguished from African Americans. Evidence from the nineteenth century indicates that the Irish rubbed shoulders with African Americans in urban neighborhoods; competed with them for, and worked alongside them at, various jobs; and socialized with them. It took awhile for the "whiteness" of the Irish to be defined, and they were active agents in this process, eventually seeking to draw a clear social boundary between themselves and blacks.[15] A curious residue of such racial perceptions is a once common epithet for Italians—"guinea." As H. L. Mencken observed in *The American Language,* the term originated in a name for slaves from the African coast. It is, in short, a color word.[16]

Over time, the racial perceptions of the most disparaged European groups shifted. The Irish, and perhaps other groups, initially struggled to create racial and social distance between themselves and African Americans. But as these groups climbed the socioeconomic ladder and mixed residentially with other whites, their perceived distinctiveness from the majority faded. (World War II also had a powerful impact on attitudes toward European and Asian ethnics, as discussed earlier.) Intermarriage both marked this shift and accelerated it.

We see no a priori reason why a shift in the perception of racial difference could not take place for some contemporary immigrant groups and some segments of others. We think here particularly of newer Asian groups and light-skinned Latinos. In the case of Asian groups, the already high intermarriage rates of their U.S.-born members suggests the absence of a deep racial divide, a by-product in part of the assimilation of the descendants of earlier East Asians. Even so, we would not claim that racial distinctions between whites and

Asians are on the verge of disappearing; indeed, the "whiteness" paradigm, which holds that groups assimilate by being redefined as unambiguously white, is probably not the right model for possible shifts in racial perceptions of the future. Much will depend on how the children of intermarriages view themselves and are viewed by others.[17] The racial diversity among Latinos creates other kinds of uncertainty. Whereas approximately half view themselves as racially white, the other half do not. Most in this group declare themselves to be racially "other"—other than black or white—on the U.S. Census. While no one is certain how racial appearance actually corresponds with census data on race, it seems a safe bet that many Hispanics with brown skin and indigenous features—the "mestizo/Indian phenotype"[18]— place themselves in the "other" category. How much of a barrier U.S. racial boundaries will pose for this group is an open question.

At this moment in time, the most pessimistic outlook concerns those with visible African ancestry. For the most intractable racial boundary in the United States remains that separating those deemed phenotypically black from so-called whites, which has been fortified by the historic legacy of the institution of slavery. Although formal rules and their enforcement have sought to dismantle racial barriers to integration, social norms, etiquette, and networks still regulate the color line. It is worth recognizing that the black-white distinction as found in the United States is not the self-evident consequence of "obvious," impossible-to-overlook somatic differences, but is, as a newly reinvented terminology would have it, a "social construct." Thus, with its "one drop of blood" rule—a norm that is a direct legacy of slavery—for assigning membership in the black category, it differs from the racial distinctions employed in most other societies of the Western Hemisphere where both African and European ancestries are represented in the population.[19] (As a cruel witticism has it, a white mother in the United States can give birth to a black child, but a black mother cannot give birth to a white one.) In particular, the American practice of racial classification is more rigid and dichotomous than the racial distinctions recognized in, say, Brazil or Puerto Rico: it lacks the spectrum of intermediate racial statuses found elsewhere and refuses the possibility that individuals with African heritage can change their racial position through social mobility. It seems virtually certain that this boundary, despite its social constructedness and potential mutability, will exert a powerful influence on the possibilities of adaptation for immigrant groups, depending on where they are situated with respect to it.

Yet even the black-white boundary could ultimately be altered by the racial dynamics unleashed by immigration. This is obviously in the realm of speculation, not a prediction; and in any event there are multiple possible scenarios, with quite different imports for racial divisions in American society. On the one hand, there is a decidedly pessimistic scenario, which foresees the United States continuing as a bipolar society, with the major line of racial cleavage separating blacks from non-blacks.[20] On the other, an optimistic scenario is that the incorporation of non-European groups into the racial majority will blur the hitherto hard-and-fast character of the black-white divide. Until now, the expansion of the racial majority to include previously disparaged groups, such as the "swarthy" southern Italians, has not altered the taken-for-granted character of the black-white divide because the inclusion of these groups occurred by their being redefined as fully "white." But this divide will presumably become less and less possible to maintain as Asian ethnics, rapidly increasing in number (4 percent of the U.S. population in 2000), are brought into the majority. In other words, as the ethnic and racial diversity that makes up contemporary society becomes part of the mainstream, prevailing conceptions of American racial identities will likewise undergo alteration. This could undermine the transparency of these distinctions for many Americans and thus affect the distinctions that set African Americans racially apart. A continuing increase in the frequency of black-white marriage, which has grown since the 1960s, and the demands of the children of these marriages for social recognition of their multiracial ancestry could also contribute to the muting of America's most salient and hitherto indestructible racial divide.[21]

Impact of Economic Restructuring on Second-Generation Opportunity

The assimilation of Americans of European and Asian ancestry was linked to opportunities for social mobility that, within a brief historical period, brought about a rough parity of average life chances across many ethnic groups (though not within them, as life chances remained structured by social class origins and other factors). These opportunities were in turn based on historically contingent periods of economic expansion that allowed immigrants of peasant origin with few work skills of relevance in an urban, industrial economy nevertheless to gain a foothold through steady employment, often in manufacturing sectors to start with. Similar openings, it is commonly said, are not to be found with the same frequency in the contemporary economy because of economic restructuring, which has led to the elimination of many manufacturing jobs and the degradation of others; instead there are low-level service jobs, which do not offer comparable wages, stability of employment, or mobility ladders. This result of economic restructuring is often described in terms of the "disappearing middle," sometimes pictured as an "hourglass economy," with a narrowed band of mid-level jobs and bulging strata at the bottom and the top.[22] The presumption is that it will be more difficult for the descendants of contemporary immigrants, many of whom enter the labor force at or near the bottom, to make the gradual intergenerational transition upward, because footholds in the middle of the occupational structure are relatively scarce. Movement into the top strata requires substantial human capital, particularly higher educational credentials, not likely to be within reach of most members of the second generation. A possible conclusion is that, to a degree not true of European ethnics, the current second generation is at risk of experiencing no mobility or even downward mobility.[23]

Without question, economic opportunities are critical to the assimilation prospects of new immigrant groups. But we think that the hourglass analogy conveys an extreme view of the restructuring of the economy and consequently leads to an unduly pessimistic reading of the prospects. This reading also insists on what is probably a false parallelism, namely, that assimilation is likely only if the situation of contemporary groups fairly exactly parallels that of earlier ones. With respect to mobility, such an insistence overlooks the ability of individuals and groups to adjust their sights and strategies to whatever economic structures they find and the opportunities these afford. Perhaps the pathways followed by earlier groups have been narrowed over time, but others are likely to have opened up.

There do appear to be dualistic tendencies at work in the American economy.[24] They can be seen in the wages and social standing of new jobs, for these are disproportionately in service sectors, which include both "good" jobs in health and legal services, education, and finance, and "bad" jobs such as those in fast food restaurants, and therefore clump at both the high- and low-wage ends of the socioeconomic spectrum. Nevertheless, the overall distribution of jobs is still close to unimodal: that is, its characteristic feature is a large bulge in the middle.[25] The hourglass analogy, while it does reflect tendencies associated with restructuring, extrapolates them well beyond the changes they have so far brought about. Moreover, these tendencies came to the fore only during the 1970s and 1980s; it is quite risky to project them indefinitely into the future, as would have to be the case for the pessimistic scenario mentioned earlier to come true. The hourglass analogy was introduced at a time of pessimism for the future, when many analysts believed that Japan would soon overtake the American economy. During the 1990s, however, structural transformation of the economy as well as technological changes resulted in sustained improvements in productivity, tight labor markets, declines in unemployment, and economic growth that both opened and expanded avenues for mobility.[26] Hence, whether the economy will ever resemble an hourglass it is premature to say.

The theory of segmented labor markets suggests the existence of institutionalized barriers to mobility which are in effect impermeable for minorities and women.[27] American society before World War II and the civil rights movement was *truly* segmented by race insofar as racial difference posed an insurmountable barrier to social mobility for African and Asian Americans. In the post–civil rights era, race has declined as a barrier to mobility.[28] This is not to say that racism no longer matters; it does, but it is manifested today mainly in informal constraints rather than in formal rules as it was in the past. Research has shown that metropolitan areas make up a single labor market, not separate suburban and urban labor markets, nor segmented labor markets divided by impermeable structural barriers.[29] Segmentation has served more as a heuristic idea than as an empirically confirmed concept. As an adjective preceding the word assimilation, "segmented" loses its heuristic meaning of an impermeable barrier. The segmented assimilation hypothesis does not claim segmentation in the standard meaning of the term; instead it points to divergent outcomes. The concern is that, although some immigrant minorities manage to move upward into the middle class, many immigrant youths are at risk of experiencing mostly *horizontal* and *downward* mobility in merging with underclass blacks in the central city.[30] Nathan Glazer and Patrick Moynihan in *Beyond the Melting Pot* were perhaps the first to observe that West Indians were merging with the native-born African American population in New York City.[31] In this light, it seems reasonable to expect that Afro-Caribbean youths may come to share similar life chances with black youths in the inner city. Yet, while the concern for second-generation immigrant minorities in central cities is warranted, the undifferentiated view of inner-city black youths as having negative attitudes toward education and being destined to join the underclass is not. It is not supported by studies that show, for example, a convergence of high school completion rates among blacks with those of whites during the last decades of the twentieth century.[32]

Studies of local labor markets sustain the image of economic vitality commonly associated with immigrant groups. One of the major puzzles is why immigrants continue to throng into metropolitan areas where so-called postindustrial economies are highly developed and therefore the entry points needed by greenhorn immigrants are presumably limited.[33] The New York City area exemplifies this paradox, since it remains one of the most popular destinations for immigrants even though its labor market has been contracting for some time and its loss of manufacturing jobs in particular has been massive. New immigrants, however, have been able to penetrate and colonize a number of economic niches that whites have been leaving, including the garment industry, construction, and technical positions in public service.[34] Even though some of these niches have undergone very substantial downsizing in the last quarter century—the "rag trade," or garment industry, is a prime example—positions are still available to new groups, because whites are leaving these positions even more rapidly than they are declining, and African Americans have concentrated elsewhere in the urban economy, especially in public employment. In the case of the garment industry, the new generation of whites, more specifically Italians and Jews, are not willing to take over even the top ownership positions from their parents, so these too are falling by default to the new immigrants. The jobs in the niches where immigrants have established themselves should not be overestimated, for many pay poorly. But the point is that the immigrant groups are able to get started in surprising ways in a difficult regional economy.

Insofar as the sometimes subtle alterations in mobility patterns can be measured, it would appear that the structural changes have so far not diminished overall mobility opportunities. Moreover, the children

of human-capital immigrants—professionals and technical workers—
who constitute a large part of the contemporary immigration, are experiencing more rapid integration into the mainstream middle class
than the children of the turn-of-the-twentieth-century labor migration
from southern Europe. Their educational and occupational attainment differs from that of the second generation of labor migrants,
past and present, in the large proportions who attend and graduate
from four-year colleges. Structural mobility, which played a crucial
role in the assimilation of the second and third generations of European immigrant groups, may be less for the descendants of labor migration, as one would expect from the claims about economic restructuring—though this conclusion is premature in light of the continued
expansion of job opportunities for skilled workers and professionals
in newly emergent growth sectors of the American economy. But exchange mobility, which comes about through openings created by the
downward mobility of the children of relatively well-placed parents,
is now greater. This is another way of saying that an individual's socioeconomic origins are now less determinative of his or her adult position than they used to be: there is "more universalism, less structural
mobility."[35] The net effect of these changes, at least through the last
decades of the twentieth century, is that the gross amount of mobility
has remained about the same as in the post–World War II period despite increasing levels of relative inequality.

The weakening hold of parental socioeconomic position on the
next generation ("more universalism") is partly attributable to increases in educational opportunity, and this factor looms as especially
significant for many of the new immigrant groups. The role of the educational system is slighted by the hourglass analogy, which focuses
on the labor market. But the gradual extension of college education
into more and more strata of the population—a process that, as we
noted in Chapter 3, greatly accelerated in the two decades following
World War II—has had a positive impact on social mobility, because
for those with college degrees, there is little or no measurable connection between their socioeconomic position and that of their parents.[36]
Even for those who attend college but do not graduate, that association is less than it is for individuals who do not continue their education after high school. In other words, a progressive weakening of the
linkage between socioeconomic origin and destination occurs with
advancing education. In addition, the connection between social ori-

gin and educational attainment has itself weakened over time. This has happened because high school completion has become so widespread as to be nearly universal (currently, nearly 90 percent of twenty-five- to thirty-four-year-olds are graduates), because with acquisition of a high school diploma, socioeconomic origins have less impact on educational transitions, and because the college and university sector has expanded to accommodate ever larger fractions of the high school graduate pool.

The mobility pathway through a college education would appear to be especially strategic for many new immigrant groups because of their geographic location and their parents' limited human capital. New immigrant groups concentrate in metropolitan regions and states where the opportunities for higher education are unusually abundant. California and New York, in particular, have very large higher educational systems, including the largest public systems in the country, and these enroll many children of new immigrants, as well as some of the immigrants themselves. The new immigrant presence has ironically been reflected in the tensions over affirmative action on the elite campuses of the University of California, since first- and second-generation Asian students believed that their numbers in the student body were being reduced by affirmative action admissions for African Americans and Latinos (discontinued as of 1996). On the other coast, the City University of New York has continued through its open admissions policy its historic mission of educating the children of immigrants, though here, too, there has been controversy.[37]

Of course, the restructuring of the economy—even should it deepen and make the hourglass analogy more accurate in the event of a protracted economic downturn—could not have an equally negative impact on the opportunities of all groups because of the enormous variety in the financial, human-cultural, and social capital they bring with them and in the degree of support provided by the communities they enter.[38] The significance of economic restructuring for the second and subsequent generations would appear to be greatest for the "labor migrant" groups such as the Mexicans.[39] Even here, we caution that contrasts with the experiences of comparable European groups, such as the southern Italians, can be overdrawn, for they too did not enter an economy that was continuously generating a generous supply of opportunities for secure employment and upward mobility. A large portion of the second generation of southern and eastern European groups came of age in the teeth of the Great Depression. Like the children of some contemporary immigrants, many responded to their perceived lack of opportunity and rejection by constructing what are now called "reactive identities," premised on value schemes that invert those of the mainstream. We know, for instance, that during the 1930s and perhaps afterward, the children of southern Italian immigrants were widely perceived as posing problems in the educational system—they had high rates of dropout, truancy, and delinquency—all signs that they were rejecting the conventions and values of a system that they perceived as rejecting them.[40] Yet analyses demonstrate that the U.S.-born members of these groups experienced a fairly steady upgrading in educational and occupational attainment, even in the cohorts whose life chances would have been most affected by the depression.[41] And, as we saw in the last chapter, these groups have now joined the mainstream. All of this suggests that pessimism about the assimilation chances for contemporary immigrant groups owing to economic restructuring is premature and perhaps exaggerated.

Changes in the Ideological Climate Regarding Ethnic and Cultural Diversity

It is widely argued that societal expectations about the assimilation of ethnic groups have fundamentally changed in recent years and that, accordingly, the descendants of contemporary immigrant groups will face diminished pressure to assimilate compared with those of earlier immigrations. Indeed, European and East Asian immigrants and their children did at times face intensely expressed demands that they surrender their cultural distinctiveness, such as the campaign for "100 percent Americanization" during World War I. The intensity of the drive to force acculturation on early-twentieth-century immigrants and their children sometimes took forms that read today like parody, as in the case of Henry Ford's compulsory English School, described by John Higham in his magisterial analysis of nativism, *Strangers in the Land:*

> The first thing that foreign-speaking employees learned in the Ford school was how to say, "I am a good American." Later the students acted out a pantomime which admirably symbolized the spirit of the enterprise. In this performance a great melting pot (labeled as such) occupied the middle of the stage. A long column of immigrant students

descended into the pot from backstage, clad in outlandish garb and flaunting signs proclaiming their fatherlands. Simultaneously from either side of the pot another stream of men emerged, each prosperously dressed in identical suits of clothes and each carrying a little American flag.[42]

A compulsory dip in a pot that churns out streams of identical Americans hardly represents a mature version of the melting pot ideal, but when such a version did emerge after World War II, it too could be seen as strong encouragement of assimilation and implicitly as a disparagement of what were then seen as the parochial, limiting bonds of ethnicity.

Claims that the ideological climate has changed usually refer to multiculturalism, a term of ambiguous meaning, which is nevertheless understood by its advocates as a revocation of earlier American cultural beliefs about assimilation, and to bilingual education, which holds out the possibility of institutional support for cultural diversity. Both seem rather narrowly focused on educational institutions and curricula. This is obvious in the case of bilingual education, but multiculturalism too is most often discussed in the context of academic disciplines, especially in the humanities and social sciences, and thus the resonance of multiculturalist thinking outside of educational spheres is unclear.[43] The term, moreover, has a range of possible meanings. At one end of this spectrum, it refers to an undeniable empirical fact: namely, that plural cultures (as represented, say, by languages) can be found in the United States. But in this sense of the term, there is no novelty in multiculturalism, for the existence of multiple cultures has long been part of the American experience, and in fact a plausible case can be made that in the past the United States has been more culturally heterogeneous than it is today.[44] At the other end, the term suggests a grand ambition, to raise minority cultures to parity with the majority one (or ones). If so, then it has failed to spell out how such parity might be attained. One critical dilemma it fails to surmount is an asymmetry of expectations: while members of a minority culture are expected to be bi- (but not multi-) cultural if they are to be successful in the mainstream society, members of the majority culture face no similar normative expectation and, in general, reject one categorically. Language exemplifies this dilemma: that is, native speakers of other languages are expected to master English, unless they are prepared to suffer social and economic disadvantages. But there is no equivalent expectation for native English speakers; learning another language such as Spanish, probably not to the point of fluency in most cases, is an option, perhaps one that will be widely exercised in the future, but it will not be a normative requirement. Bilingualism, then, is an issue for immigrant populations but not for native speakers of English.

We have no doubt that Americans today are generally more tolerant of ethnic difference than was previously the case, but the question is how far that tolerance extends. Survey data suggest that it does not go as far as strong forms of multiculturalism presuppose. Granted, many Americans are prepared to endorse cultural diversity when it is stated in vague terms and leaves unclear whether diversity is limited to symbolic items such as food, holiday customs, and ethnic music or whether it encompasses more fundamental differences of language and behavior that manifest themselves in daily life. When, in 1994, the General Social Survey asked a representative sample of English-speaking Americans whether "racial and ethnic groups should maintain their distinct cultures" or "groups should change so that they blend into the larger society," opinions were rather evenly divided: 38 percent took an assimilationist stance, while 32 percent opposed it, and the rest were squarely in the middle. (Asked again in 2000, the question drew virtually identical results.) Further, when a question was posed in very general terms about support for bilingual education, a clear majority (68 percent) endorsed it.[45] When, however, specific bilingual options were presented, a rather different picture emerged. The options were as follows:

1. All classes should be conducted in English so that children have to learn English right from the start;
2. Children who don't know English should have classes in their native language just for a year or two until they learn English; or
3. Students who want to keep up with their native languages and cultures should be able to take many of their classes in Spanish or other languages all the way through high school.

Eighty-four percent of respondents viewed bilingual education as no more than a temporary aid to immigrant students. Specifically, 36 percent favored the first option and 48 percent the second. Only 16 percent endorsed bilingual education as a support for ethnic cultural maintenance. Such data suggest that most Americans have not fundamentally revised their understanding of what Nathan Glazer identified in 1975 as the "American ethnic pattern": ethnic difference is acceptable so long as it is voluntary and confined to private spheres of family and community; the public sphere, especially its political sector, requires a common, English-language-based culture.[46] It is not surprising, therefore, that, among those respondents who affirmed that "groups should maintain their distinct cultures," the overwhelming majority, nearly 90 percent, believed that cultural maintenance should be left up to the groups themselves and should not receive government support. Also consistent with this understanding is the high degree of approval for making English the "official" language of the United States. The survey defined this as meaning that "government business would be conducted in English only," and a law to require this was favored by 63 percent of all respondents. In 2000, three-quarters agreed with the statement that "speaking English as the common national language is what unites all Americans."

In describing the American ethnic pattern, Glazer pointed to the resistance of Americans to recognizing "subnational entities," giving official status to racial and ethnic groups. There are, of course, ways that government does recognize racial and ethnic status, ranging from census data categories to affirmative action.[47] But most Americans are still suspicious of organization along racial and ethnic lines. Thus, asked by the 1994 General Social Survey whether "political organizations based on race and ethnicity promote separatism and make it hard for all of us to live together," 70 percent agree that they do. With respect to immigration more specifically, 73 percent of respondents expressed the opinion that "as a result of more immigrants coming to this country," it would become "harder to keep the country united."

Thus, survey data offer little evidence that increased tolerance of individual difference extends to the point of endorsing a full-blown multiculturalism, in which minority cultures attain something approaching parity with the mainstream one. Even at its most tolerant, the American viewpoint seems better characterized as laissez-faire, accepting cultural practices and beliefs that depart from mainstream norms so long as they do not infringe on the paramount status of the mainstream. Insofar as this view represents a change from the past, the shift is better described as bringing opinions with respect to ethnic difference into conformity with the traditional American core value of individualism than as a revocation of past understandings about ethnicity and assimilation. This interpretation is bolstered by ethnographic studies of the interaction between contemporary immigrant groups and the mainstream society, which indicate that expectations of assimilation, particularly for the second and later generations, have not been surrendered by most other Americans. For instance, Margaret Gibson's fascinating account of Punjabi Sikh children in a California school system reveals persistent expectations from Anglo children and teachers that immigrant children will acculturate to a white, middle-class American standard.[48]

Even if the United States were to embrace officially an affirmative policy of multiculturalism, of lending support to group efforts to maintain cultural difference, it is far from clear that this would have much impact on the informal, ground-level pressures to assimilate. A comparison with Canada, which adopted multiculturalism as its official policy at the federal level in the early 1970s and has even modified its constitution accordingly, is illuminating. Multiculturalism, as opposed to the biculturalism of the English-French divide, was intended to hold out to new immigrant groups, mostly coming from Europe, the prospect of avoiding assimilation into the two dominant cultural blocs. Concretely, the policy offered government support for efforts at cultural maintenance. A study of the Canadian experience concludes, however, that in terms of cultural retention by immigrant groups, the United States and Canada are more similar than different, and that any differences between them are the consequence of the greater proportion of immigrants in the Canadian population rather than the workings of multiculturalist policy.[49] The day-to-day pressures to assimilate are powerful in both societies, and consequently "both countries are moving toward 'symbolic ethnicity' at about the same pace—a movement, it should be recalled, that can be observed clearly only over generations."[50] This statement does not apply to the gulf between English- and French-speaking Canada, a division rooted in a history of colonial settlement and conquest rather than immigration into an established society.

Finally, the contrast between the ideological climate confronting earlier, European immigrant groups in the United States and that faced by contemporary groups is overdrawn, like other distinctions we have discussed. A position with apparent similarities to multiculturalism—namely, cultural pluralism—was articulated with intellectual vigor in the final decades of mass immigration from Europe and enjoyed the support of some prominent Americans, such as John Dewey.[51] Earlier immigrant groups also managed to find or create institutional support for their cultural diversity, which ranged from the establishment of Catholic school systems by Irish and other Catholic immigrants to the use of German as a language of instruction in public school systems in many parts of the Midwest. At the end of the nineteenth century, the public schools in cities such as Baltimore, Cincinnati, Cleveland, and Indianapolis, as well as in many smaller cities and towns, offered "truly bilingual programs with the school day divided between German and English."[52] If programs that involved an hour of German instruction *per day* are counted, then bilingual education was available to the children of German immigrant parents in as many as twenty-five states. Ohio was in the vanguard because of a law that permitted a German language program wherever a sufficient number of parents asked for one; and it appears that there, at the beginning of the twentieth century, about half of the children of German immigrants were in such programs.[53] (One of the many ironies of American history is that Dwight D. Eisenhower, the commander in chief of Allied forces in Europe at the end of World War II, came from a German-speaking Kansas family; Eisenhower's grandfather, the fourth generation of the family in America, was a preacher who delivered his sermons in German, the language he also spoke at home.)[54] Other mother tongues, French and Polish among them, also found institutional anchors in public or parochial school systems.

The Emergence of Transnationalism

Transnationalism refers to the possession of ties to two (or even more) societies and, at its extreme, implies that individuals can be literally at home in, and participate in the life of, places that are separated by national borders and may even be at quite distant points on the globe.[55] It encompasses "the processes by which immigrants forge and sustain multi-stranded social relations that link together their societies of origin and settlement" and leads to "social fields that cross geographic, cultural, and political borders."[56] This phenomenon has long been associated with international migration. Transnationalism existed during previous eras of immigration to the United States, especially during the late nineteenth and early twentieth centuries, when the advent of steamship travel rendered the transatlantic journey more predictable and thus made it feasible for some Europeans to become seasonal labor migrants, who returned annually to their home villages. Among the Italians, "many young men crossed to the United States in the spring, worked until the late fall, saving and sending money home, and returned for the winter."[57] Abundant data demonstrate that many immigrants from other countries intended their stays in the United States to be short; to return home with money in one's pocket was the goal of the majority. Ties to the village and family left behind were also kept up through remittances of a portion of the money immigrants earned in the United States. The sojourner orientation of the new immigrants from southern and eastern Europe was one reason why this immigration was disparaged by early-twentieth-century nativists. Among observers more sympathetic to the new immigrants was Randolphe Bourne, who wrote in his famous 1916 essay "Transnational America": "Along with dual citizenship we shall have to accept, I think, that free and mobile passage of the immigrant between America and his native land. . . . To stigmatize the alien who works in America for a few years and returns to his own land . . . is to ignore the cosmopolitan significance of this migration."[58]

To distinguish present-day transnationalism from that of the past, contemporary analysts argue that the quantum leap in the ease of international transportation and communication has meant a qualitative shift in the locus and substance of migrants' lives. Air travel, telephone, videotapes, and E-mail have transformed the linkage of immigrants to homeland communities.[59] In the past, "it was not possible for would-be transnational entrepreneurs to travel to Poland or Italy over the weekend and be back at their jobs in New York by Monday."[60] It is possible today.

Further, the significance of these technologically engendered possibilities is enhanced by several contemporary forces. One is the globalization of capitalism, which allows firms to integrate facilities located in countries widely separated from one another into a single system of production, one that takes advantage of the labor economies obtainable in Third World nations and is flexible enough to adjust quickly to product changes required by market shifts or technological upgrading. Globalization thus makes it possible for Third World entrepreneurs—often recruited from the ranks of migrants who possess valuable ties in the advanced economies—to establish small factories whose products then enter into the streams flowing across national boundaries. Alejandro Portes points to "hundreds of small and medium-size factories, commercial ventures, and financial agencies" in the Dominican Republic founded and operated by former immigrants to the United States and notes that the entrepreneurs are "not 'return immigrants' in the traditional sense of the term," for they "travel back and forth to take advantage of economic opportunities in both countries."[61] Globalization also contributes to the motivation to become a transnational entrepreneur, since this form of capitalism, according to Saskia Sassen and others, makes immigrant workers more vulnerable than ever. Leaving the ranks of the employed (and, sometimes, of the unemployed) to become an employer is then a way of gaining greater security as well as a form of resistance to the powerful tentacles of international mega-firms.[62]

Another force lies in the attempts by sending states to hold onto the loyalties of their sons and daughters on American shores. Some observers claim, for example, that the Korean community in New York has been regarded by the Korean government as an outpost of the homeland, to be used to promote its interests under the guidance of the Korean Consulate General.[63] In an action with far wider potential ramifications, Mexico in 1998 amended its constitution to permit Mexican-born U.S. citizens and their U.S.-born children to regain Mexican nationality. This action was intended to grant them the economic rights of Mexican citizens (e.g., to own land), not the political rights, but it caused an uproar in the United States nevertheless, especially in regions where many Mexican Americans live. Although some commentators feared that this could rekindle the homeland loyalties of Mexican Americans and transmute them into a force exerting influence in U.S. politics on behalf of Mexico, the practical significance may turn out to be limited. The change appears to have unleashed not a wave of applications for Mexican passports but a trickle: only 26,000 in the first three years.[64] The promotion or exploitation of homeland ties for state ends has not been a one-sided process involving only sending nations. During the cold war, the United States used immigrant communities for its own ends, as exemplified by the attention lavished on Baltic émigrés (Estonians, Latvians, and Lithuanians) from the so-called captive nations, as a means of broadcasting the contrast between American freedoms and communist totalitarianism.

Such examples have led some observers to extrapolate to the concept of "de-territorialized nation-states," whose membership does not just encompass resident citizens but extends also to immigrant diasporas.[65] Adding to the potential for political transnationalism is the growing acceptance in U.S. law of involvement by U.S. citizens in the life of other nations. In principle, the law still discourages dual citizenship in that it supposedly requires aliens who are naturalizing to renounce their previous citizenship. Dual citizenship nevertheless arises with some frequency among contemporary immigrants, who are no longer required to surrender their previous passports (and even if they were, they could apply to regain their original nationality if homeland law allows dual citizenship). It also is found among the U.S.-born children of immigrants, who are American citizens by virtue of the *jus soli,* or birthplace, principle in U.S. law but may also be citizens of another nation, if the laws of that nation attribute citizenship through parents (the so-called *jus sanguinis* principle). A number of countries with large immigrant populations in the United States—the Dominican Republic and Ireland, to cite two examples—permit dual citizenship; and U.S. law does not require that passively acquired citizenship in another country be relinquished. More surprising is that it also no longer penalizes active citizenship in another nation, as indicated by serving in its army or voting in its elections. While such actions were once seen as disqualifications for American citizenship and potential grounds for expatriation, this has not been the case since the Supreme Court decided in *Vance v. Terrazas* (1980) that only "subjective intent" to relinquish U.S. citizenship, rather than an action connoting allegiance to another nation, precipitates expatriation. Further, there is no bar preventing American citizens, whether U.S.-born or naturalized, from acquiring citizenship in other nations, where the laws of these nations permit them to do so without renouncing their American citizenship. Ireland, for instance, has established a procedure for Americans and others with Irish-born grandparents rather painlessly to obtain Irish citizenship. Developments such as these have led some legal and political scholars to foresee a dawning era when plural citizenship will have become common and even "normal."[66] We are not there yet, though.

The novelty and significance of contemporary political transnationalism can be exaggerated, however. As Nathan Glazer pointed out half a century ago, some Old World nationalisms have had a more vigorous life in the freer atmosphere of the United States than they could in their original homelands.[67] This was true in particular for European immigrant groups from minority populations submerged in multiethnic states dominated by others, nations that were not yet states, such as the Czechs of the Austro-Hungarian Empire. Glazer notes that "the first newspaper in the Lithuanian language was published in this country, not in Lithuania," and that "the Erse revival began in Boston, and the nation of Czechoslovakia was launched at a meeting in Pittsburgh."[68] Occasionally, actions on behalf of oppressed fellow ethnics across the seas took extreme forms, as when in 1866 an armed force of Irish Americans, organized by the Fenian Brotherhood, which "conducted itself as an important international power," staged an abortive invasion of Canada in the hope of dealing a damaging blow to England.[69] More generally, the domestic political pressures exerted by Irish Americans on behalf of Irish freedom were a staple of American politics through much of the nineteenth century, providing the occasion for the derisive slogan "Rum, Romanism, and Rebellion," which contributed to the defeat of the Republican presidential candidate, James G. Blaine, in 1884. The early twentieth century witnessed similar transnational involvements, as when more than 40,000 Greek Americans were recruited by the Pan-Hellenic Union to fight for their homeland in 1912–13.[70] Too numerous and obvious to describe in detail are the efforts since then by ethnic groups to pressure the American government into actions to further the interests of their brethren overseas.

To cite past parallels is not to deny that there are some new elements in contemporary transnationalism. And certainly there are some suggestive examples of its force, such as the Mexican immigrants in the New York City area who meet regularly to plan and contribute to improvements in their home village of Ticuani in southern Mexico and even fly home for the weekend to chart the progress of these projects.[71] Nor are the instances of transnationalism necessarily confined to a modest scale. The Cuban and Nicaraguan communities of Miami have prospered in part from the access to Latin American business circles resulting in some cases from direct personal connections as well as common language and cultural bonds.[72] Thus, these Miami communities can be seen as nodes where the filaments come together, creating networks that leap over national boundaries and move capital, projects, and information across great distances. This is the sort of image that contemporary analysts of transnationalism have in mind when they see in it a larger significance than it has had in the past.

Such examples, while they demonstrate the continuing involvement of many immigrants and their families in the life of the places from which they came, seem less conclusive to us. It is hard to be sure from examples alone just how different the transnationalism of the present is from that of the past and what the long-run significance of any difference is. It is also very difficult to be sure about the quantitative extent of contemporary transnationalism. Obviously, examples by themselves cannot say what percentage of immigrant populations is affected by transnationalism and whether this is a larger fraction than in past immigration eras.

An even bigger question mark hovers over the ability of transnationalism to cross generations on a large scale. Chinese immigrants sustained transnational migration for up to three to four generations from the late nineteenth century to the mid-twentieth century as an adaptation to exclusionary immigration laws. Once racist immigration laws were abrogated, however, Chinese American transnationalism shifted to the now familiar pattern of nuclear and extended families migrating to establish permanent residence and acquire naturalized citizenship.[73] Neither the common examples nor the arguments about the distinctiveness of transnationalism in the contemporary context are persuasive that U.S.-born generations will be transnationalist in orientation. An interview one of us conducted with an Italian immigrant in southern Germany gives concrete shape to our doubts. Transnationalism is extremely common among the immigrants to Germany because of the proximity for many to their homelands. Italy, for example, is just a long drive away. The respondent described his regular trips to his hometown (in northern Italy) and the relationships he maintains there with individuals he grew up with. The questioning then turned to his adult children and whether they also visited his hometown with such regularity and had an experience similar to his. They were less interested, he observed almost with detachment, for there were few *paesani* with whom they could make a *passeggiata* around the town square (the stroll that is an Italian social ritual); they lacked the dense web of connections originating in childhood. In short, they were not at home there as their father was.

We suspect that a similar degradation will happen across generations in most immigrant families in the United States, even when the immigrant generation is able to maintain ties in multiple places. Few families will be truly *at home* in more than one place. Having multiple domiciles generally requires unusual economic circumstances, either considerable affluence or reliable employment (serial or simultaneous) in different places; a special case occurs when an individual's employment has a transnational character—such as importing—but this is not common. Thus, most immigrant children are unlikely to grow up in two societies; they will be like the children of the Italian immigrant in Germany.[74] Moreover, if the long-standing three-generation pattern of mother-tongue attrition applies on a large scale to contemporary immigrant groups—and so far there is no evidence to suggest that it will not (see Chapter 6)—then the second and even more the third generations will not be fluent enough in the mother tongue to maintain close ties with natives in the homeland. In sum, transnationalism is an important phenomenon, but its ramifications for U.S.-born generations are at best unclear, and more than likely to be modest in magnitude.

Moreover, transnationalism in the form of political attachment to the homeland may run afoul of the desire of many ethnics to demonstrate their patriotism to their new country. This is an old theme in the American experience: the second generation has often been zealous in its expression of American patriotism, partly out of a need to compensate for uncertainties about its acceptance in American society. It is too early to pronounce any final judgment about the contemporary extent of American patriotism among immigrants and their children, but there is evidence that Mexican Americans are quite patriotic, supporting core elements of American political culture, "the American creed."[75]

Political transnationalism may also come under threat from the host state. There is a risk in extrapolating into the future from very recent developments, such as the spreading possibilities for plural citizenship. Threats to transnational involvements do not generally develop in strictly linear relation to the phenomenon itself but emerge with suddenness, and sometimes finality, when transnationalism comes into open conflict with the interests of the state on whose territory immigrants reside. Perhaps no transnational project on American soil has ever been as vigorous as the case of the Germans in the nineteenth and early twentieth centuries. German immigrants sometimes thought of themselves as recreating a separate German cultural sphere in the United States, and numerous towns where they settled were given German names (such as King of Prussia, Pennsylvania, and Frankfort, Kentucky). At a relatively late point in American history, the great majority of the foreign-language press was published in German. As described earlier, the German language was unusually tenacious across the generations, supported by bilingual public education in many states. Germany also did not lose sight of its sons and daughters abroad, in the United States and other nations, the so-called *Auslandsdeutsche*. In 1913, on the eve of World War I, a new citizenship law there made German parentage the key determinant, thus allowing the *Auslandsdeutsche* and their descendants to retain German citizenship. Yet the vigor of German transnationalism in the United States came to an abrupt end within a few years. When World War I broke out, German Americans agitated on behalf of their embattled fatherland, campaigning in 1914–15 for an embargo on the export of war supplies with the goal of depriving England of American munitions. Their activities fed the suspicions of other Americans about the reliability of German American loyalties. Theodore Roosevelt responded with a thundering denunciation of "hyphenated Americans"; some states banned the teaching of German, the publication of German-language newspapers, even the use of the language on the streets or over the telephone; intense anti-German feeling produced occasional violence against those who dared to display German cultural loyalty. By the end of the war, many Americans of German ancestry had surrendered to the crusade for their "100 percent Americanization," as individuals and even towns changed their names to become more innocuous.[76] The hold of German *Kultur* had been decisively broken.

Perhaps the German case is too extreme to form a basis for judgments about contemporary transnationalism since it involves loyalties to a nation that became an enemy in war to the United States. Nevertheless, the heightened government monitoring of American Muslim communities after the September 11, 2001, destruction of the World Trade Center suggests the power of exogenous events to create suspicion about loyalty. The potential for conflict with state interests is present, however, even without war or overt enmity. The political news immediately following the 1996 election was dominated by the alleged fund-raising improprieties of the Clinton reelection campaign, in which an important element was the reported attempts by foreign firms and governments to influence U.S. decisions through donations made by some Asian Americans. More conflicts of this sort undoubtedly lie ahead.

Legitimation of Racial/Ethnic Categories by the State

A final line of argument frequently introduced to distinguish between past and contemporary immigrations looks to changes in state policies, specifically the rise of affirmative action and related regulations and laws. These are held to create fundamentally different circumstances from those faced by the descendants of previous waves of immigration. Today the state, by favoring minority groups in promotion and hiring, the awarding of contracts, and the drawing of voting districts, creates incentives for members of these groups to maintain some ethnic connections or otherwise lose the potential benefits of membership. Indeed, the state may have created "group interests" that will be defended even by minority individuals who perceive no direct benefit for themselves. In addition, such policies institutionalize racial and ethnic categories by requiring individuals to identify their racial/ethnic origins on numerous occasions, as when applying to a school or for a job. These data are used in turn to produce reports on the representation of different groups in various spheres—for example, in managerial and professional occupations or among college students—and many of these filter into public consciousness, generating an atmosphere of discourse apparently permeated by racial and ethnic categories. In more than one respect, then, the policies enhance racial/ethnic identification and militate against assimilation.[77]

Affirmative action may have been devised to assist black Americans and other domestic minorities to overcome the handicaps resulting from centuries of legal and social disadvantage, but it has been extended over time to encompass many contemporary immigrant groups.[78] Its extension to some Latino immigrant groups, Mexicans and Puerto Ricans in particular, was logical, since these could also be construed as long-resident domestic minorities that had suffered systematic disadvantage (in the Mexican case, to be sure, this characterization applies strictly to only a small percentage, since the great majority of the group is descended from immigrants who have arrived over the last hundred years). But since nonwhite color is understood in common discourse to be the source of these disadvantages, preferential policies were also extended, almost ineluctably, to nonwhite immigrant groups, despite the absence of any burdens from past discrimination in the United States. Thus, the Small Business Administration included immigrants from Sri Lanka and Tonga among those eligible for preferential treatment in the granting of loans, and Indian entrepreneurs have been among the beneficiaries of minority set-asides for public contracts in Ohio.

The hypothesis that state actions can positively affect racial and ethnic identities would seem to be supported by developments in the Native American population. Since 1960, when the census converted to the self-identification of race, the number of Americans claiming to be American Indian has soared, increasing by more than 100 percent in just the following two decades—well beyond what can be explained by natural increase. Evidently, many individuals who previously claimed to be "white," or in some other racial category, have switched their identity to American Indian. Most plausibly, they are of mixed Native American and other ancestry and no longer feel the need to present themselves as non-Indian. Several logical hypotheses connect this switch with changes in the political and legal environment of autochthonous groups—such as the enactment of more favorable federal policies; an increase in tribal wealth, largely as a consequence of successful suits over land claims and of the legally privileged position of tribal lands as sites for casinos; and greater Native American militance.[79] Yet there is at present no convincing evidence for any of these hypotheses; the link tying individual claims of American Indian ancestry with tangible benefits is vague, and the practical ramifications of switching to such an identity—for instance, in terms of involvement with tribes and their cultures—insufficiently investigated as yet. The surge in the number of American Indians remains to be explained. It may simply be that labeling oneself "Indian" has a cachet in many parts of the United States that it lacked before. All that has been demonstrated at this point is that the number of individuals filling in the box next to "American Indian" on U.S. Census forms has increased.

The impact of affirmative action and related "categorical" policies on immigrant group identities is even more uncertain. For one thing, these policies do not benefit all nonwhite immigrant groups equally; in fact, they have worked against the interests of Asian Americans in some settings. The arena where preferential policies have probably had their most pervasive impact is that of college and university admissions. But this is precisely the area where Asian Americans need little help, and the evidence indicates that minority preferences in admission usually lower, rather than raise, the chances of Asian students for admission. This is indisputably the case for admission to the elite campuses in the California system, and for this reason many Asian Americans supported the 1995 decision of the California Board of Regents to end affirmative action in admissions.[80]

Nor is it clear that all of the current forms of affirmative action and racial/ethnic preferences will survive indefinitely. As of the late 1990s, they are under siege and have suffered defeats on several fronts, including the California decision. In addition, the University of Texas Law School had its preferential admissions policy voided in court in the *Hapwood* decision (1996), which applied to all public institutions of higher education in the state. Congressional boundary lines drawn up in several states to create majority-black districts in accordance with the Voting Rights Act were thrown out by the Supreme Court. In California, voters in 1996 passed a "Civil Rights Initiative," also known as Proposition 209, which bars state government from granting "preferential treatment" based on race or ethnic origin in employment, contracts, or education. Support for this resolution may have been premised in part on the questionable notion that it was a pro–civil rights, rather than anti–affirmative action, proposal. But there is no reason to think that the electorate will generally support affirmative action if it is put to a vote, since surveys have usually shown that the sentiment of the majority is against any preferential treatment, even for black Americans.[81] Support is undoubtedly even lower for the notion that new immigrants, recently arrived in the United States, should be the beneficiaries of such treatment, giving them advantages over, say, poor white Americans.[82] Calls to eliminate new immigrants and their descendants from affirmative action policies seem certain to grow in intensity as the proportion of these groups in the population does.

In any event, here too the dividing line in the experiences between the newer and older immigrant groups seems indistinct. True, there were no affirmative action policies, as these are currently understood, for the Irish, Jews, or Poles. But to a significant extent these and other Europeans inserted themselves *qua* groups into political processes and the labor market in ways that created tangible payoffs for ethnic membership and thus should have promoted ethnic identities. That ethnic groups constituted themselves into interest groups in the domain of politics is one of the truisms of American history.[83] Electoral slates in many cities and states were overtly devised with ethnic considerations in mind. In New York City it was long a political requirement that the major parties nominate a Protestant (a WASP), a Catholic (Irish or Italian), and a Jew, though not necessarily in this order, for the top three city offices. Irish Catholics so dominated the political structure of some major cities that they were able in the late nineteenth and early twentieth centuries to convert municipal employment into an ethnic preserve.[84] Similar preferential schemes skewed hiring in specific industrial sectors in cities where immigrants and their descendants were concentrated. Especially where craft union membership was a job requirement, ethnic niches were carved out by groups in control of union locals, as exemplified by the construction unions in the New York City area, which were—and to some extent still are—dominated by the Irish and Italians.[85] Granted, the use of racial/ethnic categories in many such instances may have been informal and tacit, rather than formal and overt, as in affirmative action. But does this necessarily mean that they had less of a fortifying effect on ethnic identities? We doubt that this was the case.

We have now discussed six objections that are commonly raised regarding the relevance of the European and Asian American assimilation experience for contemporary immigrant groups. Our purposes in this discussion should not be misunderstood. We have not intended to demonstrate the falsity of the objections, which contain important kernels of truth. Thus, we are not denying that there are differences, and potentially important ones, between the immigrations of the past and present, nor are we claiming that the parallels between the situations faced by the descendants of contemporary immigrants and those of earlier ones are so strong that nineteenth- and twentieth-century patterns of assimilation can be inferred as a likely outcome for new immigrant groups. History rarely repeats itself exactly. But the distinctions between immigration eras are not nearly as clear-cut as they appear in the objections, which generally overlook the complexity of the historical record and oversimplify the European American experience in particular. A telling instance is the anachronistic assertion that assimilation was relatively straightforward for past immigrants because they were white and will be more difficult for many contemporary immigrants because they are not. This claim ignores a far more complex story about the racial categories imposed on groups such as the Jews and Italians and glosses over the fluidity of racial boundaries. No one of the objections is, in our judgment, sufficiently strong to rule out a priori the possibility of assimilation as a widespread outcome for contemporary immigrant groups. They must not forestall the hard work of evaluating, theoretically and empirically, the assimilation prospects of the new groups.

Competing Models of Ethnic Incorporation

Another way to inquire about the suitability of the new assimilation theory we laid out in Chapter 2 is by examining the strengths and weaknesses of the two main alternative models of ethnic and racial incorporation: segmented assimilation and reinvigorated pluralism. Are they inherently more plausible than the assimilation pattern for new immigrant groups? If there are uncertainties hovering about the assimilation model, perhaps there are equally weighty uncertainties hanging over the alternatives.

The alternatives respond, in different ways, to the racial subordination and exclusion that have indisputably occupied a central place in the American experience. They are less attuned to the typically fluid situation of immigrant minorities. Of relevance here is the problematic distinction between "race" and "ethnicity" (or "ethnic group"). Scholars in the field of minority-majority relations differ on whether these terms should be defined as distinct concepts or as different expressions of the same underlying phenomenon. Typical of the former approach are the following definitions: "We . . . use the term race . . . to refer to a group that is *socially* defined but on the basis of *physical* criteria. . . . Ethnic groups . . . are socially defined but on the basis of *cultural* criteria."[86] These definitions in effect portray ethnic and racial groups as distinct types, to which different social dynamics might logically be seen to apply. The definitions lend themselves to the view (though they do not require it) that members of ethnic groups have the potential to assimilate into the mainstream through acculturation but that this possibility is foreclosed to members of racial groups because of their identifiability.

By contrast, we prefer to cast "ethnicity" as the general concept and to see "race" as a form of ethnicity. As discussed in Chapter 1, we base the general concept on Max Weber's definition, whose core is the notion that an ethnic group involves a "we-they" distinction where "we" are defined, in "our" own eyes and those of others, on the basis of a belief in shared ancestry or point of origin (whether the belief is true or not). A racial group is, then, a type of ethnic group, one that is socially identified mainly on the basis of putative phenotypical characteristics. Admittedly, the concept of race stretches the Weberian definition since racial membership is generally more imposed by outsiders than elected by group members, but ethnicity is also to some degree a function of outsiders' perceptions (thus, Italian immigrants in the United States became "Italians" rather than "Sicilians" and "Neapolitans" partly through common treatment at the hands of native-born Americans). Defining racial and non-racial ethnic groups along Weberian lines makes it easier to see the important features they share, such as cultural traits that set them apart from others and a group consciousness defined in part on the basis of a distinctive history. These "ethnic" characteristics of racial groups require additional explanation when race and ethnicity are defined as distinct phenomena. (Of course, groups that are seen as ethnic but not racial, such as the Irish and Italians, may also have some "racial" characteristics, such as stereotypical physical features, by which members are sometimes identified and which in fact can enhance their sense of identification with the group.)[87]

A paradigmatic discussion of racial subordination and exclusion is found in Robert Blauner's *Racial Oppression in America*. Blauner identifies "racial privilege," defined as a "systematic 'headstart' in the pursuit of social values," as an intrinsic feature of American society, deeply woven into its institutional fabric.[88] This privilege has an economic dimension, but it is not reducible to strictly economic terms—to social class, in other words—for it also includes social and psychological dimensions: racial minorities provide a form of social basement to which whites, on the main floors of the societal edifice, need not descend. Further, Blauner stresses the institutional basis of racial exclusion, arguing that "institutional racism" is more important than individual-level prejudice and discrimination in accounting for racial inequalities. He points in particular to institutions, such as schools and police forces, that have a salient presence in minority communities and are charged with keeping minorities in their place and, if possible, reconciling them to their lesser potentialities in the larger society.[89]

According to Michael Omi and Howard Winant's highly influential racial formation approach, race is an absolutely central and inescapable feature of U.S. society, and its paramount status cannot be perceived adequately through the lens of what they describe as the "ethnicity paradigm," the "mainstream of the modern sociology of race."[90] A distinctive emphasis in their approach falls on the social construction of racial categories: far from being self-evident and thus treatable as "givens," these categories have often been painfully assembled over long periods. A racial formation—the central concept in their theory—represents the intersection of "race consciousness," the bricolage of meanings that has built up around race, on the one hand, and economic, social, and political institutions into whose structure and functioning racial meanings are interwoven, on the other. Such a formation is a bulwark from which racial privilege is exercised in everyday affairs—to the benefit of some and the detriment of others, obviously.

If racial categories are the sites of socially assembled meanings—signifying and symbolizing "social conflicts and interests by referring to different types of human bodies"[91]—then it follows that these categories can be altered by collective efforts. An unusual note sounded by their approach is the fluidity of racial dividing lines, which are not imposed by forces so deeply seated in the large-scale movements of history as to render them beyond the reach of contemporary struggle. Thus, their model allows more room for minority groups to challenge and even alter the significance and meaning of racial categories than is generally presupposed by other models of racial subordination. Although they emphasize the possibility of change, they do not provide a road map to attaining it, and it remains far from certain in their theory that minorities will *successfully* challenge the racial system in the United States. Change, one could say, is visible as a distant horizon, but the road to get there is obscured by fog immediately ahead.

Models of economic segregation also are prominent in the background of the debate over assimilation versus the alternatives. Such models view racial and ethnic distinctions as emanating from, or at least reinforced by, structures embedded in the labor market of a capitalist society and imply that, absent a fundamental transformation of the economic and social order, these distinctions will persist. The economic model with the deepest influence on discussions of contemporary immigration is the dual (or segmented) labor market model, developed in application to immigrant and other ethnic/racial groups by the economist Michael Piore.[92] Its point of departure is an analysis of the labor market as divided between sectors that are associated with distinctive monetary compensation, mobility prospects, employment stability, and other conditions of work. This dualistic structure originates with capital operating in a system where labor has achieved power sufficient more or less to guarantee itself job security and a high standard of living. Because of the costs of labor in the primary sector, constituted by the "good" jobs there, capital requires a sector where wages are low and jobs are insecure. The low ceiling on job prospects in this sector implies that inequality *within* the sector is low, and this in turn implies that the human-capital investments of its workers, say, in education, are not rewarded as consistently or as amply as is human capital in the primary sector.

These economic structures take on specific ethnic colorations because the sectoral placement of workers corresponds strongly with their racial and ethnic origins (and also with gender). Non-immigrant white workers represent the privileged stratum of the labor force and typically prefer unemployment to accepting jobs in the secondary sector. In a modern welfare state, where the economic free fall of unemployment is broken by a safety net, members of the privileged strata are not generally forced down into the secondary sector (except perhaps as a temporary expedient). Minorities and immigrants, then, are shunted into the positions that white workers refuse. Indeed, the economic raison d'être of immigration is to provide a supply of workers willing to take these degraded positions. Dual labor market theory thus provides an account in which immigrant minorities suffer more or less permanent social and economic disadvantage. They are segregated into a separate structure in the labor market, and their prospects for escape (i.e., mobility into the primary sector) seem poor.

Dual labor market theory has been expanded and deepened by the globalization theorist Saskia Sassen, who has used it as one cornerstone of her influential general theory of international migration in the contemporary era.[93] Sassen's theory encompasses the forces that generate immigration waves in the countries where they originate as well as in the receiving societies that call for immigrant labor. Immigration streams flow into global cities, such as London, Los Angeles, and New York, whose economies have entered a postindustrial phase following the loss of the greater part of their industrial jobs to regions where labor costs are cheaper. These postindustrial urban economies have strongly dualistic tendencies. At their upper end an expansion is taking place in the number of "good" jobs in and around growing headquarters of globalized firms. At the lower end, there is increasing need for low-level service workers (e.g., janitors) in the headquarters complexes and the other firms that develop around them, and for more personal service workers, exemplified by immigrant maids and nannies. Additionally, manufacturing does survive, but mainly in a "degraded" sweatshop form that reproduces the exploitative conditions associated with the early twentieth century. Immigrant workers are needed for all these low-end positions, and many of them are forced into the informal economy, where jobs are by definition "off the books" and offer no benefits or claims on the welfare state (e.g., unemployment insurance). For obvious reasons, jobs in the informal economy are the special province of undocumented immigrants.

A salient feature of all these approaches is their rigidity with respect to ethnic/racial inequality. This is in no sense to portray them as static, for they capture important shifts in the larger society. But all lodge ethnic/racial inequalities in what would appear to be very durable structures with boundaries that, if not actually impermeable, are nearly so. The approaches contribute in different ways to the explanation of these substantial inequalities but leave unclear that they will be altered. Blauner's analysis, for instance, tracing these cleavages back to the modes by which groups have entered U.S. society, in some cases centuries in the past, implies that they must be highly resistant to change. At best, then, change would appear to require revolutionary alterations to the U.S. racial order, a process not likely to be accomplished in the near future.

The segmented assimilation model combines rigid ethnic/racial boundaries and economic segmentation.[94] It envisions the second and third generations as shunted along trajectories of incorporation largely determined by their class origins, position in the U.S. racial system, and residential location. While some members of these generations will experience assimilation into the mainstream, others will undergo "downward" assimilation, that is, incorporation as disadvantaged racial minorities. The latter is especially likely for dark-skinned Hispanics and Afro-Caribbeans who grow up in economically struggling families residing in the inner city. They have at close hand the cultural models of the African American underclass and are drawn to them as they experience at first hand racist discrimination, especially in schools and other institutions, and come to recognize their very limited prospects for advancement.

The value of this model lies in its demonstration that assimilation into the mainstream is not the only possible form of assimilation. Yet, while risks of racial exclusion certainly exist for today's second and third generations, they do not foreclose assimilation of the more positive sort. The segmented assimilation model hinges on assumptions that are not unproblematic. One is that racial boundaries will remain inflexible and nearly impermeable. As we have seen, this has not been true historically. We believe that it is unlikely to prove true in the near future, because assimilation will modify boundaries by "blurring" them; this possibility is foreshadowed in the already high rates of intermarriage involving the U.S.-born generations of new immigrant groups and in the residential assimilation of their middle-class, linguistically acculturated members (see Chapters 6 and 7).

A second key assumption is that upward mobility will remain out of the reach of many in the second generation; in fact, they may even suffer downward mobility, or they may experience the same socioeconomic position as their parents as a form of downward mobility, judging its low status with the eyes of a native-born American rather than with those of an immigrant. As we argued earlier, we think that a pessimistic reading of the prospects for mobility is unwarranted. Moreover, many critics of the conventional assimilation model often seem to assume tacitly that a vault into the middle class is the prerequisite for assimilation into the mainstream. This overlooks the import of the modest upward movement experienced by many members of previous second generations, such as the children of Italian immigrants during the 1930s and 1940s.[95]

The crux of the matter, in any event, is the perception of realistic opportunities for social mobility rather than actual attainment of middle-class status. Even what appears to be no more than horizontal intergenerational movement to an outside observer can be perceived as an improvement by the children of immigrants. They may see gain in working less hard or more regularly than their parents did, in moving to a better neighborhood, or being able to provide their children with educational opportunities superior to their own. In this respect, they are probably not any different from those who are already part of the mainstream. Assimilation generally is rooted in individualistic experiences of intergenerational mobility not dissimilar from those in the mainstream. A comparative study of mobility in sixteen countries, including the United States, has found a pattern of "severe immobility at the two extremes of the occupational hierarchy and considerable fluidity in the middle."[96] Moreover, the mobility regime of modern industrial societies entails *divergent outcomes* insofar as most individuals remain in the same strata as their parents, and others experience downward mobility. An expectation of universal upward mobility for any large group is unrealistic.

The pluralist alternative to the segmented assimilation model represents an attempt to chart a safe route between the Scylla of racial subordination and exclusion and the Charybdis of assimilation. A forerunner is Nathan Glazer and Daniel Patrick Moynihan's *Beyond the Melting Pot,* which depicted the persisting importance of group membership in New York and, by extension, American society. The authors argued that ethnic/racial groups compete for niches in the urban economy and for political power. The competition is unequal because groups differ in their resources, which lie partly in the realm of culture, partly in their prior occupational experience, and partly in the solidarity each group is able to muster. Yet in these respects, inequality would appear to be "soft" and malleable; Glazer and Moynihan speak of a "Northern model" of group relations, "perhaps best realized in New York City," where "an open society prevails," and "over time a substantial and rough equalization of wealth and power can be hoped for even if not attained."[97] But they do not present any definite scenario whereby ethnic/racial inequalities will be overcome. In fact, the coincidence of resources and groups reinforces ethnicity, as individuals find it in their interest to be group members.

The contemporary pluralist model also draws on ideas about solidarities rooted in economic situations and interests, building on the notion that immigrants and their children can draw socioeconomic advantages from ethnic solidarity and from the group's cultural and socioeconomic resources. (It also makes use of the notion of a new transnationalism, which we have already addressed.) Such advantages have been invoked to explain the exceptional entrepreneurial success of some immigrant groups. In between is the concept of an ethnic niche, which refers to any economic position—a type of job, say—where a group is sufficiently concentrated to draw advantage from it, typically by being able to steer its own members into openings.[98] Much more extensive is the notion of a full-fledged ethnic enclave economy, encompassing a substantial number of firms in which ethnic bosses employ co-ethnic workers.

According to its proponents, such an economy—a sub-economy, really—represents the strongest and most protective of communal contexts for receiving immigrants, who can expect not just the usual help from kin and co-ethnics during the initial settlement process—such as finding a place to live—but even jobs in firms owned by co-ethnics, where working conditions are supportive of their cultural and social needs. Alejandro Portes and his various collaborators have made strong claims about the advantages that ethnics derive from such sub-economies. These include economic returns to their human capital on a par with those for native-born workers in the primary sectors of the economy. Further, working in ethnic firms offers routes of mobility to immigrants, who can move into supervisory positions or can even learn enough of the business to open their own firms, perhaps with advice and financial assistance from their former employers. Insofar as the enclave economy is a viable equivalent to the primary sectors of the mainstream economy, it provides an economic motive to remain within an ethnic social and cultural milieu and thus constitutes a disincentive to assimilation.[99]

These claims about the benefits of ethnic enclave economies for workers have been challenged, and research shows that the principal economic benefits flow to owners rather than employees of enclave firms.[100] But even if the enclave economy model were fully persuasive about the compatibility of ethnic solidarity and socioeconomic success, it is not one that holds this promise for every immigrant group. For only some groups—such as the Cubans of Miami and the Koreans of Los Angeles—possess the wherewithal to follow this route. No doubt there will be others, but it would appear that some unusual conditions must come together for such an enclave to emerge. Consider the Cuban ethnic economy of the Miami area, the prototype for the model. Because of its origins in the Castro revolution, the Cuban immigration in its early years included a large portion of the island's former political and business elites, some of whom brought financial capital with them and many of whom possessed business acumen. As a refugee group, the Cubans also benefited from government programs not available to ordinary immigrant groups, ranging from the immediate financial support, resettlement assistance, and job retraining offered by the Cuban Refugee Program to the access to American colleges opened up by an Office of Education loan program targeting Cuban refugees, and finally to the unusual concentration of business loans granted by the Small Business Administration.[101] It is very unlikely that many other groups have the capacity to assemble as robust an ethnic sub-economy as have the Cubans in Miami, and studies of the sectoral concentrations of owners and workers from new immigrant groups have found very few comparable examples.[102]

An ethnic enclave economy encompasses numerous ethnic niches, but not all niches need be embedded in such sub-economies. One can speak of an entrepreneurial niche, such as the Koreans have established in the retail greengrocery trade in New York City, or of an occupational niche, exemplified by the former dominance of the Irish and then the Jews among public school teachers in some cities. An ethnic niche presumes that the group has a sufficient grip on the position to serve as a gatekeeper for new openings, able thus to favor co-ethnics. Demographic and socioeconomic shifts may result in a group's withdrawing from a niche, as white ethnics have from some lines of small business in many American cities, and another group's moving in. Thus the niche idea is frequently linked to that of an ethnic queue, a hierarchical ordering among ethnic groups that determines which groups are best positioned to take advantage of the newly contestable niches.[103]

But not all niches encompass "good" jobs that individuals would be happy to keep if they had alternatives. This seems especially true of many immigrant niches, such as in the ethnic restaurant or garment industries, both of which usually provide low pay. Thus, ethnic loyalty may entail a cost where niche employment is concerned, and there is evidence that as immigrants acculturate and become aware of a wider range of possibilities, they gravitate away from niche positions. In any event, most immigrant niches would seem to hold little attraction for the second generation, assuming that its members find the mainstream economy open to them. Why, for instance, should second-generation Korean Americans want to follow their parents into such demanding lines of work as running fruit-and-vegetable stands or dry-cleaning establishments? Indeed, the choices of their parents seem premised on the possibility that the second generation can take full advantage of the American educational system and catapult well beyond their own economic level.[104] This is, in truth, an old story: the children of entrepreneurially successful parents often prefer to convert their advantaged origins into valuable educational credentials and enter the professions rather than take over the family business. This is what many Jewish garment factory owners found, sometimes to their dismay.[105]

In this chapter, we have examined the reasons why, according to many students of immigration, assimilation might not apply to current immigrant groups as other than an exceptional pattern; and we have scrutinized alternative models. In our view, nothing considered here rules out assimilation as a widespread outcome for the new immigrants and their American-born descendants. The claims that definitive distinctions exist between the new immigration and its Asian and European predecessors, by and large, oversimplify the complex history of immigration to the United States and gloss over the seriousness of the hostility and adjustment problems faced by earlier immigrants and their children. Too often, in our view, these claims seem to read history backward, starting from our present knowledge of the extensive assimilation of European ancestry groups. Obviously, many differences do exist between current and past immigrant groups and their situations in the United States, but to this point at least, the implications are not sufficiently unambiguous as to exclude serious consideration of assimilation on a mass scale. Likewise, the alternative models of ethnic/racial incorporation seem to underplay the fluidity of ethnic boundaries and to understate the incentives for members of the second and third generations to join the mainstream. Our objections do not mean that the alternatives are not also true in some ways: like the assimilation pattern, they are useful as templates that can be applied to some parts of the immigration experience. But if they are true *to the exclusion of the assimilation pattern,* American society will in the future be locked into an elaborate and rigid system of ethnic stratification. This could come to pass, we recognize; but before such a pessimistic prognosis is accepted, the evidence that assimilation also is occurring deserves a full airing.

CHAPTER FIVE

The Background to Contemporary Immigration

Unlike many other societies that harbor large immigrant populations, the United States conceives of itself as an immigration society through and through. (In Germany, by way of contrast, where postwar immigrants and their children make up nearly 10 percent of the population, a familiar refrain is "Wir sind kein Einwanderungsland": "We are not a country of immigration.")[1] Yet what this self-conception has meant for Americans has not been constant throughout our history. In this chapter we consider in greater depth the sociopolitical and legislative background behind contemporary immigration to the United States and how that background has shaped the contemporary streams. We then turn to thumbnail sketches of some of the streams themselves, preparing the way for the empirical evidence of assimilation that occupies the next chapter.

The Ethnocentric Prelude to the Present

The characterization of the United States as an immigration society, while certainly true in comparison to some other economically advanced nations such as Germany and Switzerland, conceals the contested role played by immigration throughout much of American history. A thorough consideration of that history, which is beyond the scope of this chapter,[2] reveals ethnocentric biases that have come to the fore at pivotal moments but that also have been challenged by the powerful momentum of migration flows and by Americans' sense of their mission as an immigrant nation.

Without question, the early European settlers conceived of the new nation as one dominated exclusively by whites.[3] This was underscored by the naturalization law passed in 1790 by the first Congress, which limited citizenship to immigrants who were "free white persons." Though modified after the Civil War to allow naturalization of Africans, this racial stipulation essentially stood for more than a century and a half, barring Asian immigrants from U.S. citizenship. Racial exclusivity was also very apparent in the barriers erected to immigration from Asia, beginning with the Chinese Exclusion Act of 1882, a response to intense agitation by whites in California, and culminating in the restrictive legislation of 1924, which permanently prohibited immigration by Asian "aliens ineligible for citizenship."

In the early twentieth century, ethnocentric biases also came into play with respect to immigration from Europe. After 1896, the countries of northern and western Europe no longer constituted the dominant element in the immigrant flow; now immigrants came mainly from southern and eastern Europe, from the Austro-Hungarian Empire, Italy, and Russia. As immigration crested in the first decade of the twentieth century to reach its then high-water mark, the enormous wave of southern and eastern Europeans provoked spasms of xenophobic anxiety in many native white Americans concerned about their assimilability.[4] Laws to restrict their immigration were not long in coming. Two related laws, passed in 1921 and 1924, set the parameters for immigration for the next four decades.

For Europeans, the parameters were inscribed in a system of quotas based on national origin that favored immigrants from northern and western Europe, for the United States desired not only that there be fewer immigrants but that, in the aggregate, they mirror the ethnic composition of American whites. The logic was that U.S. law should favor immigrants who presumably could most readily assimilate into American society. (Interestingly, though, except for establishing a tiny border patrol, the legislation of the 1920s left untouched immigration from the Western Hemisphere, mainly from Canada and Mexico.) The 1924 act looked toward a system of permanent quotas based on the ethnic origins of the white population as of 1920. Since the census did not then inquire into the ethnic origins of all whites, the difficult inferential task of estimating this composition fell first to a special board of governmental statistical experts and then, when their estimates proved politically unacceptable (too few Americans of German, Irish, and Scandinavian stock), to a study by the American Council of Learned Societies. The ACLS study, led by the famous immigration historian Marcus Hansen, found that the earlier investigation had erred in estimating the ethnic composition of the American population in 1790. Correcting this estimate produced a larger share for northern and western European countries other than Great Britain. The ACLS estimates were more or less accepted as the basis for the permanent quotas, which went into effect in 1929.[5]

This ethnocentric background is an inauspicious prelude to the contemporary immigration, which draws from all corners of the world; and it is not obvious at first glance how the United States got from there to here. The story line that leads to contemporary immigration begins during World War II, which, paradoxically, represents the nadir of immigration: in the war years, 1941–1945, there were only 34,000 immigrants per year, fewer than during the depression years (see Figure 5.1). But the war period demonstrated some of the flaws of the immigration regime established during the 1920s, and the doubts about the wisdom of such a highly restrictive and ethnocentric system would grow and lead to change during the more optimistic and racially progressive 1960s. For one thing, during the war, the United States and its allies strove to present themselves as bastions of democracy and human rights, in strong contrast to the openly racist regimes they opposed. Yet the citizens of one of these allies, China, were not welcome in the United States as immigrants. The affront posed by U.S. immigration policy was symbolically unacceptable once the Chinese were fighting and dying on behalf of the Allied cause. In 1943, Congress repealed the Chinese Exclusion Acts and established a token quota of 105 Chinese immigrants per year, symbolically opening the door again to Chinese immigration. To be sure, during that same period Japanese Americans on the West Coast were interned in concentration camps; so one must be careful not to overstate the degree to which white Americans became attuned to the sensitivities of Asians and Asian Americans. Yet wartime circumstances did create doubt as to the consistency of America's democratic and tolerant self-image with its race- and nationality-based immigration system.

The war also highlighted the nation's inability to deal with the temporary immigration crests associated with refugees. The unwilling-

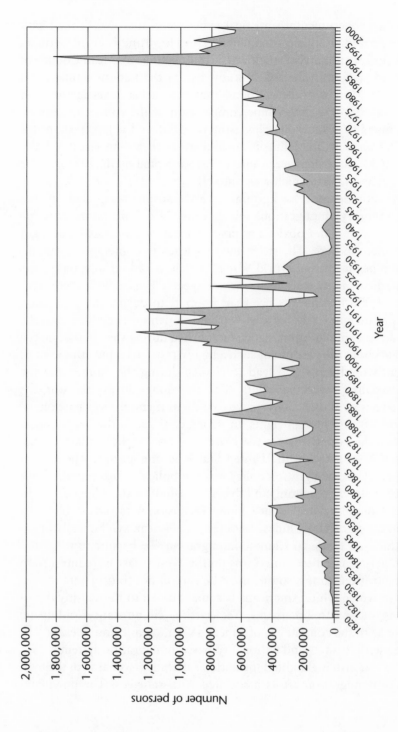

Figure 5.1. Legal immigrants to the United States, 1820–2000.

ness to accept more Jews fleeing Nazi persecution, which might have saved many thousands from Auschwitz and other concentration camps, has rightly been seen as a moral failure of enormous magnitude. Working within the tight constraints of immigration law, President Roosevelt did try to offer sanctuary to some European Jews. In 1941, for instance, before America's entry into the war, he authorized U.S. consulates outside Germany to use the immigration quota for Germans to admit refugees who had fled that country. But, undoubtedly because of nativist and anti-Semitic currents, American public opinion was against any relaxation of immigration laws in behalf of threatened Jews. Even after the war, when the horror of the Holocaust was known and Europe was awash in refugees (including millions of ethnic Germans driven from their eastern European homes), the United States was reluctant to lower its drawbridge. President Truman followed the example of Roosevelt in authorizing the use of national quotas for Germans and Austrians to admit refugees, but between 1946 and 1948, only 40,000 were allowed to enter the United States under this program. In 1948 the administration succeeded in getting the Displaced Persons Act through Congress. This act again followed the principle of using national quotas (including future ones) as the basis for admission, and eventually some 410,000 of the displaced were given refuge. Even so, Truman complained about a provision of the bill that discriminated against some Jewish refugees (based on their date of arrival in displaced persons camps). Ethnic considerations were not dropped even in this attempt to assist those who had been persecuted on ethnic grounds.

The war also revealed the need of the American economy for immigrant labor, especially on its lowest rungs. With the mobilization of many young men into the military and the absorption of many other workers, including women, into essential defense jobs, American agriculture found it impossible to recruit the labor it needed. Consequently, the U.S. government entered into an agreement with Mexico to allow Mexican laborers to migrate temporarily in the United States, a guest worker policy that came to be known as the bracero program. Though conceived as a way to fill a wartime need, the policy survived the war by two decades, ending only in 1964. By then the program had given millions of Mexican workers a taste of life in the United States. Many observers have commented on the connection between the program and the subsequent rise in immigration from

Mexico. The program prefigured subsequent immigration in another way, namely, the post facto legalization of migrants already present in the United States. Although workers were supposed to be recruited in Mexico, in fact many had crossed illegally into the United States before being recruited by growers. This early form of amnesty even had its own demeaning sobriquet: it was known as "drying out the wetbacks," "wetbacks" being a derogatory name for Mexican illegals (who were all imagined to have swum across the Rio Grande).[6]

The pressures on U.S. immigration policy intensified in the postwar period, when the United States was recognized as the leader of the "free world" in the ideological cold war against communist states. Contradictions between the rhetorical stance of the United States and its treatment of racial minorities at home and through its immigration policy were impossible to overlook for long, and so movement toward reform haltingly began to make itself manifest. A first attempt was the McCarran-Walter Act, also known as the Immigration Act of 1952. This law finally did away entirely with the remaining racist restrictions on naturalization; Asians born outside the United States were no longer "aliens ineligible for citizenship," and annual quotas were established for the various Asian nationalities previously lacking them. The law further contributed to immigration from Asia by allowing American citizens to bring their spouses into the country outside of any national origins quota. At the time, this mainly affected the numerous Japanese and Korean women who had married American servicemen. The principle that reunification of close family members with their U.S.-citizen relatives was not to be restricted by quotas was to become a pillar of the immigration system after 1965.

The McCarran-Walter Act made no fundamental change to the system of national origins quotas, leaving intact this patently ethnocentric element of U.S. immigration law, but it introduced one other innovation that became central to subsequent reform: it set up a preference system for allocating immigrant visas among the applicants from each nation. Yet in one respect the act was distinctly retrograde, sliding back toward the ethnocentrism of earlier legislation. It established for the first time distinct quotas for the colonies of other nations, whose inhabitants previously could enter the United States under the quotas of their metropoles. Since these colonial quotas were pegged at just one hundred immigrants per year, this provision was effectively a form of discrimination against Third World peoples. It especially constrained the residents of the English-ruled Caribbean islands, who were overwhelmingly of African ancestry.

During the 1950s and early 1960s, the problems of refugee populations, especially from communist-ruled nations, continued to pose challenges for the U.S. immigration system. In 1953, Congress passed new legislation to allow approximately 200,000 refugees to enter during the next three years. In 1956, just as this legislation was about to expire, the failed Hungarian revolt produced hundreds of thousands of new refugees, who initially fled to nearby European countries. At least in part for ideological reasons, the United States wanted to recognize its responsibility for these refugees from communist "tyranny," so the Eisenhower administration introduced yet another innovation in the field of immigration policy: the use of the parole power of the U.S. attorney general to grant temporary permission to reside in the United States en masse to 30,000 Hungarians. Subsequent legislation, in 1958, made their residence permanent. The biggest refugee crisis of the period resulted from the Cuban revolution of 1959. When Fidel Castro overthrew the dictatorship of Fulgencio Batista, tens of thousands of the country's former elites and middle classes fled. From 1959 to 1962, 200,000 were admitted to the United States on temporary visitors' visas. This first wave inaugurated a refugee migration that has continued, with ups and downs since then.

Immigration as of the early 1960s was not just a matter of refugee inflows. Indeed, the immigration stream was once again widening, recovering from the drought that followed the restrictive legislation of the 1920s and was exacerbated by the Great Depression and World War II. From 1950 on, the number of immigrants again exceeded 200,000 per year, and between 1961 and 1965, it averaged close to 300,000 annually. The quota system was in disarray, as two-thirds of the immigrants entered outside of the national origins quotas.[7] The sources of immigration were shifting once again. Europe was still an important source, though not nearly as much as it had been before the 1930s. Of the 297,000 immigrants who came in 1965, for instance, fewer than 40 percent (114,000) were from Europe, and only a few European countries—the United Kingdom, Germany, Italy, and Poland, in order of magnitude—were the source of more than a few thousand. An increasing number came from the Western Hemisphere, particularly the other countries of North America. Canada and Mexico, each with nearly 40,000 immigrants that year, contributed more

than any European country. Immigration from both countries had figured importantly during the early decades of the century and experienced a rapid recovery throughout the postwar period. In the case of
Mexico, the bracero program may have been a contributing factor,
though Mexican immigration might have swelled anyway, along with
that from the United States' northern neighbor. Immigration from
other continents was still of minor significance. Yet immigration was
poised to play a major role once again, and the case for the reform of
immigration law was becoming irresistible.

Immigration Reform: The 1965 Law and Its Aftermath

The 1960s were a triumphal period for American optimism about social reform, especially in the area of race relations. The civil rights
movement pushed race relations further and faster than they had gone
at any point since Reconstruction. The Kennedy presidency held out
the promise that the barriers to racial equality would be rolled back;
and after Kennedy's assassination, President Johnson made known his
own determination to make substantial progress. The civil rights im-
pulse had significant effects in the field of immigration; indeed, the racial and ethnocentric biases of immigration law could not withstand
the scrutiny generated by the drive to achieve formal racial equality.
Kennedy had entered his presidency intending to reform the immigration system, a goal he had articulated in *A Nation of Immigrants*
(1958) while a U.S. senator; and the momentum created by his proposal to Congress in 1963 was not blunted by his death. The legislation that resulted, the Immigration Act of 1965, has probably had, in
the long run, an impact on American society as deep as the initially
more acclaimed civil rights laws of the decade.

To begin with, this law, also known as the Hart-Celler Act, dismantled the offensive system of national origins quotas in favor of a uniform annual quota of 20,000 for each country in the Eastern Hemisphere. No quotas were established for the countries of the Western
Hemisphere (they were to come later in the Immigration Act of 1976).
The law did not allow the enormous number of immigrants that the
national quotas in aggregate might seem to imply, for total immigration from each hemisphere was capped in any year at 170,000 for
the Eastern Hemisphere and 120,000 for the Western (this latter being
the first such restriction ever placed on immigration from this hemisphere). These caps were not absolute, however, because close rela-

tives of U.S. citizens—parents, spouses, and minor children—were exempt from numerical limitations, and their arrival could lift the immigration totals well above the legislated ceilings.

To distribute immigration visas among the applicants from each country of the Eastern Hemisphere, the law applied a greatly revised version of the preference system inaugurated by the earlier McCarran-Walter Act. The highest priority was given to family reunification: three-quarters of the immigration slots were to be awarded on the basis of a family connection to U.S. citizens and permanent residents. Thus, one preference was reserved for the adult children of citizens, who were not exempt from quota restrictions, as were their minor-age siblings; another was for the siblings of U.S. citizens. Other slots (20 percent) were to be allocated based on labor market qualifications. In addition to highly trained individuals (i.e., professionals and scientists), these preferences allowed the entry of workers in any occupations in which the supply of American workers was not adequate (domestics, for example). Finally, a small number of places, about 10,000, were reserved for refugees.

While the 1965 legislation took a giant step in the direction of a universalistic immigration system, its practical impact was felt most heavily in a few regions of the world. The racist notion of an "Asiatic Barred Zone" was finally consigned to the junk heap of history. Immediately, immigration from Asia surged: in 1965, just 21,000 Asian immigrants were permitted to enter, but by 1970 the figure had nearly quintupled, to 93,000. The new law had beneficial effects also for Afro-Caribbeans by doing away with the hundred-person quotas that had been in place since the early 1950s. As a consequence, immigration from the English-speaking West Indies shot upwards, increasing nearly sixfold in just five years, from 4,700 in 1965 to 27,300 in 1970. And it also opened the door to an expansion of the then minimal immigration from Africa (totaling just 3,000 immigrants from the entire continent in 1965). Perhaps because of the pervasive racism that Africans would face in the United States, they took less than full advantage of the opening, but even so their immigration had increased 250 percent by 1970. For Latin America, however, the effect of the law was actually constraining because of the new numerical limit on immigration from the Western Hemisphere. Total North American immigration consequently remained relatively stable between 1965 and 1970.

Much has been written about the ethnocentric impulses that lay behind the universalistic formulation of the 1965 law, whose ultimate effects were certainly not foreseen by its creators. They expected that, because of the overwhelming priority given to family reunification, the law would ethnically recalibrate immigration, effectively achieving the goal of the 1920s legislation of generating a stream that would not alter by much the racial/ethnic composition of the American people. It was anticipated that southern and eastern Europeans in particular, who by then had found acceptance as mainstream Americans, would make up for the shortfall in their immigration imposed by the previous, discriminatory system. Explicit reassurances were given to Congress, by Attorney General Robert Kennedy among others, that few Asians would immigrate if the law were adopted.[8] Other observers have pointed out that the significance of the law has been overstated because the increase in immigration and the shift away from Europe predated the 1965 act.[9] But these points, though factually valid, do not deter us from seeing the 1965 Immigration Act as the watershed for U.S. immigration. Even if the consequences were initially misunderstood, the United States was in effect declaring that it was prepared to accept newcomers from all over the world. When it became clear that the new law in fact encouraged unanticipated sources of immigration, the United States did not repudiate it. Subsequent legislation has instead expanded immigration.

The 1965 act set in place the main outlines of the system of immigration that exists today, though some elements have been significantly altered in the interim. The most fateful of the subsequent changes has probably been the 1976 Immigration Act, which brought the Western Hemisphere under the same regime of uniform country quotas and preferences for allocating visas that applied to the Eastern Hemisphere. While at first glance this seems only logical, it fails to take into account the unique immigration role of the United States' neighbors, especially Mexico. The failure to find a formula that would allow for a larger immigration from Mexico has contributed greatly to the problem of illegal immigration from south of the border. Given the willingness of American employers—not just the growers of the agricultural Southwest and California but increasingly those in urban industries needing low-wage labor—to hire Mexican workers regardless of their residence papers, and given also the long and inadequately patrolled border, it was inevitable that a narrowing of the legally permitted flow would divert others into illegal channels.[10]

Soon afterward, the subject of "illegal" or "undocumented" immigration—the alternative names reveal something of the political charge in the topic—came to dominate discussions of immigration and legislative efforts to regulate it. A number of attempts were made to estimate the size of this largely hidden population, which leaves only imperfectly detectable traces in government statistics such as the census.[11] The estimates varied wildly. In 1974, Commissioner Leonard Chapman of the Immigration and Naturalization Service (INS) stated that the number was "possibly as great as 10 or 12 million," and he subsequently attempted to ring alarm bells with a declaration that "we're facing a vast army that's carrying out a silent invasion of the United States."[12] Other estimates—made, one hopes, by cooler heads—came in considerably lower. When the Select Commission on Immigration and Refugee Policy, appointed by Congress in the late 1970s, made its report, it tried to avoid a specific estimate, recognizing that the absence of hard data undermined the credibility of any single number. Its experts argued, however, that the number was "almost certainly below 6 million" and "possibly only 3.5 to 5 million."[13] This population was (and is) considerably more diverse than is suggested by the popular stereotype of the clandestine border crosser (also known in INS bureaucratic parlance as an EWI, or "entry without inspection"). A large fraction, perhaps close to half, of undocumented immigrants have entered the United States legally, on tourist or student visas, for instance, but overstayed the period of validity.[14] Mexican nationals constitute the largest fraction of the illegal population, but it is otherwise quite diverse in its sources.[15] When a ship named the *Golden Venture* ran aground off New York City in the early 1990s, it revealed the scale of the smuggling of Chinese illegals, and in the 1980s, the presence of a sizable Irish illegal population became known. Many of the undocumented are not permanent residents but sojourners who come to the United States temporarily to make money and then return home. Surveys in areas of Mexico from which many legal and illegal migrants come reveal surprisingly large fractions of the population who have made one or more trips across the border.[16] Yet some illegals do in the end seek a way to stay legally in the United States. They can be found among the large number of "immigrants" counted each year in INS statistics who are not new arrivals but residents who have managed at last to obtain the coveted "green card" (actually now pink) of the permanent resident alien.[17] (In 1997, for example, about half of the approximately 800,000 immigrants "admitted" were already residing in the United States, most of them legally so.)

The main legislative attempt to manage the undocumented flow was the Immigration Reform and Control Act of 1986 (also known as IRCA). It illustrates the difficulties of controlling clandestine immigration, especially when these immigrants meet domestic economic needs. The act offered three main prongs for attacking the problem. First, and in hindsight foremost, was a complex amnesty program. It gave legal status to those who could prove that they had resided in the United States for a long period: those who had been continuously resident for a number of years were entitled to receive green cards immediately, while others in residence more recently could become temporary legal residents with the right to apply subsequently for permanent status. In a more controversial provision, which gave rise to a considerable amount of fraud, individuals who could demonstrate that they had worked in U.S. agriculture for periods of three months in certain years could also obtain legal resident status. The impact was enormous. By the end of 1992, more than 2.7 million people had gained legal residency as a result of IRCA, about 1.6 million by demonstrating long residence and 1.1 million under the agricultural worker provision. The large majority of those amnestied, about 2 million in all, were Mexicans.

The amnesty afforded by the law reduced the size of the illegal population already present in the United States. The other two prongs of the attack aimed to reduce future flows. One was straightforward: increased funding for the border patrol. The other, more contested, was intended to weaken the economic magnet through employer sanctions. The idea was to penalize employers who knowingly hired illegals; but between idea and legal implementation, something was lost in translation. In fact, there was substantial political resistance to punishing employers, and in the end Congress settled for a requirement that employers be able to demonstrate that they had examined some document showing that a prospective employee was legally present. They were not, however, required to check its validity. The employer sanctions were thus rendered toothless, since even counterfeit documents could keep an employer from suffering any sanctions.

The impact of IRCA on the flow of illegals and on the size of the illegal population was difficult to measure for obvious reasons. But in retrospect it is clear that it provided no more than short-term relief.

Indirect measures of the cross-border flow, such as the number of border patrol apprehensions, suggest that there may have been a several-year dip in clandestine entries after IRCA was passed; but the decrease was temporary.[18] The hot economy of the 1990s lured many undocumented immigrants to the United States, with the consequence that the 2000 U.S. Census counted millions more people than anticipated, many of them part of an illegal population that amounted to perhaps 8 million at that time.[19] IRCA may itself have encouraged some to become documented residents by holding out the hope of a future amnesty.

Those legalized under IRCA were counted in the immigration statistics of the early 1990s, and they created a huge bulge in the apparent number of immigrants. For fiscal year 1991, for instance, that number was more than 1.8 million, 1.1 million of whom were due directly to IRCA. The act generated further immigration because Congress had subsequently (in 1990) given legal residence to the spouses and children of immigrants legalized under it. Finally, IRCA created a large class of people who are able under U.S. immigration law eventually to bring in their relatives.

The problems of refugees have also received attention in the post-1965 period. The Refugee Act of 1980, written in the aftermath of overlapping waves of refugees from Cuba, the Soviet Union, and Southeast Asia, attempted to bring some coherence to the treatment of those seeking haven in the United States. To start with, it brought the U.S. definition of a refugee in line with the international standard set by the United Nations Protocol on the Status of Refugees: namely, a refugee is someone who has left her or his country and is unwilling to return because of "a well-founded fear of persecution due to race, religion, nationality, membership in a particular group, or political opinion."[20] It also aimed to allow some flexibility in dealing with the unpredictable nature of refugee flows, while keeping them within a predetermined numerical limitation, by permitting the president, in consultation with the Congress, to declare annual ceilings on the number of refugees the United States will accept. What it could not do was eliminate the essentially political decision of determining who will be recognized as a refugee. Hence, during the 1980s, the Cubans and Nicaraguans fleeing from communist regimes were recognized as refugees (or asylum seekers, in cases where they were already present on U.S. territory), whereas Guatemalans and Salvadorans generally were not. Throughout the 1980s, when many Haitians attempted to flee the oppressive political and economic conditions in their country, U.S. policy under Presidents Reagan and Bush was to intercept their boats at sea and turn them back. The contrast with the reception accorded Cuban *balseros* traveling the same waters could not have been stronger.

By the 1990s, the system inaugurated by the 1965 law was yielding an immigration as large and diverse as any previously experienced by the United States, or any other nation for that matter.[21] The system remained under adjustment. Thus, immigration legislation in 1990 substantially increased the size of the pool of preferences reserved for economic immigrants—that is, those who could qualify based on the need for their occupations or the skills, qualifications, or wealth they possessed—without reducing the number of slots to be allocated according to family connections. The law thereby raised the total number of immigrants who would be allowed in within the framework of numerical limitations (to 675,000 at the time). The per country limit also was allowed to float based on an annually set formula; in 1997 the limit was determined to be 25,620.[22] But the ability of certain immediate family members to enter outside of any numerical limitations remained as before. In addition, the act added a new category, the "diversity" immigrants, coming from countries with low volumes of immigration in recent years, whose immigration had presumably been adversely affected by the emphasis on family ties and labor market qualifications. Following an entirely new tack, the law specified that these diversity slots, 55,000 per year, were to be awarded by lottery, subject only to the provision that, for the first several years, 40 percent would go to natives of Ireland. The reservation of so many slots for the Irish reveals the ethnic currents that are in play whenever matters of immigration policy are decided, but the diversity of immigration guarantees that, unlike in the past, these currents will now come from many directions.

The diversity of immigration is displayed in Tables 5.1 and 5.2. The first shows the distribution by region of origin and the second the fifteen leading nations in immigration for the three-decade period 1968–2000, and specifically for the last five years of that period. The data for the longer period capture the immigration following the 1965 act, which did not take full effect until 1968; the immigration of 1996–2000 allows us to see how the diversity of contemporary immi-

Table 5.1. The regional origins of U.S. immigration, 1968–2000 and 1996–2000

	1968–2000		1996–2000	
	N	% of total	N	% of total
Africa	683,121	3.12	222,771	5.76
Asia & Oceania	7,696,170	35.10	1,284,043	33.22
Europe	3,194,045	14.56	583,397	15.10
North America	9,009,824	41.09	1,517,194	39.25
Caribbean	2,565,455	11.70	457,502	11.84
Central America	1,102,988	5.03	233,303	6.04
Other N. Amer.	5,341,381	24.36	826,389	21.38
South America	1,342,426	6.12	257,699	6.67
Total Immigration	21,925,586		3,865,104	

Source: Annual Reports of the U.S. Immigration and Naturalization Service, Washington, D.C.

gration differs from that of the period as a whole. One difference has to be noted at the outset: the volume of immigration has increased over the three decades. The average number of legal immigrants for the 1996–2000 period was 773,000, far above the number that prevailed in the pre-1965 period but also 16 percent above the annual average since 1968. (According to the National Research Council's 1997 report on immigration, an additional 200,000–300,000 illegal immigrants enter the United States each year.)[23]

There is a remarkable consistency between the entire period and the more recent one in the contributions made by large regions as well as by specific nations. If one disaggregates the North American immigration into its various regional components (the Caribbean area, Central America, and other North America, including Canada and Mexico), then the leading region of immigration since 1968 has been Asia. It has been the source of slightly more than a third of all immigrants for the entire period, and this fraction is virtually identical for the most recent period. Following close on its heels have been the U.S. neighbors, Canada and Mexico. They account for nearly a quarter of the immigrants over the entire period; since this fraction, however, is partly due to the contribution of IRCA legalizations to Mexico's total, the fraction drops somewhat in the recent period, when "other North American immigration" accounts for a bit more than a fifth of the total. Despite the common depiction of contemporary immigration as

Table 5.2. The top fifteen sources of U.S. immigration, 1968–2000 and 1996–2000

	1968–2000			1996–2000	
		N	% of total		N	% of total
1.	Mexico	4,534,426	20.68	Mexico	763,504	19.75
2.	Philippines	1,427,607	6.51	Philippines	212,959	5.51
3.	China[a]	1,361,648	6.21	Mainland China	197,615	5.11
4.	Vietnam	1,005,243	4.58	India	191,695	4.96
5.	India	840,379	3.83	Vietnam	145,375	3.76
6.	Korea	800,863	3.65	Dominican Republic	122,444	3.17
7.	Dominican Republic	769,822	3.51	Cuba	112,391	2.91
8.	Cuba	746,246	3.40	El Salvador	87,646	2.27
9.	USSR[b]	645,427	2.94	Haiti	85,788	2.22
10.	Jamaica	576,422	2.63	Jamaica	82,808	2.14
11.	United Kingdom	458,576	2.09	Russia	77,286	2.00
12.	El Salvador	465,038	2.12	Korea	75,362	1.95
13.	Canada	431,338	1.97	Ukraine	70,156	1.82
14.	Haiti	391,824	1.79	Pakistan	66,611	1.72
15.	Colombia	352,575	1.61	Colombia	63,587	1.65
	Total Immigration	21,925,586			3,865,104	

Source: Annual Reports of the U.S. Immigration and Naturalization Service, Washington, D.C.

Notes: a. For 1968–2000, the count of Chinese immigrants includes those from Taiwan and Hong Kong. In U.S. immigration statistics, Mainland China and Taiwan were not separately tabulated until 1982. b. Although the USSR no longer exists, it was the political unit from which emigrants were leaving through most of the 1968–2000 period, and we therefore must retain "USSR" in reporting data for the whole period.

non-European, Europe is far from negligible as a source: for the entire period, about one of every seven immigrants was European. Currently, European immigration is sustained by immigrants from the former Eastern bloc nations (including Russia), who were unable to leave their countries at the beginning of the new immigration era. The Caribbean region and the countries of Central and South America are about equal in their representation in the immigrant flow. Each region accounts for 11 to 13 percent of the immigration of the entire period and of the more recent one. In terms of region of origin, the most notable change in the more recent period is the growing contingent of immigrants from Africa, who constitute 6 percent more recently compared to just 3 percent overall since 1968.

The consistency of representation of each country among immigrants is quite striking. The more recent period shows few gross changes from the rank ordering that prevailed for the thirty-three-year period as a whole. In first place is Mexico, the country of origin of 20 percent of the immigrants in 1996–2000. Four of the next five nations in the more recent rank order are Asian—the Philippines, China, India, and Vietnam, in closely spaced order—each of which represents roughly 4 to 6 percent of the immigration of the 1996–2000 period. These nations all have figured prominently throughout the post-1965 period. The only substantial change to this grouping has been the decline of Korea as a source of immigrants: for the three-decade period it is in sixth place, but more recently it has fallen to twelfth. Another change worthy of note is the appearance during the 1990s of separate immigrations from Russia and other states once part of the Soviet Union.

Except for the nations of the former communist bloc, which tightly restricted emigration prior to its breakup, all of the contributing nations in the more recent top fifteen have been central to the entire new immigration era in the United States; and, with the modest exceptions of Canada and the United Kingdom, no nation with an equivalent role for the entire three-decade period fails to appear among the top fifteen for 1996–2000. The top nations, moreover, account for a large fraction of the total—two-thirds for the immigration of the entire period. Hence, while there has certainly been variability in immigration because of external events, such as the arrival of tens of thousands of Iranians in the decade following the overthrow of the shah in 1979, there has also been a great deal of continuity. Thus, studying what has happened to the immigrants and their descendants coming from the top fifteen countries should tell us a great deal about the prospects of the new immigration as a whole.

Major Immigrant Groups

We focus in this section on the non-European groups, for they are thought to represent the hard test for assimilation. In what follows, we briefly describe the nature of each of the main non-European streams. For this purpose we have selected from Table 5.2 the five leading sources of immigration from the Western Hemisphere (Mexico, the Dominican Republic, Cuba, Jamaica, and El Salvador) and from the Eastern Hemisphere exclusive of Europe (Philippines, China, Vietnam, India, and Korea). These descriptions provide the essential backdrop to our analysis of assimilatory patterns in Chapter 6.

Mexicans

Of the contemporary immigration groups, the Mexicans have the longest record of significant continuous inflow. Mexican Americans are not all immigrants, for tens of thousands remained in the territory that the United States acquired by virtue of the Treaty of Guadalupe Hildalgo (1848) and the Gadsden Purchase (1853) following the U.S.-Mexico War. (They remained in part because the treaty promised that their property and cultural rights would be respected, a promise that was not kept.)[24] Exactly how many migrated between Mexico and the new U.S. territories in the subsequent decades is impossible to know because the border was highly porous and largely unmonitored. But by the end of the nineteenth century, Mexico had developed a railroad system that linked its internal regions as far south as Mexico City to the northern border. This system promoted migration directly, as a means of rapid transportation to the border, and indirectly, as a conduit for goods and ideas that originated in the Anglo society to the north.[25]

The first large wave of immigration from Mexico came in the period 1900–1930. It has been estimated that this large and only partly counted flow (the United States did not begin to keep any records of crossings at its southern border until the first decade of the twentieth century) caused a loss of 10 percent in the Mexican population.[26] There were multiple factors at work on both sides of the border in stimulating it. On the American side, the demand for unskilled labor in the Southwest and California grew in tandem with the region's population and the development of its agricultural, mining, and railroad industries. Moreover, other sources of low-wage labor were drying up as the United States excluded any further immigration from China (in 1882) and Japan (in 1908), and the influx of European immigrants was mostly cut off by World War I and then by the restrictive legislation of the 1920s. It was logical, in any event, for employers in California and the Southwest to look southward toward the nearest source of cheap labor, and the U.S. government obliged them by leaving the border unpatrolled until 1924. Even then, impediments to crossing the border undetected were not serious, and so many Mexicans were able to avoid the literacy test and fees then required of legal immigrants. On the Mexican side, economic changes occurring in the late nineteenth and early twentieth centuries, promoted by the policies of the Mexican government, led to the consolidation of land tracts in large, privately owned haciendas, at the cost of the small-holdings of independent farmers and communally owned lands known as *ejidos*. Consequently, many in the countryside were deprived of an independent livelihood and driven into a precarious existence in the agricultural proletariat. Then, from 1910 to 1920, the Mexican Revolution brought intermittent periods of bloody strife, making parts of the countryside unsafe. In 1910, the U.S. Census counted just 162,000 Mexicans (an underestimate, granted), but in the next decade more than 200,000 arrived, and during the 1920s almost 450,000.[27]

This immigration was tolerated by the United States only so long as cheap Mexican labor was needed. Americans were even more skeptical of Mexicans as part of the American nation than they were of southern and eastern Europeans. So, when the Great Depression ended the need for Mexican labor and made unemployed Mexicans and their families a burden on the relief rolls, hundreds of thousands were repatriated.[28] The repatriation, which has no parallel in the experiences of other U.S. immigrant groups, was organized at both federal and local levels. The federal government undertook to locate and deport illegal immigrants. But more offensive to a sense of justice were the efforts at the local level, which at times ignored such niceties as legal rights. Local governments financially sponsored voluntary repatriations insofar as possible—Los Angeles paid the train fare home for unemployed migrants, for instance—but immigrants often were cajoled or coerced into cooperating. Some had resided in the United States for decades and were U.S. citizens. Once back on Mexican soil, the former U.S. residents were not allowed to return. In Los Angeles, the repatriation reduced the Mexican population by one-third and transformed the community into one dominated by the second generation.[29]

Then, as soon as the need for Mexican labor became apparent at the start of World War II, American policy swung in the other direction. In 1942 the bracero program began, and with it were planted the seeds of the immigration that continues today. Although the braceros—several million by the time the program ended in 1964—were intended to be only seasonal workers, they brought home from the United States not just dollars but also information about job opportunities and wages. Legal and illegal immigration sprang up in response. If one is willing to accept the number apprehended at the border as an indication of the number who got through illegally, then their numbers appear to have risen tremendously: in 1943, only about 12,000 were caught trying to cross the border, but little more than a decade later, in 1954, the number surpassed 1 million.[30] Illegal immigrants surveyed in the 1950s asserted that they had come to the United States after learning by word of mouth about employment opportunities.[31] While legal immigration had numbered less than 10,000 a year in the late 1940s and early 1950s, in 1956 it soared to its first postwar peak, 65,000 Mexicans, constituting 20 percent of all immigrants in that year.

Thus began an era in which Mexico was rather consistently the largest single source of U.S. immigrants. Initially, immigration from Mexico was favored by the absence of any numerical quotas; other requirements involving health, literacy, and means of support, however, kept the number from rising even further. The 1965 law for the first time placed a ceiling on total immigration from the Western Hemisphere, though in a bow to the need for Mexican labor in the Southwest, especially given the ending of the bracero program the year before, it imposed no per nation limit (that of 20,000 from any country was set for the nations of the Eastern Hemisphere, it will be recalled). The law did make immigration from Mexico more difficult for some, however; and waiting lists developed in Mexico and other Latin American countries.[32] In the late 1970s, Congress added to the restrictions by extending the 20,000-person limit to all nations. This was particularly hard on the Mexicans, whose immigration had consistently exceeded that total since the early 1950s.

Yet legal immigration from Mexico has continued to grow. During the 1970s, more than 600,000 arrived; the number increased in the next decade to more than 1 million. The figure for the 1990s was much larger still, 2.6 million, partly because of the legalizations under the amnesty provisions of the 1986 IRCA law. While nothing in the intricate maze of immigration law can be considered entirely simple, the single most important explanation for the growth of legal immigration from Mexico beyond the IRCA amnesty program is the ability of U.S. citizens to bring in their immediate relatives outside of numerical limitations. This provision guarantees the potential for a large immigration from Mexico for the foreseeable future (but, as we noted in the last chapter, the demographics of the young adult population in Mexico will stabilize the pool of those most likely to immigrate). The importance of the provision is indicated by the fact that in 1995–1997, the parents, spouses, and children of U.S. citizens accounted for 34 percent of all immigrants.[33] Illegal immigration from Mexico remains a powerful force also. According to INS estimates, the undocumented population from Mexico grew at an annual rate of at least 150,000 during the first half of the 1990s.[34] In light of the larger than expected total undocumented population revealed by the 2000 U.S. Census, this is probably an underestimate.

Mexican immigrants have mostly gone to areas of traditional settlement, which have large Mexican American communities, though there are now signs of change in their distribution across the United States. In the quarter century between the late 1960s and the early 1990s, the premier area of settlement was southern California, especially the Los Angeles region. Texas is another common area of settlement: in the 1960s, El Paso was the third most common destination, but in the early 1990s it was overtaken by Houston. The other top destination, Chicago, is a bit surprising in view of the stereotypical assumption that Mexicans are concentrated near the border; but it has rather consistently appeared among the top three since the 1960s and ranked second in 1993.[35] Concentrations of Mexicans are now appearing in numerous places where they have not settled before. One of the more surprising is New York City, whose Hispanic population was dominated until recently by Puerto Ricans, with no visible presence of Mexicans at all. According to the 2000 U.S. Census, however, the Mexican population in the New York City region swelled more than threefold during the 1990s. Also noteworthy is the appearance of Mexican communities in places that have not received immigrants in the modern era, such as rural parts of the South. Mexicans, then, have become the ubiquitous face of contemporary immigration.

The socioeconomic character of Mexican immigration has not altered very much in recent decades, and it still represents the largest supply of low-wage labor coming to the United States. The 1990 census, which counted much of the resident illegal population, shows Mexicans ranking at the bottom in educational attainment among all immigrant groups, with just a quarter of adults having completed high school. Correspondingly, the Mexican immigration contains one of the highest proportions of low-skilled workers: in 1993, for instance, nearly half of all immigrants were counted as operators and laborers.[36] When critics of current U.S. immigration policy speak of the relative decline in the skill levels of recent immigrants, it is the Mexican immigration they have in mind as the prime example. Taking the wage gap between native-born Americans and immigrants as an indicator of underlying disparities in labor market skills, the 1997 report of the National Research Council notes that the wages of recently arrived Mexican male immigrants declined from 62 percent of natives' wages in 1970 to 50 percent in 1990.[37] Despite this evidence, there can be little doubt that immigration from Mexico is socially selective and generally includes individuals with above-average levels of education. Moreover, such a huge immigration is almost of necessity more diverse than averages can reveal. While only 2.6 percent of immigrants born in Mexico were engaged in professional occupations in 1990, this still represented more than 75,000 professionals, a relatively large contingent compared to other foreign-born groups.[38]

The social machinery seems in place for a continuation of large-scale immigration from Mexico for the foreseeable future, even if it becomes pinched somewhat by demographic changes in the young adult population. Prior experience in the United States gives individuals detailed knowledge about the legal and illegal pathways into the country and about specific job opportunities and how to take advantage of them. The dissemination of this knowledge throughout social networks brings it within reach of ever larger fractions of the Mexican population. This stock of human and social capital has been growing over time in Mexico.[39] The impact of future immigration is virtually certain to be felt not only in the traditional receiving grounds for Mexican immigrants in the Southwest but in other parts of the United States as well. If the present is any indication of the future, there is certain to be considerable illegal as well as legal immigration from Mexico. One of the large unanswered questions surrounding Mexican immigration concerns the disadvantages transmitted by illegal immigrant parents, who are generally pushed to the margins of the U.S. labor market, to their children, many of whom reside legally in the United States by virtue of their birth on this side of the border.

Cubans

Cuban immigration has a very different origin. Prior to the late 1950s, immigration from Cuba was quite modest: the 1960 census, taken when the exodus of refugees from the Castro regime was already under way, found only 124,000 Cubans and Cuban Americans in the United States. But that number was to grow rapidly over the next few years. Not only were virtually all Cubans welcomed in the United States as refugees if they could reach its territory (from 1959 until 1994, when President Clinton ended the policy), but also many received generous government assistance in resettling.

The first in a series of distinct waves lasted from 1959 until fall 1962, when commercial flights between Cuba and the United States ceased as a result of the Cuban missile crisis. Approximately 200,000 Cubans landed in the United States during this period; and at the high point of the inflow, 3,000 arrived each week.[40] This first wave, sometimes dubbed the "golden" wave, disproportionately included the military, political, and economic elites of pre-Castro society. Individuals who had held high positions in the previous regime, which was propped up by U.S. support, obviously had reason to flee. But business and professional elites, recognizing that the new regime intended a thoroughgoing social revolution in Cuban society, also saw that their chances would be dim in the new Cuba and took advantage of the opportunity to leave. These refugees came primarily from Havana and other cities, and their educational attainment averaged well above that of Cuban society as a whole. They also tended to be light-skinned, a fact of no small significance, given the fateful role of skin color in the country they were entering.[41]

The immigrants of this first wave laid the foundation for the subsequent economic success of the Cuban community in Miami. This was not because its members brought significant wealth with them; despite their previous affluence, most arrived with little money. But what many did bring was business and professional know-how; and despite an initial economic setback as a result of the exodus and loss of status in the United States, many subsequently rebounded, and some rather quickly achieved success. Carlos Arboleya, a bank official in Cuba who left in 1960 when the banks were nationalized, arrived with his family and $40. Though initially forced to work as an inventory clerk in a shoe factory, by 1968 he was president of a bank in Miami.[42] He and the hundreds of other Cubans who became bank officials in Miami helped to fuel the Cuban sub-economy by providing "character loans" to prospective Cuban entrepreneurs, which were based not on the tangible assets of a Miami business but on the Cuban reputation of its owner.[43]

Besides the initiative and business acumen of these immigrants, the policies of the U.S. government also played a pivotal part in Cuban success. As refugees from the only communist regime in the Western Hemisphere, they were welcomed with open arms. Although the Cuban Refugee Program, initiated by the Eisenhower and Kennedy administrations, was based on the premise that the stay of the exiles was to be temporary, the reality of its permanence soon set in. Therefore, in 1966, Congress enacted the Cuban Adjustment Act, which allowed the refugees then present in the United States to become permanent residents and eventually U.S. citizens if they so desired. In addition, through the Cuban Refugee Program, the U.S. government provided $1.4 billion in resettlement aid, some of it in the form of small-business loans.[44]

The second major wave of refugees took place between 1965 and 1973, after President Johnson declared that the United States would accept all Cubans who reached its shores, and airline flights were resumed by agreement between the two governments. More than a quarter million Cubans immigrated during this period, but not everyone was free to come. Both governments regulated the selection of refugees, with priority given on the U.S. side to the relatives of Cubans already here. The Cuban government for its part prevented the emigration of young men of military age and of many individuals whose skills would represent a loss for the Cuban economy. Nevertheless, this wave brought over large numbers of the island's petite bourgeoisie, including many small merchants, craftsmen, and other skilled workers.[45] The motives for immigration were shifting over time, and many of the immigrants came as much in search of economic opportunity as out of opposition to the Castro regime and the socialist society it was creating.

Airline flights ceased again in 1973, and few Cubans arrived until the third wave started in April 1980. These immigrants, the "Marielitos," were by far the most controversial of the Cuban émigrés. Approximately 125,000 new arrivals were brought to the United States by a chaotic "freedom flotilla," set in motion by Castro's decision to open the port of Mariel to any Cuban who wanted to leave. Thousands of private boats piloted by Cuban Americans set out from Florida and returned with human cargo. This wave was stigmatized in the minds of Americans by the allegation that the Cuban regime was using this means to get rid of many criminals and other undesirable elements. Subsequent research, however, indicates that the Marielitos were primarily members of the Cuban working class who could no longer bear the privations of Cuban life and who were young enough to have hopes of achieving higher status in the United States. This third wave included a large number of black Cubans. There was also, it is true, a high proportion—about 20 percent—of Cubans who had spent time in jail. But since the Castro regime had criminalized all forms of dissent and many other behaviors, such as homosexuality, that were tolerated in the United States, a jail term by itself was not a strong indicator of what Americans would view as criminal inclinations.[46]

After Mariel, another lull set in, only to be broken by the desperation of many Cubans to leave for the United States. Although Cuba and the United States agreed in the mid-1980s to allow 20,000 or more immigrants per year, only a tenth as many visas were being issued. This time, Cubans set out to sea on their own, frequently attempting to cross ninety miles of open water on tiny rafts or even on car tires. The *balseros*, as they came to be known, were putting their lives at risk, but hope or desperation drove increasing numbers to make the attempt. After some 37,000 Cubans were rescued at sea by the U.S. Coast Guard in 1994 and untold others perished, President Clinton reversed American policy and declared that the United States would no longer accept all Cubans. This declaration was coupled with a promise that the U.S. government would issue at least 20,000 immigrant visas each year. In fact, in 1996–97 the number of Cuban immigrants exceeded 60,000, making Cuba once again one of the top ten countries of origin for immigrants.

The Cubans have tended to concentrate in south Florida, but this is not their only region of settlement. During the early years of the Cuban Resettlement Program, the U.S. government attempted to disperse the refugees; consequently, other Cuban settlements grew up in places such as Union City and West New York, New Jersey. But the preeminence of the south Florida concentration has grown over time, as Cubans originally settled in other parts of the country eventually migrated there.

Although the Cubans stand out among Hispanic immigrant groups for their relative economic success, the distinction is not so striking when they are compared to all immigrants, regardless of origin. According to 1990 census data for the foreign-born, the educational attainment of Cuban immigrants was slightly below the average for all immigrants: for instance, 16 percent of Cubans had completed college, compared to 20 percent of immigrants in general. Median household income was also slightly below average ($27,292 versus $28,314 for all immigrants and $30,176 for the average native-born household in 1989). The Cuban ethnic economy of south Florida has commanded a good deal of attention, but when it comes to business ownership, the Cuban rate of self-employment (73 per 1,000 employed persons) was only slightly higher than its equivalent for all immigrants (68 per 1,000). Although this was decidedly above the self-employment figures for the Mexicans, Dominicans, and other Hispanic immigrant groups (typically between 45 and 50 per 1,000), it was not close to the self-employment rates for the Koreans and Greeks, the most entrepreneurial of immigrant groups (180 and 147 per 1,000, respectively). Still, among immigrant minority firms with employees, the Cuban-owned ones reported the highest income.[47]

Dominicans

Like its Cuban analogue, immigration from the Dominican Republic is historically quite recent and has been ignited by political events at home. Economic motivations to emigrate overtook political ones even more quickly than was the case for Cubans, however. Because Dominicans were not seen as a refugee group by the U.S. government, their immigration has been more constrained by U.S. law, which has been unable to satisfy the high demand for immigrant visas. As a consequence, a significant illegal immigration has sprung up.

Until the early 1960s, the government of the Dominican Republic was a dictatorship in the hands of Rafael Trujillo, whose regime maintained tight controls over emigration. Few Dominicans were allowed even to have passports, and immigration to the United States was necessarily meager.[48] This changed with the assassination of Trujillo in 1961 and the several years of political turmoil that followed, which included a military coup against an elected president in 1963 and military occupation of the capital by U.S. Marines in 1965. During this period, many Dominicans sought to leave for political reasons; and even though a large fraction of them were leftists aligned against what the United States saw as its interests, for the most part they were allowed to come, perhaps in the hope that their departure would help stabilize the political situation at home.[49]

In 1969 legal immigration from the Dominican Republic exceeded 10,000 for the first time, and in 1983 it climbed over 20,000; during the first half of the 1990s it remained close to or above 40,000 but fell off at the end of the decade. Illegal immigration is obviously much harder to estimate, but there is little doubt that it is substantial. One estimate is that, of the Dominicans counted in the 1980 U.S. Census, at least 11 percent were illegals,[50] many of whom enter legally on tourist or other temporary visas but remain after these have expired. This route of entry is most open to middle-class Dominicans or those who can appear so, because the U.S. consulate in Santo Domingo, wary of the use of tourist visas for illegal immigration, requires evidence, such as proof of financial assets, that visitors are highly likely to return home.[51] Other Dominicans first go to Puerto Rico by boat and then, posing as Puerto Ricans, whose entry to the U.S. mainland is unrestricted, fly to New York.

The Dominican immigration appears to be fairly selective. The immigrants, typically youthful, come mainly from urban areas rather than from the countryside; those originating in rural areas frequently have first migrated to a Dominican city or town. On average, the immigrants are better educated than the Dominican population as a whole, and their educational credentials appear to have improved over time. Eleven percent of those arriving between 1985 and 1990 were college graduates, compared to 5 percent in the previous two decades.[52] A factor no doubt driving their immigration has been the rapid rise in access to a university education without a concomitant expansion in suitable job sectors.

Though many come from the most highly trained strata of society, Dominican immigrants frequently find themselves at a disadvantage in the U.S. labor market. For one thing, their educational attainment is below average by comparison with that of the average immigrant or native-born American. Only 42 percent of the Dominican immigrants counted by the 1990 census had completed high school and only 8 percent had graduated from college, significantly fewer than among all foreign-born residents—59 percent and 20 percent, respectively—to say nothing of the U.S.-born. For another, their skin color may place them at a disadvantage. While all Hispanic groups are racially mixed, a smaller fraction of Dominicans than of Hispanics in general describe themselves as white: three-quarters of Dominicans in New York City, for instance, identified themselves as either black or of "other" race.[53] Legal status, or lack of it, also plays a role, as illegal immigrants are forced into the lowest tiers of the labor market and often work off the books for low pay and no job benefits.

Geographic concentration is a final factor. As of 1990, more than three-quarters of Dominicans in the United States lived in and around New York City, many of them in the crowded Washington Heights area of upper Manhattan. The New York City economy has lagged behind that of the nation in recent years and has experienced a very dramatic downsizing in its manufacturing sectors, where newly arrived immigrants might be expected to get a start. Consequently, many Dominicans work in what has been described as the city's "downgraded" manufacturing sector—in garment factories, for instance, where illegal immigrants work off the books—or in poorly paying service jobs. According to 1990 census data, half the Dominican workers in the city were operators or laborers or performed personal services (e.g., as maids), and only 10 percent held professional, managerial, or technical jobs—in aggregate, a poorer labor market picture than for other immigrant groups prominent in the city's economy such as Jamaicans and Haitians.[54]

Indeed, the Dominicans have been described as possibly the poorest racial/ethnic group in the city. They are also among the poorest immigrant groups in the nation. According to the 1990 census, the median income for Dominican immigrant households was approximately $20,000, despite their concentration in a high-income (and quite expensive) region; and 30 percent lived below the poverty line. Only Cambodians, Laotians, and a disproportionately elderly group of immigrants from the former Soviet Union had lower median incomes.

Complicating the economic adjustment of Dominican immigrants has been the increase in single-parent households. In New York City, for instance, almost 40 percent of Dominican households with minor-age children were headed by women.[55] This development can be understood as a result of the sojourner orientation of many Dominicans, especially men, and the changed gender relations among immigrants in the United States. For many Dominican men, the goal is to return to the Dominican Republic as soon as possible. Their byword is, "Five dollars wasted today means five more years of postponement of a return to the Dominican Republic." When women arrive, however, they frequently find that their relationships with their husbands are more egalitarian than was true at home. This is due in part to their entry into the labor market; the wages they earn empower them to renegotiate such fundamental matters as control over the family budget. Over time, they become less eager to return; many Dominican women say, "The Dominican Republic is a country for men, the United States is a country for women."[56] In some families these diverging interests develop into a conflict over ultimate goals and lead to family breakup, with the man returning home and the woman and children remaining in the United States.[57]

Nevertheless, the Dominican immigration is one of the most transnational in the sense that many immigrants maintain lives in the home country and return there with some frequency. Dominicans from a community based in Boston, for example, move back and forth, with some also sending their children back to their home villages to receive some of their schooling there.[58] If this phenomenon occurs on a large scale, then obviously it carries enormous implications for the incorporation of the Dominican second generation. The Dominican immigration is one that will be watched carefully by social scientists interested in evaluating the significance of contemporary transnationalism.

Salvadorans

Immigration from El Salvador is another in the sequence of Latino immigrations that owe their origins to political upheaval. It differs from the Cuban and Dominican cases in that many immigrants were motivated by fear for their lives in the context of a bloody civil war, and also in that their ability to remain permanently in the United States is uncertain in many cases. As late as the 1970s, Salvadoran immigration amounted to at most a few thousand arrivals per year, but the civil war that started in 1979 and lasted until 1992 changed that. The war involved atrocities committed by both sides, often against the civilian population, causing many to flee the country. Consequently, during the 1980s the number of legal immigrants soared to more than 200,000, and the total immigration figure was considerably higher because of the large number of illegal immigrants known to have arrived.[59] The 2000 census enumerated 655,000 Salvadorans, but this is almost certainly an underestimate. For one thing, a substantial fraction of illegal and/or illiterate immigrants in the Salvadoran population are likely to have been missed.

Legal status is an issue of great consequence for the Salvadorans. Although many were emigrating in fear for their lives, the U.S. government was reluctant to recognize them as refugees. The refugee designation is a political decision on the part of a receiving government, and it is generally refused when the government of the nation of origin is a political ally, as was the case during the El Salvador conflict. Consequently, Salvadorans arriving at U.S. borders were not welcomed in the same manner as Cubans. They usually did not even apply for asylum unless they were apprehended by immigration authorities; the rate of acceptance of Salvadoran asylum applications initially was very low, under 3 percent (compared to 60 percent or more for Iranians, for instance), and the immigrants were afraid that such an application in the United States would be used against them in El Salvador should it be refused.[60] The rate of acceptance did eventually climb after the U.S. government agreed to set up a new review system in the 1990 settlement of a lawsuit brought by advocates for Central Americans, but it still remained well below the 50 percent mark. Meanwhile, many Salvadorans already here were able to take advantage of the amnesty provisions of the 1986 Immigration Reform and Control Act. Nationwide, 150,000 previously undocumented Salvadorans regularized their situation under the law; in fact, the IRCA legalizations account for about half of the legal immigrants tallied from 1981 to 1990. Once legalized, these immigrants gained the right to bring in close family members, and so the IRCA legalizations have contributed to the higher legal annual immigration evident during the 1990s.

Many other Salvadorans are still in a form of legal limbo. To forestall their deportation to what was then still a war zone, Congress passed a law in 1990 to give them temporary protected status, which would allow them to live and work in the United States until the civil war ended. Nearly 200,000 Salvadorans asked for this status, whose initial duration was eighteen months. Despite the end of the war in 1992, this status was extended several times before expiring in 1994, but by then those who had been covered were waiting for new asylum hearings granted under the 1990 lawsuit settlement. As of the late 1990s, many Salvadorans were living in the United States from one extension of their stay to another.[61] Others, especially numerous among post-1990 arrivals to whom the temporary protected status did not apply, remain without any legal authorization to reside in the United States, and frequently lead a fearful, largely underground life.

Salvadorans are concentrated in a few metropolitan regions, Los Angeles above all, where half of those counted in 1990 were resident. In part because of the liabilities inherent in uncertain legal status and in part because of limited educational histories, their place in the labor market tends to be quite humble. Many lacked the documents necessary to work legally in the United States until the temporary protection program became effective in 1991; and especially once the IRCA legislation was passed in the mid-1980s to target the employment of illegals, they found themselves unable to take regular work in aboveground businesses. Accordingly, many Salvadorans find jobs in the underground service economy or at the margins of the legitimate one. Many Salvadoran men on Long Island are employed, for example, by landscaping services. Others find work on a day-by-day basis, appearing at shape-up locations where contractors may pick out a few men for a specific job. Women often work as domestics, providing cooking, housekeeping, or child care services to affluent native-born families or even to compatriots. Even when Salvadorans have legal authorization to work, their jobs tend to be at the bottom of the ladder, for instance, as kitchen and janitorial help in fast food restaurants.[62]

Jamaicans

Jamaicans are only the most numerous of a diverse Afro-Caribbean immigration that has sprung up in the aftermath of the 1965 law. This new immigration is writing another chapter in a little-known history of immigration from the English-speaking West Indies. In the early twentieth century, this immigration drew selectively from the more educated and skilled strata of the island societies, attracting individuals who "saw greater economic opportunities in the United States."[63] There has been much speculation about the reasons for the relative economic success of these immigrants in African American communities in the northern states, where they and their children have been disproportionately represented in the business, professional, and political elites. To cite just a few instances of civil rights leaders, Marcus Garvey, Malcolm X, and Shirley Chisholm, the first black woman elected to Congress, were all of West Indian birth or ancestry, as is Colin Powell, the first black U.S. secretary of state. Nevertheless, the ability of distinctive West Indian communities to maintain themselves appears to have been limited, given the paramount power of race in the United States.[64]

The earlier West Indian immigration was disrupted by the Great Depression, and then very low quotas were set for the Caribbean colonies by the Immigration Act of 1952. In any event, at that time immigration to Great Britain offered an alternative outlet for those who sought greater opportunity than they could find at home.[65] The result was a decades-long hiatus in immigration to the United States. The 1965 law, which removed the discriminatory quotas for Jamaica and the other island nations, reopened a door that had been largely closed since the 1930s. At about the same time, Great Britain enacted legislation to reduce immigration there from its former Caribbean colonies.

Although U.S. law had eliminated the quotas, immigration from the Western Hemisphere was not at first determined by the same preference system applied to the Eastern Hemisphere. Instead, immigrants from Jamaica had to be certified by the U.S. Labor Department as filling a labor market need and not having an adverse impact on U.S. workers.[66] This made the Jamaican immigration quite unusual because women, rather than men, were better positioned to receive certification. It was women who could gain entry as domestics (who made up half the immigrants of the late 1960s) and bring their families later.[67] (When the system of preferences was subsequently applied to immigration from the Western Hemisphere, in 1978, the family reunification emphasis aided this process.) In some cases, these early immigrants deliberately took jobs considerably below their qualifications in order to gain entry to the United States; once here, they were able to change jobs and improve their occupational situation. Other female immigrants entered as skilled or professional workers, among whom nurses and others in health-related occupations have been numerous.

According to 1990 census data, the socioeconomic profile of Jamaicans places them roughly in the middle of the contemporary immigration spectrum. In educational terms, their rate of high school completion, 68 percent, is somewhat above average for the entire foreign-born population, while their rate of college graduation, 15 percent, is somewhat below average. Their median household income, $30,600 in 1989 dollars, is also above average for immigrants in general ($28,300) and even slightly above that for all the native-born ($30,200).[68]

While Jamaican immigrants have attained some degree of economic success in the United States, an unanswered question is whether they are able to translate it into commensurate social advantages such as residential situation. The Jamaican immigration, like most other Afro-Caribbean immigrant streams, has flowed heavily to the New York region. Within New York City, some neighborhoods, such as Crown Heights/Flatbush in Brooklyn, have become known for their concentrations of West Indian immigrants. In general, these areas are on the edges of large African American neighborhoods, and there is some evidence to suggest that West Indians are frequently the forerunners for African American entry into a neighborhood, as has happened in Brooklyn.[69] Race severely constrains the ability of Jamaicans and other West Indians to translate the initial economic advantages they attain as immigrants into residential advantages with long-run consequences.

The West Indian immigrations are of particular interest because they straddle what appears to be a major line of division among minorities in the United States—between immigrant groups and African Americans. The evidence suggests that the immigrant generation is able to manage the resulting tensions despite frequent encounters with racial prejudice because their identities as West Indians are firmly anchored and they are able to compare their U.S. situation favorably against their prospects had they not immigrated. But the tensions become less manageable for the second generation, who evaluate their situation by U.S. standards rather than those of their parents' homeland. Their adaptation is influenced by their parents' social class and the neighborhoods they live in. Many see themselves as defined mainly by their race in the eyes of other Americans, and their second-generation status is much less consequential, while some strive to hold onto an ethnic identity derived from their West Indian origins.[70] The contest between these self-definitions may prove a litmus test for possible shifts in the potency of racial status.

Chinese

Chinese immigration to the United States was the first to be affected by an exclusionary law prohibiting immigration by an entire ethnic group. Thus, it provides a useful benchmark for American experience with nonwhite immigration.

Following the discovery of gold in California in 1848, Chinese miners and merchants began arriving in San Francisco in large numbers. The Chinese population grew rapidly, mirroring the boomtown growth of San Francisco and the mining industry.[71] Chinese merchants and former miners built a diversified ethnic economy in the city, centered on light manufacturing, retail, and services. Chinese labor contractors recruited men from the Pearl River Delta in Guangdong Province to meet the growing labor demand. Chinese were the mainstay of the workforce that built the transcontinental railroad from California through the Sierra Nevada into Utah, and Chinese labor developed California's early agricultural economy, from constructing the levees and irrigation systems in the Sacramento River Delta and San Joachin Valley to cultivating new farmland.

By 1870, there were more than 63,000 Chinese immigrants in the West; in California, Chinese made up a quarter of the state's workforce. Although initially the Chinese were welcomed, soon complaints from white gold miners about competition ignited a three-decade-long buildup of anti-Chinese sentiment among whites in the western states.[72] A long series of legislative efforts aimed to restrict Chinese entrepreneurial activity and labor market competition.[73] They culminated in the passage of the Chinese Exclusion Act in 1882, ending the immigration of Chinese laborers. A decade later, a follow-up exclusion law extended the ban to include all classes of Chinese, including merchants. Citizenship law excluded Chinese immigrants from naturalization. Moreover, as nonwhites, they could not testify in court, a rule that exacerbated their vulnerability to racist violence. It was during this period that "not a Chinaman's chance" became a well-known adage.

The Chinese exclusion laws were stringently monitored and enforced by the federal government because public opinion was so firmly behind their intent. Following their passage, the anti-Chinese movement spawned violent mob action, driving Chinese from their niches in the mainstream economy in fishing, mining, agriculture, and industry. As they were driven out, Chinese laborers returned to the Pearl River Delta—if they could afford the passage home—or found shelter in the larger Chinatowns in San Francisco and Oakland, or moved to the East (New York City and Boston) and South (the Mississippi Delta and Louisiana). The Chinatown merchant elite tried its best to defend Chinese interests through legal action in the courts. Though unsuccessful, these actions established a record of protest against the harsh treatment meted out to the Chinese American community.

In the aftermath of the virulent anti-Chinese movement, Chinatowns emerged as segregated ghettos. Well into the early decades of the twentieth century, older residents could recall being stoned and beaten by whites if they ventured elsewhere. The immigrant enclave economy was cut back as restrictive legislation curtailed Chinese entrepreneurial activity in manufacturing and in agriculture and fishing. What remained of the diverse range of Chinese-owned businesses in California was concentrated in areas in which Chinese did not compete directly with white firms and workers—mainly specialty shops serving a Chinese ethnic clientele, as well as the laundry business, domestic service, and tourism.

In Chinatowns, a sizable second generation was slow to emerge.[74] Chinese laborers had come to America as male sojourners, leaving their wives and children in their home villages in the Pearl River Delta. The few Chinese women who migrated to the United States during the period of open immigration were either wives of merchants or prostitutes. After the passage of the Chinese Exclusion Act, the Chinese laborers who remained in America were forbidden by law to bring their wives and children to join them. Gradually, the merchant families and the prostitutes who married laborer husbands produced a second generation, who grew up in a community dominated by aging bachelors, the laborers who had remained in America. The second generation acculturated, but it was not until after World War II that the American-born Chinese assimilated, as we noted in Chapter 3.[75] A quasi-second generation also appeared after the San Francisco earthquake of 1906 destroyed the city's records, when Chinese immigrant men could claim that they were born in America and were therefore citizens entitled to bring immediate family members to the United States. This opened the way for some Chinese to immigrate by pretending to be the sons of these men. The pattern of "paper son" migration continued for years and in some families involved multiple generations migrating to America. Though reduced to a trickle compared to what it was in the mid-nineteenth century, immigration continued through such loopholes. During World War II, a revision of the immigration law opened the door slightly, setting a quota of 105 legal Chinese immigrants a year. Additionally, the War Brides Act allowed American-born Chinese veterans to bring back wives married in China. Likewise, "stranded students" who were studying at American universities at the time of the Chinese Communist victory in 1949 were allowed to become permanent residents.

There were 105,465 Chinese immigrants in 1880; not until 1920 did the Chinese American population return to its size prior to the Chinese Exclusion Act, as a second generation slowly emerged. From 111,010 in 1920, the Chinese American population grew slowly to only 141,768 in 1950.[76] The McCarran-Walter Act of 1952 finally did away with the exclusion of Chinese and other Asian immigrants from naturalization as U.S. citizens.

Only with the passage of the Immigration Act of 1965 did large-scale immigration of Chinese resume. More than 1.3 million legal immigrants came to the United States between 1968 and 2000, making this the third-largest immigrant stream (following those from Mexico and the Philippines), and far surpassing numerically the scale of the earlier nineteenth-century Chinese immigration. The new Chinese immigration has also been substantially more diverse in its social and geographic origins. Rather than emanating from the rural counties of the Pearl River Delta, these immigrants come from Taiwan, Hong Kong, Southeast Asia, and the Chinese mainland. Some have arrived through the family reunification clause of the 1965 immigration law, which allowed the families of the descendants of the earlier immigration to bring over their relatives. These immigrants, many of whom come from mainland China, have tended to settle in existing Chinatowns, where they find employment in ethnic firms. Others are highly educated professionals who, after earning their postgraduate degrees in American universities, find jobs in mainstream firms and settle in suburban communities.

Koreans

Although Koreans originally came to the United States in the early-twentieth-century immigration from Asia, they remained a very small immigrant group, never more than 2,000 to 3,000 per year. Within the first years of immigration after 1965, new Korean immigrants quickly surpassed the total number of Koreans who had arrived in the first wave. An average of 30,000 to 35,000 Korean immigrants arrived annually in the United States from 1976 to 1990. By the end of the 1980s, Koreans were among the top five immigrant groups (after Mexicans and Filipinos). In the 1990s, however, the group's rate of growth fell, as the attractiveness of the immigration option apparently declined with the growth of the South Korean economy: the annual number of arrivals was cut in half, while the number of returns, much more difficult to estimate, grew.[77] The main center of Korean American population is southern California, in and around Los Angeles, where 260,000 were residing in 2000. The second-largest population center is the New York–New Jersey metropolitan area, with about 170,000 Koreans. Once established, the large Korean ethnic economy in these areas provided ethnically bounded opportunities, which in turn drew more immigrants.[78]

The selectivity of the Korean immigration, despite its relative size, is striking. First, Koreans came primarily from one city, Seoul. South Korea's export-led economic development strategy in the 1950s and 1960s sparked rapid industrial growth and urbanization that transformed Seoul into one of the most densely populated cities in the world. Urbanization brought masses of rural migrants into the city at a time when South Korea was experiencing an explosive population growth.[79] In addition, refugees from the North settled there after the Korean War. As a means of coping with urban population growth, the government encouraged emigration. Second, Korean immigrants are predominantly from the urban middle class. Over 70 percent have college and postgraduate degrees. Professionals and technical workers—physicians, nurses, engineers, pharmacists, dentists—outnumber any other occupational group. Unlike, for example, Chinese professionals from Taiwan and mainland China, many of whom earned their postgraduate degrees at American universities, Korean professionals generally earned their degrees in Korean universities and were already employed in their areas of training prior to immigration. Third, Koreans come with the aim of settling in America as immigrants. They are generally already married couples who arrive with their children. Usually, they sell their homes and other fixed assets before emigrating and bring their savings as financial capital to facilitate the transition to working lives in the United States.[80]

The similarity in social background has given rise to a close-knit Korean immigrant community. Flourishing membership in Korean Protestant churches reflects the social cohesiveness. In the New York metropolitan area alone, Korean Protestant churches increased in number from six in 1971 to over three hundred in 1986. More than sites of worship, these churches serve multiple purposes as centers of Korean communal life.[81] Korean ministers are heavily involved in community service, from matchmaking to interpreting for newly arrived immigrants and helping them find jobs and housing. Korean immigrants seek help from friends and acquaintances when they are looking for a job, obtaining timely business information and contacts, and even negotiating business deals. The churches foster a family atmosphere useful in promoting cooperation within the Korean community.

Although relatively few come from business backgrounds, Korean immigrants have the highest self-employment rate of any of the post-1965 immigrant groups. Over a third of Korean households are involved in operating a small business—more than twice the percentage for comparable immigrant groups such as the Cubans, the Chinese, and the Indians. The large proportion of Koreans going into small business can be accounted for by the difficulty of finding jobs in their area of training, given their foreign credentials and problems in adapting to an English-speaking cultural environment.[82] (Although Filipino professionals also have foreign credentials, their familiarity with English prior to emigration accounts in part for why so many seek employment in the mainstream economy even when unable to find jobs in their area of professional training.) Yet another reason why Koreans have concentrated in small business may be the effectiveness of their ethnic business associations. Korean entrepreneurs concentrate in specific niches, such as greengroceries, liquor and food stores, gas stations, dry cleaning, and garment subcontracting. For each of these niches there is a Korean business association that provides valuable services for its members, including group insurance, tax advice, legal services, and business seminars. The business associations also promote ethnic solidarity. They enable Korean small businesses to cooperate in reducing intragroup competition, negotiate for better terms with non-Korean suppliers and contractors, fight against discriminatory treatment of Korean firms, work on improving relations with blacks in the central city, and pursue a host of other activities that promote their interests.[83]

The pattern of incorporation of Korean immigrants resembles the experience of other middleman minorities. Korean small businesses have specialized in serving the inner city, in part because this market offers a relatively high profit margin. Despite the risks involved in operating businesses in the ghetto, the opportunity to accumulate capital rapidly is viewed by Korean entrepreneurs as outweighing the dangers they confront, even in the face of growing hostility toward them from the black community. The average gross annual profit of Korean small businesses is substantially higher than for either Cuban- or Chinese-owned businesses.[84] Such success offers a relatively quick ascendance into the upper-middle class for many Korean households. Although Korean immigrant entrepreneurs may rely heavily on the ethnic economy for their livelihood, the aim of assimilating into American life is evident in the choice of residence in the more affluent suburban neighborhoods and in the rapid acculturation of the second generation and its high educational attainment.

Filipinos

The early Filipino migration to the United States began in the 1920s and reached its height in the 1930s during the Great Depression. Filipinos arrived as single male laborers to fill the niches left vacant by the exclusion of Japanese, Koreans, and South Asians following the Immigration Act of 1924. After Spain ceded the Philippines to the United States at the conclusion of the Spanish-American War, Filipinos acquired the legal status of American nationals. Although they were not granted citizenship, they were not barred by the exclusionary laws that ended other Asian immigrations. Filipinos were employed principally in agriculture, where they formed a mainstay of the migrant labor force, working on farms in the central valley of California, from Stockton down through the Imperial Valley to Los Angeles, as well as in Oregon and Washington, and in the salmon fisheries in Alaska. Filipino laborers were also in demand as household servants and porters. By the 1930s, the Filipino population numbered about 45,000.

The pattern of labor migration was similar to that of the other Asian groups that preceded them. Filipinos came as sojourners drawn by the high wages of the American labor market, but with the intention of eventually returning to the Philippines. They worked from dawn till after sunset in crews under the supervision of a co-ethnic labor contractor, lived in makeshift bunkhouses, and moved on after the harvest to another area. Unlike the earlier Japanese laborers, Filipinos did not shift into self-employment to establish their own farms or businesses. They also did not establish communities with an ethnic economy to provide a differentiated base of small businesses and employment for professionals. Nor did they send for wives from the home country. Instead they remained on the lowest rungs of the labor force, where few earned enough to accumulate savings that would enable them to return to the Philippines.[85]

As migrant laborers, Filipinos quickly acquired a reputation for independence, as reflected by the organization of the Filipino Labor Union based in Stockton and Salinas, which led them in a number of militant strikes, sometimes violently suppressed by armed vigilantes and local police forces. Filipino laborers soon provoked a backlash among both white farm owners and laborers from Oklahoma with whom they competed. Interracial dating and marriage between Filipino laborers and white women also provoked the anger of whites, resulting in the extension of the anti-miscegenation law by the California state legislature to include the "Malay" race in its general prohibition of interracial union applying to the black and "mongolian" races. By the early 1930s, the frequency of sporadic but violent racial conflicts had increased in California. Anti-Filipino sentiment culminated in the passage of the Tydings-McDuffie Act in 1934 by the U.S. Congress, aimed at stopping Filipino migration. The sponsor, Senator Millard Tydings, argued: "It is absolutely illogical to have an immigration policy to exclude Japanese and Chinese and permit Filipinos en masse to come into the country. . . . If they continue to settle in certain areas they will come in conflict with white labor . . . and increase the opportunity for more racial prejudice and bad feeling of all kinds."[86]

Not until 1965 did Filipino migration to the United States resume. The second-wave migration, markedly different in composition from the first, has involved predominantly professionals and technical workers who come not as single male sojourners but as families with the intent to settle. The Philippines has been a major source of nurses and medical doctors for the United States, providing staff for hospitals in most major metropolitan areas. These immigrants also include large numbers of engineers, scientists, teachers, and lawyers. Only 10 percent of Filipino immigrants now arrive as laborers. A striking aspect of this, the second-largest immigration stream, is its lack of visibility. Professionals and technical workers have assimilated rapidly in some areas, acquiring jobs in mainstream institutions and residing in mixed neighborhoods, mostly in the suburbs.[87] Like the earlier wave of Filipino migrants, the English-speaking middle-class Filipino immigrants have established few ethnic enclaves, whether residential or business. This is not to say that Filipino immigrants have not encountered difficulties in their accommodation to American society. Many, especially physicians, lawyers, and pharmacists, have trouble securing licenses to practice their professions; and some consequently take jobs well below their training, as clerks, secretaries, mechanics, or technicians.

Both supply and demand account for the professional and technical nature of the new Filipino migration. Higher education in the Philippines expanded rapidly in the post–World War II period, so that by the 1970s, 25 percent of the college-age population was enrolled in colleges and universities. The Philippines then ranked second only to the United States in the proportion of youth enrolled in higher education. Only approximately 60 percent of college graduates, however, can find employment other than in menial work.[88] Moreover, jobs requiring college education and professional training pay poorly relative to salaries in advanced industrial economies. On the demand side, the U.S. labor market has faced chronic shortages of skilled and professional workers, notably nurses, engineers, accountants, and physicians. Hospitals, for instance, actively recruit nurses in the Philippines to meet their staffing needs. The nursing shortage stems from a convergence of a number of trends: the rapid growth in demand in health care following the establishment of Medicare, the shift from reliance on private practice to health management organizations, and the decline in the prestige of the nursing profession owing to relatively low salaries and the opening of traditionally male occupations to women.[89] As a result, hospitals find that they need to recruit nurses as well as physicians from abroad.

East Indians

As with the other Asian groups, migrants from India first arrived in the United States in the early twentieth century in response to the demand for cheap labor.[90] By the 1920s, about 6,400 laborers from the farming region of Punjab were working in sawmills and on railroads in the state of Washington. The Western Pacific Railroad recruited laborers from India to construct and maintain railway tracks, but their use as replacements for striking white workers sparked violent confrontations. As racial conflict intensified, Indian immigrants fled to California, where they were welcomed by white farmers as replacements for the aging Chinese laborers who were returning to retire in China and for Japanese who were leaving migrant labor for self-employment in small farms. Although their total number remained relatively small, Indians soon became one of the main groups of migrant laborers in the San Joachin and Imperial valleys, where they traveled from farm to farm in small bands organized by labor contractors.

Like the other Asian immigrant groups, Indian laborers came as single male sojourners. Their social organization centered on their lives as migrant laborers. They did not settle to form ethnic communities as did the Chinese and Japanese, but instead they lived in temporary shelters as itinerant workers, in bunkhouses provided by their white employers, or in the open fields. Eventually some left migrant labor to start their own small farms, leasing the land from white landowners. They proved to be skillful farmers, growing crops such as rice and cotton that were familiar to them from their native farms in the Punjab region.

Nominally Caucasian but treated like other Asians, Indians suffered from an anomalous racial classification that led them to challenge the application to themselves of the exclusion rules then applied to other Asian immigrants. In two of the early court cases, *U.S. v. Balsara* (1910) and the *Ajkoy Kumar Mazumdar* decision (1913), the courts ruled that they were entitled to naturalized citizenship as Caucasians. In 1923, however, the Supreme Court ruled in *U.S. v.*

Bhagat Singh Thind that despite their Aryan origin, Indians could not be regarded as white. The definition of a white person, argued the Court, must be based on the understanding of the common man, which the Court interpreted as meaning whites from Europe.[91] As nonwhites, Indians became ineligible for naturalization, and they were excluded from immigration by the 1924 Immigration Act.

Very few Indian women came to the United States in the first wave of migration. After the enactment of the 1917 immigration law, Indian immigrants were legally barred from bringing their wives to America. Although some farmers married white women despite the anti-miscegenation law in California, from 75 to 90 percent of Punjabi men who married in central and southern California took Mexican wives. Others lived out their lives in California as lonely bachelors (although many had wives in India whom they visited infrequently on return trips home). Little is known about the first wave of Indian immigrants after the early part of the twentieth century, but by the mid-1960s the Punjabi presence in California had all but disappeared as a visible coloration in the state's ethnic fabric.[92]

The second wave of immigration from India began after the passage of the Immigration Act of 1965. By 2000, more than 800,000 Indians had settled in the United States; together with their children and the descendants of the earlier wave, they constituted a group of more than 1.6 million.[93] By contrast to the first wave of largely illiterate laborers, the new Indian immigrants were predominantly highly educated professionals who came to the United States for their postgraduate education and stayed or who had emigrated as physicians, engineers, and technical workers with educational credentials from Indian universities. The Indian professionals are urban cosmopolitans fluent in English and with the human capital to enable them to adapt smoothly to life in the United States. They originate principally from three states: Gujarat, Punjab, and Kerala.[94] More than 80 percent are of the Hindu faith and about 14 percent are Muslim. Many are married and arrive with the intention of settling as naturalized citizens. They tend to live in large cities on the East and West coasts, with the largest number in the Northeast region, where a third of the immigrant Indian population resides. California has about 20 percent, the largest concentration of any state, followed by New York and New Jersey.

Although over 90 percent of East Indians live in urban areas, they have not established many visible ethnic communities, preferring instead to live in ethnically mixed urban neighborhoods, whether in the central city or in older suburban residential areas.[95] On New York City's Lower East Side, East Sixth Street has come to be known as "Little India," though it is not a residential enclave but a street lined with Indian restaurants; the borough of Queens, however, can boast of an area that contains both commercial and residential concentrations of Indians, though the population density of the group is low (that is, the majority of residents are non-Indian).[96]

As of the 1990 census, 71 percent of Indians have college or postgraduate degrees, making them the most highly educated of any ethnic group in the United States. Three-quarters are in professional, managerial, technical, and administrative service occupations, compared to 60 percent for non-Hispanic whites. The occupational profile of the immigrants has carried forward to the second generation; in 1990, 74 percent were in the same occupational categories as their parents, representing a remarkably smooth transfer of human-cultural capital from one generation to another.[97] They are concentrated in industries such as finance, health care, hospitality, and retail trade. In New York, Indians have established ethnic niches in the municipal bureaucracy, such as the Metropolitan Transport Authority and the Engineering Division.

Vietnamese

At the time of the passage of the Immigration Act of 1965, only six hundred Vietnamese were living in the United States. They were not an ethnic group in formation since they came to the United States not as immigrants but as students, language instructors, and diplomats. Vietnamese began to arrive in large numbers in 1975 as refugees from the communist victory in South Vietnam. During the final days of American military and diplomatic presence in Saigon, 86,000 Vietnamese were airlifted out of the besieged city. They were mainly members of the South Vietnamese political and military elite and their dependents, who during the course of the Indochina war had become closely identified with the American intervention.[98] The evacuation was hurriedly organized. Many refugees remember desperate airlifts aboard military helicopters from the rooftop of the U.S. embassy; last-minute dashes by car or truck to the Saigon airport in the midst of relentless bombing by communist forces; or pell-mell nighttime escapes to the beaches near Saigon, where they set off into the open sea on small boats in the hope of being picked up by U.S. naval vessels patrolling offshore and transported to refugee camps in Guam and the Philippines.[99]

The Vietnamese refugees arrived in the United States in several waves from 1975 to the early 1980s, until by 1985 there were 643,000 Vietnamese living in American communities. The first 130,000 Vietnamese refugees came as part of a well-organized American resettlement program. From processing camps set up in California and Arkansas, they were later dispersed by design across the country to private settlement centers set up by churches and local institutions; but within a short time, many moved to warmer regions, mainly in Orange County and San Jose, California, and in southern states such as Texas and Louisiana. As suggested by their social origins in Vietnam, this initial wave of refugees was relatively well educated, with 16 percent college graduates and almost two-thirds of adults reporting some fluency in English. They were predominantly from Saigon, most were Christian, and most came with intact families. In 1977, as the realities of the harsh conditions imposed by communist rule in Vietnam sank in, hundreds of thousands from the urban middle class and from small coastal cities and villages fled by boat to form a second wave of refugees. These so-called "boat people" endured horrific experiences of hardship at sea. Pirates attacked most of the boats, often several times, plundering, killing, and raping the defenseless refugees. Others drowned as their boats capsized and sank in tropical storms. Those who survived the ordeal gathered in refugee camps in Southeast Asia and Hong Kong to await resettlement in the United States and Europe. Unlike the first group, most in the second wave were unable to speak English and were less westernized; a large number were ethnically Chinese.[100]

When the refugees arrived in the United States, the American public was still deeply divided over the long and costly Indochina war. Nonetheless, the resettlement program went smoothly, accomplishing its mission of finding families and community organizations to offer assistance. Despite sporadic incidents involving racial insults and threats, within a relatively short period of time Vietnamese adults (95 percent of males and 93 percent of females by 1978) found jobs in the communities where they had settled. Refugees from the professional middle class experienced downward job mobility, but those from blue-collar occupational backgrounds usually found jobs comparable to those they had held in Vietnam.[101]

The arrival of large numbers of Vietnamese refugees in secondary migrations from their original settlement areas was met by outright hostility in some communities—in Seadrift, Texas, for example, where the growing settlement of Vietnamese was viewed by white fishermen as a threat to their livelihood.[102] Whites charged that Vietnamese fishermen used unfair means to compete, worked longer hours, and lacked an understanding of long-established etiquette and norms involving fishing rights in the coastal town. The Ku Klux Klan sought to mobilize anti-Vietnamese sentiment, and rumors of thousands more refugees arriving in Seadrift added to the volatility of the confrontation. Tension mounted and violence erupted as Vietnamese fishermen sought to establish a niche in the fishing industry on the Gulf Coast. Elsewhere, the settlement of Vietnamese did not provoke the same intensity of reaction, in part because those settling in Orange County and San Jose did not pose a competitive threat to local business interests. In San Jose, for example, Vietnamese refugees quickly found blue-collar jobs in the high-tech industry, meeting the labor needs of a rapidly expanding sector of the economy.

The largest Vietnamese communities are in California, where onethird settled, many after moving from their initial resettlement sites. As in the Cuban refugee community, the politics of the Vietnamese community were shaped by commitment to the anticommunism of the deposed political and military elite. The former vice president of South Vietnam, General Nguyen Cao Ky, a liquor store owner in Huntington Beach, California, and other former military officers promoted a desire to return to Vietnam to overthrow the communists, similar to the anticommunist stance of the political refugees in the Cuban community in Miami. Former political and military leaders lobbied Washington to secure a commitment to support their return to Vietnam. Given this orientation, it is not surprising that many refugees saw themselves as sojourners in America, believing that they would eventually return to Vietnam.

The realities of making a living and settling into family life in the United States soon shifted their attention to the practical tasks of accommodation. Vietnamese merchants set up retail shops and restaurants on Bolsa Avenue in Orange County which catered to the immigrant community and became known as "Little Saigon." In San Jose,

Vietnamese shops became a visible presence in the downtown shopping area. The Vietnamese ethnic economy flourished as more refugees arrived from their original settlement areas, but it remained almost entirely an ethnic retail economy that served the immigrant community with specialty foods and professional services. Ethnic Chinese Vietnamese, who previously had occupied the small-business niche in Vietnam, operated many of the shops. In Los Angeles, Chinese Vietnamese entrepreneurs opened restaurants and grocery stores in the old Chinatown in the downtown district.

Close-knit networks of families and friends pooled resources through patchwork arrangements of mutual assistance as the need arose among friends and acquaintances. As is common in all immigrant communities, networks helped to distribute resources efficiently among families, providing an informal welfare system that supported them during the difficult periods of adaptation. Often several nuclear families shared the same dwelling to save on rent. In Philadelphia, middle-class immigrants were wary of forming ties with ethnic associations led by members of the former elite in Vietnam.[103] Rather than building formal organizations to promote ethnic interests, Vietnamese immigrants have instead tended to use network mechanisms to promote communal interests.[104]

The entry of married women into the labor force changed the pattern of family life for middle-class Vietnamese families, which had been built on the ideal of patriarchal authority. As parents worked long hours to reclaim in America their former middle-class status, the generations growing up in urban communities acculturated as they progressed through public education. Their experiences ranged from those of the well-publicized academic high achievers who became valedictorians of their high school class to those of juvenile delinquents who roamed urban neighborhoods in youth gangs. As a new ethnic group arising from recent migration, the Vietnamese suffer from social problems that appear to be rooted in the familiar tensions and conflicts arising from changes in gender roles and intergenerational differences and that reflect the effects of acculturation in a family context in which New World conventions and practices clash with Old World values.[105]

Our brief sketches of ten of the largest immigrant streams point to the diversity of contemporary immigration. The post-1965 immigrants come from many more countries than did earlier immigrants from Europe. Some immigrant groups are new to the American scene, including smaller ones we did not mention because there are literally too many of them (moreover, little is known about the smaller immigrant groups). The list of identifiable ethnic groups in the 2000 census has grown to include nearly every nationality represented at the United Nations, as well as subnational groups such as the Kurds. This dazzling array of ethnic groups has made the United States arguably the most ethnically diverse country on the planet.

CHAPTER SIX

Evidence of Contemporary Assimilation

Assimilation is by its nature a multigenerational process. This fact imposes limits on our ability at the beginning of the twenty-first century to infer all the trajectories in American society initiated by a largely post-1960s immigration. While the immigrant generation experiences some changes as it accommodates to life in a new society, these are of necessity constrained for individuals who have been socialized in another, usually quite different society. Hence, changes that are evident in the immigrants themselves cannot serve as the basis for ultimate conclusions about assimilation. It is only with the U.S.-born, or the foreign-born who immigrate at an early age and are raised mostly in the United States (usefully labeled the 1.5 generation),[1] that there is any possibility of assessing the true prospects for the assimilation of immigrant groups.

But even for the second generation, the experience of the ethnics of the past offers reason to be cautious about bold conclusions. For most European and East Asian groups, the assimilation of this generation was partial. Indeed, the well-known studies (to say nothing of a huge imaginative literature) depict the children of immigrants as individuals whose lives were profoundly affected by their ethnic origins, who resided mostly in ethnic communities and exhibited in a variety of ways thinking and behavior that were characteristic of the group. It was only with the third and, in some cases, the fourth generations that the powerful undercurrent of assimilation came unmistakably to the surface.

For the new immigrant groups, the second generation is still largely young, and thus studies generally can track it at best through the initial phases of adulthood. The third generation, insofar as it exists at all, is small and composed chiefly of children; its distinctive characteristics *as a generation* will emerge only in the future. The fourth (and later) generations are to be found only among those groups in the contemporary stream whose immigration history reaches back into past eras; this includes Mexicans, Canadians, a few European groups (such as Russians and other eastern Europeans), and the Chinese. Only for the Mexicans, whose immigration into the Southwest and California has been continuous, though growing, over the past century, is there a plausible case to be made that the characteristics of the third and later generations are indicative of changes to be expected across the generations for recent immigrants and their descendants.[2] For other groups, especially the Europeans and East Asians, there is such a long temporal gap between the immigration of the earlier era, which accounts for the overwhelming majority of the contemporary third and fourth generations, and the new immigration that the characteristics of these generations are, quite obviously, of very dubious prognostic value for the descendants of present immigrants. There is simply no compelling reason to believe that the lives of, say, third-, fourth-, and later-generation Chinese Americans, whose immigrant ancestors may have arrived anytime in the latter half of the nineteenth century, are indicative for the future grandchildren and great-grandchildren of recent arrivals from Taiwan, Hong Kong, or mainland China. In short, for most groups stemming from post-1960s immigration, evidence of assimilation must be taken largely from the first and second generations. The picture is of necessity a fragmented and truncated one, and the conclusions must be regarded as provisional.

In what follows, we review the record in a number of key areas: language assimilation, socioeconomic position, residential change, and intermarriage. We have to acknowledge that the relevant data in published research are limited, as much research on the new immigration concentrates on the immigrants themselves or on the ethnic groups as wholes, which are dominated by large immigrant generations. Our attention focuses mostly on the groups from south of the Rio Grande, from the Caribbean, and from Asia. They are by no means the entirety of the new immigration, which includes significant streams from Canada and Europe, but they do constitute its great bulk—"more than eight out of ten arriving in the 1980s and 1990s."[3] And because of their non-European ancestry, they constitute the litmus test of the relevance of assimilation for immigration today.

To assist in our assessments, we draw on conceptual models that abstract the assimilation process as it was experienced by the descendants of European immigrants. By cautiously comparing the changes observed among the descendants of contemporary immigrants to those expected under these models (for instance, the three-generation model of conversion to English monolingualism), we attempt to add further plausibility to our main conclusion, namely, that assimilation will manifest itself among many descendants of the post-1965 new immigration. In truth, some aspects of assimilation, especially in the domains of acculturation, could be described as close to universal. Nevertheless, we recognize that models reflecting the experiences of past eras cannot be translated intact into the present, for much has changed. In invoking these models, we remain attentive to the respects in which they need modification. What we attempt, then, is a careful balancing act.

Acculturation and Language Assimilation

There is universal agreement that some degree of acculturation is inevitable, but its precise extent and ultimate significance are subject to considerably more debate. As we showed in Chapter 2, the view in the classical conception of assimilation was that acculturation was overwhelmingly a one-directional and substitutive process, in which immigrants and their descendants acquired the culture of mainstream America, with commensurate loss of their own. As we noted, there are difficulties with this simplistic depiction. But what should the alternative be? One of the most influential and frequently invoked ideas is the anthropologist Margaret Gibson's notion of "multilinear acculturation," according to which immigrant groups selectively acquire linguistic and other cultural practices of the majority culture without rejecting their own ethnic identity and culture.[4] Hence, acculturation is, in Gibson's view, an "additive" process involving purposive selection of cultural practices that are useful to the immigrant group. This is contrasted with the subtractive nature of one-way acculturation. Gibson also stresses the practical possibility of multiculturalism—of coexisting commitments to multiple cultural universes—which, obviously, is also assumed by those who view transnationalism as a major phenomenon of the future, for this requires that immigrants and their children continue to feel at home in the countries of their ancestors.

Selective acculturation can be read as minimalist: the children and grandchildren of immigrants must of course be proficient in certain aspects of American culture, the English language above all, if they are to enjoy any success outside the confines of ethnic enclaves. But with the exception of such inevitable concessions to the host society, they preserve a salient cultural distinctiveness. The concept assumes parental choice and ethnic community constraint in the adoption of American cultural practices by the second generation. Ethnic community norms would therefore have a determinative influence on major life decisions of immigrants and perhaps their children—about jobs, residential location, and marital choice, for instance.[5] Whether this communal influence can maintain its effectiveness beyond the immigrant generation is questionable. Indeed, accounts of generational tension between parents and adolescent children, common in every immigrant group, suggest that a weakening of social control may often occur relatively early in the American experience, especially when both parents work long hours away from home.[6] Illustrative of this are the well-known problems associated with youth gangs in large immigrant communities. The fact is that acculturation is only partly the result of intentional choices; instead, much also stems from the unintended consequences of accommodation to schooling and everyday life in the United States. Gibson notes, for instance, that Punjabi Sikh students in a rural California community generally aspire to college education and professional jobs—occupations far removed from the farming life of their immigrant parents. College and subsequent job choices are likely to scatter successful young Sikhs away from their home community and one another, adding obvious complexities and difficulties to the problem of maintaining an ethnic cultural base. The concept of selective acculturation may also underestimate the seductiveness of American culture and, in particular, of the individualism and materialism that permeate American life.[7] In any case, the forms of social controls available to parents in bounded immigrant communities can be expected to attenuate with successive generations, if the experiences of the earlier immigrations from Europe, East Asia, and Central America are any indication.

One trajectory of acculturation that can be directly glimpsed is that of linguistic change, for which a large, albeit imperfect, body of data exists. Language is in fact quite crucial for the persistence of a broad-gauge cultural differentiation, since many aspects of ethnic culture are embedded in a linguistic matrix and are weakened or lost if the mother tongue is no longer used or even known. To take just one example, the numerous pronouns of the Vietnamese language register the respect traditionally accorded family elders, who may berate youths who address them in English.[8] Language can thus be seen as a handy and tangible index of cultural differentiation. The paradigm of multilinear acculturation finds ready application in this domain, acknowledging that, as a practical matter, acquisition of English is imperative for immigrants and, even more so, for their children, but holding out the prospect that English competence can be acquired without loss of the mother tongue. Bilingualism, then, is the outcome anticipated as an alternative to full linguistic acculturation.

There is, however, considerable evidence from the experiences of past immigrations to suggest difficulties for bilingualism in the long term. The speed of the shift toward the host language in the United States appears to be unusual, if not unique. One paradigm of language shift—a three-generation transition to English monolingualism, first codified by the sociolinguists Joshua Fishman and Calvin Veltman—held, with few exceptions, for earlier (mainly European) immigrant groups.[9] Schematically, the process of Anglicization occurs in the following way. Some individuals of the immigrant generation learn English, though they generally prefer their native language, especially at home. Thus, their children usually grow up as bilinguals, but many of them prefer English, "responding to their parents in the dominant language while understanding what the parents say in the mother tongue."[10] Members of the second generation generally speak English at home when establishing their own households and rearing children. Consequently, by the third generation, the prevalent pattern is English monolingualism, and knowledge of the mother tongue for most ethnics is fragmentary at best.

Infiltration of English into the home, a critical factor in the Anglicization process, often begins when children enter school. As English becomes accepted out of necessity by immigrants and the second generation as the dominant language in the public sphere, the mother tongue is more and more restricted to use with social intimates, especially family members.[11] Consequently, if the private use of the minority language attenuates, then effectively there is no refuge left for it. There are some exceptions to the three-generation pattern of Anglicization: one is the Navajo language, whose retention has little bearing on immigrant languages, but another may be Spanish. Whether Spanish is truly an exception or simply undergoes linguistic shift at a slower pace is an important and debated question. One view has been that Spanish speakers are on average a generation or so behind others in converting to English monolingualism, but another view sees in the huge size of the Spanish-speaking group and in the proximity of Latin America factors that make Spanish unique among immigrant languages in its ability to resist the hegemony of English.[12]

Language acculturation begins in the immigrant generation. Of course, some immigrants learn English even before they come to the United States. Indian and Filipino immigrants, for example, come from countries where English is widely spoken, and consequently most know some English before they arrive. Once immigrants are here, their acquisition of English is affected by a series of factors including age at arrival, education, and length of residence in the United States.[13] Also, immigrants who come with the intention of taking up permanent residence are more likely to acquire English than those who view themselves as sojourners. Adult immigrants who come with their families are more likely to invest in learning English since they usually have school-age children, whose success in American schools is an obvious parental concern. The immigrants' social context in the United States further influences their acquisition of English, because it determines the incentives and opportunities to use one language rather than the other. For instance, a group's size and degree of segregation have been found to influence its rate of shift to English: the larger, more segregated language groups shift more slowly.[14]

Whatever the regularity of mother-tongue use, some proficiency in English generally is apparent among immigrants who have resided in the United States for more than a few years, and English proficiency attains a high level among their U.S.-born children. Even in the largest enclave economies—the Cubans in Miami, Koreans in Los Angeles, and Chinese in San Francisco—U.S.-born generations are, to an overwhelming degree, fluent in English. The concern, voiced at times in hysterical tones in the public debate about immigration, that the volume of immigration threatens the status of English is misplaced.[15] All of the studies of the new immigration indicate that linguistic assimilation in the form of English acquisition is a quasi-universal pattern.[16] We would add that, given the prestige of English throughout the world as a result of globalization and the attempts of parents in many countries to make sure their children are exposed to English, the receptiveness of immigrants and their children to English is scarcely surprising.

For the U.S.-born generations, the issue, then, is not fluency in English, which can more or less be taken for granted, but maintenance of the mother tongue. In contrast to the sociolinguistic theory and praxis of a generation ago, which discouraged bilingualism on the ground that it retarded the intellectual development of children—and in dissent from alarmism about the status of English—Alejandro Portes and Rubén Rumbaut have constructed a thoughtful case for bilingualism, emphasizing its positive contribution. They point out that bilingual individuals possess two (or more) symbols for every object and that, accordingly, bilingualism is conducive to intellectual flexibility; they also present evidence that it contributes to success in American schools. For positive outcomes to be attained, however, bilingualism must not pose a barrier to mastery of the majority language; it must, in other words, be "fluent," as opposed to "limited," bilingualism.[17]

Such bilingualism remains a hypothesis, however; the practical extent to which it can be created and maintained across generations is unknown, especially given the tradition of English monolingualism in the United States. Portes and Rumbaut's longitudinal study of school-age members of new immigrant groups suggests that the pressures to convert to English remain potent.[18] At the time of their first interviews, in 1992, with first- and second-generation eighth- and ninth-graders in the Miami and Fort Lauderdale areas and in San Diego, the overwhelming majority were already proficient in English, though a large proportion at that point retained fluency in the mother tongue. Yet even where such fluency persisted, the prestige of English was high: overall, nearly three-quarters of respondents preferred to speak English, and this figure was greater still among the members of the second generation. By the time of the second interviews three years later, the position of English had been strengthened while that of the mother tongue had deteriorated. The preference for English had expanded to nine-tenths of the youngsters overall. Moreover, reported competency in English had also grown, while that in the mother tongue declined.

This study strengthens the doubts about whether bilingualism can be maintained across the generations as other than a minority pattern in the face of the virtually universal proficiency in English and clear preference for it as the language of everyday interaction.[19]

We catch a glimpse of the contemporary pattern of language shift with linguistic data compiled from the 1990 U.S. Census. The census asks whether each member of a household speaks a language other than English at home, and if so, what is his or her level of speaking ability in English; unfortunately, there is no self-assessment of competence in languages other than English. Given the way the census question is posed, there is a risk that even occasional use of a language other than English is reported, and thus that the data overstate mother-tongue retention.[20] Yet, this limitation notwithstanding, the census data about languages spoken at home are probative for the course of bilingualism. Particularly telling is the absence of a mother tongue: where the exclusive use of English is rising, the level of bilingualism almost certainly is falling.[21] This must be the case for the children of the current generation of adults, for the roots of mother-tongue ability lie in the parental household; if a language is not spoken by children with their parents, the likelihood that they will ultimately have fluency in it is small. (Not many Americans, after all, fluently speak a language they learned mainly at school, and much evidence demonstrates that oral ability in a language is best acquired before the mid-teenage years.)[22]

Initially, we focus on the twenty-five to forty-four age group. This is a critical age range for language usage, since the individuals at this stage have generally established their own households and are raising their own families; they also are frequently in the workforce, where the economic disadvantages of limited English competence become apparent. We restrict our examination to groups whose U.S.-born members are not mainly the descendants of immigrants from earlier eras. (Decennial census data do not allow us to separate out the adult second generation from subsequent generations.) For this reason, we examine language shift among the Chinese, Filipinos, Indians, Koreans, and Vietnamese (but not the Japanese, whose U.S.-born are predominantly in the third and later generations) and also among the Cubans, Dominicans, Mexicans, and Salvadorans.[23] Some of these groups, notably the Chinese and Mexicans, have a longer history in the United States than the others, and their U.S.-born include some third- and even fourth-generation members, but all of them have a substantial second generation. Since we are focusing on U.S.-born adults who were twenty-five and older in 1990, the second generation represents the children of immigrants who arrived before the 1965 changes to immigration law that are widely seen as ushering in the new immigration era. There is, at the time we write this, no way around this limitation. Nevertheless, our list includes the major groups whose immigrants report below-average English proficiency (in ascending order of proficiency, these are Mexicans, Dominicans, Salvadorans, Cubans, Koreans, and Vietnamese).[24] Contemporary immigrants from other areas of the world, especially western Europe and Africa, tend to have very high levels of English competence. In sum, the groups we examine constitute the most rigorous test of language assimilation that can be attained at this time.

Figure 6.1 presents the percentages of adults aged twenty-five to forty-four who speak only English at home for immigrants by period of arrival, and for the second and later generations of these groups. Quite predictably, the exclusive use of English at home is infrequent in the immigrant generation, almost regardless of length of residence. Thus, the rate is generally below 5 percent for immigrants who have

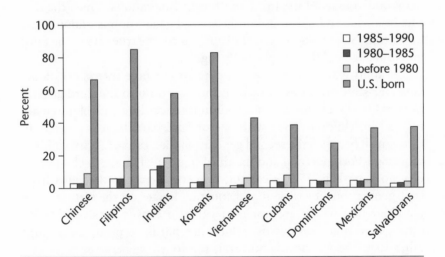

Figure 6.1. Percent who speak only English at home (1990), 25–44-year-olds by immigrant cohort and generation. *Source:* Tabulations from the 5% Public Use Microdata Sample of the Census.

been in the United States for ten years or less, with Filipinos and Indians as mild exceptions.

Among the U.S.-born generations in all groups, there is a sharp rise in the exclusive use of English at home. In all the Asian groups but the Vietnamese, more than half appear to maintain a monolingual English-speaking home; among the Filipinos and Koreans, this is reported by 80–85 percent. Conversion to English only is substantially lower among the Spanish-speaking groups. Even so, the use of Spanish at home has been dropped by more than a quarter of U.S.-born Dominicans and by more than a third of U.S.-born Cubans, Mexicans, and Salvadorans. The Mexicans offer the acid test, given the large size of the group, their frequent residence in extensive Mexican neighborhoods, and the concentration of large portions of the group within a few hundred miles of the Mexican border, where the airwaves are permeated by Spanish-language media. All of these factors should be conducive to the retention of the mother tongue. Yet 36 percent of their U.S.-born generations use exclusively English at home. Since Mexican immigration has a longer history than that of other Spanish-speaking groups (and includes the descendants of families that were present when the United States acquired the territory that became the southwestern states and California), the U.S.-born group includes many individuals of the third and fourth generations. Thus, the true rate of exclusive English use in the second generation is undoubtedly lower than 36 percent, but by the same token, the true rate in the third and fourth generations is probably higher.

A second way of using census data to examine intergenerational language shift brings us directly to the transition to the third generation and to the obviously crucial circumstances in which children are reared. For children living with one or both parents, it is possible to distinguish between the second generation (i.e., the U.S.-born children of foreign-born parents) and the third (i. e., the U.S.-born children of U.S.-born parents).[25] (We cannot, however, separate the third from later generations, because that distinction hinges on the birthplace of grandparents, which are not retrievable in census data, except for three-generation households, which are hardly typical; for groups other than the Mexicans, however, the fourth generation is small.) The percentages who speak only English at home are shown for these two generations of children (ages six to fifteen) in Figure 6.2. These data appear to indicate that the three-generation model of language shift, while not universal, is broadly applicable to immigrant groups.

For the Asian groups with substantial numbers in the third generation—the Chinese, Filipinos, and Koreans—90 percent or more of
this generation speak only English at home. For the Chinese and Koreans, these proportions represent marked increases from those in
the second generation, where 40 percent or fewer do not speak the
mother tongue at home. For the Latino groups with sizable third
generations, the Cubans and Mexicans, the proportions of this generation who are monolingual in English are less than the proportions
among Asians, but they are still high, from two-thirds (Mexicans) to
three-quarters (Cubans). For the Mexicans in particular, given all of
the reasons why Spanish is expected to persist among them, the figure
seems remarkably high, even if it should be discounted somewhat because of the presence of individuals who belong to the fourth (or
later) generations. It does seem clear that loyalty to Spanish erodes
over the generations.

In alarmist discussions of immigration, the possibility is sometimes
raised that parts of the United States may effectively become bilingual
in the near future, with Spanish attaining virtual parity with English

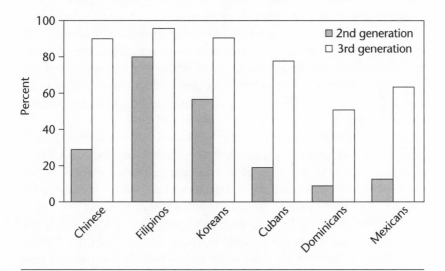

Figure 6.2. Percent who speak only English at home (1990), 6–15-year-olds by
generation. *Source:* Richard Alba, John Logan, Amy Lutz, and Brian Stults,
"Only English by the Third Generation? Loss and Preservation of the Mother
Tongue among the Grandchildren of Contemporary Immigrants," *Demography*
39 (August 2002): 467–485.

as a language in which the ordinary business of daily life is conducted. This possibility seems to some a threat to the hitherto unquestioned hegemony of the English language and the American culture that is embedded in it.[26] Such alarmist prospects have fed the "English only" movements that have arisen in many states. We are skeptical that Spanish, or any other language, for that matter, can in the foreseeable future reach parity with English, at least within the present fifty states. (Puerto Rico, should it attain statehood, would be another matter.) Those who raise this prospect have, in our view, lost sight of the asymmetry that reigns in matters of language in the United States. For speakers of mother tongues other than English recognize that they must learn English or suffer economic and social disadvantages, while native speakers of English generally reject categorically the premise that they must learn another language. English speakers may learn Spanish or another minority language, but they generally do so as a matter of choice, not to satisfy an imperative.

We can test the notion of a bilingual territory in the United States by examining the language situation near the Mexico-U.S. border, where the forces promoting Spanish ought to be at their strongest. Among Mexican Americans, the retention of Spanish should be very common there and the transition to English monolingualism relatively weak.[27] For this purpose, we examine the linguistic situation of both U.S.-born adults and children in three geographic zones: areas in close proximity to the border (a band whose width, because of the geographic restrictions in micro-level census data, varies between 35 and 215 miles);[28] elsewhere in a border state; and the remainder of the United States. The data are given in Table 6.1.

Without question, proximity to the U.S.-Mexico border does support the persistence of bilingualism among Mexican Americans, but it does not appear to retard English proficiency, at least insofar as this is measured in census data. U.S.-born Mexican American adults are much more likely to speak Spanish at home if they reside in proximity to the border: nearly 85 percent of such residents say that they do. This percentage drops off noticeably, to about 70 percent, for those who live elsewhere in a border state and to slightly less than 50 percent further in the U.S. interior. Among second- and later-generation Mexican Americans who live in the U.S. interior, at least half have dropped Spanish and speak only English at home. But for proficiency in English, proximity to the border makes little difference: more than

Table 6.1. Language characteristics of Mexican Americans by proximity to the U.S.-
Mexico border (1990)

	Proximate to border	Elsewhere in border state	In the U.S. interior
% speak English well, U.S.-born 25–44-year-olds	95.6	96.9	97.6
% speak only English at home, U.S.-born 25–44-year-olds	16.0	31.3	52.1
% speak only English at home, third-generation 5–14-year-olds	31.4	58.7	73.3

Source: Tabulations from the 5% Public Use Microdata Sample of the 1990 U.S. Census.

95 percent of the U.S.-born Mexican Americans in each geographic zone can speak English well. For third-generation children, the percentage speaking Spanish at home also varies substantially by location. Near the border, only 30 percent have converted to English monolingualism at home; in other words, the majority have remained bilingual. Elsewhere in border states, nearly 60 percent of these Mexican American children speak only English at home, as do about three-quarters of those in non-border states. The great majority of third-generation children do not live in the vicinity of the border, it should be noted; this majority includes such huge Mexican American concentrations as that in and around Los Angeles. The border zone appears to sustain a culture of bilingualism for Mexican Americans, but the U.S.-born still attain competence in English, and a nontrivial level of conversion to English monolingualism occurs anyway. When Mexican American families move away from the border, the probability that their children will retain Spanish appears to be greatly reduced.

All in all, the evidence of powerful currents of acculturation is simply undeniable in the realm of language. Competence in spoken English is characteristic of the great majority of immigrants once they have been in the United States for more than ten years, and it is virtually universal among their children who are born here. The acquisition of English leaves room for continuing competence in a mother tongue; bilingualism is extremely common among immigrants and is also frequently encountered among the second and later generations. But our analysis of census data appears to demonstrate unequivocally that a substantial proportion of the second generation do not maintain a bilingual pattern at home, and thus a large percentage of the third generation grow up speaking only English. As others have noted,[29] this is especially the case among Asian groups. It appears unlikely that bilingualism will persist into their third and fourth generations, except under unusual circumstances such as regular travel to homelands by families that maintain business and professional links abroad. There is greater evidence of persisting bilingualism among Spanish-speaking groups. Whether the Spanish-speaking, because of their numbers and proximity to Latin America, are simply a generation or so slower in converting to English monolingualism or will be able to maintain bilingualism, at least for some fraction, into the fourth generation and beyond is a question that cannot be answered with confidence at this time. But by any standard, linguistic assimilation is widespread, and more or less complete assimilation—that is, English monolingualism with at best fragmentary knowledge of a mother tongue—would appear to be the experience of the majority in the third generation of all contemporary immigrant groups.

Might the rate of intergenerational conversion be slowed appreciably, even for the Asian groups, as the presence of various contemporary immigrant groups grows in the future as a result of continuing immigration? This could happen; but we think that the outer limit of bilingualism is probably established by the Mexican American case. Mexicans have a long-standing history of immigration, which persisted throughout the twentieth century: they represented in 2000 more than 7 percent of the total American population; their language (insofar as they are Spanish speakers; some Mexicans speak Indian languages) was supported by a variety of U.S. institutions, such as Spanish-language newspapers, radio, and television; and their homeland is near at hand. Yet, as we have seen, more than 60 percent of Mexican children of the third and later generations speak only English at home. Bilingualism persists into the third generation for a substantial portion of the group, but conversion to English monolingualism appears to be at least as strong a pattern. We doubt that its power can be broken. Indeed, the compatibility of Asian languages with English is undoubtedly much less than for Spanish, as they are linguistically far removed from European tongues.[30]

Of course, the conversion of substantial portions of the U.S.-born generations to English monolingualism does not mean that the current immigrant languages will ever cease to be spoken in the United

States. The languages brought by the immigrants of the 1820–1930 period have not died out, even though we are now three-quarters of a century beyond the end of mass immigration from Europe. For as far into the future as the eye can possibly see, then, the United States will be a polyglot society, displaying a robust linguistic pluralism. Large parts of the first and second generations, along with smaller parts of the third, will be bilingual, and their numbers will grow if immigration continues at its present clip.[31] The pattern of more complete linguistic assimilation, which is especially detectable in the third and later generations, should not be allowed to cloud this bilingualism; but conversely, neither should persisting bilingualism be allowed to disguise the potent force of assimilation in language.

Language does not offer the right paradigm for understanding other forms of acculturation because linguistic acculturation is of necessity one-directional. Yet the point that the United States will remain a polyglot society finds an echo in other domains of culture, for the rapid or complete extinction of the cultures brought by immigrants is not to be expected in the American environment. Certainly this did not happen among groups of European origin either. Some aspects of culture are capable of persisting independently of the mother tongue. They are exemplified in the persistence of ethnic associations in the Chinese communities stemming from the mid-nineteenth-century migration, despite the long hiatus from 1882 to the 1960s when legal migration from China was curtailed by anti-Chinese immigration laws.[32] To judge by the experiences of European immigrant groups, religion, with its capacity to give rise to ethnically separate institutional structures, especially endures, supporting the continuation of various cultural practices. The experience of both Jews and Irish Catholics bears witness to its efficacy. Since some of the new immigrant groups bring with them religions, such as Buddhism, not previously established in the United States or are capable of forming their own congregations within established American religions (e.g., Korean churches), the role of religion as a cultural matrix is certain to continue. Aspects of culture also survive because they are absorbed into the mainstream, as we have already observed. The incorporation of some ethnic cultural elements, along with the broad acculturation we have documented through language, narrows the band of cultural distinctiveness for ethnic groups arising from immigration. In the case of Europeans, this lowered the cultural barriers to social relationships across ethnic lines and thus contributed to the spread of interethnic marriage. Whether it will do the same for the newer groups remains to be seen, but data showing an increase in intermarriage for Asian Americans and Hispanics point to an emerging public acceptance of interracial marriage in American society.

Socioeconomic Attainment

A hallmark of the new immigration is the diversity of social background of the immigrants. Rather than hailing primarily from rural communities, they come from both rural and urban areas, from underdeveloped regions of the Western Hemisphere as well as from industrially developed areas of East Asia. Both the poorly educated and the highly educated are represented in large numbers. Their occupations encompass the full spectrum, from unskilled labor in the informal economy to skilled professional and technical jobs in the mainstream economy. This range reflects two distinct streams of immigrants into U.S. labor markets: *traditional labor immigrants* and *human-capital immigrants*.[33] At the lower rungs of the market are labor migrants who, like the earlier European immigrants from peasant origins, take jobs involving manual work in garment shops, restaurants, hotels, parking lots, and bakeries, on farms, and in light manufacture and assembly. As with the labor migration from Europe, contemporary labor migrants come predominantly from villages and rural towns in areas on the periphery of the world market economy.[34] Strikingly new in the current era of mass immigration is the sizable increase in the proportion of highly educated "human-capital" immigrants who come from urban backgrounds. Nearly one-fourth of legal immigrants report their occupation at the time of arrival as professional. Such human-capital immigrants come from all regions of the world, but especially from Asia. There are many Asian engineers, technicians, computer scientists, mathematicians, physicians, and nurses now living in the United States. The passage by Congress in October 2000 of a bill to increase significantly, to 195,000 a year, the number of visas for human-capital immigrants contributes to the relative size and importance of this migration stream.[35] The presence for the first time of large numbers of human-capital immigrants raises the question whether some earlier theories of immigration require rethinking.

The influential theory of labor migration developed by Michael

Piore in his seminal book *Birds of Passage* emphasized the function of immigrant labor in filling the jobs at the bottom of the labor market that native workers do not want. These positions are characteristically unskilled and menial, generally low paying, and stigmatized by inferior status, and they often entail hard or unpleasant working conditions and job insecurity. Piore maintained that employers initially must actively recruit poorly educated and unskilled workers from rural areas of underdeveloped countries to fill these jobs; but once a labor migration has begun, it becomes self-sustaining as networks of migrant workers establish the basis for chain migration linking firms in the advanced industrial society with their home villages. Should a source of labor dry up or legislation stemming from the opposition of natives curtail further immigration, employers will seek and find alternative sources of temporary labor; hence, this form of labor is inexhaustible. The theory's core proposition is that the labor market in advanced industrial economies is segmented into primary and secondary sectors: "There is thus a fundamental dichotomy between the jobs of migrants and the jobs of natives, and the role of migrants in industrial economies can be traced to the factors that generate the distinction initially, to the role and function of the secondary sector in which migrants are found, and to the evolution of its labor requirements."[36]

To be sure, immigration from Mexico and Central America—the largest stream of contemporary immigrants—conforms to the pattern of labor migration theorized by Piore, as described in Chapter 5. Human-capital immigration, however, does not.[37] The jobs these immigrants fill are generally located in what Piore identifies as the primary-labor market. Moreover, human-capital immigrants do not come as "birds of passage," temporary workers who have little incentive to participate in the cultural and social practices of the society in which they work. Instead, they generally seek permanent residence, now often through the family reunification portal of the legal immigration edifice.[38] To secure the commitment of human-capital immigrants, employers extend the same long-term contracts as for native workers. In sum, the presence of large numbers of human-capital immigrants challenges the confined role of immigrants in the labor force posited by the theory of the segmented labor market.

Human-capital immigrants have been less a focus of research than traditional labor migrants in part because they tend to assimilate economically and culturally within a relatively short time after their arrival. Those educated abroad, after a period of downward adjustment, appear to shift into jobs commensurate with their education, as they acquire local work experience and facility with the English language.[39] Many human-capital immigrants also enter the labor market directly from professional and graduate schools in the United States. Their movement into jobs in the mainstream economy involves a school-to-job transition not dissimilar from that of native-born professional workers. (This is not to deny that foreign-born professionals may still face some discrimination in the U.S. labor market, which typically confronts them with a "glass ceiling" capping their ultimate rise.) Because human-capital immigrants frequently are exposed to Western culture before arrival and typically seek to find employment in organizations and firms where English fluency is required, they acculturate relatively quickly to workaday life in the United States. Although they may encounter difficulties in the early years, human-capital immigrants soon obtain returns on their education similar to those of natives in the same occupational group.[40] Traditional labor migrants and immigrant entrepreneurs, in contrast, tend to clump together in visible ethnic communities and economies. Researchers have thus concentrated on them in discussing the problematics of assimilation. A growing concern (as we shall see) over the declining "quality" of immigrants and the consequences for their prospects of economic assimilation has also focused attention on labor migration.[41]

What is obvious from this brief discussion is that the socioeconomic circumstances of contemporary immigrant groups are quite diverse, considerably more so than was the case for the earlier immigration from Europe. This makes for a complicated picture. We next survey the extensive literature on the economic incorporation of the immigrant generation, first in ethnic economies, then in the general one. We then proceed to an assessment, necessarily somewhat tentative, of the second and subsequent generations.

Immigrants in the Ethnic Economy

Traditionally, labor migrants have concentrated in immigrant communities and found low-wage jobs in the ethnic economy or through labor contractors who recruit for firms owned by natives. Research on the economic progress of immigrant minorities has thus focused on the role of ethnic economies in providing a protected niche.[42] Employment there has been of especial importance for minorities facing harsh societal hostility. Thus, despite institutional racism that excluded the Chinese and Japanese from opportunities for mainstream advancement, they were able to sustain themselves during the first half of the twentieth century through a small-business economy that created alternative ladders of opportunity. This provided the economic basis for rearing and educating a second generation. In addition, the ethnic economy provided a means for survival and economic gain when racial discrimination barred even the college-educated second generation from opportunities in the mainstream economy.

In many respects, ethnic economies served a similar role for early Chinese and Japanese immigrants as for Jewish immigrants, whose success through an ethnic economy is renowned. What set the experience of these groups apart from the traditional form of labor migration was that the ethnic economy freed them from dependence on low-wage employment in firms owned by natives. Immigrant entrepreneurs relied instead on ethnic resources to build small-business economies that were often competitive with native businesses and that provided immigrant workers alternative employment. Immigrant entrepreneurship has remained predominantly a matter of small family-operated businesses. The odds of entering into self-employment appear to be greater for immigrants with either a high school or college education who come with family members. The immigrant family provides the social organization and labor power that facilitate starting up a small business despite very modest financial resources.[43] The Korean-owned businesses in the New York region, typified by greengroceries, nail salons, and dry cleaners, illustrate this pattern.

There can be no question that ethnic economies have constituted an important form of incorporation for immigrants. Their viability, however, may be contingent on continued immigration and the persistence of institutional barriers to mobility in the mainstream society. Following the abatement of societal hostility during and after World War II, the Chinese ethnic economy declined steadily in size, and many smaller Chinatowns disappeared as the American-born generation assimilated. Even the largest Chinatowns declined prior to the resumption of Chinese immigration after 1965. The Japanese ethnic economy was largely a first-generation phenomenon. Though it was reconstituted after the internment during World War II, it never regained its prewar level. Once the color line broke down, the second generation (nisei) abandoned parental small businesses to seek jobs in the mainstream economy. Implied in their choice was a perception of the limited nature of the economic mobility and choice provided by the ethnic economy, constituted by very small firms with limited capital and bounded markets.[44] In the contemporary immigration, this is already becoming evident in the Vietnamese ethnic economy in Orange County, popularly known as Little Saigon. As Vietnamese immigrants and their children assimilate economically and move out of the ethnic community, demand for products and services in Little Saigon is beginning to decline. The second generation apparently prefers the shopping malls in Orange County. Consequently, competition has intensified among shopkeepers in Little Saigon, which in turn has driven down profits; this has resulted in an increased mortality rate for Vietnamese firms. In a five-year period during the mid-1990s, 929 businesses opened up in Little Saigon, but 811 closed down.[45]

Although job opportunities in the ethnic economy are limited in comparison to the larger and more extensive labor markets of the mainstream economy, there may be little alternative, at least initially, for immigrant workers who are disadvantaged by educational, language, and ethnic factors, and a significant number of them still find employment within ethnic confines.[46] The advantages of working in the enclave rather than the mainstream economy have been the subject of considerable debate, focused on the optimistic hypothesis that immigrant workers in the enclave economy would derive returns on human capital comparable to those available to workers in the primary sector of the economy. Reviewing the debate stimulated by Alejandro Portes's influential "enclave economy" hypothesis, however, Ivan Light and Stavros Karageorgis conclude that "empirical tests of relative wages have generally failed to substantiate . . . [the] enclave economy hypothesis."[47] This conclusion seems acutely borne out by the Chinese case. For immigrant workers in San Francisco, jobs in the Chinatown economy appear to provide even lower earnings than those in the low-wage, competitive secondary sector. There have been similar findings for Asian immigrant workers in Los Angeles.[48] The fact that Chinese men earn the lowest net wages of any immigrant group in the nation has been attributed to the ethnic economy's effect on workers' wages: "More so than other streams of current immigrants, it appears that the uneducated from China are concentrated in or trapped in a low-wage enclave economy, helping to explain why the Chinese are less effective than other immigrants in translating their characteristics into earnings."[49]

Although the ethnic economy remains important for contemporary immigrants, one must question whether it does, or can, provide the main route for their economic advancement. Especially for the Latino groups other than Cubans, the ethnic economy cannot employ more than a small fraction of Latino workers. According to the 1992 census of minority-owned businesses, Latino-owned firms controlled only 700,000 jobs. Even under the very generous assumption that these firms hired only other Latinos, it is obvious that they could take in just a tiny portion of the Latinos then in the labor market.[50] Moreover, the principal economic advantages of the enclave accrue to firm owners rather than to their employees. Only for immigrant owners does it appear to be true that the income returns to human capital in the enclave match or exceed what can be achieved in the primary sectors of the mainstream.[51] And while we agree that "self-employment represents an important component of the immigrant experience in the U.S. labor market,"[52] it is useful to keep in mind how uncommon self-employment (which includes some forms of professional employment as well as small-business ownership) is: just 14 percent of native-born non-Hispanic whites are self-employed; only Korean immigrants show a higher concentration than this (28 percent). Despite the emphasis on immigrant entrepreneurship in the literature on contemporary immigration, all other immigrant groups report a lower level of involvement in self-employment than whites.[53] It is doubtful that the modal labor market experience of immigrants takes place in the ethnic economy, and it is certainly not in small-business ownership. Immigrant workers may first establish a foothold in the immigrant labor market by working in the ethnic economy, but over time the direction of job changes tends to be toward jobs that offer better remuneration and working conditions, and these are mostly available in the mainstream labor market.[54]

We find it implausible that the constrained horizons in the ethnic economies established by most contemporary immigrant groups will prove attractive to substantial segments of the second generation. In any event, this generation, generally fluent in English and possessing American educational credentials, will not be as disadvantaged in the mainstream economy as its parents are. Few will be satisfied with lives as restaurant or garment workers. Even in those cases where the ethnic economy has expanded beyond a narrow base to infiltrate more desirable sectors of the economy—this is famously true for the

Cubans of Miami, and it appears to be increasingly so for the Chinese, Indians, and Koreans[55]—we doubt that it can retain the loyalty of large numbers of the second generation. In the main, the groups that have made this breakout are ones that bring high levels of human capital to the United States, and their second generations have educational attainments that exceed those of the non-Hispanic white majority. In our view, the most successful ethnic economies, where high rates of entrepreneurship are found, are most likely to serve as a springboard for entry into professional occupations by the second and third generations. This was indeed their role for eastern European Jews, for Chinese descended from the earlier nineteenth-century immigration, and for the Japanese, and the popular literature has already identified the Koreans as following this well-trodden path, with immigrants making self-conscious sacrifices for the sake of the educational and professional prospects of their children.[56]

Immigrants in the Open Labor Market

The experiences of immigrants in the general labor market have been as intensely debated as have those associated with ethnic enclaves. The pioneering studies by the economist Barry Chiswick indicated that after an initial period of income decline, which he interpreted as the "cost of immigration," the earnings of immigrants gradually achieved parity with those of natives. George Borjas challenged these findings, however, because Chiswick relied on a cross-sectional research design, which conflated the effects of lengthening residence in the United States with possible differences across immigration cohorts. By examining cohort differences, Borjas's analysis suggested that over the previous five decades there had been a substantial decline in the *relative* education of immigrants entering the U.S. labor market. Pooling data from multiple censuses, he found that the income growth of recent cohorts failed to surpass the earnings levels of the native-born and was lower than the growth experienced by earlier cohorts of immigrants. His controversial conclusion was that the "quality" of immigrants had declined as the source of immigrants shifted from Europe to the Third World, and that the low level of formal schooling of Mexican and Central American labor migrants was likely to impose a lower ceiling than in the past on the extent of economic assimilation for the first generation.[57]

The debate on the rate of economic assimilation has been largely inconclusive. The limitations of existing data prevent any truly longitudinal analysis. Although Borjas pooled data from two decennial censuses, he was unable to examine changes in earnings for the same immigrant workers as they acquired work experience in the United States. One possibility his analysis cannot rule out is that on-the-job learning and adult education may result in greater economic assimilation than might be inferred from the initial low levels of formal schooling; a second is that the undetected return to their home countries of some of the more successful immigrants reduces the apparent economic success over time of an immigrant cohort. In any event, if the comparison group is the U.S.-born members of the same ethnic group, then Chiswick's results are confirmed: even recent cohorts of immigrants quickly achieve economic parity with native-born Americans. Immigrants who come to the United States as children also achieve economic parity.[58]

As we noted earlier, the issue of economic assimilation is relevant mainly for labor immigrants rather than human-capital entrants. Overall, the literature suggests that the labor immigrants in the post-1965 streams are handicapped not so much by race as by their relatively low stocks of human capital interacting with structural changes in the U.S. economy.[59] If earnings growth is slow, this is accounted for in part by the low level of education of recent cohorts of immigrants from developing economies who make up the traditional labor stream. This is a matter of relative educational levels, for in absolute terms (i.e., amount of schooling), the educational levels of labor immigrants have been going up; but they have not risen as fast as the average educational level of native-born workers. Further, the slower pace of economic assimilation is the result of the transformation of the American economy, in particular the gradual erosion of demand for unskilled labor and the increasing demand for highly skilled workers, a trend that of course affects natives and immigrants alike. The low human-capital stock of labor migrants from Mexico and Central America could cast a long shadow into the future through the influence of parental education on school attainment of the U.S.-born generations.

A problem of a different order with respect to economic assimilation is posed by the large number of illegal or undocumented immigrants, estimated to be as many as 8 million in 2000.[60] Many of the undocumented have no more than a primary school education, although there is considerably more educational heterogeneity among them than is often recognized. In particular, visa overstayers, who legally enter the United States but remain beyond the validity of their visas, make up nearly half of the total undocumented population, and they tend to be relatively well educated. This is understandable in terms of the social selectivity involved in obtaining a tourist visa to enter the United States.[61] But undocumented migrants who cross the border clandestinely, the greatest number of whom are Mexicans, the largest nationality group among the undocumented, generally have low levels of education. Undocumented immigrants tend to concentrate in particular locations. Geographic concentration, which enables employers to depend on their cheap labor, may exacerbate the effects of poor education on their labor market experience.

But above all, the problems of the undocumented have to do with their legal vulnerability. In the post–civil rights era, as we discussed in Chapter 2, Title VII and other civil rights legislation have made it more costly for firms (except small businesses, which are difficult to monitor) to discriminate by gender and race. As a result, the workplace is more regulated today than it was at the time of the earlier mass immigration to the United States. The principle of equality under the law has been definitively extended to legal immigrants and naturalized citizens.[62] It does not extend to illegal immigrants, however, even though they are entitled to due process and possess limited rights of access to public services. Consequently, illegal undocumented immigrants are likely to concentrate in jobs in the underground informal economy not regulated by the state. Undocumented status restricts labor market mobility because it effectively closes off job opportunities in large firms and government, which in part accounts for the fact that there are relatively few human capital immigrants among the undocumented. Even so, studies have shown some earnings growth, albeit relatively slight, for illegal immigrants. The fact that "wages of undocumented immigrants increased at all is remarkable," given the performance of the U.S. economy during the period covered by one study (the 1980s) and the restrictions on labor mobility.[63] A study of Latino day laborers in Los Angeles County shows that the lowest-level manual laborers from Mexico are surprisingly adroit and entrepreneurial in negotiating the informal labor market of Los Angeles.[64] The hourly wage of day laborers in this study was higher than the state's minimum wage.

Educational Attainment of the Second Generation

Because the new immigration is so recent, the number of second-generation adults in most groups is still comparatively small. Consequently, studies of how this generation is faring have focused largely on educational performance rather than labor market outcomes. The distinction between human-capital and traditional labor immigrants has great relevance here because of the predictability of children's educational attainment in light of their parents'. As many have noted, the contemporary immigration stream harbors large numbers of both the very highly and the very minimally educated. Immigrants are overrepresented among the holders of postgraduate degrees, especially doctorates, and also among those whose education has not extended beyond primary school. In fact, they make up more than half of all U.S. residents who attended school for less than five years, and include a sizable number who never attended school at all. Specifically, the migrations from Taiwan, India, Iran, and many African countries are human-capital immigrations, dominated by individuals with relatively high levels of education, while those from Mexico, Haiti, and the Dominican Republic conform largely to the image of traditional labor migrants, bringing proportionately few highly educated individuals. Although such data can lead to a temptation to overgeneralize and classify African and Asians in general as human-capital immigrants and Latinos as traditional labor migrants, the reality is not quite so neat. Some Asian immigrations include many with the characteristics of traditional labor migrants; this is true of the Cambodian immigration, largely made up of refugees. The Chinese and Cuban immigrations are mixed cases, with large proportions of both the highly and the minimally educated. Moreover, the Mexican and Dominican immigrations contain substantial contingents of the highly educated, but they are lost statistically among the much larger numbers of low-wage workers.[65]

Studies of the educational attainment of children from immigrant families, whether they belong to the 1.5 or the second generation, demonstrate that their school performance is frequently superior to that of the general population. One reason is that highly educated human-capital immigrants are typically able to translate this capital, which is partly cultural, into relatively high educational attainment for their children. In addition, immigrant parents, regardless of their own educational attainment, appear to emphasize to their children the importance of education as a route to success in the United States and to maintain relatively strict homework regimens.[66] Hmong children from Southeast Asia, whose parents are frequently not literate, nevertheless achieve high grades because they devote so much time to homework each day.[67] The success of the children of immigrants depends obviously on their proficiency in English, and this factor favors the second generation, born in the United States, as well as members of the 1.5 generation who arrived when they were still young.[68]

There are, however, threats in the American setting to the drive for school success. For one thing, the zeal of immigrant children for schoolwork appears to diminish over time, perhaps as they gradually perceive the lesser effort put in by native-born Americans and adjust their own accordingly. A study of immigrant schoolchildren in Miami and San Diego has found that, with additional years in the United States, the average number of hours devoted to homework declines while the time spent watching television increases.[69] In this respect, assimilation to American norms appears to produce a negative outcome. Even more threatening are the seductions of an "oppositional" identity, which scorns the drudgery (and uncertainties) of school success for the more instantaneous respect afforded by low-achieving, defiant peer groups.[70] Of course, this is an old story in the history of American immigrant groups and minority groups in general, as studies of Italian American youth in the mid-twentieth century illustrate.[71] The risk that children will adopt an oppositional identity is greater insofar as they perceive that their own chances of success through school are low or likely to be reduced by discrimination. It is heightened by racial difference from the mainstream, especially by black skin, and by inner-city residence, particularly by proximity in school and neighborhood to an already existing lower-class culture, with its alternative models of behavior and thinking.[72]

Yet, on average, the educational attainment of the U.S.-born generation appears relatively strong, with the children of human-capital immigrants surpassing the average attainment of white Americans, sometimes by a large margin, and the children of labor immigrants improving substantially on the educational records of their parents. Figure 6.3, which is drawn from research by Reynolds Farley and Richard Alba, compares the educational attainments of the first and second generations of the major immigrant populations to those of third- and later-generation non-Hispanic whites as of 1998–2000.[73] The second generation (along with the white comparison group) is limited to those aged twenty-five to thirty-nine, implying that its members were born after the late 1950s and thus are mostly the children of post-1950 immigrants; the lower age limit guarantees that most will have completed their schooling. The immigrant generation is confined to those at least fifty years of age to approximate the educational attainment of the parents of the second generation. To simplify the data presentation, the focus is on the extremes of the educational distribution: college completion at one end and failure to complete high school at the other. Specific groups have mostly been aggregated into larger populations here because the data source, the Current Population Survey, which provides the latest available data and affords an ability to isolate the second generation from later ones, is much smaller than the decennial census.

For groups with large numbers of low-wage labor migrants, there is an unmistakable tendency for educational attainment to improve—

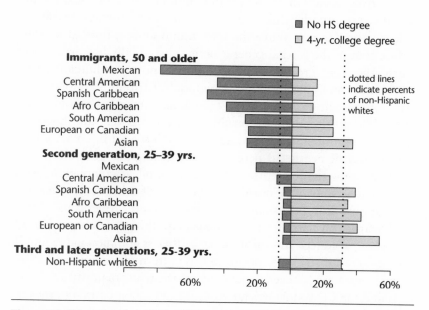

Figure 6.3. Educational attainment by generation, 1998–2000. *Source:* Reynolds Farley and Richard Alba, "The New Second Generation in the United States," *International Migration Review* 36 (Fall 2002). Used with permission.

usually substantially—in the second generation. This is not surprising, since many immigrants from these groups have only a few years of education. Therefore, if their children merely remain through the mandatory years of schooling in the United States, they will have surpassed their parents. Half or more of immigrants from countries such as Mexico, El Salvador, and the Dominican Republic (in the Spanish Caribbean group) have not completed high school. The rates of high school completion are much higher in the second generation; on average, the groups from the Spanish-speaking Caribbean have attained the norm for third-generation whites, and those from Central America have nearly done so.[74] This cannot be said of second-generation Mexicans, whose high school dropout rate is well above that of non-Hispanic whites. The U.S.-born Mexicans, however, do far better in this respect than their immigrant parents.

Improvements are not limited to the lower end of the educational range and to labor migrant groups. The percentage completing college generally rises sharply in the second generation and, except for Mexicans and Central Americans, attains or exceeds the level found among whites. Second-generation advance is noteworthy even for the groups from Asia, where the greatest number of human-capital immigrants are found: while even the immigrant generation's rate of college completion is above the level found among third-generation whites, that in the second generation is substantially higher still. (Of course, the Asian groups are not composed entirely of human-capital immigrants, and education has a bimodal distribution among some Asian immigrant groups, such as the Chinese, many of whom arrive with minimal formal education. By the second generation, however, the failure to obtain the equivalent of a high school diploma, which is at a level of nearly 30 percent in the immigrant generation, has dropped below the white American norm.) College completion levels are also at or above the norm for a number of other second-generation groups: Europeans and Canadians, South Americans, Afro-Caribbeans, and those from the Spanish-speaking Caribbean. For all these groups, college education is markedly less common in the immigrant generation. The exceptions to this pattern of second-generation convergence with (or even superiority to) the white majority are Mexicans and the Central American groups. But in their cases too, the educational attainment of the second generation still represents an advance over that of the first.

The educational picture for the second generation so far shows no signs suggestive of widespread intergenerational decline or stagnation. Nevertheless, one should be cautious about drawing very firm conclusions—optimistic ones, in this case—about the educational progress of the second generation, because the adult segment of this generation is still small and may not be representative of the children of contemporary immigrants.[75] Moreover, any forecast from these data for the third generation of Mexicans and perhaps some other Hispanic groups is even more problematic. According to the most widely accepted analyses, the educational record of third-generation Mexicans does not reach the level of the second generation. For instance, although members of the third generation are no more likely to drop out of high school than are members of the second generation, and they do not slip back toward the limited schooling characteristic of the immigrant generation, they are less likely to go on to college and thus to gain ground on the native white majority. Specifically, in younger cohorts as of the late 1980s, about a quarter of the Mexican American third generation attended college, compared to a third of the second—significantly fewer in both groups than among non-Hispanic whites, approximately half of whom attended college. Nevertheless, one analysis appears to indicate that the third generation is continuing to narrow the educational gap.[76] A possible explanation for the more pessimistic conclusion, which seems to have greater research weight behind it, is that some third-generation Mexican students are attracted to an oppositional subculture because they perceive a limited horizon of opportunity for themselves; they take on what has been described as a "Cholo" or "Chicano" identity and derogate the children from immigrant families for their diligence and ambition. This pattern is consistent with the concept of segmented assimilation.[77] Of course, Mexicans are the prototype of low-wage labor immigration, and there is little reason to think that this pattern will carry over to the third generation of human-capital migrations. Whether it will apply to other labor migrations is the crucial question. For now, this cannot be answered.

Labor Market Position in the Second Generation

As a rule, the average occupational position of the second generation represents a considerable advance over that of the first, and in a number of cases equals or even exceeds the average job status of native whites. These patterns are displayed in Figure 6.4, which shows executive, managerial, and professional occupations grouped on the right, representing the high end of the occupational spectrum, and service, operative, and laborer jobs grouped on the left, representing the low end. Immigrants tend to concentrate in the latter kinds of jobs, so a decline between the first and second generations in the fraction of a group working in these jobs indicates both occupational advance and a greater dispersion of the group throughout the labor force.

Occupational advance for the U.S.-born can be found even among some of the groups with large numbers of human-capital immigrants. Such immigrants, who frequently arrive with foreign educational credentials but a limited ability to communicate in English, do not always attain jobs commensurate with their education; it is by no means uncommon to see foreign college graduates toiling at humble jobs, at least for a period of time. For the Asian second generation, the percentage in high-end positions is substantially greater than for the first generation and for third-generation non-Hispanic whites, and the

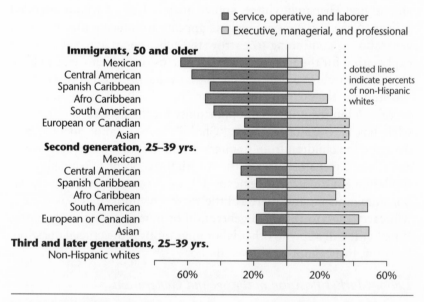

Figure 6.4. Occupational position by generation, 1998–2000. *Source:* Reynolds Farley and Richard Alba, "The New Second Generation in the United States," *International Migration Review* 36 (Fall 2002). Used with permission.

percentage in the jobs at the low end is smaller. There is occupational advance even in the European and Canadian groups, which probably are the least disadvantaged in the immigrant generation because, for one thing, most are fluent in English when they arrive. While their occupational profile in the second generation is not as favorable as that of Asians, it does not lag behind by much.

Among groups dominated by low-wage labor immigrants, the picture of advance is generally uncomplicated: a considerable improvement in average occupational position occurs between the immigrant and U.S.-born generations, though usually not to the point of matching that of native whites. Nonetheless, from the perspective of findings on intergenerational mobility in the status attainment literature, the pattern reported here would exceed expectations based on findings of structural rigidities in transitions from the bottom strata.[78] Especially salient in Figure 6.4 is the decline in the second generation in the proportion holding low-level jobs. While half or more of the immigrant generations of the groups from the Americas (other than Canada) work in service, operative, and labor occupations, this is not true for any of their second generations. In general, the number of U.S.-born in these jobs is close to, and in a couple of cases less than, that of third- and later-generation whites. For all these second generations, moreover, the proportions in the "better" jobs have risen in comparison with the immigrant generation. The proportions in executive, managerial, and professional jobs among the South Americans and the Spanish-speaking groups from the Caribbean have attained the white norm; the proportion for Afro-Caribbeans is not far behind. But even for those second-generation groups that have not achieved parity with whites, Mexicans being the preeminent case because of their prominence in the contemporary immigrant stream, a summary index of labor market position given by mean occupational score would show that the distance from the labor market situation of the immigrant generation is greater than that from the white majority.[79] A substantial upgrading seems apparent in the second generation as of the end of the twentieth century.

Once again, we must point out the need for caution about inferring an overly optimistic conclusion. A number of objections could be made to the necessarily sketchy analysis we present: most important, we cannot directly link the second generation to its family origins, so our statements about the advances of the second generation in comparison with the immigrant one are true only in an aggregate sense. Moreover, because of the data limitations, our national analysis does not examine how the second generation fares in terms of the regional labor markets in which its members actually work. Nor could we distinguish specific groups other than the Mexicans; the aggregate nature of the analysis could cloud the picture. Thus, as of the late 1990s, second-generation adults from the Spanish-speaking Caribbean were disproportionately Cuban, the most advantaged of the major Hispanic groups; hence, the overall occupational standing of the Spanish Caribbean aggregate could sink as, say, the number of second-generation Dominicans in the workforce, a much more disadvantaged group, increases. Moreover, the status of the second generation as a whole could founder if the most pessimistic readings of immigration trends, which see the overall human capital of immigrants as declining over time relative to that of native-born Americans, turn out to be correct.

Yet, when all is said and done, we see no sign here of a mass second-generation decline or stagnation. In general, there is much evidence of occupational advance in the second generation; to judge by our findings, members of the second generation have ample reason to perceive incentives here to merge with the mainstream. Even if they personally do not experience the mobility that is reflected in the aggregate in the second generation, they are likely to have friends and relatives who do. So, even though we might well find patterns of decline or stagnation were we able to analyze some subgroups of the U.S.-born generation, such as those who grew up in inner-city neighborhoods, the evidence that a good part of the U.S.-born generation is doing rather well seems unassailable.

Overall, we find reasons for cautious optimism about the second generation in the evidence regarding socioeconomic attainment. A pattern of second-generation decline or stagnation does not appear to be widespread—which of course does not mean that it does not exist at all. For the groups with many human-capital immigrants, "stagnation" in the second generation implies a position of socioeconomic advantage in the United States, characterized by college graduation and frequent entry into the ranks of professionals and managers. The real issue, at any rate, concerns the U.S.-born generations from groups dominated by traditional labor migrants, such as Mexicans and Dominicans. The evidence here suggests that not only does the second generation exceed its parents' educational attainments, which is only to be expected in light of the limited schooling of the immigrant generation, but also it is less likely to be found in typical immigrant jobs and more likely to attain professional and managerial positions.

Yet reasons remain for concern about the socioeconomic attainments of the U.S.-born. One, certainly, is race, which in the North American context is most constraining for those with perceptible African ancestry. Studies of Afro-Caribbean immigrants reveal the inescapable nature of their contact with institutional and interpersonal racism, which limits the parents' ability to find housing outside of segregated neighborhoods and the children's ability to escape inadequate schools and to avoid being stopped by the police.[80] While the trajectory of the second generation is very much affected by the social class position of the parents, part of it is at risk of segmented assimilation and thus of exclusion from the economic mainstream. The same pattern may appear on a diminished scale among other groups in which African ancestry is common but not universal, such as the Dominicans. Racism may also limit opportunities for Mexicans and other Latin Americans with an indigenous appearance, but here the research record is not clear.[81]

A second concern encompasses the third generation from traditional labor immigrations, which thus far exists in substantial numbers only among the Mexicans (and cannot be distinguished among adults in decennial census data). Studies of that generation among Mexican Americans find a stagnation in educational attainment relative to the second generation; and qualitative studies of Mexican American schoolchildren reveal the emergence of an oppositional culture deriding school achievement among some who are not immigrants themselves. The precise circumstances under which this culture appears among Mexicans must still be clarified, but it offers sufficient reason to be concerned about the socioeconomic trajectory of Mexicans and of some other groups, such as the Dominicans.

Finally, there are the as yet unmeasured disadvantages associated with being the child of undocumented parents. The labor market situation of the undocumented is clearly a difficult one; many undocumented workers are located in the underground economy and thus work for low pay and without benefits.[82] Almost certainly there is an impact on the socioeconomic horizons of their children, even though many of them are U.S. citizens by virtue of their birth on American soil. The fact that traditional labor immigrations, which originate for the most part in Latin America and the Caribbean,[83] also harbor the largest contingents of the undocumented adds to the concern about the position of the second generation. Indeed, it appears that the number of the undocumented has been rising sharply in the aftermath of the amnesties of the early 1990s and was around 8 million at the time of the 2000 census. While some of these immigrants may subsequently attain legal status, it is likely that, without a further mass amnesty, many will remain illegal.

Spatial Patterns

One of the most salient features of the new immigration is its heavy concentration in a small number of states and metropolitan areas.[84] Of the immigrants who arrived during the 1990s, two-thirds ended up in only six states: California, New York, Texas, Florida, Illinois, and New Jersey, in order of share. Concentration within specific metropolitan areas is nearly as extreme: more than half the immigrants of the 1990s settled in and around New York City, Los Angeles, San Francisco, Chicago, Miami, Houston, and Dallas. The new immigration is overwhelmingly urban and suburban, as opposed to rural, in destination, even though its largest nationality component, Mexicans, is also engaged in agricultural work. As of 2000, only twenty-five of the nation's largest metropolitan areas (over 500,000 population) had above-average concentrations of the foreign-born (see Table 6.2). These regions accounted for nearly three-quarters of all immigrants.

Geographic concentration is an inevitable by-product of immigration, which is guided by social networks. Settlement patterns are determined partly by the need of immigrants, unfamiliar with American society and frequently lacking proficiency in English, for assistance from kin and co-ethnics. Even so, the degree of geographic concentration among new immigrant groups appears to exceed that of older ones at a comparable stage. Moreover, its ethnic impact is undoubtedly enhanced by the exodus of a considerable number of U.S.-born Americans, both white and black, from these metropolitan areas, thus intensifying immigrants' relative presence.[85] Only groups with a large professional stratum, such as Indian immigrants, appear to be exceptions—understandably so, since for professionals, job considerations typically override the tendency to settle in ethnic communities and particular regions. Places of settlement are also initially more dispersed for refugees, whose original destination in the United States is usually determined by government agencies and private sponsorship. But secondary migrations tend to bring about greater ethnic concentration, exemplified by Miami as a mecca for Cubans and Orange County, California, for Vietnamese.[86]

Nevertheless, the concentration of immigrant groups in a small number of metropolitan areas appears incompatible with the rapid growth of ethnic populations that is projected if immigration remains at the current level. The National Research Council suggests a middle-of-the-road scenario which projects that by 2020, Latinos and Asians, the two racial/ethnic populations receiving the bulk of the new immigration, will account for nearly a quarter of the population, which would represent almost a doubling of their proportion in a thirty-year period.[87] It seems self-evident that these groups cannot remain concentrated in a few states and metropolitan areas if growth occurs on this scale. The data from the 2000 census provide considerable evidence of the dispersal of Mexican and Asian immigrants, who, for instance, are showing up in larger numbers throughout the South, a region that heretofore has received very little immigration. Moreover, the statistics of regional concentration cited earlier are significantly reduced from those of 1990, when more than 80 percent of recent immigrants were found in six states. A rigorous analysis of 2000 census data indicates that racial and ethnic diversity is increasing over time in most parts of the United States, implying that the impact of immigration is not limited to the few metropolitan regions that are currently the main reception areas.[88] One future possibility is the emergence of a much larger number of immigrant cultural centers, especially of Spanish speakers. Other areas of the country might begin to resemble the immigrant concentrations found in metropolises such as Los Angeles, Miami, and New York. Yet the hypothesis that movement away from areas of original settlement tends to be associated with a ratcheting up of assimilation, which seems generally borne out in the experiences of European-descent groups, is also plausible in application to new immigrant groups. There is some evidence that suggests a moderate deconcentration by the second generation, which is consistent with the assimilation hypothesis, but no firm conclusion is warranted as yet.[89]

Table 6.2. Top metropolitan areas of immigrant concentration, 1990 and 2000

Metro area	1990		2000	
	Number of foreign-born (in thousands)	Percent of population	Number of foreign-born (in thousands)	Percent of population
Areas of 1,000,000+				
Miami–Fort Lauderdale	1,073	33.6	1,558	40.2
Los Angeles–Riverside–Orange County	3,945	27.1	5,068	30.9
San Francisco–Oakland–San Jose	1,251	20.0	1,902	27.0
New York–Northern N.J.–Long Island	3,554	19.6	5,182	24.4
San Diego	429	17.2	606	21.5
Houston–Galveston–Brazoria	460	12.4	896	19.2
West Palm Beach–Boca Raton	105	12.2	197	17.4
Las Vegas	74	8.7	258	16.5
Chicago–Gary–Kenosha	910	11.3	1,467	16.0
Dallas–Fort Worth	315	8.1	785	15.0
Sacramento–Yolo	140	9.5	260	14.5
Phoenix–Mesa	162	7.2	457	14.1
Washington, D.C.–Baltimore	572	9.1	981	12.9
Boston–Worcester–Lawrence	436	10.4	721	12.4
Austin–San Marcos	56	6.7	153	12.2
Providence–Fall River–Warwick	119	10.3	143	12.0
Orlando	82	6.7	197	12.0
Seattle–Tacoma–Bremerton	202	7.9	414	11.7

Areas of 500,000–1,000,000

McAllen–Edinburg–Mission, Texas	95	24.7	168	29.5
El Paso	142	23.9	186	27.4
Fresno	133	17.5	193	21.0
Stockton–Lodi	79	16.4	110	19.5
Honolulu	131	15.7	168	19.2
Bakersfield	66	12.2	112	16.9
Tucson	60	9.0	100	11.9
N as % of national total	73.8	7.9	71.6	11.1
National totals	19,767		31,108	

Source: "The New Americans," Lewis Mumford Center, University at Albany, SUNY; "Census 2000: Demographic Profiles," U.S. Census Bureau.

Within the metropolitan areas where they concentrate, immigrants and the second generation appear to be segregated from the majority population to a substantial extent, but no more so than were the immigrant groups of the early twentieth century. "Segregation," gauged by the most conventional measure, the so-called index of dissimilarity, has a specific technical meaning that must be kept in mind: namely, that the spatial distribution of a group (across units such as census tracts) differs from that of a comparison group, often the majority. Such a difference may be produced by the existence of immigrant residential enclaves, where immigrants and their children are surrounded by fellow ethnics and have limited contact with outsiders, or by a dispersal of immigrants in some parts of a region but not others. In the latter case, immigrants may live mainly in the midst of people who differ ethnically from them. Or both patterns may combine for any group.

Most studies find moderate levels of segregation for ethnic populations growing from immigration but measure this only for the largest populations, that is, Asians and Latinos. Analysis of 1990 census data for metropolitan regions throughout the United States found that the average index of dissimilarity between Hispanics and non-Hispanics was .43, virtually unchanged from the 1980 index calculated in an equivalent way. That of Asians from non-Asians is also .43, representing in this case a slight increase from the 1980 value (.41). By contrast, the average 1990 value for blacks was .64. Another study comparing average segregation index values between 1990 and 2000 found the same pattern of stable segregation levels (though the segregation of Hispanics, calculated this time from non-Hispanic whites, came out higher, around .51).[90] Remarkably, there appears to have been no increase during the 1980s and 1990s in the segregation of Asians and Hispanics, even though these populations were growing very rapidly because of immigration.

But analyses of large aggregates can conceal higher levels of segregation for specific immigrant groups. For instance, the 1990 index-of-dissimilarity values for specific immigrant ethnic groups in the New York and Los Angeles metropolitan regions generally are in the .5–.7 range, indicating a "high moderate" to "low high" level of segregation; such values, in fact, are not much below those for African Americans in the same regions. In Los Angeles, a city that is a mecca without equal for immigration streams from Asia and Latin America, the index of dissimiliarity between Mexicans and Anglos (i.e., non-Hispanic whites) was .59, and that between Salvadorans (the second-largest Latino group in the region) and Anglos was even higher, .77.[91] The index values were also relatively high for the major Asian groups: Chinese, .60; Filipinos, .54; Koreans, .58; Vietnamese, .66.[92] Yet, except for that .77, these values do not seem very remarkable by historical standards, for analysis of data from the early twentieth century for New York finds rather similar values for the immigrant groups of that era.[93]

Moreover, when the racial/ethnic composition of the local areas where the typical member of an immigrant group resides is taken into account, using a different type of segregation measure (the indices of isolation and exposure, which belong to the so-called P* family of measures), then the degree of immigrant segregation usually appears more modest. For the typical member of such a group lives in a very mixed neighborhood where other immigrant and non-immigrant groups are present. In fact, it is quite common for non-Hispanic white neighbors to outnumber co-ethnic ones. This is especially true for Asians: for instance, though in 1990 the Chinese were the second-largest non-Anglo group in the Los Angeles region, the average Chinese Angeleno resided in a census tract that was only 14 percent Chinese, while approximately 40 percent of the neighbors were Anglo. Only for the large Hispanic groups in regions of heavy immigrant concentration—for instance, the Mexicans of Chicago or the Los Angeles region, the Cubans of Miami—do co-ethnic neighbors outnumber Anglo ones. Even in these regions, moreover, it is usual for at least half of a group to reside outside of its areas of concentration: in 1990 this was the case for 52 percent of New York's Chinese, despite the existence of Chinatown and satellite neighborhoods, and of 55 percent of Los Angeles Mexicans.[94] In these respects there is a sharp distinction between the typical residential situation of immigrant minorities and that of African Americans, who are more likely to reside in areas where their own group is in the majority and white neighbors are rare. Correspondingly, black immigrants tend to be more segregated: both West Indians and dark-skinned Latinos are very likely to be channeled into or near black neighborhoods, especially if they reside in cities.[95] The extent to which immigrant minorities reside with co-ethnics in metropolitan regions such as Los Angeles will almost certainly increase in the future as immigration continues. But they are likely to continue to live with non–group members, including whites, in their midst, or even in the midst of whites, unless there is a massive flight of whites from areas of immigrant concentration. This seems unlikely, as many of the areas where immigrants go are global metropolises with concentrations of headquarters complexes and associated professional and high-level service jobs.[96] Whites will not abandon them completely.

In clear contrast to earlier, European immigrant groups, which generally first established urban enclaves and only after a generation or more migrated to suburbs, the new immigrants frequently settle in suburbs immediately upon, or soon after, arriving in the United States.[97] According to 2000 census data, 48 percent of those who arrived during the 1990s and were living in metropolitan areas already resided outside the central cities. The percentages of suburbanites were particularly high and growing among Asian groups. Within the first decade after their arrival in Los Angeles, many Asian immigrant families "buy up" into suburban neighborhoods. In 2000, 61 percent of East Indian households in metropolitan areas of the nation were located in suburbs. The comparable 2000 figure for whites is only modestly higher, 71 percent. The lowest percentage among Asian groups is found for the Chinese, who have long-standing urban enclaves; but as of 2000, almost half were located outside the central cities—a noticeable increase from 1980 (40 percent), despite the heavy immigration of ethnic Chinese during the 1980s and 1990s. Rates of suburbanization are on average lower for Latino groups, except for Cubans, who are as likely to reside in suburbia as non-Hispanic whites.

Will suburbanization have the same meaning for new immigrant groups as it had for older ones, for whom it was usually associated with the maturity of the residential assimilation process? There cannot be a definitive answer at this point in the history of the new immigration; and in any event, one needs to recognize that the term "suburbia" now covers such a vast range of residential contexts that a single, unqualified answer is ultimately unlikely. But the existence of extensive suburban ethnic enclaves, such as of the Chinese in Monterey Park in Los Angeles, suggests that the contemporary settlement pattern is distinctive. The huge Los Angeles barrio is also for the most part outside the central city. These examples, along with other evidence, suggest that barriers to suburban entry have fallen for freshly arrived immigrants, who may not speak English well. They can now reside in suburbia without detriment to their ability to function in daily life (e.g., shop or participate in recreational activities), presumably because they find sufficient numbers of co-ethnics and an ethnic infrastructure in their vicinity.[98]

One has to be careful not to exaggerate the magnitude of the new suburban areas of ethnic concentration. Many of them still have, at least to date, a thin ethnic presence, amounting to 10–30 percent of residents, the majority of whom are whites. Further, most suburbanized members of the immigrant and second generations live outside these areas.[99] Nevertheless, the existence of suburban ethnic concentrations has the potential to undermine one of the principal mechanisms that propelled residential assimilation for European ethnics, namely, the search for improved residential amenities, which typically led them away from urban ethnic areas. If the new immigrants are able to establish suburban ethnic communities that already have qualities such as good schools and clean streets, then presumably their motivation to leave these communities is weakened.

These questions lead us to a more systematic consideration of the conceptual model that represents the most developed understanding of the process of residential assimilation. Labeled the "spatial assimilation model" in its most recent formulation (by the sociologist Douglas Massey), its intellectual roots lie in the early-twentieth-century theorizing of such Chicago School figures as Robert E. Park and Louis Wirth, based on their observations of immigrant groups in that city (see Chapter 2). One can think of the model as a distillation of the "average" or "typical" residential processes experienced by European groups, recognizing at the same time that these were undoubtedly too complex to be entirely compressed into a single template. But the model gives us a standard by which to evaluate in a rough way the degree of fit between the settlement patterns of past and present groups. Based on its underlying assumptions that neighborhood location and housing are largely determined by market processes and that ethnics are motivated to improve their residential assimilation once they have acculturated to some extent and made some socioeconomic gains, the model leads to several clear-cut hypotheses. Residential exposure to the majority group and various qualities of the neighborhood are hypothesized to improve in tandem with an ethnic family's socioeconomic standing, acculturation (as measured, say, by its members' proficiency in speaking English), and generational status or, in the case of the immigrants themselves, length of residence. Suburbanization also enjoys a special role in the model as a stage enhancing residential assimilation.[100]

A series of studies of spatial assimilation for some of the main metropolitan regions where the new immigrants concentrate has tracked these hypothesized linkages as of 1990. By and large, the findings uphold the spatial assimilation model.[101] In some critical respects, they sustain the analogy between the residential trajectory of contemporary immigrant groups and that of past European groups, despite the existence of obvious differences. The studies focus especially on the median household income of the census tract of residence—a measure not only of its affluence but also of the residential amenities a neighborhood is likely to provide—and the percent of non-Hispanic whites, the majority group, among residents. For Asians and Latinos,[102] the most powerful determinant is their own socioeconomic position: the greater their income and the higher their educational status, the larger, for instance, the percentage of non-Hispanic whites in the population of the neighborhood where they reside. Linguistic acculturation is a second-order determinant. The difference it makes is particularly sizable among Latinos and is most pronounced between those who speak only English at home and those who do not speak English well. Bilinguals, who speak a mother tongue but are proficient at English too, are in between.

Race also matters, however, and not only for black West Indians but also for Latinos. Light-skinned Latinos (i.e., those who describe themselves on the census form as "white"—about half of all Latinos in 1990) are better able to enter neighborhoods with large numbers of non-Hispanic whites, and thus more advantaged areas. As we have noted before, the residential patterns of Latinos who describe themselves as "black" (fewer than 5 percent of all Latinos in 1990) tend to conform to those of African Americans, the most segregated group in the United States; and thus they live in neighborhoods with greater disadvantages (e.g., lower median household income) than one would otherwise expect given their own socioeconomic characteristics. Latinos who describe themselves as other than black or white usually fall in between.

After socioeconomic standing, residence in a suburb rather than a city is the strongest predictor of the percentage of the majority group present in the neighborhoods where Asians and Latinos live. Even in the metropolitan regions most affected by the new immigration and where, therefore, many new immigrants are potential neighbors, this variable still typically adds about 10–20 percentage points to the non-Hispanic white share of the neighborhood. In cities, the neighbors in mixed areas are typically members of other minority groups.[103] Perhaps the mixed nature of most neighborhoods has little bearing for immigrants, who may find enough co-ethnics in their vicinity to live in comfortably ethnic ways. But it is likely to have a considerable impact on their children, who as they grow up are frequently brought together with whites and members of other ethnic groups in schools and in playgroups.

Figure 6.5 summarizes these findings for the two principal regions of immigrant concentration, Los Angeles and New York. On the left in each quadrant are the predicted values for a poor urban immigrant from one of the four major racial/ethnic populations (Asians, blacks, light-skinned Latinos, and whites); on the right those for a middle-income, suburban, native-born group member. (To provide a suitable standard, the whites are assumed to be native-born in both cases.) The left-hand bars portray substantial racial/ethnic inequality. In every case, the residential situation of whites is the most privileged: the affluence of their neighborhoods is well above that expected for poor immigrants from the other groups, in part because poor whites live mainly with other whites while poor minorities do not. According to the right-hand bars, however, the middle-class, linguistically assimilated members of the second generation from the immigrant minorities approach residential parity with whites, something that is not true for socioeconomically successful African Americans. In other words, the characteristics of the neighborhoods where these Asians and light-skinned Latinos reside are nearly the same as those where similarly situated whites live—implying that these are frequently not just similar but indeed the same neighborhoods.

This is not to say that, in a strict sense, spatial assimilation requires residence in largely white neighborhoods. Certainly, the residential integration of the European American second generation was frequently a matter of entry into ethnically mixed neighborhoods, not those dominated by Protestants of British ancestry. But the entry of many middle-class Asians and Hispanics into the neighborhoods of the majority population is a strong demonstration of contemporary

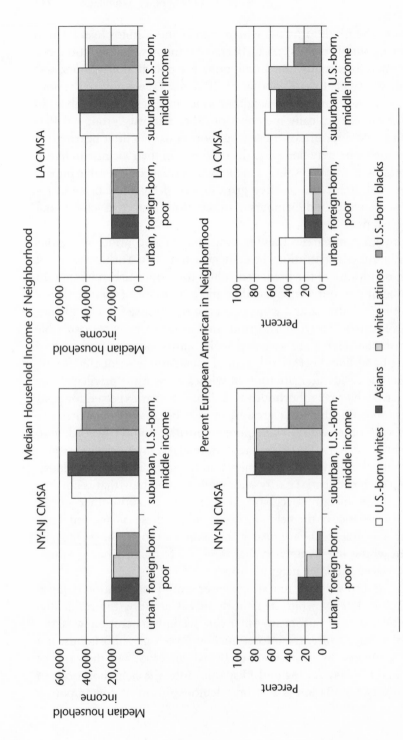

Figure 6.5. Residential situations of Asians and light-skinned Latinos compared to those of socio-economically similar whites and blacks, 1990. *Source:* Richard Alba, "Immigration and the American Realities of Assimilation and Multiculturalism," *Sociological Forum* 14 (March 1999): 3–25.

spatial assimilation. Could this feature of spatial assimilation be undermined by the continuing immigration into the metropolitan regions where immigrants and their children are most concentrated? This, combined with the inclination of some natives to move away from these regions, is altering the racial/ethnic composition of neighborhoods in a way that reduces the availability of majority group members as neighbors for upwardly mobile immigrant households. Still, even in the areas most heavily affected by immigration, middle-income, linguistically assimilated Asian and Latino suburbanites tended as of 1990, the latest date for which the relevant analyses are available, to live in areas where non-Hispanic whites predominate. Only in Los Angeles and Miami, the two regions with the highest proportions of foreign-born in their populations and where, therefore, the racial/ethnic shifts spurred by immigration are the furthest developed, was this generalization at risk. In other regions of immigrant settlement, such as San Francisco and New York, which have the third- and fourth-highest concentrations of new immigrant groups, the neighborhoods of even modestly affluent Asians and Latinos generally had non-Hispanic white majorities, which were quite substantial in the suburbs. Presumably the same would have been even more true for most other metropolitan regions, where the concentration of new immigrant groups is necessarily more modest. In such areas it will be a long time, if ever, before immigration modifies the racial/ethnic composition of neighborhoods to the point where the residential integration with whites for middle-class, acculturated Asians and light-skinned Latinos is endangered.

That residential patterns exhibit somewhat contradictory qualities is probably inevitable at an early stage in the unfolding of the consequences of large-scale immigration. Indeed, results from the 2000 census indicate both that immigrant enclaves have grown during the 1990s and that processes of spatial assimilation continue to function. In particular, the stability of the overall segregation levels for Asians and Hispanics implies that, despite the enormous increase of these populations during the 1990s because of immigration, their distribution across different types of neighborhoods held steady. Given the increased sizes of the groups, this implies some increase in ethnic density of group enclaves; yet at the same time, the numbers who live outside these enclaves, often in neighborhoods with many whites but also in some multihued neighborhoods where many groups mix, are rising. Perhaps the most interesting signal of all is the declining racial and ethnic exclusivity of the neighborhoods where whites live: as of 2000, the average white in the metropolitan regions of the nation resides in a census tract where 20 percent of the residents are nonwhite or Hispanic (up from 15 percent in 1990 and 12 percent in 1980).[104] Given the historic role of the majority's exclusion of minorities from its residential bastions, the increasing diversity in white neighborhoods suggests that the way is open to further spatial assimilation, at least for some contemporary immigrant minorities.

But even as we underscore the continuities in spatial assimilation, we are aware that, as a totality, the residential picture is more mixed: that elements of persisting segregation appear alongside those of integration. The high walls of residential segregation confronting Americans with visible African ancestry, native-born and immigrant, are crumbling very slowly. Moreover, the evidence is convincing that Hispanics who are black are as affected by this segregation as are African Americans. And the other Hispanics who do not have a European appearance are also residentially disadvantaged, though not to the extent that blacks are. New areas of ethnic concentration are developing as a result of the clustering of immigrant groups, and some of them offer suburban amenities, making them much more attractive as places to live than the inner-city enclaves typical of immigration a century ago. Thus, the spatial assimilation of some will not dilute the patches of racial and ethnic colorations on future social mappings of U.S. metropolitan regions, but by the same token the visibility of those patches should not obscure the occurrence of such assimilation.

Social Relations

Ethnicity characteristically carries with it a tendency to privilege those of similar ethnic origins when it comes to various kinds of social relations, especially those involving degrees of trust and intimacy. This tendency typically lessens as an ethnic assimilates. Data about social relations are thus crucial to any evaluation of the ultimate course of assimilation. But at this point systematic data about social relations among contemporary immigrants are hard to find. The impression given by ethnographic studies is that primary-group relationships are largely confined within the immigrant community, even for young members of the second (and 1.5) generation. Many of these studies depict immigrant families during their first decade in the United States, describing the difficulties of the settlement process, the need to rely on family and immigrant networks, and the limited extent of acculturation.[105] They also show how prejudice and hostility can reinforce the tendency to stay within the confines of common ethnic origin. For example, in a rural community in California studied by Margaret Gibson, Punjabis were a growing minority who had bought up 50 percent of the farmland in the area. White residents viewed Punjabi immigrants with ambivalence and hostility, expressed as envy or worry over competition for resources. The immigrants themselves were aware of underlying tensions in their relationship with local whites. Gibson reports that all those she interviewed had experienced prejudice but were quick to point out that it did not interfere with their pursuit of daily activities. Punjabi farmers emphasized that they got along well with local white farmers, and underscored their growing economic interdependence. They recounted hostile incidents, usually involving local white youths, but they balanced these with accounts of friendship with white neighbors and unexpected kindness. Even so, social interaction between whites and Punjabis generally occurred as a by-product of commercial transactions, and tended to be superficial. Gibson's description of selective acculturation and limited interaction with natives is consistent with accounts of the early stages of accommodation in the mass immigration from eastern and southern Europe.[106]

This is also seen in the case of Mexican immigration to the United States. The sheer size of this immigration, its geographic concentration, linguistic isolation, and low level of formal education, make it more resistant to social assimilation than the smaller immigrant streams. Notwithstanding, Mexican labor migrants undergo a gradual transition from a sojourning pattern of seeking temporary work in U.S. labor markets to a more settled pattern of labor migration. In the early years, immigrants commute regularly between work in the United States and home communities in Mexico. They live frugally, often in communal housing arrangements, sending remittances home to support their families. But over time, many labor migrants settle down in daughter communities in the United States and bring their spouses and children to live with them. Especially after the birth of a child in the United States, their orientation shifts away from Mexico as they establish permanent commitments in Latino communities. In the early years, the web of personal relationships is predominantly embedded within a society of fellow labor migrants. Even in the first year of residence in the United States, however, 11 percent of rural migrants and 17 percent of migrants from urban areas report having Anglo friends. By the fifteenth year, 63 percent of the former and 71 percent of the latter have such friends; moreover, the friends of rural migrants are *more* likely to be Anglo than Chicano. The development of English language competency is a key factor in promoting social assimilation.[107]

The social relations of contemporary immigrants themselves are for obvious reasons very unlikely to resemble a pattern of full-fledged social assimilation, except in unusual cases where highly educated immigrants are isolated from co-ethnics. The social relations of the U.S.-born are more likely to show such assimilation. This brings us to the most commonly available data on social relations—data about intermarriage. These provide a sort of sociological x-ray to observe what changes, if any, may be taking place within ethnic social structures. Clearly, such data are of great interest in and of themselves for a prognosis of assimilation. Because the norm of endogamous marriage has served throughout the world as a regulative mechanism maintaining the social boundaries of ethnic groups, its diminishment can be interpreted as reflecting changes in ethnic identities and boundaries. In the United States, intermarriage between Anglo-Saxons of native stock and European immigrants from outside the circle of northwestern Protestant countries was uncommon as late as the mid-twentieth century. But as white ethnic groups progressed toward cultural and social assimilation, the sense of violation of the norm of endogamous marriage diminished to the point where marriages between descendants of northwest European stock and other white ethnics have come to be viewed as unremarkable, even endogamous.[108] The fading of norms hindering intermarriage among white Americans of different ethnic and religious backgrounds reflects the great decline of segregating social boundaries among European Americans.[109]

What inferences can we make from the occurrence of interracial marriage about possible changes in the salience of ethnic/racial boundaries between white and nonwhite Americans? Heretofore, interracial marriage has been uncommon in the United States. This is not surprising, since interracial marriage was illegal in a number of states until 1967, when the Supreme Court finally ruled so-called anti-miscegenation laws unconstitutional. Since then, even though interracial marriages have increased somewhat, from 0.7 percent in 1970 to 1.3 percent in 1980 and to 2.2 percent in 1992, they still represent a very small percent of all marriages in the United States.[110] But, although such an increase may seem slight in the aggregate, when viewed from the vantage point of racial minorities it looms larger as a significant rise in the rate of out-marriage that may indicate a weakening of social and cultural norms maintaining racial boundaries. It is useful, therefore, to examine the variation of intermarriage across minorities to understand better its extent and implications.

Provoked by what appear to be relatively high intermarriage rates, considerable attention has focused on Asian ethnic groups. One study examined out-marriage rates through marriage license applications in Los Angeles during the 1970s for those with East Asian surnames. Of the three Asian American groups studied, the Japanese had the highest rate of marriage with non–co-ethnic spouses: in 1975, 55 percent of Japanese-surname marriages were with a non-Japanese mate, and in 1979, 61 percent. In the latter year, 11 percent of these Japanese out-marriages were with spouses from other Asian ethnic groups. Excluding such intra-Asian marriages, the rate of interracial marriage in 1979 was 30 percent for Chinese, 50 percent for Japanese, and 19 percent for Koreans (then a new Asian ethnic group in Los Angeles). Out-marriage increased significantly with the second and third generations. Half of all second-generation Chinese marriage license applications involved out-marriage. Third-generation Japanese Americans displayed a similarly high rate. Asian American females were more likely to intermarry than males, a pattern also observed in national studies of intermarriage. In Hawaii in 1980, rates of out-group marriage were mostly higher still: 76 percent for the Chinese, 59 percent for the Japanese, 65 percent for Filipinos, and 83 percent for Koreans. Because Hawaii has a majority Asian American population, Asian out-marriage there reflects a stronger propensity toward a pattern of pan-Asian intermarriage, not dissimilar to the pattern of intra-religious interethnic marriage of Europeans embodied in the concept of "the triple-melting pot." As the size of the Asian American population grows on the West Coast, a similar trend toward increased pan-Asian intermarriage might also become more evident.[111] Pan-Asian intermarriage among U.S.-born Asians can be viewed as part of the larger process of assimilation in which social barriers created by ethnic boundaries attenuate as social relations expand across ethnic groups.

There has been less systematic attention to intermarriage among Hispanics (and very little to the marriage patterns of black immigrants, as compared with African Americans).[112] But it appears that intermarriage is generally less common for Hispanics than for Asians, partly because of larger group sizes, which are associated with higher endogamy. A study of Mexicans found that their intermarriage prevalence in 1980 averaged 23 percent across fifty-three metropolitan areas with large Mexican populations. This study did not separate immigrants from the native-born and thus cannot address intergenerational changes. Another study, however, limited to New York City and based on marriage records for 1975, found extremely high intermarriage rates for the second-generation non–Puerto Rican Hispanic groups, ranging from 75 percent to more than 90 percent. But these groups, including Cubans, Dominicans, and Central and South Americans of various national origins, were still mostly small in 1975, which would tend to make intermarriage more likely.[113]

Broad changes in marriage patterns in American society over the course of the twentieth century are likely to have a notable influence on racial minorities emerging from contemporary immigration. Two major studies have found strong evidence of increasing educational homogamy in marriages. As the number of years of school attendance has lengthened for Americans, single persons have become increasingly likely to meet their mates in the final stages of school and thus to marry persons of similar, if not the same, educational attainment. Reinforcing this pattern is the increased importance of educational credentials as a determinant of future earnings. With women joining the labor force in greater numbers, men as well as women have come to value such credentials as a guide to the future earning power of their mates.[114] Significantly, the trend toward increased educational homogamy has occurred during a period of substantial expansion of American secondary and higher education, which has resulted in a diminished effect of parents' social class on the educational attainment of their children. An implication is that the increase in educational homogamy need not entail increased homogamy according to social class origin.[115]

Do racial barriers become easier to cross as education grows in importance as a basis for mate selection? An important study of interracial marriage has addressed this question, among others, using 1980 and 1990 census data for native-born married couples twenty to twenty-nine years of age, thus focusing on recent marriages and excluding those contracted decades ago when interracial marriage was far more difficult.[116] This study shows that between 1980 and 1990 the percentage of racial endogamy for both males and females declined for all racial groups. In 1990 it was highest for blacks (males, 92 percent; females, 97 percent) and lowest for Asian Americans—defined to include Chinese, Japanese, and Koreans—(males, 39 percent; females, 34 percent). The proportion of endogamous marriages for Hispanics was 64 percent for males and 63 percent for females. When group size is controlled for, the tendency to endogamy is lower for Hispanics than Asian Americans. But interracial marriage for Asian Americans is almost exclusively with whites, whereas this is not true for Hispanics. Overall, interracial marriages are highest between whites and Asian Americans followed by whites and Hispanics and lowest between whites and blacks. The decline in racial endogamy over the decade was highest among men and women with high educational attainment (Figure 6.6). The odds of interracial marriage with whites increased sharply for Asian Americans with college and postgraduate educational attainment. This suggests a significant weakening of racial boundaries between whites and Asians. The socioeconomic attainment of Asian Americans—high levels of educational attainment and occupational mobility, along with parity in earning power—appears to make Asian Americans more attractive as marriage partners.[117]

According to this analysis, interracial marriages with whites tend to be educationally homogamous for all three racial minorities. In marriages between spouses with unequal educational attainment, however, "hypogamy for white women" remains the dominant pattern in Latino/black marriages with whites. In hypogamous marriages, white women trade their higher racial status as whites for their nonwhite mate's higher earning power, an exchange which, as Robert K. Merton observed, may not result from an intentional choice, but nonetheless operates in the background. Merton's classic paper, written more than half a century ago, inferred from hypogamy the existence of caste-like racial barriers between whites and blacks—for in hypogamous marriages, both parties are compensated for violating strongly held social and cultural norms prohibiting interracial marriage

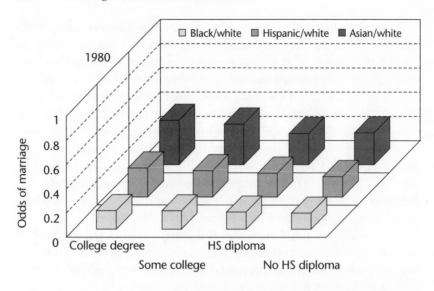

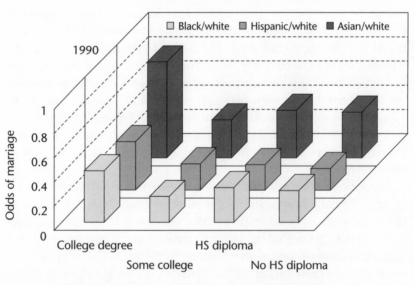

Figure 6.6. Relative odds of intermarriage with whites, 1980 and 1990, by education level (relative to odds of a marriage between two whites with some college). *Source:* Zhenchao Qian, "Breaking the Racial Barriers," *Demography* 34 (May 1997): 272. Used with permission.

through the exchange of complementary values.[118] Significantly, however, hypogamous marriage does not appear to extend to interracial marriages involving Asian American men. Instead, white women are, if anything, less likely to marry Asian American men higher in education than to marry those lower in education.[119] To follow Merton's logic, this finding suggests that racial barriers between whites and Asian Americans have moderated in the United States.

Despite what appear to be relatively high intermarriage rates on the part of the second and later generations of contemporary immigrant groups, no bold prognostications about ultimate assimilation are warranted on this basis alone. Although intermarriage has received more attention than other kinds of social relations for new immigrant groups, research has not sufficiently established the individual and contextual determinants of intermarriage to be confident about marriage patterns over the long run. In view of the well-established principle that endogamy increases in proportion to the size of a racial/ethnic population, more research is needed especially to understand better the population dynamics of intermarriage in the context of sustained high-volume immigration. Moreover, it has long been accepted that a key issue for interpreting the long-term effect of intermarriage involves the racial/ethnic identity of the married couple and, even more so, of their children.[120] Although the importance of this issue is widely acknowledged, it is only now beginning to draw attention in relation to intermarriage in new immigrant groups, which frequently cross racial lines. As of 1990, "about one quarter of the 2 million children with at least one Asian parent, and of the 5.4 million with at least one Hispanic parent live in inter-racial households with a white parent or step parent."[121] Researchers are discovering that multiracial or multiethnic identities are common among those descended from such marriages.[122] The ramifications of such identities for racial/ethnic populations are far from clear, and little is known in particular about their implications for everyday behavior and ethnic boundaries.

The evidence reviewed in this chapter demonstrates, we believe, that assimilation remains a potent force affecting immigrant groups in the United States. Our focus throughout has been on signs of intergenerational shift, and there are plenty to be found. Some forms of assimilation appear to be widespread, if not virtually universal, as one looks across the generations. Almost everyone learns English, and conversion to English monolingualism is clearly widespread, even among Spanish-speaking groups. Acculturation, we must note, is not always benign: studies of health outcomes show that acculturation to fatty American foods and to lack of physical activity sometimes brings about a worsening of health status.[123] Ethnic cultures will nevertheless persist in some respects, as they did among European groups. For many of the new ethnic groups, even those that are Christian, religion will provide an institutional carapace protecting some cultural differences. But the scope of ethnic cultural difference will narrow, and cultural commonalities with other Americans will expand, thus allowing for more intergroup interactions.

Other forms of assimilation are likely to characterize certain segments within many of the new ethnic groups. This seems a plausible prognosis for socioeconomic assimilation. The distinction between human-capital and traditional labor migrants is of great relevance here. In general, the descendants of immigrant streams with many human-capital migrants retain socioeconomic advantages into the second and probably later generations. On average, their educational attainment and their position in the labor force are at least as favorable as those of native whites. To be sure, these advantages result in large part from the human-cultural capital brought by immigrants rather than the social mobility across the generations that characterized the experiences of many European groups; and this raises a question about the application of the term "assimilation," which to some implies improvement in socioeconomic position. For the second generation of human-capital immigration, assimilation mostly involves horizontal intergenerational educational and occupational attainment. This is *horizontal* mobility because many in the second generation remain in the same or similar occupational categories as their immigrant parents. The concept of segmented assimilation appears to conflate horizontal mobility with downward assimilation. The relatively high level of social and economic resources of many in these groups permits them to participate in the mainstream society on rather favorable terms and thereby encourages other forms of assimilation, such as social mixing across ethnic lines.

For traditional labor migrants the pattern of socioeconomic assimilation is more ambiguous. This may seem a puzzling assessment inasmuch as they generally show unmistakable signs of educational and occupational upgrading between the first and second generations. If we view Mexicans as the modal labor migrant group, some degree of intergenerational mobility must be expected because of the first generation's entry at the bottom of the job ladder, especially the undocumented migrants from Mexico. The mobility that we find on average allows for the possibility of a dominant pattern of horizontal mobility between generations, in which lower-class Mexican culture merges with lower-class cultural and behavioral patterns prevalent in poor neighborhoods of American central cities. In short, the average pattern of upward mobility in the second generation may disguise a great deal of diversity in socioeconomic trajectory, with a substantial portion of the group experiencing stagnation or, at best, limited mobility. The presence of a large pool of undocumented immigrants in the Mexican and some other low-wage labor groups contributes to this diversity of outcome in the second generation. By the third generation, the average intergenerational mobility of the Mexican group appears on the basis of some evidence to stagnate, at least when measured in terms of college education. Yet this average, too, leaves room for considerable diversity, and a sizable portion of the Mexican group has undoubtedly entered the middle-class realm.

A mixed picture is also evident when we turn to forms of social assimilation, which we measure by residential assimilation and intermarriage. Both can be revealing of the narrowing of social distances between ethnic groups and the white majority. Studies of residential patterns indicate that some aspects of the model of spatial assimilation still appear to hold: thus, suburbanization and improving socioeconomic position both increase the likelihood of residing outside an ethnic neighborhood and in one where whites are in the majority; linguistic assimilation also has this effect for Latinos. But there are also some differences from the classic pattern experienced by most of the European groups: these are epitomized by the appearance of affluent ethnic communities in suburbs. Moreover, there is evidence here, too, of segmented assimilation, for black skin color substantially reduces the likelihood of entry into a majority group area. Residential assimilation into majority group areas is more likely for Asians and for light-skinned Latinos than for others. This conclusion seems consistent with the intermarriage data, which show quite high intermarriage rates for second- and later-generation Asians and lower, though still considerable, rates for Latinos. The impressive Asian intermarriage rates suggest that the social and cultural barriers to marriages with whites, the main intermarriage partners, are not high. The lower rate among Latinos, together with the greater racial diversity of their intermarriage partners, seems to hint at a racial gradient in Latino intermarriage, with light-skinned, middle-class Latinos perhaps most likely to intermarry with non-Latino whites.

Assimilation among the descendants of the new immigrants will not be a simple repetition of the story line for European Americans. But history rarely, if ever, repeats itself exactly. Many circumstances have changed; the American society in which the second and third generations find themselves differs in numerous ways from that faced by the second and third generations of the past. But it remains true that a broader set of opportunities is found in the mainstream than in the social and economic niches where ethnic groups are dominant; and this difference will provide a motivation for many to move toward the mainstream. It would be foolhardy to forecast that assimilation will have as corrosive an impact on the ethnicities created by the new immigration as it did for those created by European immigration. But it would be equally foolhardy to discount the relevance of assimilation for the new immigration. Assimilation remains a pattern of major import for immigrant groups entering the United States, and it is likely to reshape the future ethnic contours of American society, as it did those of the past.

CHAPTER SEVEN

Conclusion: Remaking the Mainstream

Imagine that the contemporary immigration continues for a century, rising in the future to a level above the present one, thus adding in each decade 4–8 percent to the U.S. population, and occasionally even more. (In general, this would exceed the high level of immigration of the 1990s, which, augmented in part by the amnesty provision of the 1986 Immigration Reform and Control Act, appears to be just under 4 percent of the mid-decade population.)[1] Suppose, too, that the immigrants continue to be ethnically, sometimes racially, and frequently religiously different from mainstream America. They settle with great density in a number of metropolitan regions, where ethnic enclaves are a prominent feature of the social landscape and immigrant languages are to be heard on the streets and seen on the signs of many ethnic businesses, while in other parts of the country their presence is thinner and much less noticeable. In some of the areas of densest concentration, languages other than English are used for a good portion of the instruction in schools. Eventually, the levels of citizenship in the immigrant population rise through naturalization and the birthright citizenship of the second generation to the point where the groups dominate the politics of some cities and states and exert control over much municipal employment. Because of the economic niches developed by specific groups, strong associations arise between specific jobs and particular groups, giving rise to stereotypes such as, in a previous era, the Irish policeman and the Italian barber.

Many might think that the result would be an America different from what we have known, but in fact what we have just described derives not from the future but from the history of immigration from Europe during the century of mass immigration, 1820–1924. Starting in the 1830s, the immigration of each decade added more to the U.S. population than has that of any decade since 1965, except for the 1990s (see Figure 7.1). In several it contributed about 10 percent: during the 1850s, when the numbers were swollen with Irish fleeing the famine; during the 1880s, when immigration from Germany attained its high-water mark; and during the early 1900s, when the immigration from southern and eastern Europe crested. Moreover, from its beginnings, the immigration of this period brought mostly arrivals who were ethnically and religiously different from Anglo-America, overwhelmingly composed at the time of Protestant British stock. The largest group of immigrants in the 1830s were the Irish, who, because of their long history of conquest and subordination at the hands of the English, were viewed as members of an inferior race; and the immigration of mid-century was dominated by a combination of Irish and Germans. The Irish were mainly Catholic, of course, and the Ger-

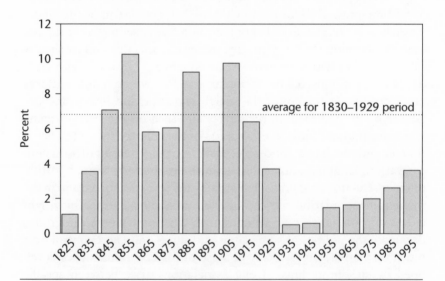

Figure 7.1. Legal immigrants per decade as percent of the mid-decade U.S. population.

man immigration included many Catholics and Jews. By the early twentieth century, immigrants and their children made up the majority of the population in many American cities (and there were scarcely any suburbs for the native urban population to flee to). In some cities, public and parochial education was bilingual or even conducted largely in the language of the immigrant group; this was true throughout the Midwest, where the Germans had settled in large numbers, and in some parts of New England, where the Catholic population was heavily French-speaking. The politics of many cities were, moreover, dominated by political machines headed by Irish Catholics but relying on the votes of other immigrant groups; the Irish also controlled municipal employment in these cities to a degree that would likely be impossible to attain today because of civil service examinations and affirmative action.

Yet assimilation has been the master trend among the descendants of prior waves of immigration, which originated predominantly in Europe but also in East Asia. Groups once regarded as racial and religious outsiders, such as Jews and Italians, have joined the American institutional mainstream and social majority. Among whites, ethnic boundaries have not entirely disappeared, but they have become so faint as to pale beside other racial/ethnic boundaries. Assimilation is unlikely to achieve the same preeminence among the descendants of contemporary immigrants, but that it will be a force of major consequence we have no doubt. In arguing for the importance of assimilation as a social process, we are not asserting its inevitability, as the early writing on assimilation appeared to. Perhaps in the long run, assimilation will turn out to be as predominant in the future as it has been in the American past, but even if it does, the time scale of such a "long run" may be so long that the Keynsian witticism "in the long run we are all dead" is a suitable retort.

We, in any event, are thinking about the patterns that will be observable during the first half of the twenty-first century. The unfolding of the consequences of renewed mass immigration is in its early stages, and as we have repeatedly noted, the new immigration is very diverse. The contemporary immigration scene displays complex, contradictory patterns, from rapid assimilation apparent among some professionals and their children to the new way of sojourning apparent in transnational circuits, and to the potential among other immigrant groups for incorporation as racialized minorities. But the key conclusion for us is that there will be some continuity in assimilation between past and present; in this spirit, it is reasonable to consider what the impact will be on American society as well as on the immigrant minorities.

The Contingencies of Assimilation

Clearly, assimilation will not apply to all immigrant minorities to the same extent, and this is one way in which the incorporation stories of the past and present are likely to differ. The contemporary immigration is more diverse than that of the past, in terms of the forms of capital immigrants bring, the nature of the communities they enter, and their race and legal status. That the members of some groups enter American society at a high level almost from the start because they bring educational and professional credentials or wealth with them has obvious effects on the character of their integration. Whether as immigrant professionals or entrepreneurs, human-cultural and financial capital enables them to benefit most directly from the institutional changes that have taken place since the 1960s. Frequently enough, they pursue professional occupations and live in suburbs, often where whites predominate, and their children are able to attend selective American schools. Stories of this type are too well known to require any emphasis from us. But even among these groups there will not be a uniform assimilation scenario. What can be expected is that individuals and groups will acculturate at different rates and often selectively, by shedding some aspects of immigrant cultural practices while retaining others (though these will often be altered by the American experience, which should not be surprising, since the same was true of earlier immigrant groups).

Members of other groups face quite different conditions. Low-wage laborers with low levels of formal schooling, who are found in great numbers in the immigrations from Mexico and Central America, compete for jobs on the bottom rungs of the labor market. The reliance of labor migrants on ethnically based social capital may reinforce social closure within the ethnic enclave; moreover, initial disadvantages in human-cultural capital are likely to persist into the second generation. Although the second generation may graduate from high school, substantially fewer will go on to college, especially in comparison to the children of professionals and entrepreneurs of the same immigrant groups. As a result, some of the children of labor migrants may stall in terms of their socioeconomic attainment, though their fate should not be treated as a foregone conclusion, given the widespread pattern of second-generation advance documented in Chapter 6. Moreover, for some groups, racism enters as a complicating factor, limiting not only the chances for social mobility but also the opportunities to convert socioeconomic success into more favorable residential contexts and other societal values. The overlap of West Indian and African American neighborhoods, for example, is evidence that Afro-Caribbeans are subject to racial segregation in a manner not so different from that affecting native-born African Americans.[2]

A final major complication, which we understand the least about, in part because it has almost no analogue among European immigrants, is that of legal status. Since there were no practical legal limits on European immigration until 1917, there was no issue of undocumented status on a sizable scale that could impinge on the chances of the second generation. But for some of the contemporary immigration streams, especially those from Mexico, Central America, and also the Caribbean, illegal status frequently drives immigrant parents into a social and economic underground, where they are afraid to insist on the rights that legal residents and citizens see as their due. We have no systematic evidence yet about how undocumented status intrudes, directly or indirectly, on the second generation, whose members are U.S. citizens by virtue of birth but grow up in households where parents and perhaps older siblings must live with the associated uncertainties; but an impact must be suspected until proven otherwise.[3] A special case is the Salvadoran immigration, in which a large number of migrants have fled a civil war and other disruptions but are not recognized as refugees by the U.S. government. Many have been allowed to stay temporarily, but their lives in the United States are made uncertain by the possibility that their permission to stay may be rescinded.[4]

As we have stressed, there is no reason to believe that assimilation is inevitable or that it will be the master trend for all these diverse groups, as it has turned out to be for the descendants of earlier European and East Asian immigrants. Moreover, if we take a cue from studies of social mobility, *divergent outcomes* have to be expected. Such studies suggest that large numbers in the contemporary second generation will experience limited or even no social mobility, while some will fall from their parents' position in the socioeconomic hierarchy. Insofar as social mobility is linked to assimilation, especially for the second generation from groups that have entered on the lowest rungs of the socioeconomic ladder, then a similar variability will hold for assimilation.

The alternative models—pluralism and segmented assimilation—have their own limitations, however, as we argued in Chapter 4. The pluralist model is woven from two distinct threads: the transnational connections that have become far easier to maintain in the contemporary world because of advances in transportation and communication, and the economic and social advantages that may be drawn from ethnic networks and communities. We have no doubt that these are sufficient to ensure pluralist outcomes for some portions of the current second and third generations. As we noted in Chapter 3, three-quarters of a century after the end of mass immigration from Europe, there are still ethnic communities derived from it and individuals whose lives are more or less bounded by the frames of ethnic social matrices. Yet transnationalism would seem hard to sustain on a mass scale in the second and third generations, which are far more enmeshed in the American environment than is the immigrant generation and, in most cases, lack the "thick" connections to the places and people in the homeland that are necessary for transnationalism to be viable. Further, the socioeconomic advantages to be derived from ethnic affiliations are also less clear for the U.S.-born generations than for the immigrant one. The prime virtue of many ethnic labor market niches is that they provide jobs to individuals who, because of their foreign origins, are at a disadvantage; but the jobs themselves are not often very desirable. Few ethnic economies are large or diverse enough to provide jobs that are attractive to many individuals with realistic prospects of mobility in the mainstream economy. Thus, our view is that the pluralist mode of incorporation is likely to remain confined to modest portions of the U.S.-born generations, as was true for the earlier European and Asian ethnics.

One reason why the pluralist model has received so much attention is that it develops an alternative to the third mode of incorporation, spotlighted by the model of segmented assimilation. While this model encompasses the possibility of assimilation into the mainstream—this is one segment, or trajectory—its focus of interest is on assimilation into a disadvantaged minority status. That outcome is seen as the result of changes in economic structures that reduce opportunities for upward mobility; racial distinctions that remain powerful and place the children of nonwhite immigrants at a disadvantage; and the attractiveness of an inner-city, underclass culture for those in the second generation who have experienced discrimination and rejection in schools and workplaces.

Although such lucid identification of a potential social problem for the second and third generations has value, we foresee limits on the likely scale of "downward" assimilation. (In pointing to limits, we do not intend to diminish the distress felt by those who experience discrimination and ethnically constrained opportunities or the problem these pose for the society.) For one thing, upward mobility is by no means as reduced as the model seems to assume; the socioeconomic advance in the second generation is quite broad for the children of low-wage laborers, and the children of human-capital immigrants do quite well on average, as the data in Chapter 6 show. Even what appears to be horizontal mobility on the abstract grid of the social scientist may be experienced as intergenerational improvement by those undergoing it; certainly, this is what studies of the perceptions of lateral movers appear to indicate.[5] Downward socioeconomic mobility, which the model highlights, does not appear widespread.

Moreover, the model takes as fixed something that should be viewed as potentially malleable: the rigidity of racial boundaries in the United States. As we have argued in previous chapters, this rigidity has already softened to a large extent for Asians. The extent of its relevance for Hispanics is unclear: to judge by residential patterns, it is not experienced much by the roughly half of Hispanics who view themselves as racially "white." The degree of racial discrimination suffered by brown-skinned Hispanics or those with an indigenous or "Indian" appearance is undoubtedly greater. Evidence for a linkage of racial barriers and downward assimilation is strongest among individuals and groups with visible African ancestry: Afro-Caribbeans, including some Spanish-speakers.[6] Nevertheless, this describes the contemporary situation; as we will argue shortly, we see reasons to hypothesize that racial boundaries could become less rigid in the future.

In developing a theory to specify the mechanisms of assimilation, in Chapter 2 we claim that incentives matter: insofar as entry into the mainstream expands the structure of opportunities ranging from education, occupation, and areas of residence to greater latitude in a variety of private choices, many immigrants and their children are likely to consider courses of action that, whether intended to do so or not, improve their probability of assimilating. Whether or not they commit themselves to these courses, however, and advance on trajectories of assimilation is contingent to a large measure on the predictability of their chances of success, especially in terms of social mobility; and these in turn depend on the reception they anticipate from members of the majority and other racial/ethnic groups. Consequently, our theory emphasizes the institutional mechanisms that ensure predictability and thus the role of the state in maintaining an institutional environment in which the civil rights of minorities are safeguarded and barriers to entry imposed by racism have been lowered (albeit not eliminated). While the cost of discrimination has been increased for workplaces and public organizations by these formal mechanisms, cultural changes have reduced informal racism in the private domain of personal relationships and in choice of residential neighborhoods. In making these statements, we do not wish to be misunderstood as claiming that institutional and informal racism have all but disappeared; the systematic data about persisting residential segregation are sufficient to dispel such chimeras.[7] We also acknowledge that the changes have been more effective in reducing the costs of racism for some groups, such as Asians, than for African Americans and others with visible African ancestry. Nevertheless, we believe that the theoretical alternatives to assimilation have not factored into their schemas the enormous institutional and cultural changes that have taken place between the first half of the twentieth century and the beginning of the twenty-first.

In the not so distant American past, the rights of membership in civil society were limited to people of European ancestry, as reflected in the laws governing immigration, citizenship, marriage, housing, education, and property, which were aimed at excluding nonwhites from civil society. Even access to many public facilities, from public beaches to partitioned areas of theaters, was denied to racial minorities. These formal rules of racial separatism were buttressed by the informal constraints—the customs, conventions, norms, and etiquette of race relations—which in combination effectively barred nonwhites from assimilation into the mainstream society. Exclusionary rules were justified by the ideology of manifest destiny and white supremacy, which were perceived to be threatened by racial minorities at home as well as by the flood of unwelcome immigrants from outside the traditional sources of northern and western Europe. Early in the twentieth century, the view of the United States as a threatened Anglo-American nation was widespread, as reflected in the influential movie *The Birth of a Nation* (1915), which sympathetically depicts the rise of the Ku Klux Klan and the events leading to the Jim Crow era in the South. Around this same time, the immigration acts of 1917 and 1924 were passed, ending immigration from Asia and imposing national origins quotas to restrict immigration from southern and eastern Europe.

The post–World War II institutional and cultural changes should be assessed not only by the standard of racial equality, which has not yet been achieved, but also from the vantage point of the early twentieth century. The aim of civil rights legislation was to confer on nonwhites equal rights of membership in civil society. Similarly, the change in immigration policy brought about by the enactment of the 1965 immigration law ended the national quota system and opened legal immigration to non-Europeans on an equal footing. These legislative reforms have brought about a watershed change in the formal rules regulating entry into the American mainstream for native-born minorities and immigrants. From schooling to the workplace, government has sought to impose costs to discrimination through institutional mechanisms of monitoring and enforcement of formal rules that outlaw discrimination by race or gender. To be sure, persistent opposition by whites to specific programs such as school busing and affirmative action has been effective in limiting the impact of civil rights–era legislation. Nonetheless, the broad support for the core idea of outlawing racial discrimination has fundamentally altered the institutional environment. The integration of the American armed forces provides a dramatic example of just how effective federal regulatory interventions can be in remaking the racial boundaries of a mainstream organization that as recently as World War II fought in segregated units.[8] Similarly, the integration of elite educational institutions, from the New England boarding schools to leading universities and major U.S. corporations, though still in progress and vulnerable to reversals, nonetheless demonstrates the scope of institutional change since the early 1960s.

Concomitant with the changes in formal rules has been a subtle though profound set of changes in the attitudes of Americans toward ethnicity, race, and visible difference. This has been reflected above all in a growing, if still incomplete, acceptance of racial and ethnic inclusion as a social value—of social groupings that are diverse in terms of the origins of their members—and an increased tolerance of visible cultural difference (e.g., Sikh turbans). Tolerance in matters such as dress and food preferences makes it easier for members of previously excluded ethnic and racial groups to enter the mainstream, for it lowers the personal costs of doing so if they are not required to repudiate all signs of their own cultural distinctiveness. The valorization of inclusion has been sufficient to produce public and private policies intended to foster it within the framework of equality under the law. Although there is controversy as to whether preferential treatment through affirmative action is fair to European and Asian Americans, diversity as a social value has gained support in many sectors of the American mainstream. This cultural change is contributing to an incremental remolding of that mainstream. While the data on residential segregation demonstrate the persistence of institutional and informal racism, those on the changes in the residential environments of whites reveal the breadth of the tolerance for diversity: according to the data from the 2000 census, the *average* white now lives in a neighborhood where 20 percent of the residents are nonwhite or Hispanic.[9] The percentage of minorities has almost doubled since the early 1980s, and we infer from this change that few whites can entirely escape racial diversity in their immediate environment.

It is not a paradox, at least not a sociological one, that many nonwhites and Hispanics live in segregated communities, isolated from the mainstream, while many others are integrated into neighborhoods where numerous European Americans live as well. Yet from a contemporary standpoint, these changes may seem modest and imperfectly achieved. Episodes of exclusion and intolerance are not hard to find. It should be remembered, however, that the contemporary attitudes not only are quite different from those that prevailed a century ago, at a previous crest of immigration, but also are different from those in many other immigration societies. France, for example, sees itself as an assimilationist nation, tracing this stance to the heritage of the French Revolution and to the expansionist and radically egalitarian view of citizenship associated with it. Today, most French observers see the integration of immigrants and their descendants as unfolding according to the "Republican" model, whose foundational principles include the notions that all French citizens have equal rights and that the state should not make any distinctions among them based on ethnic origins.[10] Members of immigrant groups who fully embrace French culture will be accepted as French regardless of their origins. Some French social scientists have claimed a superiority for the French over the American style of assimilation on the grounds that French society is willing to assimilate individuals without regard for racial difference; others deride the United States as a "multicultural" society that has abandoned its assimilation model by giving recognition to racial and ethnic difference.[11] But the Republican model allows less tolerance of visible cultural difference, both because of the high value placed on French culture and because cultural differences promote ethnic distinctions. The so-called *foulard* controversy, which erupted in 1989 when three Muslim female students who insisted on wearing head scarves to school were expelled, did allow other voices, claiming a right to be different, to be heard. Yet in 1994, the French government banned "ostentatious" religious symbols, including Muslim head scarves, in public schools, basing its decision in part on the principle of *laïcité* in education.[12] While this decision was subsequently rescinded, the result has not been the establishment of the right to be different. The wearing of head scarves is still contested, and in many schools Muslim young women wearing *foulards* are harassed by teachers acting in the name of *laïcité*.[13]

Our theory does not offer a basis for predicting that assimilation will be the master trend for the descendants of contemporary immigration in the United States, but it highlights the role of the state by implicating it directly in the institutional mechanisms that ensure reasonably predictable chances of success for the second and third generations. A question naturally arises: Should the state devise additional, proactive policies to promote assimilation, such as the English-only public education system envisioned by opponents of bilingual education? While our book is not intended to speak directly to policy questions, we do not wish to be misunderstood as implicit supporters of such policies. We do not equate assimilation with Americanization, a term that is linked to an unsavory history of coercion. We believe that, in the past, assimilation has advanced most effectively when it has resulted from the choices of the individuals undergoing it, as part of a strategy intended to improve their own life chances or those of their children. (Assimilation, one could say, is something that frequently enough happens to people while they are making other plans.) Coercive assimilation, which can be seen in the state- and elite-led policies of the early twentieth century, which disparaged immigrant cultures and attempted "pressure-cooker" acculturation, is not usually very effective because it stimulates active resistance in its subjects.[14] Moreover, it has led to egregious violations of minority rights everywhere it has been attempted. If we are to break with the dispassionate tone we have striven to attain throughout our analysis, it would be to say that minority individuals and families have a right to attempt to preserve their cultural distinctiveness if they so wish. If they are to make choices that, wittingly or unwittingly, promote their assimilation, let them do so because they believe their choices to be in their own best interest.

Remaking the Mainstream

Assimilation has reshaped the American mainstream in the past, and it will do so again, culturally, institutionally, and demographically. The cultural reshaping of the mainstream that we see as resulting from immigration is not accurately conveyed by the metaphor of the melting pot, which implies that change is largely a process of fusing elements from different cultures into a new, unitary culture. Certainly, there are such syncretisms in American culture, but much cultural change appears to occur as the mainstream expands to accommodate cultural alternatives, usually after they have been "Americanized" to some extent, by shedding their more exotic aspects.

Change of this sort is very visible in the arena of religion. It was not so long ago that mainstream Americans defined the United States as a white, Protestant nation. In the early twentieth century the arrival of large numbers of eastern and southern European Catholics and Jews generated intense xenophobia among native whites. Today, in a reflection of our contemporary understanding of the differences that matter, the dimensions of this past difference are described as predominantly ethnic and even racial, but to nativist observers at the time, the religious distinctions were as salient as the ethnic/racial ones. Judaism and Catholicism, the latter perhaps to a lesser extent since it is a Christian religion, were seen as incompatible with mainstream institutions and culture. The Protestant zealotry of the Ku

Klux Klan, which reached the zenith of its membership and its influence on the national scene during the 1920s, marks only the extreme end of a spectrum of anti-Jewish, anti-Catholic attitudes.

Yet over time, these religions have become part of the American mainstream. Contemporary opponents of multiculturalism, in upholding the value of Western civilization, refer to "our" Judaeo-Christian heritage. The religions as practiced here certainly changed during the course of this incorporation into the mainstream: for instance, non-Orthodox forms of Judaism, including Reform Judaism, with its muted religious services and commitments, found wide acceptance in the United States, and what had been a minor holiday in the Jewish calendar, Hanukkah, was elevated in status to provide Jewish children with an equivalent to Christmas. American Catholics have become known within their worldwide church for combining a high level of religious observance with individualistic dissent from some Catholic teachings, such as those on birth control.[15] But the mainstream changed as well, as its boundary moved to include these alternative models of religious belief and practice.

One consequence has been to ease marriage across religious lines, as the social and cultural distances among the three "charter" religions have shrunk; this has been especially noticeable for Jews, whose rate of marriage with Christians rose from less than 10 percent to 50 percent or more in the decades between 1960 and 1990. This intermarriage cannot be understood simply as an assimilation of the Anglo-conformity type, a passing of minority individuals into the religion of the dominant group. About a third of Jewish-Christian couples participate in Jewish congregations and raise their children as Jews, while others join Christian churches or create a nondenominational family culture. An entire literature has arisen to counsel such intermarried couples.[16] It appears that, for the most part, those who affiliate with Judaism do not locate themselves at the more devout end of the religious spectrum, and their family cultures typically include some Christian elements, such as Christmas celebrations.[17] No doubt, many of those who have adopted a Christian religious identity also participate in some Jewish rituals, such as Passover seders at the in-laws', since these are, after all, family occasions as much as religious ones. In effect, the once sharp religious boundary has been blurred, in the sense that rituals from both traditions are practiced.

What is especially telling is that, in a society that once defined itself as Christian, even Protestant, and evinced substantial anti-Semitism, Christian and Jewish families accept that their sons and daughters marry across a historical religious chasm and raise their children in the other religion. This can occur on a large scale only if the chasm has been filled in. And it even appears to be linked to a revision of what often seems, in the common sense about race and ethnicity, to be the most immutable: the perception of physical difference. The social divide between Jews and Christians was "naturalized" in the early twentieth century by widespread perceptions of Jewish physical distinctiveness, epitomized by the "Jewish" nose.[18] But as we noted in Chapter 3, the decline in the frequency of rhinoplasty, intended to give Jews a less ethnic appearance, at the very moment when Jewish-Christian marriages are soaring in number suggests that the mainstream standards of physiognomic attractiveness have expanded. Standards of beauty are not immune to the changes in the mainstream resulting from assimilation.

Our conception of the mainstream emphasizes institutional structures and organizations regulated by formal rules. Rules that outlaw racial discrimination and extend civil rights to all racial groups have lowered the barriers to entry into the mainstream for nonwhites. So long as the current ensemble of rules on racial equality remain in force and are monitored and enforced, we can expect the trend toward inclusion of ethnic and racial minorities in the American mainstream to continue. The reshaping of the mainstream also involves the inclusion of what are initially defined as minority ethnic and racial groups, or at least some parts of them. Through assimilation, the mainstream has become diverse in the ethnic origins of those who participate in it; and the ethnic majority group, which dominates the mainstream population, has been reconstituted. We predict that these processes will continue. But will demographic change conform to the blending processes already well advanced in the institutional and organizational mainstream?

One of the commonplaces about the American future is that its racial and ethnic landscape will be radically transformed from that of the present. According to widely cited population projections, if immigration continues at its current pace into the middle of the century, then the majoritarian status of the white mainstream will be in jeopardy—at least numerically—as African Americans, Asians, Latinos, and Native Americans will constitute nearly half the population.[19]

This projected demographic change is often stated even more dramatically in common discourse; for instance, in a 1997 speech, President Clinton claimed that, by 2050, there will be "no majority race" in the United States, a statement that overlooks the fact that half of Hispanics, the largest minority group according to the projections, view themselves as racially white. Another common exaggeration involves a telescoping of the shift into the imminent future; even so usually astute an observer as Gary Wills fell into this trap when he wrote in 1998: "The explosion of ethnic diversity guarantees that affirmative action of some sort will be needed so that everyone feels a stake in a country that is literally changing complexion every day: *whites will be a minority by early in the next* [twenty-first] *century.* What does that imply about the education, cultural heritage, and social values of a community also undergoing technological changes of a dizzying sort?"[20] The projected changes are viewed by many commentators as implying the potential for revolutionary changes in the relationship between majority and minority Americans, including a decline of, or even an end to, the cultural and social dominance of a majority group and a flowering of multiculturalism.

We believe that this population scenario and, even more, the implications drawn from it are likely to be undermined by assimilation. The projections presume a continuing compartmentalization of the American population into mutually exclusive groups separated by unambiguously marked boundaries. As we have emphasized throughout the previous chapters, the boundaries separating early-twentieth-century immigrant groups, such as eastern European Jews, southern Italians, and East Asians, from Anglo-Americans seemed at the time insurmountable, anchored in quasi-racial, as well as religious, distinctions. The same could be said of the mid-nineteenth-century immigration of Irish Catholics, who were commonly caricatured with simian-like features. Today, the racial edge to the perception of ethnic differences among whites has disappeared; and those still perceived as nonwhite, such as the descendants of the earlier East Asian immigration, have nonetheless assimilated to a large degree.

Perhaps the single most important conclusion to take from the social assimilation of European and Asians descended from the nineteenth- and early-twentieth-century immigration is that racial/ethnic boundaries can blur, stretch, and move, as the current emphasis on the social construction of race implies.[21] Indeed, were it not for the fluidity of boundaries, there might be no racial/ethnic numerical majority in the United States today. Only between a quarter and a third of the population can trace some ancestry to Protestants from the British Isles, the former "majority" group.[22] Thus, were the ethnic definition of the majority group limited to the original Anglo-American core, it would already have become a minority of the population; only because of past assimilation can one say that an ethnic majority, in all senses of that term, exists in the United States today.

What does this suggest about the new immigrant groups? Might boundaries between ethnically and racially defined social groups change again? Of course they might, and it seems a safe bet that they will to some degree. Where changes will take place and what their nature will be are the key questions, impossible to answer definitively at present. Nevertheless, important clues to assimilatory boundary change are found in the evidence described in Chapter 6 of narrowing social distances between new immigrant minorities and the European American majority. Such narrowings are a two-sided process: members of the minority must seek entry into social contexts occupied by the majority group; and members of the majority must find their entry acceptable. Will the narrowing of social distance lead to boundary blurring, implying some decline in the salience of racial/ethnic boundaries, or to boundary shifting, which might bring the new groups, or at least large portions of them, into the mainstream society? Or will assimilation be limited to boundary crossing?[23]

That there is and will continue to be some boundary crossing—into the dominant group—is beyond question. Boundary crossing conforms to the most conventional definition of assimilation: individuals and sometimes subgroups "melt" into mainstream institutional structures and organizations, becoming fully a part of them, except perhaps for some symbolic form of identification with their ethnic origin. When this happens, their origins become to a large extent socially "invisible." Even the individuals themselves may have only sketchy knowledge of this aspect of their background. Changes in the mainstream, such as cultural incorporations, may facilitate the process of social incorporation by reducing perceptions of individuals' cultural and social distance from the dominant group. Of course, individual-level assimilation will not be spread uniformly among the new immigrants and their descendants. Boundary crossing into the dominant group will depend on forms of immigrant capital, racial appearance, and geographic location, among other factors. But boundary crossing will not by itself produce any fundamental revision in the racial/ethnic system of the United States. Rather, the "white" portion of the population will be augmented, as, for example, many South Americans of European ancestry or the offspring of Asian-white marriages live and work in mainstream milieus, blended in such a way that their origins are rarely salient.[24]

Boundary blurring occurs when an intermediate zone opens up between two racial/ethnic populations: the ethnic origins of individuals in the zone have not become invisible to those on either side of it, but the social and cultural distances separating them from either group have been reduced. Consequently, even though origins remain visible, as would, say, those of a Vietnamese American living in a largely white suburb, they are not perceived by others to be especially relevant for most interactions, which take place in an unself-conscious manner.

Boundary blurring can be brought on by the expansion of the mainstream culture to include elements of the minority cultures, a process that, we have argued, has happened throughout the history of U.S. assimilation, for this kind of cultural incorporation reduces the apparent differences between the two sides. Boundary blurring also occurs as a consequence of intermarriage and the racial and ethnic mixing that results from it. The assimilation of the descendants of earlier Chinese and Japanese immigrants demonstrates that racial perceptions do not inevitably correlate with impenetrable social boundaries. That nearly two-thirds of the young children of Japanese Americans also have some other ancestry—generally from a European ethnic origin—testifies to the extent to which once salient racial boundaries can become blurred.[25] And as boundary blurring occurs through mixed ancestry, racial/ethnic difference becomes more continuous and less sharply differentiated; eventually, perception—a highly social phenomenon, in any event—is affected, and physical differences can be seen more as individual characteristics and less as group markers.[26] The increasing social recognition being given to racially mixed ancestry, which led the Census Bureau to allow individuals to place themselves in more than one racial category starting with the 2000 census, suggests its growing importance. Mixtures spanning the main racial/ethnic divides of U.S. society, whose precise geometry has been described as a "racial-ethnic pentagon,"[27] are likely to gradually break down the neatness of the racial/ethnic compartmentalizations.

Assimilation will alter the racial/ethnic contours of American society, we predict, at a minimum augmenting the majority group by boundary crossing and expanding the mainstream by blurring the boundaries between the majority and the groups being fed by contemporary immigration. (We assume that boundaries will also be blurred between some of these groups as well.) Will the majority group of the United States then continue to be viewed as constituted by the white, European-ancestry population? We are not certain of the answer. It is conceivable that it will no longer be equated with white America as individuals who are visibly nonwhite are increasingly incorporated into the families and other intimate social milieus of whites, though we are not able to predict an alternative social definition. Even so, the "summit" positions of the society—its political leadership, for instance—are likely to remain in the hands of whites for a long time, despite their decreasing share of the population; and this could slow a redefinition of the nation's dominant group. (It is remarkable that Protestant whites whose ancestry stems from the British Isles still dominate the presidency, and this fact demonstrates the power of what are, in ordinary circumstances, minor ethnic distinctions—such as being Greek or Italian American—for attaining the most elite status.)

There is, however, one scenario that seems highly implausible to us. Until now, assimilation has meant the expansion of the racial majority to include previously disparaged groups, such as the "swarthy" southern Italians. It has not altered the racial character of that divide because the inclusion of these groups occurred by their being redefined as fully "white." But this sort of boundary shift seems ruled out by two factors: it will presumably not be possible to redefine as "white" individuals who are visibly nonwhite, such as most Asians; and many assimilating second- and third-generation individuals will be from ethnic origins that remain prominent in the social landscape, continually revitalized by new immigrant inflows. Thus, a redefinition of the racial status of an entire group seems quite unlikely. Consequently, the type of radical boundary shifts that would bring all or a substantial portion of the new groups into the majority, the type we now view as an outcome of European immigration, seems highly doubtful; the wholesale "whitening" undergone by the European groups may be ultimately tied to singular historical contingencies, such as the four-decade hiatus in mass immigration that began in the mid-1920s. The nature of boundary alteration, then, seems likely to be a key difference between the present era and past ones. By the same token, assimilation is not likely to require that non-Europeans come to view themselves as "whites," a criticism of the concept that one often hears. In this respect, multiculturalism may already be preparing the way for a redefinition of the nature of the American social majority, one that accepts a majority that is racially diverse.

A second issue concerns the ultimate significance of assimilation for racial and ethnic stratification. One idealistic, normatively tinged conception of assimilation that Americans have inherited from the past envisions an end to the ethnic inequalities that are still so salient; this was the dreamy prophecy of Israel Zangwill's early-twentieth-century play *The Melting Pot,* which helped to popularize the metaphor. But we are certain that racial and ethnic stratification is still going to have a powerful role in shaping the society of the future. In this respect, the alternative patterns of incorporation have validity. In particular, the segmented assimilation notion that one form of incorporation will move individuals into a disadvantaged minority status is part of the reality of the future. This is especially likely for individuals with combinations of family background features—low levels of parental human capital, certain racial appearances by North American standards, and illegal status—that make it difficult for them to perceive realistic opportunities to advance in U.S. society. The pluralist model indicates that some proportion of each group will remain within the confines of the ethnic social matrix, though this may turn out to be most often the case when that choice does not disadvantage them in socioeconomic terms. But that racial and ethnic groups will continue to exist on both sides of blurred boundaries we have no doubt, and they will be associated with disparities in life chances. At the same time, there will be diversity of incorporation within all groups.

If the compartmentalization among mutually exclusive racial and ethnic groups begins to dissolve as racial boundaries blur, then the membership category into which an individual is placed by social perception, and even more its apparent relevance in many social settings, will depend on more than appearance and ancestry. These will obviously count, but so too will characteristics that we think of as achieved rather than ascribed, such as exterior cultural characteristics, residential location, social class position, and the apparent race/ethnicity of one's marriage partner. A provocative way of formulating what we are suggesting is that the racial/ethnic system of the United States could begin to resemble in certain respects those of Latin America. Race/ethnicity will lose some of its clear-cut, categorical character; it will become more like a spectrum on which an individual's location will be determined by a number of social and physical characteristics and may shift from one social setting to another. We take no position as to whether such a development should be viewed as an improvement over the historical rigidities of the U.S. race system, epitomized by the infamous "one-drop" rule for determining membership in the black group. As we have noted, there will still be a racial and ethnic stratification system, and placement within it will matter for the life chances of individuals; this is true of race in Latin America as well, though some Latin societies, such as Brazil, compare their systems favorably to that of the United States.[28]

How will the changes we envision affect the social meaning of race for African Americans, who have suffered grievously from white Americans' binary vision of race? The changes could lead ultimately to a broad decline in the significance of racial/ethnic boundaries, and this could finally soften the hitherto hard-and-fast character of the black-white divide. A continuing increase in the size of the African American middle class and in the frequency of black-white marriage, both of which have grown since the 1960s, coupled with the demands of the children of these marriages for social recognition of their multiracial ancestry, could also contribute to the blurring of America's most salient and hitherto indestructible racial divide.

But a more pessimistic scenario is also plausible. As many descendants of new immigrant groups come to be included in the mainstream, the nature of the distinction between blacks and the majority could simply change without losing its social salience or its import for the distribution of social goods and statuses: instead of a division between blacks and whites, the fundamental social chasm would evolve into a distinction between blacks, a category that could expand to include Afro-Caribbeans and dark-skinned Hispanics, and everyone else. Herbert Gans has speculated along these lines, arguing that the basic distinction between "nonblacks" and blacks could be supplemented by a "residual" category "for the groups that do not, or do not yet, fit into the basic dualism."[29] Playing into such a scenario

could be new social mythologies, already at hand, about basic similarities in the characteristics of "hardworking" immigrant groups, wherever they come from, in contrast to other, especially native, minorities. This sort of scenario is supported by the strenuous efforts made
by past immigrant minorities to distinguish themselves from blacks
and advance their candidacy for membership in the white majority,
suggesting that assimilation by contemporary second and third generations could also depend on the existence of a pariah racial group to
mark the status of "other."[30] It also relies on the evidence that black
social mobility cannot be equated with acceptance in the mainstream,
that middle-class blacks continue to suffer frequent stings of discrimination from racist whites.[31]

From the standpoint of the present, there is no definitive way to
know which of these scenarios will prevail. Yet it seems likely that elements of both scenarios will play a part in America's future. The institutional and cultural changes we experienced as a society starting
with the civil rights–era legislation have long-term consequences for
the cumulative causation of progressive inclusion of ethnic and racial minorities in the American mainstream. Mainstream institutional
structures and organizations are clearly more diverse in their ethnic
and racial representation than in any previous period of American
history. Racial stratification will continue to prove potent: there will
be a black group for the foreseeable future, and membership in it will
continue to be associated with disadvantages and discrimination. But
the boundaries between blacks and other groups, including whites,
are likely to blur because of black social mobility into core institutional structures and organizations. Immigration could prove a critical lever in this process because Afro-Caribbean immigrants may be
more able to pierce the racial boundary: more willing to enter as racial
pioneers into white-dominated social settings and more likely to find
acceptance there.[32] The more black Americans appear in the mainstream—work in middle-class jobs alongside whites and participate in
core institutional structures—and take part in social life in integrated
neighborhoods and intermarry with whites, the more whites' assumptions about the social meanings attached to skin color will be eroded.

Yet assimilation is not a panacea for America's racism. In this area
especially, we are wary of the normative aspects of assimilation theory interfering with a clear-eyed assessment of prospects for change.
Assimilation theory has long been snagged on utopian concepts of

America's singular mission in the world; this strand of thought is visible in the earliest writings about the "melting pot," the letters of the eighteenth-century French American farmer J. Hector St. John Crèvecoeur, and continues through Israel Zangwill's famous early-twentieth-century play. At the utopian extreme, the expectation has been that assimilation would ultimately take care of invidious racial distinctions, but there is no evidence that this has happened to the black-white divide. Of course, one could make the same point about the multiculturalism associated with demographic projections of the growth of nonwhite populations relative to the white majority. It suggests that demography will ultimately undo the hegemony of the white racial majority, as in California, and produce a society in which racial origins increasingly count for less. Neither utopian vision has much chance of coming to pass. Assimilation, even if it expands to embrace non-Europeans, is unlikely to dissolve racial distinctions entirely in the United States and to end the inequalities rooted in them. Assimilation, then, provides no reason to end the struggle against the power of racism.

1 Rethinking Assimilation

1. Nathan Glazer, "Is Assimilation Dead?" *Annals* 530 (November 1993): 123.
2. For example, Molefe Keti Asante, "The Afrocentric Idea," *Journal of Negro Education* 60 (Spring 1991): 170–180.
3. L. Paul Metzger, "American Sociology and Black Assimilation: Conflicting Perspectives," *American Journal of Sociology* 76 (January 1972): 627–647. See also Robert Blauner, *Racial Oppression in America* (New York: Harper & Row, 1972); Nathan Glazer, *We Are All Multiculturalists Now* (Cambridge, Mass.: Harvard University Press, 1997); Stanford Lyman, *The Black American in Sociological Thought: A Failure of Perspective* (New York: Capricorn, 1973); James McKee, *Sociology and the Race Problem: The Failure of a Perspective* (Urbana: University of Illinois Press, 1993).
4. W. Lloyd Warner and Leo Srole, *The Social Systems of American Ethnic Groups* (New Haven: Yale University Press, 1945), pp. 295–296.
5. Ibid., p. 285.
6. Ibid., p. 292.
7. Blauner, *Racial Oppression*; Metzger, "American Sociology"; Stephen Steinberg, *Turning Back: The Retreat from Racial Justice in American Thought and Policy* (Boston: Beacon Press, 1995).
8. Gunnar Myrdal, *An American Dilemma: The Negro Problem in Modern Democracy* (New York: Harper & Row, 1944), p. 929.
9. Milton Gordon, *Assimilation in American Life* (New York: Oxford University Press, 1964), p. 72.
10. Ibid., pp. 111–112.
11. Ibid., pp. 109–110.

12. J. L. Dillard, *Toward a Social History of American English* (Berlin: Mouton, 1985).

13. Alejandro Portes and Rubén Rumbaut, *Immigrant America: A Portrait,* 2d ed. (Berkeley: University of California Press, 1996), chap. 6; Alejandro Portes and Robert Bach, *Latin Journey: Cuban and Mexican Immigrants in the United States* (Berkeley: University of California Press, 1985); Alejandro Portes and Robert Manning, "The Immigrant Enclave: Theory and Empirical Examples," in Susan Olzak and Joane Nagel, eds., *Competitive Ethnic Relations* (New York: Academic Press, 1986), pp. 47–68; Min Zhou and Carl Bankston, *Growing Up American: How Vietnamese Children Adapt to Life in the United States* (New York: Russell Sage Foundation, 1998).

14. Nina Glick Schiller, Linda Basch, and Cristina Blanc-Szanton, "From Immigrant to Transmigrant: Theorizing Transnational Migration," *Anthropological Quarterly* 68 (January 1995): 48–63; Michael Jones-Correa, *Between Two Nations: The Political Predicament of Latinos in New York City* (Ithaca: Cornell University Press, 1998); Robert Smith, "Transnational Localities: Community, Technology, and the Politics of Membership within the Context of Mexico-U.S. Migration," *Comparative Urban and Community Research* 6 (1998): 196–238. For a critical assessment, see Nancy Foner, "What's New about Transnationalism? New York Immigrants Today and at the Turn of the Century," *Diaspora* 6, no. 3 (1997): 355–375.

15. Portes and Rumbaut, *Immigrant America;* Portes and Bach, *Latin Journey;* Portes and Manning, "Immigrant Enclave"; Zhou and Bankston, *Growing Up American.* See also Alejandro Portes and Rubén Rumbaut, *Legacies: The Story of the Immigrant Second Generation* (Berkeley: University of California Press, 2001); and Min Zhou and Carl Bankston, "Social Capital and the Adaptation of the Second Generation: The Case of Vietnamese Youth in New Orleans," *International Migration Review* 28 (Winter 1994): 821–845.

16. Sarah Mahler, *American Dreaming: Immigrant Life on the Margins* (Princeton: Princeton University Press, 1995); Jose Itzigsohn, *Developing Poverty: The State, Labor Market Deregulation, and the Informal Economy in Costa Rica and the Dominican Republic* (University Park: Pennsylvania State University Press, 2000).

17. Alejandro Portes and Min Zhou, "The New Second Generation: Segmented Assimilation and Its Variants," *Annals* 530 (November 1993); see also Herbert Gans, "Second Generation Decline: Scenarios for the Economic and Ethnic Futures of Post-1965 American Immigrants," *Ethnic and Racial Studies* 15 (April 1992): 173–192.

18. Philip Kasinitz, "Invisible No More? West Indian Americans in the Social Scientific Imagination," in Nancy Foner, ed., *Islands in the City: West Indian Migration to New York* (Berkeley: University of California Press, 2001), pp. 257–275. The distinctiveness of later-generation West Indians

within the African American population is a matter of some uncertainty; see Matthijs Kalmijn, "The Socioeconomic Assimilation of Caribbean American Blacks," *Social Forces* 74 (March 1996): 910–930; and Suzanne Model and Gene Fisher, "Black-White Unions: West Indians and African Americans Compared," *Demography* 38 (May 2001): 177–185.

19. Kathryn Neckerman, Prudence Carter, and Jennifer Lee, "Segmented Assimilation and Minority Cultures of Mobility," *Ethnic and Racial Studies* 22 (1999): 945–965.

20. One sophisticated analysis estimates that, in the late 1980s, the underclass accounted for less than 10 percent of adult black men. Christopher Jencks, *Rethinking Social Policy: Race, Poverty, and the Underclass* (Cambridge, Mass.: Harvard University Press, 1992), pp. 143–203.

21. Elijah Anderson, *Code of the Street: Decency, Violence, and the Moral Life of the Inner City* (New York: W. W. Norton, 2000).

22. Jencks, *Rethinking Social Policy;* Orlando Patterson, *The Ordeal of Integration: Progress and Resentment in America's "Racial" Crisis* (New York: Basic Books, 1998).

23. Neckerman, Carter, and Lee, "Segmented Assimilation."

24. Mary Waters, *Black Identities: West Indian Immigrant Dreams and American Realities* (Cambridge, Mass.: Harvard University Press, 1999).

25. Todd Purdum, "California Census Confirms Whites Are in Minority," *New York Times,* March 30, 2001, p. A1.

26. We are grateful for Orlando Patterson's reminder on this point. It should be noted in this context that we use the terms "Hispanic" and "Latino" as synonyms. We do not wish to choose sides in the sometimes fierce debate over which term is more appropriate. See Himilce Novas, *Everything You Need to Know about Latino History* (New York: Plume, 1998), pp. 2–4.

27. Robert Ezra Park, "Assimilation, Social," in Edwin Seligman and Alvin Johnson, eds., *Encyclopedia of the Social Sciences* (New York: Macmillan, 1930), p. 281.

28. Talcott Parsons, *The Structure of Social Action: A Study in Social Theory with Special Reference to a Group of Recent European Writers* (1937; reprint, New York: Free Press, 1968); Talcott Parsons and Neil Smelser, *Economy and Society: A Study in the Integration of Economic and Social Theory* (Glencoe, Ill.: Free Press, 1956); Robert K. Merton, *Social Theory and Social Structure* (1948; reprint, New York: Free Press, 1968).

29. We are not alone in the attempt to rethink assimilation; see, for instance, Elliot Barkan, "Race, Religion, and Nationality in American Society: A Model of Ethnicity—From Contact to Assimilation," *Journal of American Ethnic History* 14 (Winter 1995): 38–101; Rogers Brubaker, "The Return of Assimilation? Changing Perspectives on Immigration and Its Sequels in France, Germany, and the United States," *Ethnic and Racial Studies* 24 (July 2001): 531–548; Russell Kazal, "Revisiting Assimilation: The Rise, Fall, and Reappraisal of a Concept in American Ethnic History," *American*

Historical Review 100 (April 1995): 437–472; Ewa Morawska, "In Defense of the Assimilation Model," *Journal of American Ethnic History* 13 (Winter 1994): 76–87; Peter Salins, *Assimilation American Style* (New York: Basic Books, 1997).

30. This conception of ethnicity is rooted in a classical literature that starts with the German sociologist Max Weber (see Weber's *Economy and Society* [New York: Bedminster Press, 1968], 1:389) and continues through the Scandinavian anthropologist Frederik Barth (see his introduction in Frederik Barth, ed., *Ethnic Groups and Boundaries* [Boston: Little, Brown, 1969], pp. 9–38). It is highly consonant with the social construction approach that dominates the contemporary literature (see Joane Nagel, "Constructing Ethnicity: Creating and Recreating Ethnic Identity and Culture," *Social Problems* 41 [February 1994]: 101–126). To define ethnicity precisely, all one need do is distinguish it from other kinds of social group boundary situations. We find that Weber's emphasis on the subjective belief in shared ancestry, that is, in the perception of common roots, is the most useful way of distinguishing ethnic situations. Following Weber and others, we view race as a particular kind of ethnicity, one in which physical characteristics play a central role in social perceptions of group membership. We acknowledge that the definitional relationship between ethnicity and race is a matter of dispute in the literature. The more common approach is to view these phenomena as related but distinct—to treat ethnicity as a matter of groups socially defined by cultural criteria and race as one of groups defined by physical ones. This is the standard textbook approach. A difficulty, however, is that the distinction in these definitions is not as clear as it seems because many ethnic and racial groups involve both criteria, albeit in highly varying proportions (see, e.g., Mary Waters, *Ethnic Options: Choosing Identities in America* [Berkeley: University of California Press, 1990]). For an approach compatible with our own, see Roger Waldinger and Mehdi Bozorgmehr, "The Making of a Multicultural Metropolis," in Roger Waldinger and Mehdi Bozorgmehr, eds., *Ethnic Los Angeles* (New York: Russell Sage Foundation, 1996), p. 30, where they state that "race is a special case of the broader ethnic phenomenon, in which the degree of separation from others is mainly, if not entirely, imposed by outsiders." For a different view, see Stephen Cornell and Douglas Hartmann, *Ethnicity and Race: Making Identities in a Changing World* (Thousand Oaks, Calif.: Pine Forge, 1998), chap. 2. The reader should be aware that, in this book, remarks about ethnicity are intended to apply to race as well, though we sometimes refer to "ethnicity and race" to underscore this scope. When we refer to race alone, however, the scope is narrowed to those ethnic groups that are identifiable primarily by phenotypic criteria.

31. To be rigorous, we must also add a specification that distinguishes this pool from others that could be argued to exist in American society, such as a possible black American melting pot. The mainstream overlaps with the soci-

ety's ethnic majority; it also contains numerous individuals who, because they are Hispanic or nonwhite, would not normally be considered part of the ethnic majority.

32. Kathleen Neils Conzen, "Germans," in Stephan Thernstrom, Ann Orlov, and Oscar Handlin, eds., *Harvard Encyclopedia of American Ethnic Groups* (Cambridge, Mass.: Harvard University Press, 1980), p. 425.

33. James Barrett and David Roediger, "In Between Peoples: Race, Nationality, and the 'New Immigrant' Working Class," *Journal of American Ethnic History* 16 (Spring 1997): 3–44. This article is part of the enormous "whiteness" literature which has sprung up since the early 1990s. For a couple of its core statements, see Noel Ignatiev, *How the Irish Became White* (New York: Routledge, 1995); and Matthew Frye Jacobson, *Whiteness of a Different Color: European Immigrants and the Alchemy of Race* (Cambridge, Mass.: Harvard University Press, 1998).

34. See Walter Powell and Paul DiMaggio, eds., *The New Institutionalism in Organizational Analysis* (Chicago: University of Chicago Press, 1991); Mary Brinton and Victor Nee, eds., *The New Institutionalism in Sociology* (New York: Russell Sage Foundation, 1998).

35. Victor Nee, "Sources of the New Institutionalism," in Brinton and Nee, *New Institutionalism,* pp. 1–16; Victor Nee and Paul Ingram, "Embeddedness and Beyond: Institutions, Exchange, and Social Structure," ibid., pp. 19–45.

36. For discussion of the concept of opportunity structure, see Merton, *Social Theory.*

37. See David Grusky and Robert Hauser, "Comparative Social Mobility Revisited: Models of Convergence and Divergence in Sixteen Countries," in David Grusky, ed., *Social Stratification: Class, Race, and Gender in Sociological Perspective* (Boulder, Colo.: Westview Press, 1994), pp. 275–288.

2. Assimilation Theory, Old and New

1. Quoted by David Heer, *Immigration in America's Future: Social Science Findings and the Policy Debate* (Boulder, Colo.: Westview Press, 1996), p. 12.

2. Milton Gordon, *Assimilation in American Life: The Role of Race, Religion, and National Origins* (New York: Oxford University Press, 1964), pp. 88–114.

3. Ibid., p. 116.

4. Ibid., p. 117.

5. James McKee, *Sociology and the Race Problem: The Failure of a Perspective* (Urbana: University of Illinois Press, 1993).

6. Robert Faris, *Chicago Sociology: 1920–1932* (Chicago: University of Chicago Press, 1970).

7. Stephen Steinberg, *The Ethnic Myth: Race, Ethnicity, and Class in America* (Boston: Beacon Press, 1989), p. 47.

8. Robert Ezra Park and Ernest W. Burgess, *Introduction to the Science of Sociology* (1921; reprint, Chicago: University of Chicago Press, 1969), p. 735.

9. Robert Ezra Park, "Assimilation, Social," in Edwin Seligman and Alvin Johnson, eds., *Encyclopedia of the Social Sciences* (New York: Macmillan, 1930), p. 281.

10. For contemporary echoes, see David Hollinger, *Postethnic America: Beyond Multiculturalism* (New York: Basic Books, 1995); and Peter Salins, *Assimilation American Style* (New York: Basic Books, 1997).

11. Robert Ezra Park, *Race and Culture* (Glencoe, Ill.: The Free Press, 1950), p. 150; see also Elliot Barkan, "Race, Religion, and Nationality in American Society: A Model of Ethnicity—From Contact to Assimilation," *Journal of American Ethnic History* 14 (Winter 1995): 39–40; James Geschwender, *Racial Stratification in America* (Dubuque, Iowa: Wm. Cr. Brown Company, 1978), pp. 19–26; Barbara Ballis Lal, *The Romance of Culture in an Urban Civilization: Robert E. Park on Race and Ethnic Relations in Cities* (London: Routledge, 1990), pp. 41–45.

12. Lal, *Romance*, pp. 41–45.

13. Park, *Race,* p. 150. Park has been faulted by many later writers for appearing to portray assimilation as an inevitable outcome in multiethnic societies (e.g., Stanford Lyman, *The Black American in Sociological Thought: A Failure of Perspective* [New York: Capricorn, 1973]; John Stone, *Racial Conflict in Contemporary Society* [London: Fontana Press/Collins, 1985]). The definition cited earlier, however, reveals that Park had a conception of assimilation that was more limited than the subsequent usage of the term. Further, more recent scholarship concerning Park's sociology, such as that by Lal (*Romance*), argues that the race relations cycle played but a minor role in it and that the fame of the idea rests more on the writings of Park's students than on his own (see also Everett Hughes, "Preface," in Park, *Race,* p. xi; McKee, *Sociology,* pp. 109–111).

14. See Donald Young's introduction to the 1971 reprinting of W. I. Thomas, Robert E. Park, and Herbert Miller, *Old World Traits Transplanted* (1921; reprint, Montclair, N.J.: Patterson Smith, 1971).

15. Ibid., pp. 280–281.

16. Robert Ezra Park, "The Urban Community as a Spatial Pattern and a Moral Order," in E. W. Burgess, ed., *The Urban Community* (Chicago: University of Chicago Press, 1926), p. 18.

17. Ibid., p. 9.

18. Ernest W. Burgess, "The Growth of the City: An Introduction to a Research Project," in R. E. Park, E. W. Burgess, and R. D. McKenzie, eds., *The City* (Chicago: University of Chicago Press, 1925), p. 56.

19. Louis Wirth, "The Ghetto," in *On Cities and Social Life* (1927; reprint, Chicago: University of Chicago Press, 1965), pp. 94, 96–97.

20. W. Lloyd Warner and Leo Srole, *The Social Systems of American Ethnic Groups* (New Haven: Yale University Press, 1945), p. 292.

21. For a recent general review of assimilation concepts, see Barkan, "Race"; other reviews include Harold Abramson, "Assimilation and Pluralism," in Stephan Thernstrom, Ann Orlov, and Oscar Handlin, eds., *Harvard Encyclopedia of American Ethnic Groups* (Cambridge, Mass.: Harvard University Press, 1980), pp. 150–160; Philip Gleason, "American Identity and Americanization," in Thernstrom, Orlov, and Handlin, *Harvard Encyclopedia,* pp. 31–58; and Charles Hirschman, "America's Melting Pot Reconsidered," *Annual Review of Sociology* 9 (1983): 397–423.

22. At the time, the civil rights movement was in full swing, with northern college students organizing against entrenched local white opposition to register blacks to vote in the South, while Japanese Americans were rebuffed in their efforts to buy homes in white neighborhoods in California. Gordon wrote in the introduction to his book (*Assimilation,* p. 4) that these events "activate the sense of outrage and concern which leads to investigation, discussion, and perhaps, sooner or later, to attempts at remedial action." As he indicates, a motivating interest of his work on assimilation was to inform social policy aimed at intervention.

23. This was originally Joshua Fishman's phrase (see Gordon, *Assimilation,* p. 72).

24. Ibid., p. 79.

25. No doubt he would concede, however, that the specific nature of religious practice and belief might shift to a considerable degree as a result of acculturation, as the evidence suggests happened in the case of Judaism and some ethnic variants of Catholicism. On the southern Italian practice of Catholicism, see Robert Orsi, *The Madonna of 115th Street: Faith and Community in Italian Harlem, 1880–1950* (New Haven: Yale University Press, 1985); Nicholas John Russo, "Three Generations of Italians in New York City: Their Religious Acculturation," in Silvano Tomasi and Madeline Engel, eds., *The Italian Experience in the United States* (Staten Island, N.Y.: Center for Migration Studies, 1970), pp. 195–209; on Judaism, see Nathan Glazer, *American Judaism* (Chicago: University of Chicago Press, 1957).

26. Gordon, *Assimilation,* pp. 80–81.

27. Aage Sorensen, "Theoretical Mechanisms and the Empirical Study of Social Processes," in Peter Hedstrom and Richard Swedberg, eds., *Social Mechanisms: An Analytical Approach to Social Theory* (Cambridge: Cambridge University Press, 1998), pp. 238–266.

28. Gordon, *Assimilation,* p. 110.

29. Michael Lind, *The Next American Nation: The New Nationalism and the Fourth American Revolution* (New York: Basic Books, 1995), p. 8.

30. Gordon, *Assimilation,* p. 125; Will Herberg, *Protestant-Catholic-Jew* (New York: Anchor Books, 1960); Mary Jo Reeves Kennedy, "Single or Triple Melting Pot? Intermarriage Trends in New Haven, 1870–1940," *American*

Journal of Sociology 49 (January 1944): 331–339, and "Single or Triple Melting Pot? Intermarriage in New Haven, 1870–1950," *American Journal of Sociology* 58 (1952): 56–59.

31. Gordon, *Assimilation,* pp. 127–128.
32. Bhikhu Parekh, *Rethinking Multiculturalism: Cultural Diversity and Political Theory* (Cambridge, Mass.: Harvard University Press, 2000).
33. Gordon, *Assimilation,* p. 159.
34. Herbert Gans, introduction to Neil Sandberg, *Ethnic Identity and Assimilation: The Polish Community* (New York: Praeger, 1973); Sandberg, *Ethnic Identity.* The concept originates with Warner and Srole, *Social Systems.*
35. Stanley Lieberson, "Generational Differences among Blacks in the North," *American Journal of Sociology* 79 (November 1973): 550–565.
36. Marcus Hansen, *The Problem of the Third Generation Immigrant* (Rock Island, Ill.: Augustana Historical Society, 1938); Herberg, *Protestant.*
37. Needless to say, the generational inevitability of assimilation has been questioned; indeed, if it were true, any debate over assimilation itself would be pointless. Critics argue, for example, that ethnicity is not simply imported by the immigrants but is created partly by conditions and out of materials in the host society, with the consequence that it may go through periods of re-creation, if not renaissance. See Kathleen Conzen, David Gerber, Ewa Morawska, George Pozzetta, and Rudolph Vecoli, "The Invention of Ethnicity: A Perspective from the U.S.A.," *Journal of American Ethnic History* 12 (Fall 1992): 3–41; Nathan Glazer and Daniel Patrick Moynihan, *Beyond the Melting Pot: The Negroes, Puerto Ricans, Jews, Italians, and Irish of New York City* (1963; reprint, Cambridge, Mass.: MIT Press, 1970); Andrew Greeley, *The American Catholic: A Social Portrait* (New York: Basic Books, 1977); William Yancey, Eugene Ericksen, and Richard Juliani, "Emergent Ethnicity: A Review and a Reformulation," *American Sociological Review* 41 (June 1976): 391–403.
38. Peter Blau and Otis Dudley Duncan, *The American Occupational Structure* (New York: Wiley, 1967).
39. Lisa Neidert and Reynolds Farley, "Assimilation in the United States: An Analysis of Ethnic and Generation Differences in Status and Achievement," *American Sociological Review* 50 (December 1985): 840–850.
40. For an early example, see Beverly Duncan and Otis Dudley Duncan, "Minorities and the Process of Stratification," *American Sociological Review* 33 (June 1968): 356–364.
41. Douglas Massey, "Ethnic Residential Segregation: A Theoretical Synthesis and Empirical Review," *Sociology and Social Research* 69 (April 1985): 315–350.
42. Tomatsu Shibutani and Kian Kwan, *Ethnic Stratification* (New York: Macmillan, 1965), p. 39.
43. On the social construction of racial and ethnic categories, see Joane Nagel, "Constructing Ethnicity: Creating and Recreating Ethnic Identity and Cul-

ture," *Social Problems* 41 (February 1994): 101–126; Mary Waters, *Black Identities: West Indian Immigrant Dreams and American Realities* (Cambridge, Mass.: Harvard University Press, 1999), chap. 3, provides an insightful application.

44. Shibutani and Kwan, *Ethnic Stratification*, pp. 263–271.

45. Frederik Barth, "Ecologic Relationships of Ethnic Groups in Swat, North Pakistan," *American Anthropologist* 58 (1956): 1079–89; in this way, too, Shibutani and Kwan anticipate the contemporary conception of ethnic groups.

46. Saskia Sassen, *The Mobility of Capital and Labor* (Cambridge: Cambridge University Press, 1988).

47. Shibutani and Kwan, *Ethnic Stratification*, p. 350.

48. Sorensen, "Theoretical Mechanisms."

49. Richard Miller, *Fact and Method: Explanation, Confirmation, and Reality in the Natural and Social Sciences* (Princeton: Princeton University Press, 1987); Daniel Little, *Varieties of Social Explanation: An Introduction to the Philosophy of Social Science* (Boulder, Colo.: Westview Press, 1991); Hedstrom and Swedberg, *Social Mechanisms*.

50. Miller, *Fact*.

51. Victor Nee, "Sources of the New Institutionalism," in Mary Brinton and Victor Nee, eds., *The New Institutionalism in Sociology* (New York: Russell Sage Foundation, 1998), pp. 1–16.

52. Already evident in Walter Powell and Paul DiMaggio, *The New Institutionalism in Organizational Analysis* (Chicago: University of Chicago Press, 1991), and elaborated in Brinton and Nee, *New Institutionalism*. In allied social sciences, a trend toward convergence is reflected in the writings of Mary Douglas (anthropology); Douglass North, Oliver Williamson, and Avner Greif (new institutional economics); and Theda Skocpol (historical institutionalism). See Mary Douglas, *How Institutions Think* (Syracuse, N.Y.: Syracuse University Press, 1986); Douglass North, *Institutions, Institutional Change, and Economic Performance* (Cambridge: Cambridge University Press, 1990); Oliver Williamson, "Transaction Cost Economics and Organization Theory," in Neil Smelser and Richard Swedberg, eds., *The Handbook of Economic Sociology* (New York: Russell Sage Foundation, 1994), pp. 77–107; Avner Greif, "Cultural Beliefs and the Organization of Society: A Historical and Theoretical Reflection on Collectivist and Individualist Societies," in Brinton and Nee, *New Institutionalism*, pp. 77–104; Theda Skocpol, *Protecting Soldiers and Mothers: The Political Origins of Social Policy in the United States* (Cambridge, Mass.: Harvard University Press, 1995).

53. Victor Nee, "Norms and Networks in Economic and Organizational Performance," *American Economic Review* 87 (1998): 85–99; Victor Nee and Paul Ingram, "Embeddedness and Beyond: Institutions, Exchange, and Social Structure," in Brinton and Nee, *New Institutionalism*, pp. 19–45.

54. North, *Institutions*.

55. Victor Nee and Yang Cao, "Path Dependent Societal Transformation: Stratification in Mixed Economies," *Theory and Society* 28 (1999): 799–834; Nee, "Sources."

56. Raymond Boudon, "The Individualistic Tradition in Sociology," in Jeffrey Alexander, Gernhard Giesen, Richard Munch, and Neil Smelser, eds., *The Micro-Macro Link* (Berkeley: University of California Press, 1987), pp. 45–70.

57. Max Weber's seminal study of the rise of capitalism in the West is a pioneering example of the use of context-bound rationality in explaining institutional change. He showed that the purposive action of individuals stemming from religious beliefs is the causal mechanism that explains the emergence of modern capitalism in the West. His causal analysis points to the unintended consequences of the rationalizing effect of the inner-world asceticism of Protestant faith on entrepreneurs and firms, which, through their increased levels of productivity, transformed relative prices in manufacture, adversely affecting artisans and craft production, and incrementally gave rise to modern capitalism. See Max Weber, *The Protestant Ethic and the Spirit of Capitalism,* trans. Talcott Parsons (1904–5; reprint, New York: Charles Scribner's Sons, 1958).

58. Herbert Simon, *Administrative Behavior,* 2d ed. (New York: Macmillan, 1957), xxiv.

59. Ginger Thompson, "The Desperate Risk of Death in a Desert," *New York Times,* October 31, 2001, p. 1. See also Douglas Massey et al., *Beyond Smoke and Mirrors: Mexican Immigration in an Era of Economic Integration* (New York: Russell Sage Foundation, 2002).

60. Raymond Boudon, "Social Mechanism without Black Boxes," in Hedstrom and Swedberg, *Social Mechanisms,* pp. 172–203.

61. The World Bank estimates that remittances sent back by immigrants to Latin America and the Caribbean Basin region were well over $15 billion in 2000. These have become the primary source of foreign exchange in smaller countries in the region, outpacing foreign investments, and for all countries a much larger source of revenue than foreign aid. "Making the Most of an Exodus," Economist.com, February 21, 2002.

62. Michael Spence, *Market Signaling: Informational Transfer in Hiring and Related Screening Processes* (Cambridge, Mass.: Harvard University Press, 1974).

63. Victor Nee and Jimy Sanders, "Understanding the Diversity of Immigrant Incorporation: A Forms-of-Capital Model," *Ethnic and Racial Studies* 24 (May 2001): 386–411.

64. Mark Granovetter, "Economic Action and Social Structure: The Problem of Embeddedness," *American Journal of Sociology* 91 (1985): 481–510.

65. Nee and Ingram, "Embeddedness."

66. George C. Homans, *Social Behavior: Its Elementary Form* (1961; reprint,

New York: Harcourt Brace Jovanovich, 1974); James Coleman, *Foundations of Social Theory* (Cambridge, Mass.: Harvard University Press, 1990).

67. William Foote Whyte, *Street Corner Society: The Social Structure of an Italian Slum* (1943; reprint, Chicago: University of Chicago Press, 1955).

68. George C. Homans, *The Human Group* (New York: Harcourt Brace Jovanovich, 1950).

69. Robert Axelrod, *The Evolution of Cooperation* (New York: Basic Books, 1984).

70. In collectivities involving large numbers, the "free-rider" problem arises from the availability of a public good to all regardless of whether they contribute to its production; this problem is minimized in close-knit groups where compliance with norms can be effectively secured as a routine by-product of ongoing social exchange among members.

71. Robert Ellickson, *Order without Law: How Neighbors Settle Disputes* (Cambridge, Mass.: Harvard University Press, 1991).

72. Edna Bonacich and John Modell, *The Economic Basis of Ethnic Solidarity: Small Business in the Japanese-American Community* (Berkeley: University of California Press, 1981); Alejandro Portes and Julia Sensenbrenner, "Embeddedness and Immigration: Notes on the Social Determinants of Economic Action," *American Journal of Sociology* 98 (May 1993): 1320–50.

73. Douglas Massey, Rafael Alarcón, Jorge Durand, and Humberto González, *Return to Aztlan: The Social Process of International Migration from Western Mexico* (Berkeley: University of California Press, 1987).

74. Victor Nee and Jimy M. Sanders, "Trust in Ethnic Ties: Social Capital and Immigrants," in Karen Cook, ed., *Trust and Society* (New York: Russell Sage Foundation, 2001), pp. 374–392; Victor Nee, Jimy M. Sanders, and Scott Sernau, "Job Transitions in an Immigrant Metropolis: Ethnic Boundaries and the Mixed Economy," *American Sociological Review* 59 (December 1994): 849–872.

75. John Modell, *The Economics and Politics of Racial Accommodation* (Berkeley: University of California Press, 1977); Ivan Light, *Ethnic Enterprise in America* (Berkeley: University of California Press, 1972); Bonacich and Modell, *Economic Basis;* Alejandro Portes and Robert Bach, *Latin Journey: Cuban and Mexican Immigrants in the United States* (Berkeley: University of California Press, 1985).

76. James Loewen, *The Mississippi Chinese: Between Black and White* (Cambridge, Mass.: Harvard University Press, 1971).

77. Ibid., p. 79.

78. Margaret Gibson, *Accommodation without Assimilation: Sikh Immigrants in an American High School* (Ithaca: Cornell University Press, 1989).

79. Homans, *Social Behavior.*

80. Illso Kim, *New Urban Immigrants: The Korean Community in New York* (Princeton: Princeton University Press, 1981); Pyong Gap Min, *Caught in the Middle: Korean Merchants in America's Multiethnic Cities* (Berkeley:

University of California, 1994); In-Jin Yoon, *On My Own: Korean Business and Race Relations in America* (Chicago: University of Chicago Press, 1997).

81. Oscar Handlin, *The Uprooted* (New York: Grosset & Dunlap, 1952).
82. Pierre Bourdieu, *Distinction: A Social Critique of the Judgement of Taste,* trans. Richard Nice (Cambridge, Mass.: Harvard University Press, 1984).
83. See, e.g., John Logan, Richard Alba, and Wenquan Zhang, "Immigrant Enclaves and Ethnic Communities in New York and Los Angeles," *American Sociological Review* 67 (April 2002): 299–322.
84. Douglas Massey, Luin Goldring, and Jorge Durand, "Continuities in Transnational Migration: An Analysis of Nineteen Mexican Communities," *American Journal of Sociology* 99 (May 1994): 1492–1534.
85. Nee, Sanders, and Sernau, "Job Transitions"; Nee and Sanders, "Trust in Ethnic Ties."
86. Min Zhou and Carl Bankston, *Growing Up American: How Vietnamese Children Adapt to Life in the United States* (New York: Russell Sage Foundation, 1998).
87. Dana Canedy, "Troubling Label for Hispanics: 'Girls Most Likely to Drop Out,'" *New York Times,* March 25, 2001, p. 1.
88. David Grusky and Robert Hauser, "Comparative Social Mobility Revisited: Models of Convergence and Divergence in Sixteen Countries," in David Grusky, ed., *Social Stratification: Class, Race, and Gender in Sociological Perspective* (Boulder, Colo.: Westview Press, 1994), pp. 275–288.
89. Alejandro Portes and Min Zhou, "The New Second Generation: Segmented Assimilation and Its Variants," *Annals* 530 (November 1993): 74–96.
90. Herbert Gans, *The Urban Villagers: Group and Class in the Life of Italian-Americans* (1962; reprint, New York: Free Press, 1982); Joel Perlmann, *Ethnic Differences: Schooling and Social Structure among the Irish, Italians, Jews, and Blacks in an American City, 1880–1935* (Cambridge: Cambridge University Press, 1988).
91. Modell, *Economics;* Bonacich and Modell, *Economic Basis.*
92. Bonacich and Modell, *Economic Basis,* p. 58.
93. Leonard Bloom and Ruth Riemer, *Removal and Return* (Berkeley: University of California Press, 1949), p. 85.
94. Alexander et al., *Micro-Macro Link;* Coleman, *Foundations.*
95. Nee, "Sources of the New Institutionalism."
96. Douglass North, *Structure and Change in Economic History* (New York: W. W. Norton, 1981), pp. 31–32.
97. Mary Walsh, "U.S. Joins in 2 Bias Suits against Lockheed Martin," *New York Times,* December 6, 2000, p. C1.
98. Waters, *Black Identities.*
99. Howard Schuman, Charlotte Steeh, and Lawrence Bobo, *Racial Attitudes in America: Trends and Interpretations* (Cambridge, Mass.: Harvard University Press, 1985), p. 74.

100. Ibid., p. 88.
101. Nee, "Norms"; Nee and Ingram, "Embeddedness."
102. Waters, *Black Identities*.
103. See Michael Omi and Howard Winant, *Racial Formation in the United States: From the 1960s to the 1990s,* 2d ed. (New York: Routledge & Kegan Paul, 1994); Gerald Suttles, *The Social Order of the Slum* (Chicago: University of Chicago Press, 1968). For reports of white suspiciousness toward African Americans they encounter on the street and in stores, see Joe Feagin, "The Continuing Significance of Race: Antiblack Discrimination in Public Places," *American Sociological Review* 56 (February 1991): 101–116.
104. Michael T. Hannan and John Freeman, *Organizational Ecology* (Cambridge, Mass.: Harvard University Press, 1989).
105. Edna Bonacich, "A Theory of Ethnic Antagonism: The Split Labor Market," *American Sociological Review* 37 (October 1972): 547–559.
106. Max Weber, *Economy and Society,* vol. 1 (1922; reprint, Berkeley: University of California Press, 1978), pp. 63–113.
107. Nee, Sanders, and Sernau, "Job Transitions"; Nee and Sanders, "Understanding Diversity."
108. This borrowed distinction derives from Rainer Bauböck, "The Integration of Immigrants," Council of Europe, Strasbourg, 1994; and Aristide Zolberg and Long Litt Woon, "Why Islam Is Like Spanish: Cultural Incorporation in Europe and the United States," *Politics and Society* 27 (March 1999): 5–38.
109. Whether it will work out this way is impossible to say as yet, but the adoption of mixed-race reporting by the Census Bureau in the 2000 U.S. Census suggests that the social recognition of mixed race as a social category (or a set of them) will increase. See Charles Hirschman, Richard Alba, and Reynolds Farley, "The Meaning and Measurement of Race in the U.S. Census: Glimpses into the Future," *Demography* 37 (August 2000): 381–393.
110. Sander Gilman, *Making the Body Beautiful: A Cultural History of Aesthetic Surgery* (Princeton: Princeton University Press, 1999).
111. For a good account of these blending processes in Christian-Jewish families, see Sylvia Barack Fishman, *Jewish and Something Else: A Study of Mixed-Married Families* (New York: American Jewish Committee, 2001).
112. Frederik Barth, introduction to *Ethnic Groups and Boundaries* (Boston: Little, Brown, 1969), pp. 9–38.
113. Nancy Denton and Richard Alba, "The Growth of Suburban Diversity: The Declining Number of All-White Neighborhoods," presented at the Conference on Suburban Racial Change, Harvard University, 1999.
114. This figure comes from the analyses of the Lewis Mumford Center at the University at Albany (see the Web site: www.albany.edu/mumford).
115. The moral dimensions of boundary distinctions have been explored by Michèle Lamont in *The Dignity of Working Men: Morality and the Bound-*

aries of Race, Class, and Immigration (Cambridge, Mass.: Harvard University Press, 2000). See also Mitchell Duneier, *Slim's Table: Race, Respectability, and Masculinity* (Chicago: University of Chicago Press, 1992).

116. Gilman, *Making the Body Beautiful: A Cultural History of Aesthetic Surgery* (Princeton: Princeton University Press, 1999), chap. 6; Jane Gross, "As Ethnic Pride Rises, Rhinoplasty Takes a Nose Dive," *New York Times,* January 3, 1999, sec. 4, p. 2.

3 Assimilation in Practice

1. Leonard Covello, *The Social Background of the Italo-American School Child* (Totowa, N.J.: Rowman & Littlefield, 1972); Joel Perlmann, *Ethnic Differences: Schooling and Social Structure among the Irish, Italians, Jews, and Blacks in an American City, 1880–1935* (Cambridge: Cambridge University Press, 1988).

2. John Higham's *Strangers in the Land: Patterns of American Nativism, 1860–1925* (New York: Atheneum, 1970) is the classic source on American nativism of the nineteenth and early twentieth centuries. The quote is from p. 143. See also Matthew Frye Jacobson, *Whiteness of a Different Color: European Immigrants and the Alchemy of Race* (Cambridge, Mass.: Harvard University Press, 1998), p. 72.

3. Richard Gambino, *Vendetta: The True Story of the Largest Lynching in America* (1977; reprint, Toronto: Guernica, 1998); Higham, *Strangers,* pp. 87–93; Jacobson, *Whiteness,* pp. 56–62.

4. Quoted by John Modell, *The Economics and Politics of Racial Accommodation* (Berkeley: University of California Press, 1977), p. 45.

5. Quoted ibid., p. 41.

6. Rose Hum Lee, *The Chinese in the United States of America* (Hong Kong: Hong Kong University Press, 1960); Edna Bonacich and John Modell, *The Economic Basis of Ethnic Solidarity: Small Business in the Japanese-American Community* (Berkeley: University of California Press, 1980).

7. Mia Tuan, *Forever Foreigners or Honorary Whites? The Asian Ethnic Experience Today* (New Brunswick, N.J.: Rutgers University Press, 1998), p. 159.

8. For a consonant concept, see Rogers Brubaker, "The Return of Assimilation? Changing Perspectives on Immigration and Its Sequels in France, Germany, and the United States," *Ethnic and Racial Studies* 24 (July 2001): 531–548.

9. A contrasting point of view is expressed by Andrew Greeley, *Why Can't They Be Like Us?* (New York: Dutton, 1971); Anthony LaRuffa, *Monte Carmelo: An Italian-American Community in the Bronx* (New York: Gordon and Breach, 1988); and Michael Novak, *The Rise of the Unmeltable Ethnics* (New York: Macmillan, 1971).

10. Tuan, *Forever Foreigners,* p. 167.

11. Harry Kitano, *Japanese American: The Evolution of a Subculture,* 2d ed. (Englewood Cliffs, N.J.: Prentice-Hall, 1976); William Petersen, *Japanese Americans: Oppression and Success* (New York: Random House, 1971).

12. Bonacich and Modell, *Economic Basis.*

13. For instance, fertility levels underwent rapid, dramatic shifts as high-fertility immigrant groups, such as the Italians and eastern European Jews, converted within a generation to the low-fertility patterns characteristic of other white Americans in urban areas. In 1910 the expected number of children born to Italian immigrant women by the end of their fertility was seven; for Yiddish-speaking immigrants, the figure was even higher. But by the 1930s, the number of children born to second-generation women in these groups approximated the norm for other urban white women. Other kinds of acculturation required time. See Francis Femminella and Jill Quadagno, "The Italian American Family," in Charles Mindell and Robert Habenstein, eds., *Ethnic Families in America: Patterns and Variations* (New York: Elsevier, 1976), pp. 61–85; Sidney Goldstein and Calvin Goldscheider, *Jewish Americans: Three Generations in a Jewish Community* (Englewood Cliffs, N.J.: Prentice-Hall, 1968); S. Philip Morgan, Susan Watkins, and Douglas Ewbank, "Generating Americans: Ethnic Differences in Fertility," in Susan Watkins, ed., *After Ellis Island: Newcomers and Natives in the 1910 Census* (New York: Russell Sage Foundation, 1994), pp. 83–124.

14. This massive linguistic shift is discussed by sociolinguists as a three-generation model of Anglicization, first codified by Joshua Fishman and Calvin Veltman. See Joshua Fishman, *The Sociology of Language* (Rowley, Mass.: Newbury, 1972), and Calvin Veltman, *Language Shift in the United States* (Berlin: Mouton, 1983); for additional evidence, see Gillian Stevens, "The Social and Demographic Context of Language Use in the United States," *American Sociological Review* 57 (April 1992): 171–185.

15. Richard Alba, "Cohorts and the Dynamics of Ethnic Change," in Matilda White Riley, Bettina Huber, and Beth Hess, eds., *Social Structures and Human Lives* (Newbury Park, Calif.: Sage, 1988), pp. 211–228.

16. The census question does not ask about regularity of mother-tongue use and may encourage respondents to report infrequently used minority languages or ones that are spoken poorly, thus overstating their persistence; see David Lopez, "Language: Diversity and Assimilation," in Roger Waldinger and Mehdi Bozorgmehr, eds., *Ethnic Los Angeles* (New York: Russell Sage Foundation, 1996), pp. 139–163.

17. Victor Nee and Brett de Bary Nee, *Longtime Californ': A Documentary Study of an American Chinatown* (New York: Pantheon Books, 1973).

18. For an explanation of the limits on generational distinctions in census data and the use of them, see Chapter 6.

19. Because of the prevalence of mixed ancestry for the European categories, each of them is constructed to contain individuals who either are solely of

the ancestry in question or include it as part of a mixture. The main alternatives, limiting each category to individuals of single ancestry or to those who name it first, would, in effect, eliminate or reduce the impact for that category of one of the important mechanisms of assimilation: growing up in an ethnically mixed family. Nevertheless, because of the liability of and simplifications in ancestry reports by individuals with mixed ancestry, none of the categories is complete; see Stanley Lieberson and Mary Waters, "The Ethnic Responses of Whites: What Causes Their Instability, Simplification, and Inconsistency?" *Social Forces* 72 (December 1993): 421–450.

20. The census does not record the language of children under the age of five.

21. This impact is partly a consequence of the measures taken against the German language and partly a result of the hostility against overtly ethnic German Americans. See Heinz Kloss, "German-American Language Maintenance Efforts," in Joshua Fishman et al., eds., *Language Loyalty in the United States* (The Hague: Mouton, 1966), pp. 206–252; and Higham, *Strangers*.

22. Third-generation data will be discussed in more detail in Chapter 6.

23. Felicity Barringer, "For 32 Million Americans, English Is a 2nd Language," *New York Times,* April 28, 1993, p. A18.

24. The sociologist, novelist, and Roman Catholic priest Andrew Greeley has probably done the most to develop supportive evidence. See, e.g., Greeley, *Why Can't They Be Like Us?* and Andrew Greeley and William McCready, "The Transmission of Cultural Heritages: The Case of the Irish and the Italians," in Nathan Glazer and Daniel Patrick Moynihan, eds., *Ethnicity: Theory and Experience* (Cambridge, Mass.: Harvard University Press, 1976), pp. 209–235. The survival of ethnic values and behavioral patterns in the private spaces behind closed front doors is described as part of the American compact on ethnicity by Nathan Glazer, *Affirmative Discrimination* (New York: Basic Books, 1975).

25. Nathan Glazer and Daniel Patrick Moynihan, *Beyond the Melting Pot: The Negroes, Puerto Ricans, Jews, Italians, and Irish of New York City* (1963; reprint, Cambridge, Mass.: MIT Press, 1970), p. xxxiii.

26. The application of the term "invention" to ethnicity is often credited to Werner Sollors (*The Invention of Ethnicity* [New York: Oxford University Press, 1989]). Kathleen Conzen, David Gerber, Ewa Morawska, George Pozzetta, and Rudolph Vecoli apply the idea to European Americans in "The Invention of Ethnicity: A Perspective from the U.S.A.," *Journal of American Ethnic History* 12 (Fall 1992): 3–41.

27. Tuan, *Forever Foreigners,* p. 50.

28. Glazer and Moynihan, *Melting Pot,* p. lvii; see also William Yancey, Eugene Ericksen, and Richard Juliani, "Emergent Ethnicity: A Review and a Reformulation," *American Sociological Review* 41 (June 1976): 391–403.

29. For a more complete data presentation, see Richard Alba, "Assimilation's Quiet Tide," *Public Interest* 119 (Spring 1995): 1–18.

30. There is, in fact, evidence to suggest that some of the white ethnic groups are underrepresented in the student populations at Ivy League colleges. An unpublished study of Italian-surnamed students conducted by Dr. A. Kenneth Ciongoli, then president of the National Italian-American Foundation, found such students substantially underrepresented at Ivy League colleges in comparison with their proportion in the U.S. population. The question is: Why? In general, Ivy League colleges allocate a large number of slots in entering classes to legatees, the children of alumni and alumnae. Some educationally high-achieving groups, notably Jews and Asians, occupy substantial portions of the non-legatee openings; and minorities receive special attention as a result of affirmative action policies. Thus, the low percentage of Italians may not indicate any special educational disadvantage or ethnic discrimination as such. It may result instead from the difficulties experienced by non-privileged whites in general in gaining admission to elite colleges. This explanation is not a dismissal: the problem is worthy of serious attention by elite institutions.

31. Lisa Neidert and Reynolds Farley, "Assimilation in the United States: An Analysis of Ethnic and Generation Differences in Status and Achievement," *American Sociological Review* 50 (December 1985): 840–850; Stanley Lieberson and Mary Waters, *From Many Strands: Ethnic and Racial Groups in Contemporary America* (New York: Russell Sage Foundation, 1988); Andrew Greeley, *Ethnicity, Denomination, and Inequality* (Beverly Hills, Calif.: Sage, 1976).

32. Analyzing the New York situation to 1990, Roger Waldinger, in *Still the Promised City? African-Americans and New Immigrants in Postindustrial New York* (Cambridge, Mass.: Harvard University Press, 1996), finds a particularly steep decline in Italian niche concentration but a weaker one for Jews.

33. Charles Hirschman and Morrison Wong, "Trends in Socioeconomic Achievement among Immigrant and Native-Born Asian-Americans, 1960–1976," *Sociological Quarterly* 22 (1981): 495–514; Robert Jiobu, "Earnings Differentials between White and Ethnic Minorities: The Cases of Asian Americans, Blacks, and Chicanos," *Sociology and Social Research* 61 (1976): 24–38; Victor Nee and Jimy Sanders, "The Road to Parity: Determinants of the Socioeconomic Attainments of Asian Americans," *Ethnic and Racial Studies* 8 (January 1985): 75–93; Wong, "The Cost of Being Chinese, Japanese, and Filipino in the United States, 1960, 1970, 1976," *Pacific Sociological Review* 5 (1982): 59–78.

34. See Thomas Kessner, *The Golden Door: Italian and Jewish Immigrant Mobility in New York City, 1880–1915* (New York: Oxford University Press, 1977); Steven Erie, *Rainbow's End: Irish-Americans and the Dilemmas of Urban Machine Politics, 1840–1985* (Berkeley: University of California Press, 1988); Waldinger, *Still the Promised City?*

35. Bonacich and Modell, *The Economic Basis.*

36. Lieberson and Waters, *From Many Strands*, chap. 3; on the Italians of the Sunbelt, see Phyllis Cancilla Martinelli, *Ethnicity in the Sunbelt* (New York: AMS Press, 1989).

37. Lawrence Fuchs, *The American Kaleidoscope: Race, Ethnicity, and the Civic Culture* (Hanover, N.H.: University Press of New England, 1990), pp. 302–303.

38. See Thomas Philpott, *The Slum and the Ghetto* (New York: Oxford University Press, 1978), concerning Chicago; on the concept of segregation, see Douglas Massey and Nancy Denton, *American Apartheid: Segregation and the Making of the Underclass* (Cambridge, Mass.: Harvard University Press, 1993).

39. Avery Guest and James Weed, "Ethnic Residential Segregation: Patterns of Change," *American Journal of Sociology* 81 (March 1976): 1088–1111; Stanley Lieberson, *Ethnic Patterns in American Cities* (New York: Free Press, 1963).

40. Lee, *The Chinese*.

41. *Longtime Californ': A Documentary Study of an American Chinatown* (New York: Pantheon Books, 1973).

42. We do not show figures for the Chinese in Table 3.1 because of the heavy impact of contemporary immigration on their residential distribution. This factor is not as great for the Japanese because present-day Japanese immigration is of a much smaller magnitude.

43. Our discussion is based on the work that Richard Alba has done with John Logan and Kyle Crowder (in "White Ethnic Neighborhoods and Spatial Assimilation: The Greater New York Region, 1980–1990," *Social Forces* 75 [March 1997]: 883–912). The area they analyzed represents the broadest conception of the New York region and closely approximates what the Census Bureau labels the "New York–Northern New Jersey–Long Island CMSA." A CMSA, or Consolidated Metropolitan Statistical Area, is a designation the Census Bureau reserves for huge agglomerations of large and small cities and their suburbs, which represent multiple smaller metropolitan areas.

44. Judith DeSena, *Protecting One's Turf: Social Strategies for Maintaining Urban Neighborhoods* (Lanham, Md.: University Press of America, 1990); Jerome Krase, "Little Italies in New York City: A Semiotic Approach," *Italian American Review* 5 (Spring 1996): 103–116; LaRuffa, *Monte Carmelo*; Jonathan Rieder, *Canarsie: The Jews and Italians of Brooklyn against Liberalism* (Cambridge, Mass.: Harvard University Press, 1985); Donald Tricarico, *The Italians of Greenwich Village* (Staten Island, N.Y.: CMS Press, 1984).

45. Further decline of Italian Bensonhurst is apparent in the 2000 census; see Joseph Berger, "Well, the Ices Are Still Italian," *New York Times*, September 17, 2002, pp. B1, 8.

46. Alba, "Quiet Tide"; see also Richard Alba and Reid Golden, "Patterns of Interethnic Marriage in the United States," *Social Forces* 65 (September 1986): 203–223; Lieberson and Waters, *From Many Strands*.

47. Robert K. Merton, "Intermarriage and Social Structure: Fact and Theory," *Psychiatry* 4 (August 1941): 361–374.

48. Peter Blau, *Inequality and Heterogeneity: A Primitive Theory of Social Structure* (New York: Free Press, 1977).

49. The data are reported by Peter Steinfels, "Debating Intermarriage, and Jewish Survival," *New York Times,* October 18, 1992, pp. A1, 40. The precise magnitude of Jewish intermarriage is still the subject of debate, however, because of allegations that errors in the original analysis of the NJPS data exaggerated the increase. See the op-ed piece by J. J. Goldberg, "Interfaith Marriage: The Real Story," *New York Times,* August 3, 1997. Nevertheless, the revised estimates of the recent intermarriage rate, which mostly range between 40 and 50 percent, still imply a hefty increase in a short period of time.

50. Matthijs Kalmijn's analysis ("Shifting Boundaries: Trends in Religious and Educational Homogamy," *American Sociological Review* 56 [December 1991]: 786–800) also supports this conclusion.

51. Zhenchao Qian, "Breaking the Racial Barriers: Variations in Interracial Marriages between 1980 and 1990," *Demography* 34 (May 1997): 263–276.

52. Amy Iwasaki Mass, "Interracial Japanese Americans: The Best of Both Worlds or the End of the Japanese American Community?" in Maria Root, ed., *Racially Mixed People in America* (Newbury Park, Calif.: Sage, 1992), pp. 265–279.

53. Ibid.; Teresa Kay Williams, "Prism Lives: Identity of Binational Amerasians"; and George Kitihara Kich, "The Developmental Process of Asserting a Biracial, Bicultural Identity," all in Root, *Racially Mixed People,* pp. 265–320.

54. John Leland and Gregory Beals, "In Living Colors," *Newsweek,* May 5, 1997, p. 59. The count of mixed-race Asian children comes from the 2000 census.

55. The percentage counts individuals whose race is reported in the census (by their parents) as Japanese but who also have some other ethnic origin indicated according to the Hispanic origin question or the ethnic ancestry one; also counted are those whose race is reported as other than Japanese but who are described as part Japanese on the ancestry question.

56. For the first position, see Greeley, *Why?;* Novak, *The Rise.* Herbert Gans, in "Symbolic Ethnicity: The Future of Ethnic Groups and Cultures in America," *Ethnic and Racial Studies* 2 (January 1979): 1–20, coined the concept of symbolic ethnicity, which has been substantiated in the empirical research of Richard Alba (*Ethnic Identity: The Transformation of White*

America [New Haven: Yale University Press, 1990]) and Mary Waters (*Ethnic Options: Choosing Identities in America* [Berkeley: University of California Press, 1990]).

57. Waters, *Ethnic Options.*

58. Mia Tuan *(Forever Foreigners)* sensitively documents the "hidden injuries" experienced by third- and later-generation Chinese and Japanese, but also acknowledges that her respondents' actual everyday experience of ethnicity is in many respects similar to that described for white ethnics.

59. On the so-called long-form questionnaire (received by approximately one of every six households), the 1980, 1990, and 2000 censuses asked about each household member, "What is this person's ancestry or ethnic origin?" (The "ethnic origin" phrase was added in 1990.) Some of the limits of the question as used in the census are explored by Reynolds Farley ("The New Census Question about Ancestry: What Did It Tell Us?" *Demography* 28 [1991]: 411–429) and Lieberson and Waters ("Ethnic Responses"); the latter provide an analysis of the social basis for inconsistent ancestry reporting. The inconsistencies themselves are reported by the Bureau of the Census in *Detailed Ancestry for States, 1990 Census of Population: Supplementary Reports* (Washington, D.C.: U.S. Department of Commerce, 1992). These inconsistencies alert us to take ancestry data with a dose of caution, for the "English" and "Germans" of a given census differ in unknown ways from the "English" and "Germans" of another.

60. On pan-Asian marriage, see Yen Le Espiritu, *Asian American Panethnicity: Bridging Institutions and Identities* (Philadelphia: Temple University Press, 1992); Larry Shinagawa and Gin Yong Pang, "Intraethnic and Interracial Marriages among Asian Americans in California, 1980," *Berkeley Journal of Sociology* 33 (1988): 95–114; Tuan, *Forever Foreigners.*

61. This portrait is based on Alba, *Ethnic Identity,* and Waters, *Ethnic Options.*

62. Ethnicity among whites appears much weaker in other regions; on California, see Waldinger and Bozorgmehr, *Ethnic Los Angeles.*

63. For instance, the total membership of the Sons of Italy, the largest national Italian American organization, was just 90,000 as of 1990, at a time when nearly 15 million Americans claimed some Italian ancestry. Alfred Rotondaro, "Ethnicity at Work," *Altreitalie* 6 (1991): 120.

64. See Tuan, *Forever Foreigners;* Nee and Nee, *Longtime Californ'.*

65. Nazli Kibria, "The Construction of 'Asian American': Reflections on Intermarriage and Ethnic Identity among Second-Generation Chinese and Korean Americans," *Ethnic and Racial Studies* 20 (July 1997): 523–544; Nee and Nee, *Longtime Californ';* Ronald Takaki, *Strangers from a Different Shore* (Boston: Little, Brown, 1989).

66. Glazer and Moynihan, *Melting Pot;* Ewa Morawska, *For Bread with Butter: Life-Worlds of East Central Europeans in Johnstown, Pennsylvania, 1890–1940* (Cambridge: Cambridge University Press, 1985); Yancey, Ericksen, and Juliani, "Emergent Ethnicity."

67. Alba and Golden, "Patterns"; Lieberson and Waters, *From Many Strands;* Waters, *Ethnic Options.*

68. Alba, *Ethnic Identity;* Alba, Logan, and Crowder, "White Ethnic Neighborhoods."

69. Fuchs, *American Kaleidoscope;* Glazer and Moynihan, *Melting Pot.*

70. Peter Blau, Terry Blum, and Joseph Schwartz, "Heterogeneity and Intermarriage," *American Sociological Review* 47 (February 1982): 45–62.

71. M. D. R. Evans, "Immigrant Entrepreneurship: Effects of Ethnic Market Size and Isolated Labor Pool," *American Sociological Review* 54 (December 1989): 950–962.

72. Carl Bankston and Jacques Henry, "Endogamy among Louisiana Cajuns: A Social Class Explanation," *Social Forces* 77 (June 1999): 1317–38.

73. Alba, *Ethnic Identity;* on the Italians, see John Goering, "The Emergence of Ethnic Interests: A Case of Serendipity," *Social Forces* 49 (March 1971): 379–384; Susanna Tardi, "The Traditional Italian Family Is Alive and Living in New Jersey," *Italian American Review* 5 (Autumn–Winter 1996): 1–14; and Rudolph Vecoli, "The Coming of Age of the Italian Americans," *Ethnicity* 5 (June 1978): 119–147; on Jews, see Steven Cohen, *American Modernity and Jewish Identity* (New York: Tavistock, 1983); Steven Gold and Bruce Philips, "Mobility and Continuity among Eastern European Jews," in Silvia Pedraza and Rubén Rumbaut, eds., *Origins and Destinies: Immigration, Race, and Ethnicity in America* (Belmont, Mass.: Wadsworth, 1996), pp. 182–194; Samuel Heilman and Steven Cohen, *Cosmopolitans and Parochials: Modern Orthodox Jews in America* (Chicago: University of Chicago Press, 1989).

74. David Halle, *America's Working Man: Work, Home, and Politics among Blue-Collar Property Owners* (Chicago: University of Chicago Press, 1984), p. 271.

75. E.g., John Bodnar, *The Transplanted: The History of Immigrants in Urban America* (Bloomington: Indiana University Press, 1985); Donna Gabaccia, *From Sicily to Elizabeth Street: Housing and Social Change among Italian Immigrants, 1880–1930* (Albany: SUNY Press, 1984); Kessner, *The Golden Door;* Stefano Luconi, *From Paesani to White Ethnics: The Italian Experience in Philadelphia* (Philadelphia: Temple University Press, 2001); Rudolph Vecoli, "*Contadini* in Chicago: A Critique of 'The Uprooted,'" *Journal of American Ethnic History* 51 (December 1964): 404–417; Virginia Yans-McLaughlin, *Family and Community: Italian Immigrants in Buffalo, 1880–1930* (Ithaca, N.Y.: Cornell University Press, 1977).

76. Irving Child, *Italian or American? The Second Generation in Conflict* (New Haven: Yale University Press, 1943); Covello, *Social Background;* William Foote Whyte, *Street Corner Society: The Social Structure of an Italian Slum* (1943; reprint, Chicago: University of Chicago Press, 1955).

77. But see Herbert Gans, *The Urban Villagers: Group and Class in the Life of Italian-Americans* (1962; reprint, New York: Free Press, 1982); Charles

Hirschman and Ellen Kraly, "Racial and Ethnic Inequality in the United States, 1940 and 1950: The Impact of Geographic Location and Human Capital," *International Migration Review* 24 (Spring 1990): 4–33; Vecoli, "Coming of Age."

78. U.S. Bureau of the Census, *Population 1920,* vol. 3 (Washington, D.C.: Government Printing Office, 1922), table 11.

79. Bodnar, *The Transplanted,* pp. 169–175; cf. Stephan Thernstrom, *The Other Bostonians: Poverty and Progress in the American Metropolis, 1880–1970* (Cambridge, Mass.: Harvard University Press, 1973), pp. 249–250.

80. Joel Perlmann and Roger Waldinger, "Second Generation Decline? Children of Immigrants, Past and Present: A Reconsideration," *International Migration Review* 31 (Winter 1997): 897.

81. For general treatments of occupational mobility in the middle decades of the twentieth century, see Peter Blau and Otis Dudley Duncan, *The American Occupational Structure* (New York: Wiley, 1967); David Featherman and Robert Hauser, *Opportunity and Change* (New York: Academic Press, 1978).

82. The most extended consideration of these issues is Stanley Lieberson, *A Piece of the Pie: Blacks and White Immigrants since 1880* (Berkeley: University of California Press, 1980), which has promoted the queueing concept. Hirschman and Kraly ("Racial and Ethnic Inequality") and George Borjas ("Long-Run Convergence of Ethnic Skills Differentials: The Children and Grandchildren of the Great Migration," *Industrial and Labor Relations Review* 47 (1994): 553–573) demonstrate the socioeconomic advance of the second generation in many places by the 1940s. See also Stewart Tolnay, "African Americans and Immigrants in Northern Cities: The Effects of Relative Group Size on Occupational Standing in 1920," *Social Forces* 80 (December 2001): 573–604.

83. Gary Gerstle, *Working-Class Americanism: The Politics of Labor in a Textile City, 1914–1960* (Cambridge: Cambridge University Press, 1989), p. 31 ("the most French city in the United States").

84. Ibid., pp. 326–329.

85. We are grateful to Joel Perlmann and Roger Waldinger for pointing out to us our slighting of processes of social closure and of collective mobility in an earlier version of this discussion.

86. Stephen Steinberg, *The Ethnic Myth: Race, Ethnicity, and Class in America* (Boston: Beacon Press, 1989); Leonard Dinnerstein, *Antisemitism in America* (New York: Oxford University Press, 1994).

87. Dinnerstein, *Antisemitism,* pp. 84–94.

88. Ibid., chap. 8.

89. The source of these data, Martin Trow's classic essay "The Second Transformation of American Secondary Education" (*International Journal of*

Comparative Sociology 2 [1961]: 144–166) calls attention to the emergence of "mass" higher education.

90. Keith Olson, *The G.I. Bill, the Veterans, and the Colleges* (Lexington: University Press of Kentucky, 1974), p. 43.
91. David Karen, "Access to Higher Education in the United States, 1900 to the Present," in Kevin Dougherty and Floyd Hammack, eds., *Education and Society: A Reader* (New York: Harcourt, Brace, Jovanovich, 1990), p. 267.
92. Steven Brint and Jerome Karabel, *The Diverted Dream: Community Colleges and the Promise of Educational Opportunity in America* (New York: Oxford University Press, 1989); W. Vance Grant and Leo Eiden, *Digest of Educational Statistics, 1980* (Washington, D.C.: National Center for Education Statistics, 1980).
93. David Lavin, Richard Alba, and Richard Silberstein, *Right versus Privilege: The Open Admissions Experiment at the City University of New York* (New York: Free Press, 1981); State University of New York, *SUNY 2000: A Vision for the New Century* (Albany: SUNY Press, 1991).
94. Lieberson, *A Piece of the Pie*, pp. 200–206, 328–332.
95. Kenneth Jackson, *Crabgrass Frontier: The Suburbanization of the United States* (New York: Oxford University Press, 1985).
96. Dennis Judd and Todd Swanstrom, *City Politics: Private Power and Public Policy* (New York: HarperCollins, 1994), p. 203; see also Jackson, *Crabgrass Frontier;* Massey and Denton, *American Apartheid;* Richard Polenberg, *One Nation Divisible: Class, Race, and Ethnicity in the United States since 1938* (New York: Viking, 1980).
97. Jackson, *Crabgrass Frontier*, p. 239.
98. Bruce Lambert, "At 50, Levittown Contends with Its Legacy of Bias," *New York Times*, December 26, 1997, pp. 23, 26.
99. Herbert Gans, *The Levittowners: Ways of Life and Politics in a New Suburban Community* (New York: Pantheon, 1967), pp. 23–24.
100. Tuan, *Forever Foreigners*, pp. 48–75.
101. See Alba, Logan, and Crowder, "White Ethnic Neighborhoods"; Herbert Gans, "Park Forest: Birth of a Jewish Community," *Commentary* 2 (April 1951): 300–309; Salvatore LaGumina, *From Steerage to Suburb: Long Island Italians* (Staten Island, N.Y.: Center for Migration Studies, 1988).
102. The curtailment of legal immigration for Chinese occurred earlier, and resulted in a decline in the relative size of the Chinese population, which at its peak, in the 1870s, made up 12 percent of California's population; by the 1950s, the second-generation descendants of Chinese immigrants constituted a very small minority group in California.
103. For the data, see Chapter 7 and Smith and Edmonston, *New Americans*, chap. 2.
104. For a discussion of German bilingualism, see Walter Kamphoefner, "German-American Bilingualism: Cui Malo? Mother Tongue and Socioeco-

nomic Status among the Second Generation in 1940," *International Migration Review* 28 (Winter 1994): 846–864; Higham, in *Strangers,* describes some of the wartime measures against German.

105. Quoted by John Morton Blum, *V Was for Victory: Politics and American Culture during World War II* (New York: Harcourt Brace Jovanovich, 1976), p. 63.

106. Polenberg, in *One Nation Divisible,* discusses the war's impact on European ethnics.

107. Masayo Umezawa Duus, *Unlikely Liberators: The Men of the 100th and 442nd* (Honolulu: University of Hawaii, 1987).

108. Blum, *V Was for Victory.*

109. John Hersey, *A Bell for Adano* (New York: Knopf, 1944), pp. 1–2.

110. Dinnerstein, *Antisemitism,* p. 151.

111. Leonard Dinnerstein (*Antisemitism,* chap. 8) describes these struggles in some detail for Jews, who undoubtedly had to fight the hardest and whose successes may have paved the way for other groups; see also Charles Silberman, *A Certain People: American Jews and Their Lives Today* (New York: Summit, 1985).

112. Perlmann and Waldinger, "Second Generation Decline?" p. 907.

113. Dinnerstein, *Antisemitism,* p. 159.

114. Silberman, *A Certain People,* pp. 96–98.

115. During the 1990s, a new literature on "whiteness" sprang up to document the processes involved. See, e.g., Noel Ignatiev, *How the Irish Became White* (New York, Routledge, 1995); Jacobson, *Whiteness;* David Roediger, *The Wages of Whiteness: Race and the Making of the American Working Class* (New York: Verso, 1991). On the racialization of ethnic categories, see Michael Omi and Howard Winant's enormously influential *Racial Formation in the United States: From the 1960s to the 1990s,* 2d ed. (New York: Routledge & Kegan Paul, 1994).

116. Ignatiev, *How the Irish,* p. 112.

117. Reynolds Farley and William Frey, "Changes in the Segregation of Whites from Blacks during the 1980s: Small Steps towards a More Integrated Society," *American Sociological Review* 59 (February 1994): 23–45; Massey and Denton, *American Apartheid;* William Julius Wilson, *The Declining Significance of Race: Blacks and Changing American Institutions* (Chicago: University of Chicago Press, 1978).

118. Gerstle, *Working-Class Americanism;* John McGreevey, *Parish Boundaries: The Catholic Encounter with Race in the Twentieth-Century Urban North* (Chicago: University of Chicago Press, 1996).

119. See, e.g., Blauner, *Racial Oppression.*

120. Samuel Freedman, *The Inheritance: How Three Families and America Moved from Roosevelt to Reagan and Beyond* (New York: Simon & Schuster, 1996), p. 29.

4 *Was Assimilation Contingent on Specific Historical Conditions?*

1. Alejandro Portes and Rubén Rumbaut, *Immigrant America: A Portrait*, 2d ed. (Berkeley: University of California Press, 1996), p. 7. See also Douglas Massey, "The New Immigration and Ethnicity in the United States," *Population and Development Review* 21 (September 1995): 631–652.

2. For a sophisticated reading of the comparison between past and present, see Nancy Foner, *From Ellis Island to JFK: New York's Two Great Waves of Immigration* (New Haven: Yale University Press, 2000).

3. Stanley Lieberson, *A Piece of the Pie: Blacks and White Immigrants since 1880* (Berkeley: University of California Press, 1980); Massey, "New Immigration."

4. Peter Brimelow, *Alien Nation: Common Sense about America's Immigration Disaster* (New York: Random House, 1995).

5. Massey, "New Immigration"; Douglas Massey, "A March of Folly: U.S. Immigration Policy after NAFTA," *American Prospect* 37 (1998): 22–33.

6. Frank Bean, Thomas Espenshade, Michael White, and Robert Dymowski, "Post-IRCA Changes in the Volume and Composition of Undocumented Migration to the United States: An Assessment Based on Apprehensions Data," in Frank Bean, Barry Edmonston, and Jeffrey Passel, eds., *Undocumented Migration to the United States* (Washington, D.C.: Urban Institute, 1990), pp. 111–158; Katharine Donato, Jorge Durand, and Douglas Massey, "Stemming the Tide? Assessing the Deterrent Effects of the Immigration Reform and Control Act," *Demography* 29 (May 1992): 139–157; David Heer, *Immigration in America's Future: Social Science Findings and the Policy Debate* (Boulder, Colo.: Westview Press, 1996).

7. Heer, *Immigration*, pp. 137–145.

8. Saskia Sassen, *The Mobility of Capital and Labor* (Cambridge: Cambridge University Press, 1988); Douglas Massey, Joaquin Arango, Graeme Hugo, Ali Kouaouci, Adela Pellegrino, and J. Edward Taylor, *Worlds in Motion: Understanding International Migration at the End of the Millennium* (Oxford: Clarendon Press, 1998).

9. Barry Edmonston and Jeffrey Passel, "The Future Immigrant Population of the United States," in Barry Edmonston and Jeffrey Passel, eds., *Immigration and Ethnicity: The Integration of America's Newest Arrivals* (Washington, D.C.: Urban Institute Press, 1994), pp. 317–353; James Smith and Barry Edmonston, *The New Americans: Economic, Demographic, and Fiscal Effects of Immigration* (Washington, D.C.: National Research Council, 1997).

10. We are grateful to Alex Aleinikoff for pointing out to us the German case.

11. David Reimers, *Still the Golden Door: The Third World Comes to America* (New York: Columbia University Press, 1992), p. 72.

12. On the Korean immigration, see Pam Belluck, "Healthy Korean Economy

Draws Immigrants Home," *New York Times,* August 22, 1995, pp. A1, B4; Pyong Gap Min, *Caught in the Middle: Korean Merchants in America's Multiethnic Cities* (Berkeley: University of California, 1996); on the Irish, see Warren Hoge, "Irish Eyes Turning Homeward as a Country's Moment Comes," *New York Times,* March 23, 1997, pp. A1, 12.

13. For a full discussion of the potential for change in Mexican immigration, see Agustin Escobar Latapi, Frank Bean, and Sidney Weintraub, "The Dynamics of Mexican Emigration," in Reginald Appleyard, ed., *Emigration Dynamics in Developing Countries,* vol. 3 (Aldershot: Ashgate, 1999), pp. 18–116; also relevant is Sam Dillon, "Smaller Families Bring Big Change to Mexico," *New York Times,* June 8, 1999, pp. A1, 12.

14. E.g., Foner, *From Ellis Island;* John Higham, *Strangers in the Land: Patterns of American Nativism, 1860–1925* (New York: Atheneum, 1970); Matthew Frye Jacobson, *Whiteness of a Different Color: European Immigrants and the Alchemy of Race* (Cambridge, Mass.: Harvard University Press, 1998).

15. The strategies by which whiteness was achieved are just beginning to be discerned, but it is apparent so far that cultural devices, the exclusion of African Americans from white ethnic job niches, and violence all played a part. See David Roediger, *The Wages of Whiteness: Race and the Making of the American Working Class* (New York: Verso, 1991); Noel Ignatiev, *How the Irish Became White* (New York: Routledge, 1995); Jacobson, *Whiteness.*

16. H. L. Mencken, *The American Language* (New York: Knopf, 1963), p. 373; James Barrett and David Roediger, "Inbetween Peoples: Race, Nationality, and the 'New Immigrant' Working Class," *Journal of American Ethnic History* 16 (Spring 1997): 3–44.

17. On Asian-white intermarriage, see Sharon Lee and Marilyn Fernandez, "Trends in Asian American Racial/Ethnic Intermarriage: A Comparison of 1980 and 1990 Census Data," *Sociological Perspectives* 41, no. 2 (1998): 323–342; Zhenchao Qian, "Breaking the Racial Barriers: Variations in Interracial Marriages between 1980 and 1990," *Demography* 34 (May 1997): 263–276. The phenomenon of mixed racial ancestry is discussed in Maria Root, *Racially Mixed People in America* (Newbury Park, Calif.: Sage, 1992); Paul Spickard, *Mixed Blood: Ethnic Identity and Intermarriage in Twentieth-Century America* (Madison: University of Wisconsin Press, 1989); Paul Spickard and Rowena Fong, "Pacific Islander Americans and Multiethnicity: A Vision of America's Future?" *Social Forces* 73 (June 1995): 1365–83; Mary Waters, "The Social Construction of Race and Ethnicity: Some Examples from Demography," in Nancy Denton and Stewart Tolnay, eds., *American Diversity: A Demographic Challenge for the Twenty-first Century* (Albany, SUNY Press, 2002); and Yu Xie and Kimberly Goyette, "The Racial Identification of Biracial Children with One Asian Parent: Evidence from the 1990 Census," *Social Forces* 76 (December 1977): 547–570. Asian American identities are also discussed in Yen Le

Espiritu, *Asian American Panethnicity: Bridging Institutions and Identities* (Philadelphia: Temple University Press, 1992); and Mia Tuan, *Forever Foreigners or Honorary Whites? The Asian Ethnic Experience Today* (New Brunswick, N.J.: Rutgers University Press, 1998).

18. David Lopez and Ricardo Stanton-Salazar, "Mexican Americans: A Second Generation at Risk," in Rubén Rumbaut and Alejandro Portes, eds., *Ethnicities: Children of Immigrants in America* (Berkeley: University of California Press, 2001), pp. 57–90.

19. F. James Davis, *Who Is Black? One Nation's Definition* (University Park: Pennsylvania State University Press, 1991).

20. Herbert Gans, "The Possibility of a New Racial Hierarchy in the Twenty-first-Century United States," in Michele Lamont, ed., *The Cultural Territories of Race: Black and White Boundaries* (Chicago and New York: University of Chicago Press and Russell Sage Foundation, 1999), pp. 371–390; Joel Perlmann and Roger Waldinger, "Second Generation Decline? Children of Immigrants, Past and Present: A Reconsideration," *International Migration Review* 31 (Winter): 893–922. See also Foner, *From Ellis Island*, pp. 224–231.

21. On the frequency of black-white intermarriage, see Matthijs Kalmijn, "Trends in Black/White Intermarriage," *Social Forces* 72 (September 1993): 119–146.

22. The "hourglass" image has been deployed in the immigration literature by Alejandro Portes and Min Zhou, "The New Second Generation: Segmented Assimilation and Its Variants," *Annals* 530 (November 1993): 74–96; for general discussions of trends in occupational structure and income distribution, see Reynolds Farley, *The New American Reality: Who We Are, How We Got Here, Where We Are Going* (New York: Russell Sage Foundation, 1996); and Frank Levy, *The New Dollars and Dreams: American Incomes and Economic Change* (New York: Russell Sage Foundation, 1998).

23. Herbert Gans, "Second Generation Decline: Scenarios for the Economic and Ethnic Futures of Post-1965 American Immigrants," *Ethnic and Racial Studies* 15 (April 1992): 173–192; Portes and Zhou, "New Second Generation." Not all scholars agree: see Perlmann and Waldinger, "Second Generation Decline?"; Foner, *From Ellis Island*, pp. 231–238.

24. Our discussion of general trends in social mobility owes a great deal to conversations with Michael Hout.

25. See Farley, *New American Reality;* Claude Fischer, Michael Hout, Martin Sánchez Jankowski, Samuel Lucas, Ann Swidler, and Kim Voss, *Inequality by Design: Cracking the Bell Curve Myth* (Princeton: Princeton University Press, 1996), chap. 5; Sassen, *Mobility.*

26. Levy, *New Dollars.*

27. Michael Piore, *Birds of Passage: Migrant Labor and Industrial Societies* (Cambridge: Cambridge University Press, 1979).

28. William Julius Wilson, *The Declining Significance of Race: Blacks and*

Changing American Institutions (Chicago: University of Chicago Press, 1978).

29. Christopher Jencks, *Rethinking Social Policy: Race, Poverty, and the Underclass* (Cambridge, Mass.: Harvard University Press, 1992), pp. 120–142; Victor Nee, Jimy Sanders, and Scott Sernau, "Job Transitions in an Immigrant Metropolis: Ethnic Boundaries and the Mixed Economy," *American Sociological Review* 59 (December 1994): 849–872.
30. Portes and Rumbaut, *Immigrant America,* pp. 232–268.
31. Nathan Glazer and Daniel Patrick Moynihan, *Beyond the Melting Pot: The Negroes, Puerto Ricans, Jews, Italians, and Irish of New York City* (1963; reprint, Cambridge, Mass.: MIT Press, 1970).
32. Jencks, *Rethinking,* p. 173; Farley, *New American Reality,* pp. 228–238.
33. Sassen, *Mobility.*
34. Roger Waldinger, *Still the Promised City? African-Americans and New Immigrants in Postindustrial New York* (Cambridge, Mass.: Harvard University Press, 1996).
35. Michael Hout, "More Universalism, Less Structural Mobility: The American Occupational Structure in the 1980s," *American Journal of Sociology* 93 (May 1988): 1358–1400; see also David Grusky and Thomas DiPrete, "Recent Trends in the Process of Stratification," *Demography* 27 (November 1990): 617–637; Thomas DiPrete and David Grusky, "Structure and Trend in the Process of Stratification for American Men and Women," *American Journal of Sociology* 96 (July 1990): 107–143.
36. Hout, "More Universalism."
37. Andrew Hacker, "Goodbye to Affirmative Action?" *New York Review of Books,* July 11, 1996, pp. 21–29; David Lavin and David Hyllegard, *Changing the Odds: Open Admissions and the Life Chances of the Disadvantaged* (New Haven: Yale University Press, 1996).
38. Victor Nee and Jimy Sanders, "Understanding the Diversity of Immigrant Incorporation: A Forms-of-Capital Model," *Ethnic and Racial Studies* 24 (May 2001): 386–411; Victor Nee and Jimy Sanders, "Trust in Ethnic Ties: Social Capital and Immigrants," in Karen Cook, ed., *Trust and Society* (New York: Russell Sage Foundation, 2001), pp. 374–392.
39. Portes and Rumbaut, *Immigrant America;* Portes and Zhou, "New Second Generation."
40. Irving Child, *Italian or American? The Second Generation in Conflict* (New Haven: Yale University Press, 1943); Leonard Covello, *The Social Background of the Italo-American School Child* (Totowa, N.J.: Rowman & Littlefield, 1972).
41. Lieberson, *Piece of the Pie.*
42. Higham, *Strangers,* pp. 247–248.
43. For the debate on multiculturalism, see Arthur Schlesinger, *The Disuniting of America: Reflections on a Multicultural Society* (New York: W. W. Norton, 1992); Charles Taylor, *Multiculturalism and "The Politics of Rec-*

ognition" (Princeton: Princeton University Press, 1992); Ronald Takaki, "Multiculturalism: Battleground or Meeting Ground?" *Annals* 530 (November 1993): 109–121; Will Kymlicka, *Multicultural Citizenship* (Oxford: Clarendon Press, 1995); Nathan Glazer, *We Are All Multiculturalists Now* (Cambridge, Mass.: Harvard University Press, 1997); Bhikhu Parekh, *Rethinking Multiculturalism: Cultural Diversity and Political Theory* (Cambridge, Mass.: Harvard University Press, 2000).

44. Vincent Parrillo, "Diversity in America: A Sociohistorical Analysis," *Sociological Forum* 9 (December 1994): 523–545.

45. The data in the text come from the 1994 survey except where indicated and should be understood as the percentages of those who expressed opinions; see James Davis and Tom Smith, *General Social Surveys, 1972–1996: Cumulative Codebook* (Chicago: National Opinion Research Center, 1996). These data seem broadly consistent with other survey data about immigration and multiculturalism (see, e.g., Heer, *Immigration;* Alan Wolfe, *One Nation, After All* [New York: Penguin, 1998], pp. 154ff.).

46. Nathan Glazer, *Affirmative Discrimination* (New York: Basic Books, 1975).

47. Glazer, *Affirmative Discrimination,* p. 23; cf. Joane Nagel, "The Political Construction of Ethnicity," in Susan Olzak and Joane Nagel, eds., *Competitive Ethnic Relations* (Orlando, Fla.: Academic Press, 1986), pp. 93–112.

48. Gibson, *Accommodation.*

49. Jeffrey Reitz and Raymond Breton, *The Illusion of Difference: Realities of Ethnicity in Canada and the United States* (Toronto: C. D. Howe Institute, 1994). Immigrants made up 16 percent of the Canadian population in 1991, double their percentage at the time in the United States.

50. Ibid., p. 63.

51. Milton Gordon, *Assimilation in American Life* (New York: Oxford University Press, 1964), chap. 6.

52. Walter Kamphoefner, "German-American Bilingualism: Cui Malo? Mother Tongue and Socioeconomic Status among the Second Generation in 1940," *International Migration Review* 28 (Winter 1994): 847.

53. Ibid.; see also Heinz Kloss, "German-American Language Maintenance Efforts," in Joshua Fishman et al., eds., *Language Loyalty in the United States* (The Hague: Mouton, 1966), pp. 206–252. The case of French is addressed by Gary Gerstle, *Working-Class Americanism: The Politics of Labor in a Textile City, 1914–1960* (Cambridge: Cambridge University Press, 1989). Other mother tongues are discussed by Fishman et al., *Language Loyalty.*

54. Piers Brendon, *Ike: The Life and Times of Dwight D. Eisenhower* (London: Secker & Warburg, 1987), p. 15.

55. Linda Basch, Nina Glick Schiller, and Cristina Blanc-Szanton, *Nations Unbound: Transnational Projects, Post-colonial Predicaments, and De-territorialized Nation-States* (Langhorne, Pa.: Gordon and Breach, 1994); Nina Glick-Schiller, Linda Basch, and Cristina Blanc-Szanton, "From Immigrant to Transmigrant: Theorizing Transnational Migration," *Anthropological*

Quarterly 68 (January 1995): 48–63; Peggy Levitt, *The Transnational Villagers* (Berkeley: University of California Press, 2001); Alejandro Portes, Luis Garnizo, and Patricia Landolt, "The Study of Transnationalism: Pitfalls and Promise of an Emergent Research Field," *Ethnic and Racial Studies* 22 (March 1999): 217–237; and Alejandro Portes, "Introduction: The Debates and Significance of Immigrant Transnationalism," *Global Networks* 1 (2001): 181–193. For two cogent evaluations, see Nancy Foner, "What's New about Transnationalism? New York Immigrants Today and at the Turn of the Century," *Diaspora* 6, no. 3 (1997): 355–375; and Peter Kivisto, "Theorizing Transnational Immigration: A Critical Review of Current Efforts," *Ethnic and Racial Studies* 24 (July 2001): 549–577.

56. Basch et al., *Nations*, p. 7.
57. Walter Nugent, *Crossings: The Great Transatlantic Migrations, 1870–1914* (Bloomington: Indiana University Press, 1992), p. 99. For additional discussions of earlier transnational patterns, see Foner, "What's New"; Nina Glick Schiller, "Transmigrants and Nation-States: Something Old and Something New in the U.S. Immigrant Experience," in Charles Hirschman, Philip Kasinitz, and Josh DeWind, eds., *The Handbook of International Migration: The American Experience* (New York: Russell Sage Foundation), pp. 94–119; Mark Wyman, *Round-Trip to America: The Immigrants Return to Europe, 1880–1930* (Ithaca: Cornell University Press, 1993).
58. Randolph Bourne, "Trans-national America," *Atlantic Monthly* 118 (July 1916): 187.
59. Foner, "What's New?"
60. Portes et al., "Study," p. 223.
61. Alejandro Portes, "Global Villagers: The Rise of Transnational Communities," *American Prospect* 7 (March–April 1996).
62. Sassen, *Mobility;* Alejandro Portes, "Conclusion: Towards a New World—the Origins and Effects of Transnational Activities," *Ethnic and Racial Studies* 22 (March 1999): 471–472.
63. Illsoo Kim, *New Urban Immigrants: The Korean Community in New York* (Princeton: Princeton University Press, 1981); Portes and Rumbaut, *Immigrant America.*
64. Migration News, "Hope, Dual Nationality" (May 2001), website is http://migration.ucdavis.edu/mn/.
65. Basch et al., *Nations.*
66. Heer, *Immigration;* David Jacobson, *Rights across Borders: Immigration and the Decline of Citizenship* (Baltimore: Johns Hopkins University Press, 1996); Peter Schuck, *Citizens, Strangers, and In-Betweens: Essays on Immigration and Citizenship* (Boulder, Colo.: Westview Press, 1998).
67. Nathan Glazer, "Ethnic Groups in America: From National Culture to Ideology," in Morroe Berger, Theodore Abel, and Charles Page, eds., *Freedom and Control in Modern Society* (New York: D. Van Nostrand, 1954), pp. 158–173; see also Foner, "What's New"; Mona Harrington, "Loyalties:

Dual and Divided," in Michael Walzer, Edward Kantowicz, John Higham, and Mona Harrington, eds., *The Politics of Ethnicity* (Cambridge, Mass.: Harvard University Press, 1982), pp. 93–138.

68. Glazer, "Ethnic Groups," p. 167.

69. Thomas Brown, *Irish-American Nationalism: 1870–1890* (Philadelphia: J. B. Lippincott, 1966), p. 39.

70. Harrington, "Loyalties," p. 113.

71. Robert Smith, "Transnational Localities: Community, Technology, and the Politics of Membership within the Context of Mexico-U.S. Migration," *Comparative Urban and Community Research* 6 (1998): 196–238.

72. Alejandro Portes and Alex Stepick, *City on the Edge: The Transformation of Miami* (Berkeley: University of California Press, 1993).

73. Victor Nee and Brett de Bary Nee, *Longtime Californ': A Documentary Study of an American Chinatown* (New York: Pantheon Books, 1973).

74. Some children of immigrants are sent to their homeland for part or all of their education; this record is most developed in the case of Dominicans (see Levitt, *Transnational Villagers*). But Portes concedes that the evidence of intergenerational transmission of transnationalism is negligible ("Introduction," pp. 189–190).

75. Rodolfo de la Garza, Louis DeSipio, Chris Garcia, John Garcia, and Angelo Falcon, *Latino Voices: Mexican, Puerto Rican, and Cuban Perspectives on American Politics* (Boulder, Colo.: Westview Press, 1992).

76. On the hold of German culture, see Kathleen Conzen, "Germans," in Stephan Thernstrom, Ann Orlov, and Oscar Handlin, eds., *Harvard Encyclopedia of American Ethnic Groups* (Cambridge, Mass.: Harvard University Press, 1980), pp. 405–425. Rogers Brubaker (*Citizenship and Nationhood in France and Germany* [Cambridge, Mass.: Harvard University Press, 1992]) discusses the background of the German citizenship law of 1913. The anti-German measures of the war period are described by Kloss ("German-American") and Higham (*Strangers*).

77. The relationship between state policies and ethnicity has been addressed by Nagel ("Political Construction").

78. John Skrentny, *The Ironies of Affirmative Action: Politics, Culture, and Justice in America* (Chicago: University of Chicago Press, 1996); Glazer, *Multiculturalists;* Hacker, "Goodbye."

79. Joane Nagel, "American Indian Ethnic Renewal: Politics and the Resurgence of Identity," *American Sociological Review* 60 (December 1995): 947–965.

80. Hacker, "Goodbye."

81. Larry Bobo and James Kluegel, "Opposition to Race Targeting: Self-Interest, Stratification Ideology, or Racial Attitudes?" *American Sociological Review* 58 (August 1993): 443–464; Howard Schuman, Charlotte Steeh, Lawrence Bobo, and Maria Krysan, *Racial Attitudes in America: Trends and Interpretations* (Cambridge, Mass.: Harvard University Press, 1997);

Skrentny, *Ironies;* see also the opinions of Wolfe's (*One Nation,* pp. 215–223) middle-class respondents.

82. See, for example, the remarks of Michael Lind in *The Next American Nation: The New Nationalism and the Fourth American Revolution* (New York: Basic Books, 1995); and of Hacker in "Goodbye." See also John Skrentny, "Affirmative Action and New Demographic Realities," *Chronicle of Higher Education,* February 16, 2001, p. B7.

83. Glazer and Moynihan, *Melting Pot.*

84. Steven Erie, *Rainbow's End: Irish-Americans and the Dilemmas of Urban Machine Politics, 1840–1985* (Berkeley: University of California Press, 1988).

85. Waldinger, *Promised City.*

86. Pierre van den Berghe, *Race and Racism* (New York: John Wiley, 1967), pp. 9–10; for an extended treatment of the definitional question that partly fits with van den Berghe's approach and partly with our own, see Stephen Cornell and Douglas Hartmann, *Ethnicity and Race: Making Identities in a Changing World* (Thousand Oaks, Calif.: Pine Forge Press, 1998), chap. 2.

87. Mary Waters, *Ethnic Options: Choosing Identities in America* (Berkeley: University of California Press, 1990), chap. 3.

88. Robert Blauner, *Racial Oppression in America* (New York: Harper & Row, 1972), p. 22.

89. This theme was also highly developed in the education literature of the 1970s; see, e.g., Samuel Bowles and Herbert Gintis, *Schooling in Capitalist America* (New York: Basic Books, 1976).

90. Michael Omi and Howard Winant, *Racial Formation in the United States: From the 1960s to the 1990s,* 2d ed. (New York: Routledge & Kegan Paul, 1994).

91. Ibid., p. 55.

92. Piore, *Birds.*

93. Sassen, *Mobility.*

94. Portes and Zhou, "New Second Generation."

95. Foner, *From Ellis Island,* pp. 231–234.

96. David Grusky and Robert Hauser, "Comparative Social Mobility Revisited: Models of Convergence and Divergence in Sixteen Countries," in David Grusky, ed., *Social Stratification: Class, Race, and Gender in Sociological Perspective* (Boulder, Colo.: Westview Press, 1994), pp. 275–288.

97. Glazer and Moynihan, *Melting Pot,* pp. xxiii–xxiv.

98. See Light, "Immigrant"; Alejandro Portes and Robert Bach, *Latin Journey: Cuban and Mexican Immigrants in the United States* (Berkeley: University of California Press, 1985); and Waldinger, *Promised City.*

99. The concept of an enclave economy is developed in a series of works including Portes and Bach, *Latin Journey;* Portes and Robert Manning, "The Immigrant Enclave: Theory and Empirical Examples," in Susan Olzak and Joane Nagel, eds., *Competitive Ethnic Relations* (New York: Academic

Press, 1986), pp. 47–68; Thomas Bailey and Roger Waldinger, "Primary, Secondary, and Enclave Labor Markets: A Training Systems Approach," *American Sociological Review* 56 (August 1991): 432–445; and Min Zhou, *Chinatown: The Socioeconomic Potential of an Urban Enclave* (Philadelphia: Temple University Press, 1992).

100. Jimy Sanders and Victor Nee, "Limits of Ethnic Solidarity in the Ethnic Enclave," *American Sociological Review* 52 (December 1987): 745–767; Nee, Sanders, and Sernau, "Job Transitions"; Terry Hum, "A Protected Niche? Immigrant Ethnic Economies and Labor Market Segmentation," in Lawrence D. Bobo, Melvin L. Oliver, James H. Johnson, Jr., and Abel Valenzuela, Jr., eds., *Prismatic Metropolis: Inequality in Los Angeles* (New York: Russell Sage Foundation, 2000), pp. 279–314.

101. On the factors at work in the case of Miami's Cubans, see Portes and Stepick, *City;* and Maria Cristina Garcia, *Havana USA: Cuban Exiles and Cuban Americans in South Florida, 1959–1994* (Berkeley: University of California Press, 1996). See also Lisandro Perez, "Growing Up in Cuban Miami: Immigration, the Enclave, and the New Generations," in Rumbaut and Portes, *Ethnicities,* pp. 91–126.

102. See John Logan, Richard Alba, and Thomas McNulty, "Ethnic Economies in Metropolitan Regions: Miami and Beyond," *Social Forces* 72 (March 1994): 691–724; John Logan and Richard Alba, "Minority Niches and Immigrant Enclaves in New York and Los Angeles: Trends and Impacts," in Frank Bean and Stephanie Bell-Rose, eds., *Immigration and Opportunity: Race, Ethnicity, and Employment in the United States* (New York: Russell Sage Foundation, 1999), pp. 172–193; John Logan, Richard Alba, Michael Dill, and Min Zhou, "Ethnic Segmentation in the American Metropolis: Increasing Divergence in Economic Incorporation, 1980–1990," *International Migration Review* 34 (Spring 2000): 98–132.

103. For work that develops and makes use of the niche concept, see Lieberson, *Piece;* Waldinger, *Promised City;* Suzanne Model, "The Ethnic Economy: Cubans and Chinese Reconsidered," *Sociological Quarterly* 33 (Spring 1992): 63–82; and Suzanne Model, "Ethnic Economy and Industry in Mid-Twentieth-Century Gotham," *Social Problems* 44 (1997): 445–463.

104. See, e.g., Elaine Louie, "A Korean Family's Dream, a Community's Struggle," *New York Times,* March 13, 1996, p. C1.

105. Such intergenerational mobility led to lost worlds, such as that of Jewish cattle dealers; see Rhonda Levine, *Class, Networks, and Identity: Replanting Jewish Lives from Nazi Germany to Rural New York* (Boulder, Colo.: Rowman & Littlefield, 2001).

5 The Background to Contemporary Immigration

1. Klaus Bade, *Ausländer—Aussiedler—Asyl: Eine Bestandsaufnahme* (Munich: C. H. Beck, 1994).

2. See Roger Daniels, *Coming to America: A History of Immigration and Ethnicity in American Life* (New York: HarperCollins, 1990); David Heer, *Immigration in America's Future: Social Science Findings and the Policy Debate* (Boulder, Colo.: Westview Press, 1996); John Higham, *Strangers in the Land: Patterns of American Nativism, 1860–1925* (New York: Atheneum, 1970); David Reimers, *Still the Golden Door: The Third World Comes to America* (New York: Columbia University Press, 1992); and Reed Ueda, *Postwar Immigrant America: A Social History* (Boston: Bedford Books, 1994).

3. Tomás Almaguer, *Racial Fault Lines: The Historical Origins of White Supremacy in California* (Berkeley: University of California Press, 1994).

4. This story is brilliantly told by Higham, *Strangers*.

5. Heer, *Immigration*, p. 46.

6. See Himilce Novas, *Everything You Need to Know about Latino History* (New York: Plume, 1994), pp. 102–104.

7. Reimers, *Golden Door*, p. 36.

8. Ibid., chap. 3.

9. Douglas Massey, "The New Immigration and Ethnicity in the United States," *Population and Development Review* 21 (September 1995): 631–652; Rubén Rumbaut, "Origins and Destinies: Immigration, Race, and Ethnicity in Contemporary America," in Silvia Pedraza and Rubén Rumbaut, eds., *Origins and Destinies: Immigration, Race, and Ethnicity in Contemporary America* (Belmont, Calif.: Wadsworth, 1995), pp. 21–42.

10. Douglas Massey, "A March of Folly: U.S. Immigration Policy after NAFTA," *American Prospect* 37 (1998): 22–33.

11. See, e.g., the brave attempt of Robert Warren and Jeffrey Passel, "A Count of the Uncountable: Estimates of Undocumented Aliens Counted in the 1980 United States Census," *Demography* 24 (August 1987): 375–393.

12. Heer, *Immigration*, p. 57.

13. Reimers, *Golden Door*, p. 222.

14. For an exemplary discussion of how this process works in the case of Dominican illegal immigration, see Sherri Grasmuck and Patricia Pessar, *Between Two Islands: Dominican International Migration* (Berkeley: University of California Press, 1991), pp. 171–174.

15. James Smith and Barry Edmonston, *The New Americans: Economic, Demographic, and Fiscal Effects of Immigration* (Washington, D.C.: National Research Council, 1997).

16. Massey, "March."

17. In 1995, Congress allowed illegal immigrants to apply for a change in their status without first leaving the United States. Instead, they were required to pay a penalty fee. Applications immediately jumped. See U.S. Department of Justice, "Legal Immigration, Fiscal Year 1997," Annual Report, Statistics Branch, Office of Policy and Planning, 1999.

18. Frank Bean, Thomas Espenshade, Michael White, and Robert Dymowski,

"Post-IRCA Changes in the Volume and Composition of Undocumented Migration to the United States: An Assessment Based on Apprehensions Data," in Frank Bean, Barry Edmonston, and Jeffrey Passel, eds., *Undocumented Migration to the United States* (Washington, D.C.: Urban Institute, 1990), pp. 111–158; Katharine Donato, Jorge Durand, and Douglas Massey, "Stemming the Tide? Assessing the Deterrent Effects of the Immigration Reform and Control Act," *Demography* 29 (May 1992): 139–157.

19. J. Gregory Robinson, "ESCAP II: Demographic Analysis Results," U.S. Census Bureau, 2001 (available on Census Bureau Web site: www.census.gov).

20. Heer, *Immigration*, pp. 55–56.

21. One can always argue about how immigration data should be standardized for the purpose of comparison, but from a number of points of view the United States is the dominant immigration-receiving country in the world today. According to the report of the National Research Council, "the uniqueness of the United States is not in how many immigrants it has relative to its population, but in its position as the only large country that is attracting significant numbers of immigrants" (Smith and Edmonston, *New Americans*, p. 62). See also Stephen Castles and Mark Miller, *The Age of Migration: International Population Movements in the Modern World* (New York: Guilford Press, 1998).

22. U.S. Department of Justice, "Legal Immigration."

23. Smith and Edmonston, *New Americans*.

24. On the treatment they received, see Rodolfo Acuña, *Occupied America: A History of Chicanos*, 3d ed. (New York: Harper & Row, 1988); and Almaguer, *Fault Lines*.

25. George Sánchez, *Becoming Mexican American: Ethnicity, Culture, and Identity in Chicano Los Angeles, 1900–1945* (New York: Oxford University Press, 1993), pp. 21–22.

26. Ibid., p. 18; on U.S. immigration record keeping, see Smith and Edmonston, *New Americans*, p. 31.

27. Joan Moore, *Mexicans Americans* (Englewood Cliffs, N.J.: Prentice-Hall, 1970); for a discussion of immigration in this period, see Douglas Massey, Rafael Alarcón, Jorge Durand, and Humberto González, *Return to Aztlan: The Social Process of International Migration from Western Mexico* (Berkeley: University of California Press, 1987), chap. 4.

28. L. H. Gann and Peter Duignan (*The Hispanics in the United States: A History* [Boulder, Colo.: Westview Press, 1986], p. 52) estimate the number at 415,000 "by far the largest number of aliens of any nationality forced to leave the United States."

29. See Sánchez, *Becoming*, chap. 10.

30. Gann and Duignan, *Hispanics*, pp. 58–59.

31. Ibid.

32. Reimers, *Golden Door*, p. 124.

33. U.S. Department of Justice, "Legal Immigration," p. 8.
34. Immigration and Naturalization Service, "Illegal Alien Resident Population," 2001 (available on the INS Web site: www.ins.gov).
35. Alejandro Portes and Rubén Rumbaut, *Immigrant America: A Portrait,* 2d ed. (Berkeley: University of California Press, 1996), pp. 46–47.
36. The data come from Portes and Rumbaut, *Immigrant America,* chap. 4.
37. Smith and Edmonston, *New Americans,* p. 177. The economist George Borjas has done the most to call attention to the possible growth in human-capital disparities between immigrants and natives; see, e.g., George Borjas, *Heaven's Door: Immigration Policy and the American Economy* (Princeton: Princeton University Press, 1999).
38. Portes and Rumbaut, *Immigrant America,* p. 68.
39. Massey, "March."
40. Daniels, *Coming,* pp. 373–374; Reimers, *Golden Door,* p. 159. For good overviews, see Silvia Pedraza, "Cuba's Refugees: Manifold Migrations," in Pedraza and Rumbaut, *Origins and Destinies,* pp. 263–279; Lisandro Pérez, "Growing Up in Cuban Miami: Immigration, the Enclave, and New Generations," in Rubén Rumbaut and Alejandro Portes, eds., *Ethnicities: Children of Immigrants in America* (Berkeley: University of California Press), pp. 91–125.
41. Reimers, *Golden Door,* pp. 165–166.
42. Ibid., p. 168.
43. Alejandro Portes and Alex Stepick, *City on the Edge: The Transformation of Miami* (Berkeley: University of California Press, 1993), pp. 132–136.
44. Reimers, *Golden Door,* p. 160.
45. Pedraza, "Cuba's Refugees," p. 267.
46. Pedraza (ibid., pp. 269–271) offers a good discussion of who the Marielitos were.
47. The data all come from Portes and Rumbaut, *Immigrant America,* chap. 3.
48. Our discussion of Dominican immigration relies heavily on the work of Grasmuck and Pessar (*Two Islands;* also "Dominicans in the United States: First- and Second-Generation Settlement," in Pedraza and Rumbaut, *Origins and Destinies,* pp. 280–292); and Peggy Levitt (*The Transnational Villagers* [Berkeley: University of California Press, 2001]).
49. See Grasmuck and Pessar, *Two Islands,* p. 33.
50. The estimate of Robert Warren, cited by Grasmuck and Pessar, "Dominicans."
51. Grasmuck and Pessar, *Two Islands,* pp. 172–173.
52. Grasmuck and Pessar, "Dominicans," p. 282.
53. Ibid., p. 284.
54. Ibid., p. 283.
55. Ibid.
56. Ibid., p. 286.
57. Grasmuck and Pessar, *Two Islands,* p. 158.

58. Levitt, *Transnational Villagers*.
59. See Sarah Mahler, *American Dreaming: Immigrant Life on the Margins* (Princeton: Princeton University Press, 1995), p. 4.
60. Ibid., pp. 13–16.
61. Cecilia Menjivar, *Fragmented Ties: Salvadoran Immigrant Networks in America* (Berkeley: University of California Press, 2000), pp. 80–89.
62. Mahler, *American Dreaming*, pp. 55–62.
63. Reimers, *Golden Door*, p. 147; see also Nancy Foner, "Jamaican Migrants: A Comparative Analysis of the New York and London Experience," Center for Latin American and Caribbean Studies, New York University, 1983.
64. See, among others, the essays in Nancy Foner, ed., *Islands in the City: West Indian Migration to New York* (Berkeley: University of California Press, 2001); Matthijs Kalmijn, "The Socioeconomic Assimilation of Caribbean American Blacks," *Social Forces* 74 (March 1996): 910–930; and Philip Kasinitz, *Caribbean New York: Black Immigrants and the Politics of Race* (Ithaca: Cornell University Press, 1992).
65. Foner ("Jamaican Migrants") and Suzanne Model ("An Occupational Tale of Two Cities: Minorities in London and New York," *Demography* 34 [November 1997]: 539–550) compare the West Indian immigrations to New York and London.
66. Reimers, *Golden Door*, p. 147.
67. Foner, "Jamaican Migrants," pp. 14–15.
68. Portes and Rumbaut, *Immigrant America*, chap. 3.
69. Kyle Crowder, "Residential Segregation of West Indians in the New York/New Jersey Metropolitan Area: The Roles of Race and Ethnicity," *International Migration Review* 33 (Spring 1999): 79–113; Nancy Foner, "The Jamaicans: Race and Ethnicity among Migrants in New York City," in Nancy Foner, ed., *New Immigrants in New York* (New York: Columbia University Press, 1987), pp. 195–217; Kasinitz, *Caribbean New York*.
70. Milton Vickerman, *Crosscurrents: West Indian Immigrants and Race* (New York: Oxford University Press, 1999); Mary Waters, *Black Identities: West Indian Dreams and American Realities* (Cambridge, Mass.: Harvard University Press, 1999).
71. The historical account is drawn from Victor Nee and Brett de Bary Nee, *Longtime Californ': A Documentary Study of an American Chinatown* (New York: Pantheon Books, 1973).
72. Alexander Saxton, *The Indispensable Enemy: Labor and the Anti-Chinese Movement in California* (Berkeley: University of California Press, 1971).
73. Thomas Chinn, H. Mark Lai, Philip P. Choy, eds., *A History of the Chinese in California: A Syllabus* (San Francisco: Chinese Historical Society of America, 1969).
74. Nee and Nee, *Longtime Californ'*.
75. Rose Hum Lee, *The Chinese in the United States of America* (Hong Kong: Hong Kong University Press, 1960).

76. Stanford Lyman, *Chinese Americans* (New York: Random House, 1974).

77. Pam Belluck, "Healthy Korean Economy Draws Immigrants Home," *New York Times*, August 22, 1995, pp. A1, B4.

78. Pyong Gap Min, *Caught in the Middle: Korean Merchants in America's Multiethnic Cities* (Berkeley: University of California Press, 1996).

79. Lucie Cheng and Edna Bonacich, *Labor Immigration under Capitalism: Asian Workers in the U.S. before World War II* (Berkeley: University of California Press, 1984); Illsoo Kim, *New Urban Immigrants: The Korean Community in New York* (Princeton: Princeton University Press, 1981).

80. Kim, *New Urban Immigrants;* In-Jin Yoon, *On My Own: Korean Business and Race Relations in America* (Chicago: University of Chicago Press, 1997).

81. Kwang Chung Kim, "Ethnic Resources Utilization of Korean Immigrant Entrepreneurs in the Chicago Minority Area," *International Migration Review* 19 (Spring 1985): 82–111; see also Min, *Caught in the Middle*.

82. Min, *Caught in the Middle*.

83. Ibid.

84. Ibid.

85. Carlos Bulosan, *America Is in the Heart: A Personal History* (1946; reprint, Seattle: University of Washington Press, 1981).

86. Cited in Ronald Takaki, *Strangers from a Different Shore: A History of Asian Americans* (Boston: Little, Brown, 1989), p. 332.

87. John Logan, Richard Alba, and Wenquan Zhang, "Immigrant Enclaves and Ethnic Communities in New York and Los Angeles," *American Sociological Review* 67 (April 2002): 299–322.

88. Takaki, *Strangers*, p. 433.

89. Paul Ong, Edna Bonacich, and Lucie Cheng, eds., *The New Asian Immigration in Los Angeles and Global Restructuring* (Philadelphia: Temple University Press, 1994).

90. Joan Jensen, *Passage from India: Asian Indian Immigrants in North America* (New Haven: Yale University Press, 1988); Howard Brett Melendy, *Asians in America: Filipinos, Koreans, and East Indians* (Boston: Twayne, 1977).

91. Matthew Frye Jacobson, *Whiteness of a Different Color: European Immigrants and the Alchemy of Race* (Cambridge, Mass.: Harvard University Press, 1998), pp. 223–245; Takaki, *Strangers*.

92. Jensen, *Passage;* Takaki, *Strangers*.

93. Sharon Lee, *Asian Americans: Diverse and Growing* (Washington, D.C.; Population Reference Bureau, 1998); Manju Sheth, "The Immigrants from India: Who Are They?" in Brij Khare, ed., *Asian Indian Immigrants* (Dubuque, Iowa: Kendall-Hunt, 1997), pp. 25–57.

94. Arthur Helweg and Usha Helweg, *The Immigrant Success Story: East Indians* (Philadelphia: University of Pennsylvania Press, 1990).

95. Sheth, "Immigrants."

96. Logan, Alba, and Zhang, "Immigrant Enclaves."

97. Sheth, "Immigrants."

98. Darrel Montero, *Vietnamese Americans: Patterns of Resettlement and Socioeconomic Adaptation in the United States* (Boulder, Colo.: Westview Press, 1979).

99. Takaki, *Strangers.*

100. Montero, *Vietnamese Americans;* Hien Duo Do, *The Vietnamese Americans* (Westport, Conn.: Greenwood Press, 1999).

101. Montero, *Vietnamese Americans.*

102. Hien, *Vietnamese Americans,* pp. 51–53.

103. Nazli Kibria, *Family Tightrope: The Changing Lives of Vietnamese Americans* (Princeton: Princeton University Press, 1993).

104. Min Zhou and Carl Bankston, *Growing Up American: How Vietnamese Children Adapt to Life in the United States* (New York: Russell Sage Foundation, 1998).

105. Hien, *Vietnamese Americans;* Kibria, *Family Tightrope.*

6 Evidence of Contemporary Assimilation

1. Rubén Rumbaut, "The Crucible Within: Ethnic Identity, Self-Esteem, and Segmented Assimilation among Children of Immigrants," *International Migration Review* 18 (Winter 1994): 748–794.

2. On the history of the Mexican immigration, see Douglas Massey, "The New Immigration and Ethnicity in the United States," *Population and Development Review* 21 (September 1995): 631–652; and George Sánchez, *Becoming Mexican American: Ethnicity, Culture, and Identity in Chicano Los Angeles, 1900–1945* (New York: Oxford University Press, 1993). The prognostic potential of later-generation Mexicans in the United States at the beginning of the twenty-first century is called into question by Joel Perlmann, "Young Mexican Americans, Blacks, and Whites in Recent Years: Schooling and Teen Motherhood as Indicators of Strengths and Risks," Levy Institute, Bard College, 2001.

3. Reynolds Farley, *The New American Reality: Who We Are, How We Got Here, Where We Are Going* (New York: Russell Sage Foundation, 1996), p. 162.

4. Margaret Gibson, *Accommodation without Assimilation: Sikh Immigrants in an American High School* (Ithaca: Cornell University Press, 1988).

5. On the ethnic influences on the second generation, see, among others, Gibson, *Accommodation;* Nazli Kibria, *Family Tightrope: The Changing Lives of Vietnamese Americans* (Princeton: Princeton University Press, 1993); Alejandro Portes and Rubén Rumbaut, *Legacies: The Story of the Immigrant Second Generation* (Berkeley: University of California Press, 2001); Rubén Rumbaut and Alejandro Portes, eds., *Ethnicities: Children of Immigrants in America* (Berkeley: University of California Press, 2001); Min

Zhou and Carl Bankston, *Growing Up American: How Vietnamese Children Adapt to Life in the United States* (New York: Russell Sage Foundation, 1998). For evidence that suggests a waning of communal influence, see Steven Gold, *Refugee Communities: A Comparative Field Study* (Newbury Park, Calif.: Sage, 1992), pp. 86–87, 125–126.

6. Portes and Rumbaut, *Legacies.*

7. The seductiveness of individualism is addressed by Robert Bellah, Richard Madsen, William Sullivan, Ann Swidler, and Steven Tipton (*Habits of the Heart: Individualism and Commitment in American Life* [Berkeley: University of California Press, 1985]); and Herbert Gans (*Middle American Individualism: The Future of American Democracy* [New York: Free Press, 1988]).

8. See Zhou and Bankston, *Growing Up.*

9. The remarkable power of English to overcome immigrant languages is discussed by Stanley Lieberson, Guy Dalto, and Mary Ellen Johnston ("The Course of Mother-Tongue Diversity in Nations," *American Journal of Sociology* 81 [July 1975]: 34–61); and David Lopez ("Language: Diversity and Assimilation," in Roger Waldinger and Mehdi Bozorgmehr, eds., *Ethnic Los Angeles* [New York: Russell Sage Foundation, 1996], pp. 139–163). The three-generation model of Anglicization has been developed by Joshua Fishman (*The Sociology of Language* [Rowley, Mass.: Newbury, 1972]); and Calvin Veltman (*Language Shift in the United States* [Berlin: Mouton, 1983]).

10. Lopez, "Language," p. 146.

11. Fishman, *Sociology.*

12. For discussions of the status of Spanish, see Lopez, "Language"; and Calvin Veltman, "The Status of the Spanish Language in the United States at the Beginning of the Twenty-first Century," *International Migration Review* 24 (Spring 1990): 108–123.

13. Overviews of the research on immigrant acquisition of English can be found in Thomas Espenshade and Haishan Fu, "An Analysis of English-Language Proficiency among U.S. Immigrants," *American Sociological Review* 62 (April 1997): 288–305; and Kristin Espinosa and Douglas Massey, "Determinants of English Proficiency among Mexican Immigrants to the U.S.," *International Migration Review* 31 (Spring 1997): 28–50. Gillian Stevens ("Immigration, Emigration, Language Acquisition, and the English Language Proficiency of Immigrants in the United States," in Barry Edmonston and Jeffrey Passel, eds., *Immigration and Ethnicity: The Integration of America's Newest Arrivals* [Washington, D.C.: Urban Institute, 1994], pp. 163–185) discusses immigration from countries where English is an official and/or widely spoken language.

14. The influences of group size and segregation have been demonstrated by Guillermina Jasso and Mark Rosenzweig (*The New Chosen People: Immigrants in the United States* [New York: Russell Sage Foundation, 1990])

and by Gillian Stevens ("The Social and Demographic Context of Language Use in the United States," *American Sociological Review* 57 [April 1992]: 171–185). Alejandro Portes and Robert Bach (*Latin Journey: Cuban and Mexican Immigrants in the United States* [Berkeley: University of California Press, 1985]) make the case for the role of ethnic economic enclaves.

15. See, for instance, Peter Brimelow, *Alien Nation: Common Sense about America's Immigration Disaster* (New York: Random House, 1995), pp. 88–89, 265.

16. See, among others, Espinosa and Massey, "Determinants"; Farley, *New American Reality;* Portes and Rumbaut, *Legacies,* chap. 6; and Alejandro Portes and Richard Schauffler, "Language and the Second Generation: Bilingualism Yesterday and Today," *International Migration Review* 28 (Winter 1996): 640–661.

17. Alejandro Portes and Rubén Rumbaut, *Immigrant America: A Portrait* (Berkeley: University of California Press, 1996), chap. 6; Alejandro Portes and Lingxin Hao, "E Pluribus Unum: Bilingualism and Loss of Language in the Second Generation," *Sociology of Education* 71 (October 1998): 269–294. Zhou and Bankston (*Growing Up*) present additional evidence that bilingualism can favor success at school; see also Michael White and Gayle Kaufman, "Language Usage, Social Capital, and School Completion among Immigrants and Native-Born Ethnic Groups," *Social Science Quarterly* 78 (June 1997): 385–397. Ted Mouw and Yu Xie ("Bilingualism and Academic Achievement of Asian Immigrants: Accommodation With or Without Assimilation?" *American Sociological Review* 64 [April 1999]: 232–252), however, view the benefits of bilingualism as transitional only.

18. Portes and Rumbaut, *Legacies,* chap. 6.

19. Lopez ("Language") shares these doubts.

20. Lopez, "Language"; self-reports that reveal declining mother-tongue competence over time are documented in Portes and Rumbaut, *Legacies,* chap. 6.

21. When only English is reported as spoken at home, a mother tongue may still be used outside the home, or at least known. But the home language data, if not isomorphic with bilingualism, are surely a barometer of it.

22. E.g., Stephen Krashen, Michael Long, and Robin Scarcella, "Age, Rate, and Eventual Attainment in Second Language Acquisition," *TESOL Quarterly* 13 (December 1979): 573–582.

23. These groups are defined according to categories of race and Hispanic ethnicity that are reported in the census. For instance, the Chinese category includes all individuals who report themselves as Chinese on the census race question, regardless of their place of birth (for instance, the category would include ethnic Chinese immigrants from Vietnam). This approach seems sensible for studying language because language is associated with ethnic membership.

24. Farley, *New American Reality,* p. 175.

25. To be included in a generation group in the analysis, a child had to be the son or daughter of the householder and to be linkable to a parent (either householder or spouse) of the same racial/ethnic origin; for a full description of the group samples, see Richard Alba, John Logan, Amy Lutz, and Brian Stults, "Only English by the Third Generation? Loss and Preservation of the Mother Tongue among the Grandchildren of Contemporary Immigrants," *Demography* 39 (August 2002): 467–484. The first generation was defined as the foreign-born son or daughter of a foreign-born parent, the second as the U.S.-born child of a foreign-born parent, and the third (or later) as the U.S.-born child of U.S.-born parents.

26. Brimelow, *Alien Nation.*

27. Unfortunately, census data do not allow us to pursue the acquisition of Spanish by native speakers of English, a kind of shift that is, strictly speaking, also essential to produce a complete accounting of language patterns.

28. In the primary data source, the 1990 Public Use Microdata Sample (PUMS), within-state geography is defined in terms of so-called PUMAs, or Public Use Microdata Areas. Because of the confidentiality requirements of the Census Bureau, these units must contain at least 100,000 residents, and accordingly they vary considerably in the area they cover. The border zone is defined to contain all PUMAs adjacent to the U.S.-Mexico border. Because of the idiosyncrasies of the PUMA definitions, however, this border zone varies in width from place to place. See Alba et al., "Only English?"

29. Lopez, "Language."

30. Ibid.

31. Barry Edmonston and Jeffrey Passel, "The Future Immigrant Population of the United States," in Edmonston and Passel, *Immigration,* pp. 317–353.

32. Victor Nee and Brett de Bary Nee, *Longtime Californ': A Documentary Study of an American Chinatown* (New York: Pantheon Books, 1973).

33. For overviews of the economic characteristics of the immigrant streams to the United States, see Farley, *New American Reality;* Wilawan Kanjanapan, "The Immigration of Asian Professionals to the United States: 1988–1990," *International Migration Review* 29 (Spring 1994): 7–32; Portes and Rumbaut, *Immigrant America;* James Smith and Barry Edmonston, *The New Americans: Economic, Demographic, and Fiscal Effects of Immigration* (Washington, D.C.: National Research Council, 1997).

34. Indeed, the historical context and social organization of contemporary labor migration from Mexico, the main source country, is similar to that which gave rise to and sustained mass labor migration from Europe. See Douglas Massey, Rafael Alarcón, Jorge Durand, and Humberto González, *Return to Aztlan: The Social Process of International Migration from Western Mexico* (Berkeley: University of California Press, 1987).

35. Lizette Alvarez, "Congress Approves a Big Increase in Visas for Specialized Workers," *New York Times,* October 4, 2000, p. 1.

36. Michael Piore, *Birds of Passage: Migrant Labor and Industrial Societies* (Cambridge: Cambridge University Press, 1979), p. 37.

37. Victor Nee and Jimy Sanders, "Understanding the Diversity in Immigrant Incorporation: A Forms-of-Capital Model," *Ethnic and Racial Studies* 24 (2000): 386–411.

38. Jasso and Rosenzweig, *New Chosen People.*

39. Victor Nee, Jimy Sanders, and Scott Sernau, "Job Transitions in an Immigrant Metropolis: Ethnic Boundaries and the Mixed Economy," *American Sociological Review* 59 (December 1994): 849–872; Farley, *New American Reality.*

40. Portes and Rumbaut, *Immigrant America.*

41. George Borjas, *Friends or Strangers, the Impact of Immigrants in the U.S. Economy* (New York: Basic Books, 1990); Barry Chiswick, "Is the New Immigration Less Skilled Than the Old?" *Journal of Labor Economics* 4 (1986): 168–192; M. J. Greenwood, "The Economics of Mass Migration from Poor to Rich Countries: Leading Issues of Fact and Theory," *American Economic Review* 73 (May 1983): 173–177; Smith and Edmonston, *New Americans.*

42. The best-known studies include Edna Bonacich and John Modell, *The Economic Basis of Ethnic Solidarity: Small Business in the Japanese-American Community* (Berkeley: University of California Press, 1980); Robert Jiobu, "Ethnic Hegemony and the Japanese in California," *American Sociological Review* 53 (June 1988): 353–367; Ivan Light, *Ethnic Enterprise in America* (Berkeley: University of California Press, 1972); John Logan, Richard Alba, Michael Dill, and Min Zhou, "Ethnic Segmentation in the American Metropolis: Increasing Divergence in Economic Incorporation, 1980–1990," *International Migration Review* 34 (Spring 2000): 98–132; Nee, Sanders, and Sernau, "Job Transitions"; Alejandro Portes and Robert Bach, *Latin Journey: Cuban and Mexican Immigrants in the United States* (Berkeley: University of California Press, 1985); Jimy Sanders and Victor Nee, "Limits of Ethnic Solidarity in the Ethnic Enclave," *American Sociological Review* 52 (December 1987): 745–767; and Roger Waldinger, *Still the Promised City? African-Americans and New Immigrants in Postindustrial New York* (Cambridge, Mass.: Harvard University Press, 1996).

43. Jimy Sanders and Victor Nee, "Social Capital, Human Capital, and Immigrant Self-Employment," *American Sociological Review* 61 (April 1996): 231–249. The classic portrait of the strengths of the ethnic economy is rendered by Alejandro Portes and his associates (Portes and Bach, *Latin Journey;* Portes and Robert Manning, "The Immigrant Enclave: Theory and Empirical Examples," in Susan Olzak and Joane Nagel, eds., *Competitive Ethnic Relations* [New York: Academic Press, 1986], pp. 47–68). The research of Sanders and Nee speaks to the modest magnitude of much immigrant self-employment. Their research also suggests that the low level of

self-employment found among Mexican and other Central American immigrants is to a large measure accounted for by their low stocks of human capital and a sojourning pattern of male labor migration.

44. On the role of ethnic economies, see Tamotsu Shibutani and Kian Kwan, *Ethnic Stratification* (New York: Macmillan, 1965). Rose Hum Lee (*The Chinese in the United States of America* [Hong Kong: Hong Kong University Press, 1960]) and Victor Nee and Brett de Bary Nee (*Longtime Californ'*) discuss Chinatowns in the post–World War II period. Bonacich and Modell, *Economic Basis,* is an invaluable source concerning the Japanese ethnic economy.

45. Hien, *Vietnamese Americans.*

46. See Portes and Bach, *Latin Journey;* Thomas Bailey and Roger Waldinger, "Primary, Secondary, and Enclave Labor Markets: A Training Systems Approach," *American Sociological Review* 56 (August 1991): 432–445; Victor Nee and Jimy Sanders, "Trust in Ethnic Ties"; Nee, Sanders, and Sernau, "Job Transitions"; Waldinger, *Promised City.*

47. The hypothesis was originally formulated by Kenneth Wilson and Alejandro Portes ("Immigrant Enclaves: An Analysis of the Labor Market Experiences of Cubans in Miami," *American Journal of Sociology* 86 [September 1980]: 296–319), though it is generally associated with Portes's name. Sanders and Nee ("Limits") represent one side; Alejandro Portes and Leif Jensen ("What's an Ethnic Enclave?: The Case for Conceptual Clarity—Comment on Sanders and Nee," *American Sociological Review* 54 [1987]: 929–949) the other. See Jimy M. Sanders and Victor Nee, "Problems in Resolving the Enclave Economy Debate: Comment on Portes and Jensen," *American Sociological Review* 57 (1992): 415–418. Ivan Light and Stavros Karageorgis ("The Ethnic Economy," in Neil Smelser and Richard Swedberg, eds., *Handbook of Economic Sociology* [Princeton: Princeton University Press, 1994], pp. 647–671) attempt to take stock.

48. On San Francisco, see Don Mar, "Another Look at the Enclave Economy Thesis: Chinese Immigrants in the Ethnic Labor Market," *Amerasia* 17 (1991): 5–21; on Los Angeles, see Nee, Sanders, and Sernau, "Job Transitions."

49. Farley, *New American Reality,* p. 191.

50. U.S. Bureau of the Census, *1992 Economic Census: Survey of Minority-Owned Enterprises: Hispanic* (Washington, D.C.: U.S. Department of Commerce, 1996), table 2.

51. Sanders and Nee, "Limits"; Alejandro Portes and Min Zhou, "Self-Employment and the Earnings of Immigrants," *American Sociological Review* 61 (1996): 219–230.

52. George Borjas, "The Self-Employment Experience of Immigrants," *Journal of Human Resources* 21 (1986): 505.

53. Farley, *New American Reality.*

54. Nee, Sanders, and Sernau, "Job Transitions"; Jimy Sanders, Victor Nee,

and Scott Sernau, "Asian Immigrants' Reliance on Social Ties in a Multieth-nic Labor Market," *Social Forces* 81 (September 2002): 281–314.

55. Logan et al., "Ethnic Segmentation."

56. On Jews, see Stephen Steinberg's (*The Academic Melting Pot* [New York: McGraw-Hill, 1974]) analysis of the social origins of Jewish academics. Korean self-sacrifice is documented in Edna Bonacich, "The Social Costs of Immigrant Entrepreneurship," *Amerasia* 14 (1988): 119–128.

57. The two sides of the controversy are stated by Barry Chiswick ("Sons of Immigrants: Are They at an Earnings Disadvantage?" *American Economic Review* 67 [February 1977]: 376–380; and "The Effect of Americanization on the Earnings of Foreign-Born Men," *Journal of Political Economy* 86 [October 1978]: 897–921) and George Borjas ("Assimilation, Changes in Cohort Quality, and the Earnings of Immigrants," *Journal of Labor Economics* 3 [October 1985]: 463–489; "Self-Selection and the Earnings of Immigrants," *American Economic Review* 77 [September 1987]: 531–553; "The Economics of Immigration," *Journal of Economic Literature* 32 [December 1994]: 1667–1717). The National Research Council report on immigration, however (Smith and Edmonston, *New Americans,* chap. 5), largely reiterates and amplifies Borjas's position.

58. See Marta Tienda and Zai Liang, "Poverty and Immigration in Policy Perspective," in S. H. Danziger, G. D. Sandefur, and D. H. Weinberg, eds., *Confronting Poverty: Prescriptions for Change* (New York: Russell Sage Foundation, 1994), pp. 331–365, for an overview of the debate, and Jasso and Rosenzweig, *New Chosen People,* chap. 7, concerning data limitations. Relevant findings reported in the paragraph come from Robert LaLonde and Robert Topel, "Labor Market Adjustments to Increased Immigration," in John M. Abowd and Richard B. Freeman, eds., *Immigration, Trade, and the Labor Market* (Chicago: University of Chicago Press, 1991), pp. 167–199; and George Borjas and Richard Freeman, "Introduction and Summary," in George Borjas and Richard Freeman, eds., *Immigration and the Workforce: Economic Consequences for the U.S. and Source Areas* (Chicago: University of Chicago Press 1991), pp. 1–15. James Smith ("Race and Ethnicity in the Labor Market: Trends over the Short and Long Term," in Neil Smelser, William Julius Wilson, and Faith Mitchell, eds., *America Becoming: Racial Trends and Their Consequences,* vol. 2 [Washington, D.C.: National Academy Press, 2001], pp. 52–97) provides an analysis of recent data that indicates earnings gains over time as immigrants gain experience in the United States. See also Farley, *New American Reality,* pp. 184–187.

59. This conclusion seems to be widely accepted: see Borjas, "Economics"; Smith and Edmonston, *New Americans.*

60. Frank Bean, Jennifer Van Hook, and Karen Woodrow-Lafield, "Estimates of Numbers of Unauthorized Migrants Residing in the United States: The Total, Mexican, and Non-Mexican Central American Unauthorized Population in Mid-2001," Pew Hispanic Center, November 2001.

61. See the discussion of Dominicans in Chapter 5.
62. For thorough reviews of the legal status of non-citizens, see Lance Liebman, "Immigration Status and American Law: The Several Versions of Antidiscrimination Doctrine," in D. L. Horowitz and Gerard Noiriel, eds., *Immigrants in Two Democracies: French and American Experience* (New York: New York University Press, 1992), pp. 368–390; and Peter Schuck, *Citizens, Strangers, and In-Betweens: Essays on Immigration and Citizenship* (Boulder, Colo.: Westview Press, 1998).
63. See Marta Tienda and Audrey Singer, "Wage Mobility of Undocumented Workers in the United States," *International Migration Review* 29 (Spring 1994): 153.
64. Abel Valenzuela, Jr., "Day Laborers as Entrepreneurs?" *Journal of Ethnic and Migration Studies* 27 (2001): 335–352.
65. Portes and Rumbaut, *Immigrant America,* p. 69. The book presents a good statistical overview of the educational characteristics of different immigrant nationality groups, as does Farley, *New American Reality.*
66. See Grace Kao and Marta Tienda, "Optimism and Achievement," *Social Science Quarterly* 76 (March 1995): 1–19; White and Kaufman, "Language Usage"; and Zhou and Bankston, *Growing Up.*
67. Rumbaut, "Crucible Within," p. 767.
68. Kao and Tienda, "Optimism."
69. Rubén Rumbaut, "Paradoxes and (Orthodoxies) of Assimilation," *Sociological Perspectives* 40 (1997): 481–511.
70. Mary Waters, *Black Identities: West Indian Immigrant Dreams and American Realities* (Cambridge, Mass.: Harvard University Press, 1999).
71. Leonard Covello, *The Social Background of the Italo-American School Child* (Totowa: Rowman & Littlefield, 1972); Herbert Gans, *The Urban Villagers: Group and Class in the Life of Italian-Americans* (1962; reprint, New York: Free Press, 1982).
72. The concept of an oppositional identity relies on the work of the anthropologist John Ogbu; see, e.g., "Immigrant and Involuntary Minorities in Comparative Perspective," in Margaret Gibson and John Ogbu, eds., *Minority Status and Schooling: A Comparative Study of Immigrant and Involuntary Minorities* (New York: Garland, 1991), pp. 3–33. Empirical correlates of such an identity among the children of immigrants are developed by Alejandro Portes and Min Zhou ("The New Second Generation: Segmented Assimilation and Its Variants," *Annals* 530 [November 1993]: 74–96) and Mary Waters (*Black Identities*), among others.
73. The figure is adapted from Reynolds Farley and Richard Alba, "The New Second Generation in the United States," *International Migration Review* 36 (Fall 2002): 669–701.
74. See also Charles Hirschman, "The Educational Enrollment of Immigrant Youth: A Test of the Segmented-Assimilation Hypothesis," *Demography* 38 (August 2001): 317–336.

75. See George Borjas, *Heaven's Door: Immigration Policy and the American Economy* (Princeton: Princeton University Press, 1999).

76. Frank Bean, Jorge Chapa, Ruth Berg, and Kathryn Sowards, "Educational and Sociodemographic Incorporation among Hispanic Immigrants to the United States," in Barry Edmonston and Jeffrey Passel, eds., *Immigration and Ethnicity* (Washington, D.C.: Urban Institute Press, 1994), pp. 73–100; Perlmann, "Young Mexican Americans"; Smith, "Race"; Roger Wojtkiewicz and Katharine Donato, "Hispanic Educational Attainment: The Effects of Family Background and Nativity," *Social Forces* 74 (December 1995): 559–574.

77. The observational research is reported by Maria Matute-Bianchi, "Situational Ethnicity and Patterns of School Performance among Immigrant and Nonimmigrant Mexican-Descent Students," in Gibson and Ogbu, *Minority Status,* pp. 205–247. Another pessimistic reading of the educational chances of U.S.-born Mexicans is David Lopez and Ricardo Stanton-Salazar, "Mexican Americans: A Second Generation at Risk," in Portes and Rumbaut, *Ethnicities,* pp. 57–90.

78. See David B. Grusky and Robert M. Hauser, "Comparative Social Mobility Revisited," *American Sociological Review* 49 (1984): 19–38.

79. The mean index for second-generation Mexicans is 39, versus 29 for first-generation Mexicans and 45 for third-generation whites; see Farley and Alba, "New Second Generation."

80. Waters, *Black Identities.*

81. Lopez and Stanton-Salazar, "Mexican-Americans."

82. Sherri Grasmuck and Patricia Pessar (*Between Two Islands: Dominican International Migration* [Berkeley: University of California Press, 1991]) provide a convincing analysis of the Dominican case; see Pierrette Hondagneu-Sotelo, *Gendered Transitions: Mexican Experiences of Immigration* (Berkeley: University of California Press, 1994), for a similar study of Mexicans.

83. J. Gregory Robinson, "ESCAP II: Demographic Analysis Results," U.S. Census Bureau, 2001 (available on Census Web site: www.census.gov).

84. Sources on geographic concentration include Farley, *New American Reality;* William Frey, "Immigration, Domestic Migration, and Demographic Balkanization in America: New Evidence for the 1990s," *Population and Development Review* 22 (December 1996): 741–763; Douglas Massey, "The New Immigration and Ethnicity in the United States," *Population and Development Review* 21 (September 1995): 631–652; Portes and Rumbaut, *Immigrant America;* Roger Waldinger, "Immigration and Urban Change," *Annual Review of Sociology* 15 (1989): 211–232.

85. Frey, "Immigration."

86. The network aspects of immigration are analyzed elegantly by Douglas Massey in "Understanding Mexican Migration to the United States," *American Journal of Sociology* 92 (May 1987): 1372–1403. He also compares the relative geographic concentration of current and past immigration

streams in "New Immigration." Frey, in "Immigration," has addressed the impact of out-migration from immigrant-receiving areas by native groups. Gold (*Refugee Communities*) and Portes and Rumbaut (*Immigrant America*) discuss the geographic aspects of refugee migrations.

87. Smith and Edmonston, *New Americans,* pp. 116–117.

88. Barrett Lee, Stephen Matthews, and Wilbur Zelinsky, "The Spatial Contours of Racial and Ethnic Diversity in the United States, 1980–2000," Population Research Institute, Pennsylvania State University, 2001.

89. Massey ("New Immigration") suggests a proliferation of immigrant cultural centers as large-scale immigration continues. Frey's analysis for the National Research Council report on immigration (William Frey and Kao-Lee Liaw, "The Impact of Recent Immigration on Population Redistribution within the United States," in James Smith and Barry Edmonston, eds., *The Immigration Debate: Studies of Economic, Demographic, and Fiscal Effects of Immigration* [Washington, D.C.: National Academy Press, 1998], pp. 388–448) shows that U.S.-born Asians and Latinos are less concentrated in the main immigrant-receiving areas than are the foreign-born.

90. Reynolds Farley and William Frey, "Changes in the Segregation of Whites from Blacks during the 1980s: Small Steps towards a More Integrated Society," *American Sociological Review* 59 (February 1994): 23–45; and John Logan, "Ethnic Diversity Grows, Neighborhood Integration Lags Behind," Lewis Mumford Center, State University of New York at Albany, 2001. Douglas Massey and Nancy Denton ("Trends in Residential Segregation of Blacks, Hispanics, and Asians: 1970–1980," *American Sociological Review* 52 [December 1987]: 802–825) report similar findings.

91. Throughout this section the "immigrant" groups to which we refer include the second and later generations as well as the foreign-born.

92. See Richard Alba, John Logan, Wenquan Zhang, and Brian Stults, "Strangers Next Door: Immigrant Groups and Suburbs in Los Angeles and New York," in Phyllis Moen, Henry Walker, and Donna Dempster-McClain, eds., *A Nation Divided: Diversity, Inequality, and Community in American Society* (Ithaca: Cornell University Press, 1999), p. 120. On ethnic neighborhoods, see John Logan, Richard Alba, and Wenquan Zhang, "Immigrant Enclaves and Ethnic Communities in New York and Los Angeles," *American Sociological Review* 67 (April 2002): 299–322; James Allen and Eugene Turner, *The Ethnic Quilt: Population Diversity in Southern California* (Northridge: Center for Geographic Studies, California State University, 1997), is also relevant for Los Angeles.

93. Stanley Lieberson, *Ethnic Patterns in American Cities* (New York: Free Press, 1963).

94. Logan, Alba, and Zhang, "Immigrant Enclaves."

95. Kyle Crowder, "Residential Segregation of West Indians in the New York/New Jersey Metropolitan Area: The Roles of Race and Ethnicity," *International Migration Review* 33 (Spring 1999): 79–113; Kyle Crowder and

Lucky Tedrow, "West Indians and the Residential Landscape of New York," in Nancy Foner, ed., *Islands in the City: West Indian Migration to New York* (Berkeley: University of California Press), pp. 81–114; Nancy Denton and Douglas Massey, "Racial Identity among Caribbean Hispanics: The Effect of Double Minority Status on Residential Segregation," *American Sociological Review* 54 (October 1989): 790–808.

96. Saskia Sassen, *The Mobility of Capital and Labor* (Cambridge: Cambridge University Press, 1988).

97. On the historical pattern, see Nathan Glazer and Daniel Patrick Moyihan, *Beyond the Melting Pot: The Negroes, Puerto Ricans, Jews, Italians, and Irish of New York City* (1963; reprint, Cambridge, Mass.: MIT Press, 1970); and Douglas Massey, "Ethnic Residential Segregation: A Theoretical Synthesis and Empirical Review," *Sociology and Social Research* 69 (April 1985): 315–350. The contemporary one is discussed by Richard Alba, John Logan, Brian Stults, Gilbert Marzan, and Wenquan Zhang ("Immigrant Groups and Suburbs: A Reexamination of Suburbanization and Spatial Assimilation," *American Sociological Review* 64 [June 1999]: 446–460); Alba et al. ("Strangers Next Door"); and Waldinger ("Immigration").

98. The finding about language is reported by Alba et al. ("Immigrant Groups"). Suburban ethnic neighborhoods are discussed by Alba et al. ("Strangers"); Timothy Fong (*The First Suburban Chinatown: The Remaking of Monterey Park, California* [Philadelphia: Temple University Press, 1994]); John Horton (*The Politics of Diversity: Immigration, Resistance, and Change in Monterey Park, California* [Philadelphia: Temple University Press, 1995]); and Logan, Alba, and Zhang ("Immigrant Enclaves").

99. See Logan, Alba, and Zhang, "Immigrant Enclaves."

100. The best exposition of the spatial assimilation model is by Douglas Massey ("Ethnic Residential Segregation"). Massey and Nancy Denton ("Suburbanization and Segregation in U.S. Metropolitan Areas," *American Journal of Sociology* 94 [November 1988]: 592–626) address the role of suburbanization.

101. Richard Alba and John Logan, "Minority Proximity to Whites in Suburbs: An Individual-Level Analysis of Segregation," *American Journal of Sociology* 98 (May 1993): 1388–1427; Richard Alba, John Logan, and Brian Stults, "The Changing Neighborhood Contexts of the Immigrant Metropolis," *Social Forces* 79 (December 2000): 587–621; John Logan and Richard Alba, "Locational Returns to Human Capital: Minority Access to Suburban Community Resources," *Demography* 30 (May 1993): 243–268; John Logan, Richard Alba, Thomas McNulty, and Brian Fisher, "Making a Place in the Metropolis: Residential Assimilation and Segregation in City and Suburb," *Demography* 33 (November 1996): 443–453; Logan, Alba and Zhang, "Immigrant Enclaves." See also Emily Rosenbaum and Samantha Friedman, "Differences in the Locational Attainment of Immigrant and Native-Born Households with Children in New York City," *Demography* 38

(August 2001): 337–348; and Michael White, Ann Biddlecom, and Shenyang Guo, "Immigration, Naturalization, and Residential Assimilation among Asian Americans," *Social Forces* 72 (September 1993): 93–118.

102. For technical reasons, the Alba-Logan analyses cannot be carried out on more specific groups. Because of the limitations of census data, which to preserve confidentiality prevent the analyst from combining individual-level data with small-area characteristics, it is not possible with publicly available data to improve on these aggregate categories.

103. For a good description of such a neighborhood, see Roger Sanjek, *The Future of Us All: Race and Neighborhood Politics in New York City* (Ithaca: Cornell University Press, 1998).

104. Logan, "Ethnic Diversity."

105. Nathan Caplan, John Whitemore, and Marcella Choy, *The Boat People and Achievement in America: A Study of Family Life, Hard Work, and Cultural Values* (Ann Arbor: University of Michigan Press, 1989); Gold, *Refugee Communities;* Kibria, *Family Tightrope.*

106. Gibson, *Accommodation.*

107. Massey et al., *Return to Aztlan.*

108. For historical data, see Deanna Pagnini and S. Philip Morgan, "Intermarriage and Social Distance among U.S. Immigrants at the Turn of the Century," *American Journal of Sociology* 96 (September 1990): 405–432. The evidence on post–World War II intermarriage is provided by Richard Alba ("Assimilation's Quiet Tide," *Public Interest* 119 [Spring 1995]: 1–18); Alba and Reid Golden ("Patterns of Interethnic Marriage in the United States," *Social Forces* 65 [September 1986]: 203–223); Stanley Lieberson and Mary Waters (*From Many Strands: Ethnic and Racial Groups in Contemporary America* [New York: Russell Sage Foundation, 1988]); and Waters (*Ethnic Options: Choosing Identities in America* [Berkeley: University of California Press, 1990]). See also the discussion in Chapter 3.

109. When the marks of group distinction have largely disappeared and group differences persist largely as symbolic rather than substantive differences, as in the case of third-generation native-born white Americans, then, as Robert Merton ("Intermarriage and Social Structure: Fact and Theory," *Psychiatry* 4 [August 1941]: 364) remarked, "a state of affairs is reached where the quadrisyllable, 'intermarriage,' is whittled down to a bisyllable, 'marriage.'"

110. Zhenchao Qian, "Breaking the Racial Barriers: Variations in Interracial Marriages between 1980 and 1990," *Demography* 34 (May 1997): 263–276.

111. The Los Angeles study is by Harry H. L. Kitano, Waitsang Yeung, Lynn Chai, and Herbert Hatanaka ("Asian-American Interracial Marriage," *Journal of Marriage and the Family,* 46 (1984): 179–190). See also Akemi Kikumura and Harry H. L. Kitano, "Interracial Marriage: A Picture of the Japanese Americans," *Journal of Social Issues* 29 (1973): 67–81; Larry

Shinagawa and Gin Young Pang, "Intraethnic, Interethnic, and Interracial Marriages among Asian Americans in California, 1980," *Berkeley Journal of Sociology* 33 (1986): 95–114; Harry H. L. Kitano and Lynn Chai, "Korean Interracial Marriage," *Marriage and Family Review* 5 (1982): 75–89; Harry H. L. Kitano and Wai-tang Yeung, "Chinese Interracial Marriage," *Marriage and Family Review* 5 (1982): 35–48. National data are analyzed by Sharon Lee and Keiko Yamanaka ("Patterns of Asian American Intermarriage and Marital Assimilation," *Journal of Comparative Family Studies* 21 [Summer 1990]: 287–305), Lee and Marilyn Fernandez ("Trends in Asian American Racial/Ethnic Intermarriage: A Comparison of 1980 and 1990 Census Data," *Sociological Perspectives* 41, no. 2 [1998]: 323–342), and Betty Lee Sung ("Chinese American Intermarriage," *Journal of Comparative Family Studies* 21 [Autumn 1990]: 337–352). Sean-Shong Hwang and Rogelio Saenz ("The Problems Posed by Immigrants Married Abroad on Intermarriage Research: The Case of Asian Americans," *International Migration Review* 24 [Fall 1990]: 563–576) point out the necessity to take into account intermarriages contracted abroad by American soldiers stationed in Asia.

112. On West Indian intermarriage, see Suzanne Model and Gene Fisher, "Black-White Unions: West Indians and African Americans Compared," *Demography* 38 (May 2001): 177–185.

113. The study of Mexicans is by Robert Anderson and Rogelio Saenz ("Structural Determinants of Mexican American Intermarriage," *Social Science Quarterly* 75 [June 1994]: 414–430); the New York study by Douglas Gurak and Joseph Fitzpatrick ("Intermarriage among Hispanic Ethnic Groups in New York City," *American Journal of Sociology* 87 [January 1982]: 921–934).

114. Higher education is also associated with values concerning sex roles and attitudes about lifestyle and sexual matters; see Matthijs Kalmijn, "Shifting Boundaries: Trends in Religious and Educational Homogamy," *American Sociological Review* 56 (December 1991): 786–800.

115. Robert Mare ("Five Decades of Educational Assortative Mating," *American Sociological Review* 56 [February 1991]: 15–32) and Matthijs Kalmijn ("Shifting Boundaries") are responsible for the studies of educational homogamy. The increased power of education to determine earnings is reported by David Featherman and Robert Hauser (*Opportunity and Change* [New York: Academic Press, 1978]) and David Grusky and Thomas DiPrete ("Recent Trends in the Process of Stratification," *Demography* 27 [November 1990]: 617–637). Michael Hout, Adrian Raftery, and Eleanor Bell ("Making the Grade: Educational Stratification in the United States, 1925–1989," in Yossi Shavit and Hans Peter Blossfeld, eds., *Persistent Inequality: Changing Educational Attainment in Thirteen Countries* [Boulder, Colo.: Westview Press, 1993], pp. 25–50) find that the effect of parental status on children's educational attainment has diminished.

116. Qian, "Breaking." The sample selection minimizes an inferential problem that disturbs the patterns found by some earlier, census-based studies; since census studies are of necessity cross-sectional, they risk confounding observed intermarriage prevalence with differential rates of divorce, separation, and widowhood, which are obviously more prevalent among older persons.

117. Ibid. Also relevant is Farley's intermarriage analysis, which appears in the National Research Council report on immigration (Smith and Edmonston, *New Americans,* chap. 8). Farley uses a somewhat different age group (twenty-five to thirty-four) and includes all Asian groups. His overall intermarriage rates are, for Asians, modestly lower than those found by Qian but very nearly the same for Hispanics. Farley also finds more Asian-Hispanic marriages than Qian.

118. Merton, "Intermarriage."

119. See also Sean-Shong Hwang, Rogelio Saenz, and Benigno Aguirre, "The SES Selectivity of Interracially Married Asians," *International Migration Review* 29 (Summer 1995): 469–491.

120. Milton Gordon, *Assimilation in American Life* (New York: Oxford University Press, 1964), p. 130; Mary Waters, "The Social Construction of Race and Ethnicity: Some Examples from Demography," in Nancy Denton and Stewart Tolnay, eds., *American Diversity: A Demographic Challenge for the Twenty-first Century* (Albany, SUNY Press, 2002).

121. Roderick Harrison and Claudette Bennett, "Racial and Ethnic Diversity," in Reynolds Farley, ed., *State of the Union: America in the 1990s,* vol. 2, *Social Trends* (New York: Russell Sage Foundation, 1995), p. 40.

122. David Harris and Jeremiah Joseph Sim, "Who Is Multiracial? Assessing the Complexity of Lived Race," *American Sociological Review* 67 (August 2002): 614–627. Maria Root, *Racially Mixed People in America* (Newbury Park, Calif.: Sage, 1992); Paul Spickard, *Mixed Blood: Ethnic Identity and Intermarriage in Twentieth-Century America* (Madison: University of Wisconsin Press, 1989); Paul Spickard and Rowena Fong, "Pacific Islander Americans and Multiethnicity: A Vision of America's Future?" *Social Forces* 73 (June 1995): 1365–83; Cookie White Stephan and Walter Stephan, "After Intermarriage: Ethnic Identity among Mixed-Heritage Japanese-Americans and Hispanics," *Journal of Marriage and the Family* 51 (May 1989): 507–519; Yu Xie and Kimberley Goyette, "The Racial Identification of Biracial Children with One Asian Parent: Evidence from the 1990 Census," *Social Forces* 76 (December 1997): 547–570.

123. Nancy Landale, R. S. Oropesa, and Bridget Gorman, "Immigration and Infant Health: Birth Outcomes of Immigrant and Native-Born Women," in Donald Hernandez, ed., *Children of Immigrants: Health, Adjustment, and Public Assistance* (Washington, D.C.: National Academy Press, 1999), pp. 244–285; Kathleen Mullan Harris, "The Health Status and Risk Behav-

ior of Adolescents in Immigrant Families," in Hernandez, *Children*, pp. 286–347.

7 Conclusion: Remaking the Mainstream

1. James Smith and Barry Edmonston, *The New Americans: Economic, Demographic, and Fiscal Effects of Immigration* (Washington, D.C.: National Research Council, 1997); Immigration and Naturalization Service, *Triennial Comprehensive Report on Immigration* (Washington, D.C.: Immigration and Naturalization Service, 1999). The numbers in the text and Figure 7.1 reflect legal immigration to the United States. The generalization that the mass immigration of the earlier period was proportionately larger would not be altered by the inclusion of illegal immigrants, if they could be accurately counted (see Smith and Edmonston for an estimate of the annual magnitude). One would also need to discount the past illegal flows by the number of those who have eventually legalized and are thus counted in Figure 7.1; the calculations are not straightforward.

2. Kyle Crowder, "Residential Segregation of West Indians in the New York/New Jersey Metropolitan Area: The Roles of Race and Ethnicity," *International Migration Review* 33 (Spring 1999): 79–113; Mary Waters, *Black Identities: West Indian Immigrant Dreams and American Realities* (Cambridge, Mass.: Harvard University Press, 1999).

3. For a rare study of the undocumented, see Pierrette Hondagneu-Sotelo, *Gendered Transitions: Mexican Experiences of Immigration* (Berkeley: University of California Press, 1994).

4. Cecilia Menjivar, *Fragmented Ties: Salvadoran Immigrant Networks in America* (Berkeley: University of California Press, 2000), pp. 80–89; Sarah Mahler, *American Dreaming: Immigrant Life on the Margins* (Princeton: Princeton University Press, 1995).

5. David L. Featherman and Robert M. Hauser, "A Refined Model of Occupational Mobility," in David Grusky, ed., *Social Stratification in Sociological Perspective: Class, Race, and Gender* (Boulder, Colo.: Westview Press, 1994), pp. 265–275.

6. Alex Stepick, Carol Dutton Stepick, Emmanuel Eugene, Deborah Teed, and Yves Labissiere, "Shifting Identities and Intergeneration Conflict: Growing Up Haitian in Miami," in Rubén Rumbaut and Alejandro Portes, eds., *Legacies: Children of Immigrants in America* (Berkeley: University of California Press, 2001), pp. 229–266; and Philip Kasinitz, Juan Battle, and Inés Miyares, "Fade to Black? The Children of West Indian Immigrants in Southern Florida," ibid., pp. 267–300.

7. E.g., Douglas Massey and Nancy Denton, *American Apartheid: Segregation and the Making of the Underclass* (Cambridge, Mass.: Harvard University Press, 1993). The analysis of 2000 census data by John Logan and the Lewis

Mumford Center of the University at Albany (www.albany.edu/mumford/census) demonstrates that black-white segregation indices declined only modestly between 1990 and 2000 and remained at high levels in the nation's largest metropolitan regions.

8. Charles Moskos and John Sibley Butler, *All That We Can Be: Black Leadership and Racial Integration the Army Way* (New York: Basic Books, 1997).

9. These data, compiled by the Mumford Center of the University at Albany, were discussed in Chapter 6. It should be recalled that a neighborhood is equated here with a census tract and that the data are limited to the metropolitan regions of the United States, which encompass 80 percent of the total population.

10. For expositions, see Dominique Schnapper, *La France de l'intégration: sociologie de la nation en 1990* (Paris: Éditions Gallimard, 1991), Emmanuel Todd, *Le destin des immigrés: assimilation et ségrégation dans les démocraties occidentales* (Paris: Éditions du Seuil, 1994); for a more recent assessment, see Rogers Brubaker, "The Return of Assimilation? Changing Perspectives on Immigration and Its Sequels in France, Germany, and the United States," *Ethnic and Racial Studies* 24 (July 2001): 531–548. For a sociological study of assimilation in France, see Michèle Tribalat, *Faire France: une enquête sur les immigrés et leurs enfants* (Paris: Éditions La Découverte, 1995).

11. The first claim appears in Todd, *Le destin;* for a sophisticated discussion of the French view, see Denis Lacorne, *La crise de l'identité américaine: du melting-pot au multiculturalisme* (Paris: Fayard, 1997).

12. Youssef Ibrahim, "France Bans Muslim Scarf in Its Schools," *New York Times,* September 11, 1994, p. 4.

13. We are grateful for the insights of John Bowen, who has studied Muslims in France.

14. For a description of the early-twentieth-century Americanization campaign, see John Higham, *Strangers in the Land: Patterns of American Nativism, 1860–1925* (New York: Atheneum, 1970).

15. Andrew Greeley, *The Catholic Myth: The Behavior and Beliefs of American Catholics* (New York: Charles Scribner's Sons, 1990).

16. For example, Paul Cowan and Rachel Cowan, *Mixed Blessings: Overcoming the Stumbling Blocks in an Interfaith Marriage* (New York: Doubleday, 1987); Alan Silverstein, *Preserving Jewishness in Your Family after Intermarriage Has Occurred* (New York: Jason Aronson, 1995).

17. Sylvia Barack Fishman, *Jewish and Something Else: A Study of Mixed-Married Families* (New York: American Jewish Committee, 2001).

18. Sander Gilman, *Making the Body Beautiful: A Cultural History of Aesthetic Surgery* (Princeton: Princeton University Press, 1999), chap. 6.

19. Smith and Edmonston, *New Americans.*

20. Gary Wills, "Washington Is Not Where It's At," *New York Times Magazine,* January 25, 1998, p. 67 (emphasis added).

21. Joane Nagel, "Constructing Ethnicity: Creating and Recreating Ethnic Identity and Culture," *Social Problems* 41 (February 1994): 101–126; Michael Omi and Howard Winant, *Racial Formation in the United States: From the 1960s to the 1990s,* 2d ed. (New York: Routledge & Kegan Paul, 1994).

22. The estimate was derived for us by Brian Stults from the data of the General Social Survey (available at *www.icpsr.umich.edu:81/GSS/*).

23. We return here to a distinction we introduced in Chapter 2, which originates with Rainer Bauböck, "The Integregration of Immigrants," Council of Europe, Strasbourg, 1994; and Aristide Zolberg and Long Litt Woon, "Why Islam Is Like Spanish: Cultural Incorporation in Europe and the United States," *Politics and Society* 27 (March 1999): 5–38.

24. Absorption of individuals with non-European ancestry into the white population is revealed by past assimilation: for example, the extensive intermixing of whites and Native Americans has produced a large population of Americans with varying ratios of European and American Indian ancestry, who mostly place themselves in the white population. In the 1980 census, where individuals were required to classify themselves by a single race, 77 percent of the 6.8 million Americans who claimed then to have American Indian ancestry described themselves racially as "white." Matthew Snipp, *American Indians: The First of This Land* (New York: Russell Sage Foundation, 1989), pp. 48–49.

25. The data about mixed ancestry among the Japanese were cited in Chapter 3.

26. The sociologist David Harris has produced provocative data concerning the social ambiguity of individuals with mixed-racial facial features; see David Harris, "In the Eye of the Beholder: Observed Race and Observer Characteristics," paper presented at the 2002 meeting of the American Sociological Association in Chicago.

27. David Hollinger, *Postethnic America: Beyond Multiculturalism* (New York: Basic Books, 1995).

28. See, e.g., Anthony Marx, *Making Race and Nation: A Comparison of the United States, South Africa, and Brazil* (Cambridge: Cambridge University Press, 1998).

29. Herbert Gans, "The Possibility of a New Racial Hierarchy in the Twenty-first Century United States," in Michele Lamont, ed., *The Cultural Territories of Race: Black and White Boundaries* (Chicago and New York: University of Chicago Press and Russell Sage Foundation, 1999), p. 371.

30. Noel Ignatiev, *How the Irish Became White* (New York: Routledge, 1995).

31. Joe Feagin and Michael Sykes, *Living with Racism* (Boston: Beacon Press, 1994).

32. There is abundant evidence that whites are more welcoming of immigrant blacks than of African Africans. See Waters, *Black Identities*.

Index

Acculturation, 23–25, 41–42, 98, 115, 140; one-way, 4–5, 23–24, 26; selective, 45, 217–218; evidence of, 71–76, 217–230; and health, 268

Action: purposive, 39–42, 45, 71; joint, 42

Affirmative action, 57, 139, 153–155

Africa, 59, 175

African Americans, 19, 88, 112, 119–120, 136, 137, 139, 198, 256–257; possible effects of assimilation on, 2, 8, 290–292; Chinese and, 44; Irish and, 45, 132. *See also* Racism

African ancestry, 133, 247, 277

Afro-Caribbeans, 8, 65, 137, 161, 175, 197, 199, 241–242, 245, 247. *See also* Dominicans; Jamaicans; West Indians

Agriculture, 28, 44, 51, 176, 178, 185, 205–206, 208

Alba, Richard, 95, 240–241, 244

Alien, permanent resident, 146, 148

American, 4, 17–18, 23, 124–128, 138, 143, 144–147, 149; as ancestry, 91, 94, 95

American Council of Learned Societies, study of, 169

American Indians. *See* Native Americans

Americanization, 1, 19, 20–21, 26, 115, 140–141, 152, 281–282

Amish, 65

Amnesty, 128, 172, 178, 179, 187

Ancestry, mixed, 94, 267, 349n24; among Japanese, 94; among whites, 124

Ancestry data, 95–96

Anglicization, three-generation model of, 219

Anglo-American, 25–26, 144; culture, 2, 5, 17, 25

Anglo-Conformity, model of, 17, 26, 61

Anti-miscegenation laws, 206, 262–263

Anti-semitism, 92, 171; and elite colleges, 107–108, 118; decline of, 117; in legal profession, 118–119

Asians, 47, 49, 58, 95, 98, 113, 125, 130, 133–134, 136, 139, 154–156, 168, 179, 183, 241–242, 245, 256–259; Asian-white intermarriages, 13, 82, 90, 93, 96, 131–132, 263, 265–267; South, 15; and glass ceiling, 58, 82, 232; ineligible for citizenship, 69, 150; East, 69–70, 78, 82, 86, 124, 132, 140. *See also* Cambodians; Chinese; East Indians; Filipinos; Japanese; Koreans; Vietnamese

Asiatic Barred Zone, 175

Assimilation, 7–8, 15–16, 45, 67, 70–71, 99, 114, 120, 124–126, 131, 134–136, 138, 140–141, 144, 156–157, 164, 166, 205, 215, 274–282; old conception, 1–4, 10, 17–18, 32; in disrepute, 1–6; duration of, 3, 22–23; social, 4, 19–20, 269; canonical formulation, 6, 9–10, 23–27; segmented or downward, 8, 9, 136, 161–163, 268, 276–277; definition, 10–12, 19–20, 38; theory of, 14, 30, 35, 39, 50–

Japanese-American 442nd Brigade, 116
Jews, 13, 21, 22, 24, 101, 103, 107, 155–
157, 165, 171, 282–283; in garment industry, 5, 137, 166; eastern European,
13, 122, 124; German, 45; Christian-
Jewish families, 61, 283–284; as racially
distinctive, 63, 132; collective actions by,
118–119; in law, 118–119. *See also* Anti-
semitism
Jim Crow, 44–45, 56
Johnson, Lyndon, 174, 190
Jones, James, 116
Jus sanguinis vs. jus soli, 148

Karageorgis, Stavros, 234
Kennedy, John F., 174, 190
Kennedy, Robert, 176
Kennedy, William, 76
Kingston, Maxine Hong, 76
Koreans, 46, 47, 147, 164–165, 263, 265;
in small business, 46, 204–205, 233,
236; immigration of, 130, 182–183,
203–205; second generation, 205; lan-
guage assimilation of, 223–225
Ku Klux Klan, 212, 282–283
Kwan, Kian, 30–35, 63, 64, 123

Language, 16, 72, 75, 124, 141, 142, 149;
Navaho, 7, 200; spoken at home, 41,
73–75, 145, 222–227; decline of Euro-
pean and Japanese, 75–76; islands, 76;
and ethnic neighborhoods, 124. *See also*
Assimilation, linguistic; Bilingualism;
English language
Latinos. See Hispanics
Legal profession, 118–119
Levittown, 112
Lieberson, Stanley, 110
Life chances, 57, 122; increasing parity of,
77–83
Light, Ivan, 234
Lithuanians, 147, 149
Little Italy, 89
Little Saigon, 212
Loewen, James, 45
Logan, John, 88, 225
Long, Litt Woon, 61
Los Angeles, 9, 47, 49, 70, 86, 160, 164,
186, 197, 238, 252–254, 257–259
Lutz, Amy, 225
Lynching, 69

Mailer, Norman, 116
Mainstream, 10, 15, 25, 41, 45, 51, 64, 68,
70, 77, 82–83, 121–122, 143–144, 201;
assimilation and, 11, 282–292; defini-
tion, 12
Majority group, 14, 28, 63
Malcolm X, 198
Manufacturing, 107, 135, 194
Mariel, 191
Markets, 60, 146; integrative features of,
60
Massey, Douglas, 29, 255
McCarren-Walter Act. *See* Immigration Act
of 1952
Mead, George Herbert, 31
Mechanisms, 49, 59; causal, 38–40, 64, 66,
102; collectivist vs. individualist, 39; network, 42–45, 51, 52, 66; institutional,
50, 52–53, 57, 62
Melting Pot, 7, 17–18, 23, 116, 122, 140,
289; Triple, 26
Merton, Robert K., 265, 267
Mexican Revolution, 185
Mexicans, 8, 139, 149, 153, 216, 247,
253–254, 261–262, 264, 269; immigra-
tion of, 14, 39, 171, 173, 176, 182–189;
occupations of, 171, 178, 185, 245; un-
documented, 178, 185, 238; repatriation
of, 185–186; educational attainment of,
188, 241–243; bilingualism, 223–227
Mexico, 46, 48, 128, 149, 189; future immigration from, 130–131; fertility decline, 131; change to Constitution,
147
Miami, 7, 149, 164–165, 190, 221, 240,
259
Micro level, 32, 53
Microsoft, 55–56
Middleman minorities, 66
Midwest, 83, 86, 96, 124, 145
Miller, Herbert, 20
Mining, 185
Minority group, 15, 23–25, 29, 33, 57–59,
153, 159. *See also* Ethnicity; Race
Mobility, 2, 28, 65, 67, 80, 83, 103–111,
120, 125, 129, 133, 135–137, 211; upward, 15, 21, 22, 50, 82, 104, 106, 113,
122, 124, 139, 162–163;
intergenerational, 15, 50, 162, 269; lateral, 15, 50, 268; spatial or residential,
22, 29, 111–113; divergent outcomes,